FROM THE BOG TO THE CLOUD

Dependency and Eco-Modernity in Ireland

Patrick Bresnihan and Patrick Brodie

First published in Great Britain in 2025 by

Bristol University Press
University of Bristol
1–9 Old Park Hill
Bristol
BS2 8BB
UK
t: +44 (0)117 374 6645
e: bup-info@bristol.ac.uk

Details of international sales and distribution partners are available at bristoluniversitypress.co.uk

© Bristol University Press 2025

DOI: 10.51952/9781529241976

British Library Cataloguing in Publication Data
A catalogue record for this book is available from the British Library

ISBN 978-1-5292-4194-5 hardcover
ISBN 978-1-5292-4195-2 paperback
ISBN 978-1-5292-4196-9 ePub
ISBN 978-1-5292-4197-6 ePdf

The right of Patrick Bresnihan and Patrick Brodie to be identified as authors of this work has been asserted by them in accordance with the Copyright, Designs and Patents Act 1988.

All rights reserved: no part of this publication may be reproduced, stored in a retrieval system, or transmitted in any form or by any means, electronic, mechanical, photocopying, recording, or otherwise without the prior permission of Bristol University Press.

Every reasonable effort has been made to obtain permission to reproduce copyrighted material. If, however, anyone knows of an oversight, please contact the publisher.

The statements and opinions contained within this publication are solely those of the editors and contributors and not of the University of Bristol or Bristol University Press. The University of Bristol and Bristol University Press disclaim responsibility for any injury to persons or property resulting from any material published in this publication.

Bristol University Press works to counter discrimination on grounds of gender,
race, disability, age and sexuality.

Cover design: Liam Roberts
Front cover image: Photography by Sean Breithaupt

Saoirse don Phalaistín

Contents

List of figures ... vi
Notes on authors ... ix
Acknowledgements ... x

Introduction ... 1

1 Energetic Mediation and Imperial Geographies ... 36
2 Bog Modernity and Energy Decolonisation ... 57
3 Data Centre Land ... 85
4 Atmosphere Meets Cloud ... 114
5 The Value of a Bog ... 141
6 Land, Extractivism, and Anti-Imperialist Environmentalism ... 168

Conclusion ... 197

Notes ... 207
References ... 234
Index ... 262

List of figures

Interlude 0.1	Meta Data Centre, Clonee, County Meath (photograph by Sean Breithaupt)	xiv
Interlude 0.2	Bord na Móna Peatlands near Prosperous, County Kildare (photograph by Sean Breithaupt)	xiv
Interlude 1.1	Data centre in Grange Castle, Dublin (photograph by Sean Breithaupt)	35
Interlude 1.2	The Bog of Allen, cutaway in the Irish midlands (photograph by Sean Breithaupt)	35
1.1	Scenes from the ruined foundations of the Marconi installation, with sheep grazing and cutaway scars visible in background. A production still from *Do Sheep Dream of Electric Ruins?*, directed by Matt Parker (Audiogamma, 2025)	37
1.2	The Marconi Station, Derrigimlagh Bog, County Galway, with stacks of drying turf	38
1.3	The Marconi Station, Derrigimlagh Bog, County Galway	47
Interlude 2.1	Echelon Data Centre, Clondalkin, Dublin (photograph by Sean Breithaupt)	56
Interlude 2.2	The Bog of Allen, cutaway in the Irish midlands (photograph by Sean Breithaupt)	56
2.1	Seán Keating, mural for Irish Pavilion, World's Fair, New York, 1939	58
2.2	ESB power station at Portarlington, County Laois, 1950	67
2.3	A layout plan of Cloontuskert by Frank Gibney (1905–78) for BnM housing, Cloontuskert, County Roscommon (circa 1952)	70
2.4	Stress Diagrams of Ireland, Framework for an Irish National Plan	72
Interlude 3.1	Echelon Data Centre, Clondalkin, Dublin (photograph by Sean Breithaupt)	84

LIST OF FIGURES

Interlude 3.2	Bord na Móna peatlands near Prosperous, County Kildare (photograph by Sean Breithaupt)	84
3.1	Worker Solidarity Movement sticker protesting Gardaí repression of the Shell to Sea campaign in Rossport, County Mayo	86
3.2	Ruins of the Asahi chemical plant in Killala, County Mayo	87
3.3	1980s advertisement from the IDA, indicating to US investors Ireland's competitive tax advantages amid other European economies	99
Interlude 4.1	Data Centre in Grange Castle, Dublin (photograph by Sean Breithaupt)	113
Interlude 4.2	Bord na Móna peatlands near Derrinlough Briquette Factory, County Offaly (photograph by Sean Breithaupt)	113
4.1	Driving in County Donegal on small country roads through a 'resource-scape' dominated by Sitke spruce plantations and wind turbines	115
4.2	The base of a wind turbine at Meenbog, County Donegal, stabilised on cement and gravel, dug out from the bog, in 2021	115
4.3	Homemade sign in County Donegal	128
4.4	Derrinlough Briquette Factory, County Offaly, just before closure in 2023	139
Interlude 5.1	Data Centre in Grange Castle, Dublin (photograph by Sean Breithaupt)	140
Interlude 5.2	Clara Bog Nature Reserve, County Offaly (photograph by Sean Breithaupt)	140
Interlude 6.1	Road next to Meta Data Centre, Clonee, County Meath (photograph by Sean Breithaupt)	167
Interlude 6.2	Bord na Móna peatlands in County Offaly (photograph by Sean Breithaupt)	167
6.1	Chas Jewett, Jeshua Estes, and Lewis GrassRope, visiting from the Lakota Nation, at Greencastle Peoples Office, Sperrins, County Tyrone, 2023	169
6.2	Cartoon from Resources Study Group pamphlet (1970, 32)	187
6.3	Cartoon from Resources Study Group pamphlet (1970, 13)	188

6.4	Sister Majella McCarron with members of Ogoni Solidarity Ireland at the annual Action from Ireland (Afri) Famine Walk in County Mayo, 1995	190
Interlude 7.1	Data Centre in Grange Castle, Dublin (photograph by Sean Breithaupt)	196
Interlude 7.2	Clara Bog Nature Reserve, County Offaly (photograph by Sean Breithaupt)	196

Notes on authors

Patrick Bresnihan is Associate Professor in the Department of Geography at Maynooth University, Ireland.

Patrick Brodie is Assistant Professor and Ad Astra Fellow in the School of Information and Communication Studies at University College Dublin, Ireland.

Acknowledgements

As much as this book is the result of our joint research and writing over the past seven years, it would never exist without the countless conversations and experiences shared with comrades and collaborators inside and outside the university, across the island, and beyond. We are lucky to have such nourishing intellectual and political relationships, and we value these friendships as pretty much the basis of everything we do.

Most importantly, we are privileged to be working on these ideas alongside friends and comrades in Ireland – fellow travellers in environmental and social justice struggles and research, whose conversation and support over the years has nourished our anti-imperialist collective imaginary. In particular, V'Cenza Cirefice, Laure de Tymowski, Julianna di Sassi Silva, Patrick Doyle, Louise Fitzgerald, Tommy Gavin, Criostóir King, Dylan Murphy, Rory Rowan, Kathleen Stokes, Lynda Sullivan, and Fiadh Tubridy – thanks for everything. Most of these folks are involved in a collective publishing project called *Rundale*, which is about cultivating and sharing ideas for alternative politics and environmental justice in Ireland and more broadly. Our main hope is that this book contributes to that collective project.

We are grateful to all the people and organisations in Ireland who have influenced and supported us in our thinking around Ireland in the world-system, its crucial role within (and against) empire, and the horizons of eco-socialism on this island. Bana Abu Zuluf, John Barry, Communities Against the Injustice of Mining (CAIM), Connolly Books, Sharae Deckard, Dundalk Communities United, Lex Innocentium, Love Leitrim, the Making Relatives Collective, Marc Mac Seáin, Conor McCabe, Sinéad Mercier, Niamh Ní Bhriain, James Renaghan, John Reynolds, Save Our Sperrins, Harun Šiljak, Slí Éile, Jennie Stephens, Stop Shannon LNG, and Treasure Leitrim. Also those community campaigns and activists who have been particularly active around climate justice, energy, and data centres: Rosi Leonard, Aaron Downey, Sinéad Sheehan, Emanuela Ferrari, Eoin O'Leidhin, William Hederman, Anna Pringle, Ruairí Fahy, Brian Marron, Paul Murphy, Bríd Smith, Jess Spear, Leah Sullivan, Slí Eile, Not Here Not Anywhere and Futureproof Clare. We also want to extend special thanks and acknowledgement to Phil Lawton, our friend and colleague, without whom this collaboration never would have begun. It all started on a bench at Trinity College Dublin in 2019, after Phil offhandedly suggested that we should talk about our shared investments in data centres and energy politics. It's all rolled downhill from there – so thanks Phil.

While this is a book about Ireland's dependency in the context of monopoly tech eco-modernity, and it began with data centres, we found our (soggy) footing in the bogs. Friends across community organising, the sciences, and critical research cultivated and inspired our fascination and commitment to these landscapes, whether in the midlands, out west, or farther afield. In particular, those who inspired or gave feedback on our thinking in this area include Katja Bruisch, Creative Rathangan Meitheal, Community Wetlands Forum, Laurence Fullam, Monica de Bath, Finn Valley Wind Action Group, the Intersecting Energy Cultures Working Group, Kate Flood, Kärg Kama, Cindy Lin, James Palmer, and Lily Toomey. The brilliant Naomi Millner has also been an important source of knowledge and feedback on peatlands but we owe much more to her than just that.

Our academic comrades across geography, political ecology, and media studies have provided us with the groundwork and the encouragement to follow these lines of thinking. Darin Barney, Patrick Bigger, Kay Dickinson, Mél Hogan, Fieke Jansen, Jordan Kinder, Sima Kokotović, Sebastián Lehuedé, Dillon Mahmoudi, Dan McQuillan, Rahul Mukherjee, Matt Parker, Anne Pasek, Viviane Saglier, Joaquín Serpe, Patrick Brian Smith, Nicole Starosielski, Ana Valdivia, Hunter Vaughan, Julia Velkova – to name just a few who have directly inputted on or supported this work. The Root and Branch Collective – Rob Booth, Adam Calo, Sophia Doyle, Dan Hartley, Alex Heffron, Kai Heron, José Alfredo Ramírez Galindo, Olivia Oldhan-Dorrington, and Clara Oloriz – for nurturing new friendships and vital conversations on the centrality and potential of a liberatory agrarian politics. The constant support of long-time friends and comrades across Europe, including Emanuele Leonardi, Panagiota Kotsila, and Melissa Garcia-Lamarca. Manuela Zechner and Bue Rübner Hansen for their inspirational commitment to movement building and political education, in particular through the Common Ecologies collective and the Earthcare Podcast. In Ireland, we are also lucky to have a supportive system of environmental humanities, energy studies, and critical media studies closer to home. Marguerite Barry, Tomas Buitendijk, the UCD Centre for Digital Policy, Treasa de Loughry, Caitriona Devery, the UCD Earth Institute, Liz Farries, Kylie Jarrett, Lai Ma, Paul O'Neill, El Putman, Kalpana Shankar, Eugenia Siapera, James Steinhoff - each has provided space, inspiration, and professional support for writing this book at important points.

We have had the opportunity to present and discuss versions of this work over the past seven years across Ireland, Europe, North America, and elsewhere, each time developing these ideas with the generous feedback of our hosts and comrades. We have tried to keep track, in no particular order, and with dates having escaped our brains: Stigma Damages in Sligo, thanks to Michele Horrigan; the Manchester Urban Institute, thanks to Nate Millington; the Association of Internet Researchers in Dublin, thanks to Kylie Jarrett; the Marxism Festival in Dublin, thanks to Rebel News; Annex and its associated outputs, thanks to Fiona McDermott and all members of that team; the Property Injustice project at UCD, thanks to Amy Strecker and Sinéad Mercier; Exalt Dialogues at Helsinki, thanks to Xander Dunlap; Goldsmiths University on a couple of occasions, thanks to Sarah Pennington and Dan McQuillan; Goldsmiths and IIIT Hyderabad, thanks to Aakansha Natani and Sebastián Lehuedé; a special event at the Centre for Digital Policy at UCD, thanks to Hunter Vaughan and Liz Farries; Friends of the Earth Ireland on multiple occasions, thanks to Rosi Leonard; Rethinking the Inevitability of AI at the University of Virginia, thanks to Mar Hicks and Erik Linstrum; the Data Ecologies group at Virginia Commonwealth University, thanks to Jenny Rhee and Jesse Goldstein; the Anti-Colonial Geographies panel stream at CIG/ICG, thanks to Gerry Kearns and Karen Till; the Green Extractivism and Eco-Modernity in Ireland panel stream at CIG, co-organised with comrades; the Grierson Research Group at McGill, thanks to Darin Barney and Ayesha Vemuri; Media Rurality at McGill, co-organised by Pat and Darin Barney; Climate Camp Ireland, thanks to V'cenza Cirefice; and the Green Data Centres Working Group at Utrecht University, thanks to Judith Keilbach, Anne Helmond, and Philipp Keidl. Anything we're forgetting – please know that we appreciate it, and are just bad academics and don't keep track of our professional lives as well as we should.

Our editor at Bristol University Press, Paul Stevens, and Ellen Mitchell, our editorial manager, have been enormously helpful and generous throughout the process of writing and publication. Huge thanks to both of you. We also owe special thanks to Sean Breithaupt, who has generously provided the images that illustrate this text. From the bog to the cloud, his photos capture the uncanniness of Ireland's uneven energy and data landscapes in a way that our words cannot – so we are enormously grateful for the opportunity to reproduce them here. Sean is a professional photographer based in Dublin. His work explores current environmental issues and themes. He has won the Curtin O'Donoghue award for his work on plastic waste, and his project *Prosperous*, which looked at Ireland's wild, untouched boglands, was a finalist in the recent AOP awards. Sean is an accredited member of the AOP.

Pat owes immense gratitude to his family – my mother Anne, my late father Dave, and siblings Liam, Katie, and Marissa – for their love and support. To my friends, from Ireland, Philadelphia, Montréal, and farther afield, thanks for indulging me and giving feedback when hashing these thoughts out over drinks, coffees, and cold winter walks. And finally I especially want to thank my partner Eimear, and her family in Belfast for everything they've done for us in the course of writing this book. Eimear – your personal encouragement, historical acuity, and political clarity are an inspiration. Thanks for listening to us talk about this for so long, and for always challenging us. I hope you enjoy the endnotes.

It is hard to know how to appreciate wider support networks, particularly when the past three years have involved significant health care issues and plenty of related ups and downs. Paddy's family have been amazing – Sive, Sophie, Roger, Moray, and dad – and close friends – Maggie, Davey, Conor, Danny, and Suzy, who are always there. All the doctors, nurses, and cleaners in St John's Ward and Crumlin Children's Hospital who do such important work every day and cared so well for our little boy. And most importantly, Rachel and Ted, who I am thankful for every day and love to the moon and back.

As this project has been the result of seven years of collaborative work, we have explored and experimented with these ideas in other written contexts extensively, which we should also acknowledge here. Chapter 1 shares inspiration with the chapter 'Imperial Wireless: Energetic Mediation at Marconi's Connemara Station', published in the collection *Media Rurality* (forthcoming, Duke University Press). Arguments from Chapter 3 and other parts of the book draw, in part, from our article 'From toxic industries to green extractivism: rural environmental struggles, multinational corporations, and Ireland's postcolonial ecological regime', published in *Irish Studies Review* in 2024. A very early stab at the basis of Chapter 4 appears in our 2021 article, 'New extractive frontiers in Ireland and the moebius strip of wind/data', in *Environment and Planning E: Nature and Space*. Nascent seeds of arguments in Chapter 5 appear in a 2023 article in *New Media and Society*, 'Data sinks, carbon services: waste, storage, and energy cultures on Ireland's peat bogs'. All have been heavily rewritten, revised, and updated so as to be unrecognisable – although careful readers may see the echoes from these earlier analyses. All mistakes remain our own.

Introduction

Why are there so many data centres in Ireland?

If you read the news, you will probably know that data centres use a lot of resources, especially energy and water. These warehouses of the 'cloud', which house rows of servers processing global internet activity, have come to the forefront of contemporary discourses surrounding the sustainability of the tech industry. The rise of artificial intelligence (AI) especially has caused a proliferation of debate about the astronomical energy usage of large-scale computing. The expansion of the tech industry's server requirements shows no signs of slowing. What began a few years ago as a relatively minor criticism of the tech industry from the likes of Greenpeace International (2017) has now become central to the 'sustainable' strategies and policy considerations of all major tech companies and states as they double-down on the highly speculative promises of generative AI. While some commentators fret over the existential threat of sentient robots, the far more material and present threat of AI's resource requirements is poised to derail any slim hopes of decarbonisation and a liveable planet for the majority. Channelling the accelerationist attitudes of Silicon Valley, former Google CEO Eric Schmidt casually dropped in 2024 that the energy demand for AI was infinite and, since we were never going to meet our climate goals anyway, we may as well bet on building AI to solve the problem (Woodcock 2024). This AI will require the construction of thousands of data centres to accommodate expanding computational needs.

This is not the tech-fantasy hubris of one man, or even a few powerful tech companies – it is the beating heart of capitalist eco-modernity. In this book, we contend that it is taking shape in Ireland in unique but illustrative ways, situated within longer histories of the capitalist world ecology and in close relationship to the operations of monopolistic digital technology companies. Against the grain of this eco-modernity, we also pay attention to dispersed sites and subjects of resistance, who object in distinct ways to the latest phase of capitalist 'progress'. Rather than reducing these objections to 'climate' or 'tech' politics, our book connects them to a longer history of anti-colonial, land-based, and often internationalist politics that has been actively buried in Ireland, North and South, for at least 30 years. As will become clear through the book, the stakes of our analysis, and the choice of specific historical events and struggles, orientate around the basic question: What is the place of Ireland in the world-system? Or, to paraphrase the words of Robbie McVeigh and Bill Rolston, 'are we for the Republic or Empire' (2022)? By framing it as a political choice, McVeigh and Rolston pull the question away from academic pandering that dilutes the very present political stakes of Irish imperialist alignment, and urge a more direct engagement with the unfinished project of decolonisation on the island. But we're getting ahead of ourselves: how does this relate to data centres?

Since the mid-2000s, approximately 100 data centres have been built in Ireland, largely around the capital city, Dublin. Most of these (around 60) are classified as 'hyperscale' data centres, the large-scale facilities of the big tech cloud and social media giants such as Amazon Web Services (AWS), Google, Meta, and Microsoft, making Dublin the third highest concentration of hyperscale data centres in the world – in 2024, this small island on the edge of Europe hosted 5 per cent of the world's share of these facilities (C. Donnelly 2024). This immense concentration in a relatively small country has had significant effects in the function of the energy system. In 2023, these data centres accounted for 21 per cent of electricity on the national grid (CSO 2024), a number which the International Energy Agency (IEA) estimates could jump to 32 per cent by 2026 (IEA 2024, 32).[1] In 2024, the Commission for the Regulation of Utilities (CRU) estimated that half of electricity produced in Counties Dublin and Meath was going to data centres (Lyne 2025). To sustain this digital growth, supporting infrastructures have also expanded, organised around the resource requirements of the data centre industry. As a resource-intensive and distributed supply chain, data centres and digital technologies more broadly require multiple extractive inputs and are linked to sites far from where they are ostensibly developed and advertised. The hum of electricity coming off data centres in Dublin is pulling from the public grid, but what does that actually mean?

In 2016, one of us invited an engineer working for Eirgrid, the Irish semi-state company responsible for managing the energy grid, to speak in a geography class. The engineer recalled that when he began working for the national grid operator in the early 1990s, plans for infrastructure expansion and upgrades were oriented around supporting regional towns and projected population growth. After 2010, this all changed. With the influx of data centres, decisions about energy capacity and grid development were now geared towards supporting these energy-intensive facilities.[2] We often return to this story because of what it illustrates. Better than abstract statistics, this anecdote captures both the scale of data centre expansion in Ireland over the past decade – significant enough to shift national planning strategies – as well as the unspectacular way in which relations between the Irish state and multinational tech corporations materialise through physical infrastructures, the literal wires and cables that distribute electricity and process data. It is not possible to address the question about data centre growth in Ireland without understanding how and why the state has been able to orientate the provision of 'public' energy infrastructure, at a time of climate emergency, towards the needs of these large, private companies. The core relations of the data centre 'phenomenon' are nothing new, and can't be explained unless we dig into the specific character of Irish capitalism, a postcolonial model of developmental 'modernisation' that subordinates social need and ecological care to the imperatives of global capital.

A second illustrative story came in 2021. The construction of a 91.2 MW wind farm in Donegal, under contract with the world's largest cloud provider, AWS, precipitated a catastrophic peatslide. A video caught on a phone by a local resident documented a river of peat sliding down a mountain. The construction of 19 120 m turbines and the access roads to transport them involved the significant disturbance of peat – centuries old, semi-aqueous carbon stocks, which subsequently seeped into waterways on either side of the border between the North and South (Republic) of Ireland.[3] Land ecologies that might be otherwise termed 'natural capital' on other parts of big tech sustainability ledgers, valued for their climate benefits (Chapter 5), were pulverised under the construction requirements of the cloud's energy demands. Even before planning permission had been granted for the wind farm, the then Taoiseach (Prime Minister), Leo Varadkar, had lauded the green commitments of AWS for its investment in the Meenbog wind farm. After the peatslide, AWS did everything it could to distance itself from direct involvement in the development.

Until recently, bogs like this were also a source of thermal energy for electricity – the postcolonial energetic modernity of Ireland was fuelled by the industrialised extraction and burning of 'turf' from the peat bogs of the midlands and west of the country by the state-owned peat development company Bord na Móna (BnM) and the national Electricity Supply Board (ESB). In 2021, after ceasing peat extraction at an industrial scale, BnM rebranded itself as a 'climate solutions company', with the slogan that it is now 'more than móna' – indicating a revision of its legacy as a carbon-intensive extractive enterprise, while maintaining its role in remediating and repurposing peatland holdings towards development for these now de-industrialised regions. Its role as a development organisation became explicitly orientated towards the imperatives of climate action. It plans to pair these two aims, for example, through its pilot 'Eco-Energy Park', an enclosed renewable energy campus on former peatlands that will host privately owned wind, solar, battery storage, and other energy-intensive industrial facilities such as data centres. In 2024, it announced its anchor tenant for the project: AWS (Bord na Móna nd). The 'Eco-Energy Park' offers a perfect crystallisation of capitalist eco-modernity: climate action is seamlessly folded into the energy priorities of multinational tech companies. While promoted as a 'just transition', this model of privatised decarbonisation fails to meaningfully provide jobs for former workers in the peat industry. By contracting land and energy directly to AWS, it encloses common resources and public infrastructure for one of the most powerful multinational companies in the world.

In a spectacular way, tracking from the Meenbog peatslide disaster to the industrial peatland politics of the Irish midlands reveals the uneven political ecology of the data centre industry.[4] Our first engagement with Meenbog had come prior to the peatslide, through a local community campaign objecting to the turbines. The arguments focussed on (justified) concerns that the sensitive, biodiversity-rich blanket bog was not suitable for such large-scale infrastructure. In this forgotten corner of the border region, residents argued that the underhanded tactics used by the wind developer to gain social licence were no better than counter-insurgency operations of the British state in 'securing' the border during the conflict in NI (1969–98). But they also objected to the fact that these energy infrastructures were being built to power AWS data centres in far-off Dublin – not local houses or businesses. In other words, local objectors were not protesting data centres in the abstract or at the point of their construction, but rather at a site along their extensive, ecologically disruptive energy supply chain. What may have seemed a peripheral campaign in a remote part of the country was in fact one of the most advanced sites of contestation around tech industry expansion in Ireland – providing instructive, but somehow unheard, lessons for communities facing very different implications of a 'just transition' a few hundred kilometres away in the midlands. Why was this the case? How do the uneven geographies of tech supply chains and operations map onto the familiar fault lines of Ireland's uneven development and colonial history, west and east, North and South? What does this kind of materialist analysis of eco-modernity offer in terms of locating and amplifying social resistance and political alternatives? How do we reconnect the pressing ecological dimensions of these technologies with struggles for both environmental justice and development happening in Ireland, and beyond?

The answers to these questions tell a story about the prehistories and energetic intensities of digital media writ large, facilitated by the foreign direct investment (FDI)-led development apparatus of a 'postcolonial' nation-state on the edge of Europe.[5] The task of this book will be to present the core facets of this unfolding tale of over- and under-development, colonial and postcolonial dependency, land ecologies of the capitalist world system, and unfolding infrastructural landscapes of eco-modernity structured by the resource demands of 'monopoly tech'. To do this, we will first provide the conceptual pillars which will hold up this narrative, drawing from theories across multiple fields and geographies to structure this often messy assembly of elements which make up what we refer to as Ireland's 'postcolonial ecological regime'. This framework structures the progression of development on the island and provides an analytical basis for Ireland's ongoing role as a laboratory for the 'innovative' technologies of imperial capitalism across its history. Only by understanding the circumstances of this model of development can we begin to contest the dominant narratives of eco-modern progress – from the bog to the cloud.

The political ecology of monopoly tech

This book is concerned with the globally dominant role of 'big tech'. In some circles, mobilisation against big tech has been a rallying cry – from right-wing politicians in moral panic to left-leaning proponents of 'digital rights' and tighter regulation, the reining in of big tech multinationals has become an imperative for a range of political projects. The latter's calls have become especially loud and urgent with the oligarchical influence and support of big tech CEOs such as Jeff Bezos (AWS), Elon Musk (Tesla), and Mark Zuckerberg (Meta) within the new Donald Trump administration. From whatever perspective, the primary gripe ultimately arises from the same political economic circumstances: a few companies have become increasingly powerful in controlling the platforms through which global social and economic relations are mediated. The immense growth and market power of social media, software, and e-commerce giants Amazon, Apple, Google/Alphabet, Meta/Facebook, Microsoft, as well as growing market influence by Chinese multinationals such as Alibaba, Bytedance, Huawei, and Tencent (Steinberg et al 2022), has seen the digital technologies that permeate many of our lives controlled by a small concentration of companies. As many have written extensively, the growing role of these social media and 'cloud' giants in everything from global trade to democratic governance and climate change has far-reaching societal ramifications that we are only beginning to grapple with.[6]

As Cory Doctorow contends in his book *How to Destroy Surveillance Capitalism*, where he diagnoses fundamental tech harms within this exceptional industrial concentration, the prevalence of 'digital rights' as a unifying element of mainstream political engagement with tech has often limited apertures for transformative action (2021). Critiques of these approaches have rested on their tendency to operate within already-existing industrial guard rails: this tech is here, and it is the job of digital rights advocates, scholars, and regulators to navigate its impacts and mitigate its harms. While Doctorow moves his own critiques in another direction – essentially, arguing that we need to break up 'big tech', in a vaguely cyber-libertarian way[7] – we draw inspiration from those who clearly identify both the monopolistic directionalities of these companies, and the tendency of many critical scholars and policy makers to take their operational power as a given, one that needs to be reined in rather than dismantled entirely.[8] As we show throughout this book, the increasing embeddedness of these technologies in 'green' strategies, and their industrialisation of emerging regimes of digital expansion within and through infrastructure,[9] means that the time has come to confront seriously the contradictions of paired green, digital growth. This book shows the world historical dimensions of Ireland's role in engineering the planet to support monopoly tech through the strategic mobilisation of its territory.

In confronting the contradictions of paired 'green, digital growth' on a finite planet, we thus emphasise the *state developmental dynamics* at play in the historical underpinnings of the continuously unfolding 'green, digital transition' – and its various analogues, such as the 'twin transition' of 'digitalisation and decarbonisation' that we refer to throughout this book.[10] This will help us to bridge scholarship across two areas that have scarcely been in robust conversation: (1) critical media studies focussed on the global political economy and regulatory dimensions of big tech; and (2) lively debates happening across Marxian political ecology on eco-socialism and green imperialism. The former are rightfully focussed on the social dimensions of enormously powerful digital corporations, including in the pummelling of markets and 'extraction' of data via digital platforms; the latter are concerned with the enfolding of green transition strategies, including infrastructural and resource supply chains, with historically uneven patterns of accumulation between core and periphery, Global North and South. There has yet to be a comprehensive study of how these overlap.[11]

Missing from many mainstream debates, at least until recently, was the centrality of infrastructural control as a core facet of big tech's dominance, especially in terms of the concentration of information flows through proprietary circuits and storage. The role of the 'cloud' and its immense capabilities was an almost mythologised dimension of big tech's expansion. Originating from ironic ICT industry jokes designed to spare rank-and-file office workers from the messy electronic intricacies of IT,[12] the cloud remains shorthand for the infrastructural, storage, and software services of companies such as AWS, Google, and Microsoft. However, scholars of 'media infrastructure' have long recognised the centrality of material infrastructure to these processes and their organising of social relations,[13] and at the same time political economists of telecommunication have demonstrated how the consolidation of 'content and carrier' in deregulatory paradigms since the 1990s has enabled concentrated ownership of digital media systems to advance.[14] In 2015, at a time of continued popular reckoning surrounding the transformative and potentially radical effects of participatory social media and streaming, Christian Sandvig found that platform companies were regressing towards older models of concentration, consolidating their infrastructure to ensure regular subscriptions and traffic along proprietary infrastructural pathways (2015). AWS is a famous example of such concentration – quietly, from the mid-2000s, AWS invested heavily in 'cloud' infrastructure, building hundreds of data centres worldwide and establishing regional 'availability zones' for customers across different territories.[15] In 2024, AWS controlled 31 per cent of global cloud infrastructure (Richter 2024).

AWS' model of simultaneously vertical and horizontal integration is fascinating and worrisome from an infrastructural perspective, but for now we want to emphasise that the concentration of big tech resembles, increasingly, the historical features of monopoly capitalism.[16] In this way, we use the term *monopoly tech* throughout this book to refer to the big tech multinationals that operate in Ireland. Monopoly tech helps us to conceptually clarify a few things. One, we can distance ourselves from the sometimes unhelpfully populist rhetoric against big tech as a monolithic and undifferentiated force of power. While big tech, like big oil, big pharma, or big tobacco before it, describes a bloc of power supported by powerful lobbies through which an apparatus of toxic capitalist enterprise forges ahead,[17] monopoly tech helps us to more closely understand the processual and distributed institutional mechanisms of the infrastructural power of multinational technology companies. For example, how the regimes of resource control and productive transformation they enact, whether through renewable energy monitoring systems, cloud software for offset schemes, and software integration into public governance, operate through oftentimes occluded mechanisms, disguising profit motivations, privatisation, and power grabs along the supply chain through complex intermediating systems, including through state and semi-state partnerships. It also, second, situates the stakes of analysing multinational tech companies within a longer history of imperial capitalist development, which has always been characterised by structures of economic and technological dependency, the systemic flow of value to the imperial core, and (super-)exploitation of land, labour, and resources in the periphery (Lenin 1963 [1917]).[18] Monopoly capitalism, in spite of the perceived historical friction with the state, is not antithetical to state intervention. Its very existence, in fact, depends upon the territorial integration of imperialist states via infrastructure and resources – a fact that Lenin, in his 1917 treatise on imperialism, ties directly to the capitalist tendency towards monopoly.

We should pause here, first, to emphasise that the world historical dimensions of monopoly tech are also basically about the ecological and geographical relations of production. In this way, the mainstream rhetoric of the 'fourth industrial revolution', first heralded by the World Economic Forum's Klaus Schwab in 2016, is somewhat useful as a heuristic for understanding how the industrialisation of green, digital capitalism is taking shape through powerful companies, concentrated in (US) metropolitan centres, with suppliers and intermediaries managing the extraction of land and resources from peripheralised places towards the accumulation of profits (Arboleda 2020).[19] As this book demonstrates throughout, starting with Guglielmo Marconi's establishment of a radio transmission station in British-colonised Connemara, in the west of Ireland, in the early 1900s (Chapter 1), capitalist enterprises have long negotiated partnerships with imperial powers to develop their productive capacities. In these localised sites, they manage and organise ecologies towards their operations through infrastructure. Harnessing electricity generated through the land and its resources, beamed through the air from a facility protected at times by the British and later Free State military, the Marconi Company developed and utilised an experimental technology whose primary function was in the logistics of trade and imperial seafaring. The Marconi Company would effectively monopolise this purpose-built technology for much of the early 20th century (Garland 2023).

This early example of monopoly tech capitalism, of course, looks a bit like an AWS facility today. Go to one of these data centres, and you'll be immediately struck by the extensive security apparatus around it, as well as the diesel tanks, generators, substations, and pylons feeding the infrastructure. It also tells us a lot about the durabilities of imperial ecology in AWS' location-based harnessing of ecologies towards infrastructural operations. 'Modern' technologies of electronic communication remain functionally energetic. Anne Pasek, Cindy Lin, Zane Griffin Talley Cooper, and Jordan Kinder articulate this clearly in their book *Digital Energetics*: the basic function of digital technologies is inseparable from the harnessing and deployment of energy towards the transmission of information (2023). This is a core facet of electronic media, even if the geography of those sourcing, manufacturing, controlling, and using the material technologies have changed over time.[20] As we approach a tipping point with the growth of AI and its exponential requirements for energy-, water-, and resource-intensive computing, along with the basic resource supply chains and offset regimes being put in place to support its growth alongside 'green' adaptations, the mere acknowledgement of the materiality of the 'cloud' and its energies is insufficient. We need stronger frameworks to grasp the structural centrality of a few extremely powerful companies, who disproportionately consume resources to provide digital infrastructure and dictate the terms and geographies by which it is built and sourced, especially under the current imperatives of decarbonisation.[21]

Thus, the supposed counterweight of the state in regulating these industries has given way to an exasperated acknowledgement of the speed of their development and the lack of state control over their technoscientific acceleration. The belief that AI technology will deliver competitive advantage to faltering economies is now fuelling intra-state competition, particularly between imperial blocs, foregrounding the role of the state in providing infrastructures, resources, and markets for their expansion. The mismatch between these material and political investments in monopoly tech, and rhetoric about limiting their power, is considerable. The Irish state was an early adopter and arguable innovator in this landscape, both in providing infrastructure (for example, providing pre-defined and built industrial spaces and roads, grid connections, and trained labour) and counting on multinational investment and expertise to improve existing infrastructure to guarantee access and economic growth since the late 1950s. While the (colonial) state once laid the foundations for Marconi to 'innovate' in the bogs of Connemara (Chapter 1), and the postcolonial Free State/Republic of Ireland developed sovereign peat-driven energy infrastructure through alternative technoscientific knowledge networks (Chapter 2), the contemporary Irish state is now entirely dependent on roving multinational capital, positioning itself as an enabler of these companies to utilise Ireland's land, resources, and infrastructures to generate profits, often via toxic, resource-intensive, and high-emission operations (Chapter 3). This has left Ireland disproportionately exposed to the ecologies of monopoly tech. Rather than rein this in, the state continues to manage the contradictions of their growth under shifting green, digital imperatives (Chapters 4–6).

A second point to highlight is that a materialist and world-ecological perspective on monopoly tech moves beyond the 'impacts' of capitalist technologies on local places, and demonstrates how imperialism durably *organises nature* towards capitalist accumulation. This takes shape not only through overt actions of capitalist organisations, but also through negotiations between the state and capital as they occupy imbalanced but integrated roles in contemporary capitalism (Mezzadra and Neilson 2019). This is of crucial importance if we are to fight on emerging battlefields surrounding the role of monopoly tech in delivering and supporting climate transitions. The idea that 'impacts' and 'externalities' of capitalist activity can be managed and mitigated by technoscientific innovation and efficiencies regulated and mandated by state climate aims – the hegemony of 'techno-solutionist' thinking in industry, research, and governance – becomes a moot point if we understand that *capitalism is an ecology*, taking our cues from 'world ecology' thinkers such as Jason Moore (2015) and Sharae Deckard (2016). These theorists have demonstrated that studies of the capitalist world system from scholars such as Immanuel Wallerstein and Giovanni Arrighi can be deepened by understanding where the commodity chains of capitalism and colonialism intersect with specific environmental histories. To understand imperialist durabilities in monopoly tech's eco-modernity, we have to first analyse how capitalism continues to produce rather than only destroy ecological circumstances for 'sustainable' growth and modernisation – even if the end result resembles, far more, the familiar signatures of destruction (Heron 2024).

If imperialism organises nature for capitalist accumulation in the core, then anti-imperialism organises nature for social good in the peripheries.

This insight has come to the fore recently in the context of debates over a global green new deal and eco-socialist degrowth from the peripheries (Hickel et al 2022). Here, sovereign control over land and resources, the removal of debt burdens and unequal trade relations, technological and financial transfers from the core to the periphery, and the development of scaled industrial capacity are necessary starting points for any meaningful and sustainable post-capitalist transition for the majority (Ajl 2021a). Importantly, these positions draw on the often-obscured histories of Third World[22] ecological thought and liberatory praxis, or the ecological dimensions of sovereign social metabolism as Alberto García Molinero and Alejandro Pedregal describe it (2024). In the politically vibrant post-WWII period, experimentation with postcolonial socialist development, from China to Guinea-Bissau, linked ecological questions with projects of social advancement and wealth redistribution. While these political movements were distinct, shaped by different political and economic contexts, and more or less explicit in dealing with environmental aspects, they carried the promise of radically transforming spheres of production and reproduction, including access to and use of land. These promises were hard to keep, however, in the face of enormous pressure mounted by the alliance of internal class factions and external, imperial interests led by the US. Though rarely narrated in this way, the South of Ireland, a former colony, went through a similar trajectory: after a short-lived, highly compromised period of national development between the 1930s and 1950s, Ireland aggressively re-inserted itself into the capitalist world system from the late 1950s under US, and to a lesser extent European, direction. Our book positions Ireland within this world-historical context. We cannot understand, and thus confront, the developmental mechanisms by which the contemporary Irish state manages the socio-ecological contradictions of green, digital capitalism without understanding how they operate within a world system defined by imperialist expansion, which drives the reach of extraction deeper into land and ecologies.

A final, third point to emphasise is that 'modernity' and 'modernisation' have always looked something like the split, differentiated landscapes and geographies of uneven development. This remains the central question of 'eco-modernity' as it is shaped by the resource and infrastructural demands of monopoly tech. It goes without saying that we are seeing proliferating and unequal ecological impacts and changes driven by both digital expansion and unjust forms of climate action, in themselves responding to resource shortages and planetary limitations through technoscientific and policy dimensions.[23] However, this is foundationally an issue of *development*. Arguments surrounding jobs, private investment, and prosperity at the hands of monopoly tech infrastructures remain central to the Irish developmental narrative in the midst of climate change – a bargain with empire that has disempowered and foreclosed alternative models of development that would start with public investment and ecological care. In this arena, we see techno-solutionism aligning with monopoly tech in government policy, promoting the cynical aspiration that for economic development to continue apace with climate transitions, we need to further court the digital capabilities and expertise of multinational corporations. To do so, the state mobilises FDI-led policies across all aspects of society from the private sector, to civil society and communities, to the university, to the state itself. But to understand how and why 'development' and 'modernisation' have come at the hands of multinational-led innovation in Ireland, we first have to see the entanglement of these discourses with land and ecology through embedded histories of colonialism and imperialism.

Development and dependency in the Irish postcolony

This book grew out of an initial interest in data centres, but has evolved into an account of the development of Irish capitalism within the world-system. There is no doubt that our trajectory has been strongly influenced by a resurgence of interest in coloniality, postcolonial studies, and imperialism in Ireland over the past six years. This springs from world-historical movements such as Black Lives Matter (BLM) and the Palestinian struggle for liberation that have, as elsewhere, ignited a sharpening of consciousness and desire to establish internationalist solidarity, in part through the leveraging of a shared anti-colonial history.[24] But it also springs from the ever-present, but intensifying, counter-revolutionary revisionism that seeks to cleave Ireland closer to the US and EU, both in terms of geopolitical alignment and economic dependency. One of the key aims of this book is to contest powerful revisionist currents in Irish academia and wider cultural life that have been hegemonic for decades.[25] The emergence of the 'Celtic Tiger' in the 1990s was not just a social and economic phenomenon, but an ideological one that required, and deepened, a current of thought that had been in the ascendancy since the 1960s – namely, a distancing of the South of Ireland from its colonial pasts and present, including from anti-colonial struggle in the North. The reasons for this are complex and will be addressed throughout the book, but more important for us is the task of salvaging intellectual and political threads of anti-colonial struggle in Ireland, in order to model what we call an anti-imperialist environmentalism (Chapter 6).

The starting point for any reckoning with coloniality on the island of Ireland must be the ongoing partition separating the North of Ireland from the South, today the Republic of Ireland. But the empirical focus of this book is the South, and the fact that formal independence in 1922 did not magically bring about a Republic, nor an end to political and economic dependence on Britain. From the linking of the two currencies to reliance on British markets for cattle exports, key structural features of the Irish economy were kept in place by successive Irish governments, and the establishment of the Free State as a 'dominion' of Britain demonstrates a basis of sustained imperial relationships, inside and beyond the borders of the country. Even more significant for our argument, however, is that Ireland's subordinate position within imperial capitalist formations is not limited to its relationship with Britain. As Deckard emphasises, 'Ireland's uneven development and peripheralisation cannot be understood solely in the context of British colonialism, with no ability to account for its subsequent subordination to the hegemony of US capital and to core Eurozone states' (2016). This corrective, likely directed towards those who over- rather than under-emphasise the influence of British colonialism on contemporary Irish geographies and politics, also gets to a core issue of the ongoing uneven development of Ireland: the coexistence of over- and under-development through the asymmetrical distribution of risks and benefits derived from globalisation across the island. Analysing Ireland through historical geographies of colonialism and imperialism remains essential for understanding the circumstances and strategies by which eco-modernity plays out in contemporary Ireland, both in terms of its material footprint and impacts as well as the structures of consent and dissent that drive and/or disrupt it.

Chapters 1, 2, and 3 dwell on the historical contexts of Ireland's colonial modernity from the late 19th century to formal independence in the South, a brief period of nationalist modernity between 1930s and 1950s, and, most important of all, the period of postcolonial modernity derived from Ireland's active re-integration into the world capitalist system after World War II. Here we want to briefly outline three key themes that we return to throughout the book, and which orientate our analysis: the ideology of improvement, that has a particular significance in constructing Ireland as a colonial laboratory going back to the 17th century; the centrality of land in Irish colonial and postcolonial political economy; and Ireland as a semi-periphery within the world capitalist system, understood in this book by activating a submerged intellectual history of Irish dependency theory.[26]

Ideology of improvement

William Petty was a 17th-century physician, inventor, and political philosopher. He was also an 'adventurer' in Ireland, a proto-venture capitalist, personally benefiting from his privileged role as colonial surveyor – by 1688, he had acquired 160,000 acres in County Kerry (McCormick 2009). Petty would use his estate to test out inventions and techniques for increasing the productivity and rent from his lands, including the collection of data about his tenants (Barnard 1979). As a colonial administrator, he would refine the use of the survey as a technology for quantifying the value of land. Over subsequent decades, the survey would prove fundamental for enabling the wholesale transfer of lands from an indigenous population to the 'Protestant Ascendancy' class. From Ireland, the survey would be applied in many different colonial contexts for the same purpose.

Brenna Bhandar singles out William Petty as a key progenitor of what she calls the colonial 'ideology of improvement'. This ideology combined a novel attention to labour productivity with racialised ideas about 'proper use' and cultivation of the land. With the ideology of improvement, Bhandar writes, 'land that was not cultivated for the purposes of contributing to a burgeoning agrarian capitalist economy by industrious laborers was, from the early seventeenth century onward, deemed to be waste' (Bhandar 2018, 36).[27] Across settler-colonial contexts, aboriginal claims to land were dismissed on these grounds – colonial property regimes fused the economic categories of value/waste with racial categories of civilised/savage. Particularly interesting for us is how this ideology of improvement manifests through the governance of Ireland's bogs and their native inhabitants. These recalcitrant, alien ecologies that were not easily civilised became synonymous with Irish 'backwardness' and 'laziness'. Terms such as 'bog-Irish' or 'bog-trotter' originated in this period, capturing the pejorative identification of the specific bog landscape with indigenous Irish: not only were bogs 'unproductive' land, they harboured rebellious Irish natives, stymying the civilisation of the island.[28]

Petty's Down Survey, one of the earliest national surveys, illustrated the extent of boglands on the island of Ireland, and was among the first of many colonial projects that sought to make legible the boggy Irish landscape for profit. It was not long before new landowners and colonial administrators seeking to tame and benefit from Irish territories targeted the drainage and reclamation of boglands for agriculture. From 1716 onwards, a series of Acts were passed by the Irish parliament to encourage peatland reclamation. In 1776, Arthur Young, social commentator and future establishing member of the British Board of Agriculture, undertook a travelogue of Ireland focussing on the need for improvement in what he saw as wasteland landscapes and impoverished ways of living on them. As historian Esa Ruuskanen articulates, 'Young envisioned how a country so widely covered with "wastelands" could possess a lush, cultivated countryside and wealthier population and serve as the granary of industrialising England' (2018, 22).

For us, the ideology of improvement is not simply a historical phenomenon limited to the establishment of British colonialism in Ireland. As one of the first political economists, Petty ushered in new kind of administrative state:[29] the ideology of improvement required a technoscientific apparatus of measurement, an infrastructure for capturing, comparing, and improving the productivity of land and labour over time. Petty viewed 'the corpus vile of Ireland' as an ideal laboratory for this 'experimental statecraft', petitioning the government to support the creation of 'new instruments of government' (McCormick 2009).[30]

We trace the endurance of this 'experimental statecraft', a laboratory of improvement, across Ireland's colonial and postcolonial periods, right up until today. This manifests through a relationship to land and rural populations that is mediated through shifting regimes of waste/value and efforts to construct new resource frontiers for capitalist accumulation. The political economic contexts for these projects, in particular the role of the state and relationship to the world capitalist system, vary, but key aspects of the ideology of improvement remain. A good example of such continuity/discontinuity is illustrated in Chapter 2, where we cover Ireland's partial effort to break away from energy dependence on Britain. This resulted in the large-scale transformation of Ireland's bogs, producing a national fuel source to power the sovereign development of a modern, independent Ireland. For centuries, colonial administrators had gestured towards the need to drain, plant, and utilise the vast peatlands of Ireland, resulting in novel techniques and institutions for surveying land. But little material transformation occurred until after the South of Ireland's independence. It was only by (partially) breaking colonial dependency that these plans of 'improvement' could be acted upon. In 1934, the newly founded Turf Development Board used the very same Bog Commission maps that had been completed in the 1820s – coloniality expressed through the ideology of improvement, of boglands as 'waste', untapped resources to be capitalised on.

Today, as we discuss in Chapters 4, 5, and 6, we see the eco-modernist recasting of this ideology of improvement, as post-industrial 'wasted' bogs once again become sites of resource-making, whether to store carbon or to host data centres and their energy infrastructures. It is no coincidence that the Geological Survey of Ireland (GSI), founded in 1845, continues to ensure that Ireland is one of the most intensively and extensively mapped territories in the world (Mercier et al 2022). Nor, as we detail in Chapter 5, that the funding and architecture of Ireland's third-level sector has developed hand in glove with multinational companies to develop new technologies, including digital systems, to better exploit land and labour, not just in Ireland but internationally. Neoliberal eco-modernity is fixated on environmental metrics and targets, combining calculative expertise with market opportunities. Ireland is well adapted to this confluence not only because it is particularly 'neoliberal', but also because it has been a laboratory of improvement for five hundred years.

Understanding the continuity of state logics of improvement across historical periods is also important for making sense of resistance in rural parts of Ireland. In the 1990s, the Irish sociologist Hilary Tovey distinguished between rural 'populist' environmentalism and 'official' environmentalism – a useful framework we return to in Chapter 3. 'Populist' environmentalism was place-based and resistant to the imposition of 'bigness' (Tovey 1993), in the form of state-led development projects and infrastructures that disrupted existing ways of life and livelihood. While Tovey was specifically referring to an upsurge of localised, community campaigns in the late 1980s, we connect these peripheral, 'populist' forms of resistance to a much longer tradition of subaltern, land-based politics.[31] Generally pejoratively dismissed as 'traditional' or 'anti-modern', these varied sites of objection to 'modernising' projects also offer a rich genealogy and reservoir of anti-colonial, often internationalist, political praxis, that is once again surfacing today (Chapter 6).

The land question

Petty's 'experimental statecraft' in Ireland (Carroll 2006, 57), which aligned demographic, territorial, and technoscientific strategy through the simultaneously moral lens of 'improvement', was central to the establishment of Ireland's role in the burgeoning empire – not as a full participant or 'sub-imperial centre' (Crosbie 2009), but as a colony with a population and landscape to be managed as 'problems'. This is not just ideology as discourse, but fundamentally about the colonial appropriation of land and value, via resource extraction and the super-exploitation of labour. In other words, in the 17th century, Ireland was a blank slate that first needed to be civilised and improved, before surplus value could be syphoned off to the colonial, then imperial, core. Ireland's continued status as a 'semi-periphery', according to Denis O'Hearn's analysis (Beatty et al 2016), is inseparable from these histories.

This is partially why Petty's praxis of statecraft was so central to Marx's own theories of political economy, and Marx and Engels' understanding of what would later be called the 'metabolic rift' in Ireland's colonial political ecology (Foster 2000; Slater and Flaherty 2023). The best historical materialist work on this comes from Eamonn Slater, Terrence McDonough, and Eoin Flaherty on the Irish Famine.[32] In elucidating and developing an eco-Marxist analysis of the 'metabolic rift', they analyse the socio-ecological dynamics of the colonial agricultural economy in Ireland. From the perspective of an 'ecological regime', these scholars show how Ireland's colonial agricultural economy was not only about extraction of resources (in this case soil nutrients and plants) and the exploitation of labour, but also about the undermining of local ecological conditions, transformation in social structures, reliance on unpaid ecological care work, and ultimately the catastrophe of the Great Hunger. This saw the effective clearance of large areas of rural Ireland and the arrival of a new colonial ecological regime of pasture-based, animal agriculture.

The late 19th century was also the high point of land agitation, as the colonial landlord system buckled under its own contradictions and a large population of small tenant farmers and landless workers mobilised. At this time, the land question was linked directly with the national question, explicitly orientated against this extractive economy and towards the self-determination of Ireland's people against the crown. Responding to this, the British Government moved to 'solve' the land question by offering tenant purchase – initiating the transfer of lands from landlords to tenants. While this remains a familiar historical narrative, the reality was that the land question remained unsolved in the Free State because Ireland's agrarian economy continued to be dependent on Britain,[33] focussed on the export of live cattle via a wealthy comprador class of middlemen (McCabe 2011).[34] As Connolly put it, 'Were the landlords to disappear to-morrow, and their titles to land to become extinct, the peasant proprietors remaining would still be involved in a hopeless struggle for subsistence, whilst this island remains dominated by capitalistic conditions' (Connolly 1898). After formal independence, the South remained a de-developed, agrarian economy. Land agitation continued and was central to the short-lived and partial efforts at achieving economic self-sufficiency that took place between the 1930s and 1950s (Chapter 2).

The relative absence of Ireland's land politics from historical accounts of the first half of the 20th century and its imbrications with anti-colonial, anti-imperialist politics is not accidental. From the 1950s, Ireland embarked on a new developmental path which involved active re-integration with the world capitalist system, now dominated by the US, and moving away from the 'Catholic austerity' of national self-sufficiency and the small, peasant farmer.[35] Export-led industrialisation replaced import-substitution and domestic industry; attracting multinational companies to locate in Ireland was now the state's priority. By the 1990s, Ireland's FDI-led development strategy appeared to have worked: the Celtic Tiger was born, and with it a wave of revisionism that buried Ireland's (anti-)colonial past and present.

While we will return again and again to these histories, the point we want to emphasise here is less about Irish capitalist development per se than about the waning of a materialist analysis of Irish capitalism centred on land and resources – or, to put it another way, the absence of the land question within contemporary analysis of Irish capitalism. This may seem obvious: Ireland's economic model relies on its ability to capture a fraction of the surplus value generated by the highly exploitative, globally extensive supply chains of multinational companies. Paraphrasing Moore, Deckard argues that Ireland's Finance Services Centre (IFSC), established in the late 1980s as a tax-reduced special economic zone in Dublin, is the engine for 'organising nature' in Ireland (2016). Conor McCabe has likewise demonstrated how the institutional arrangements of the IFSC and its enablers in the state have historically laid the groundwork for this tax haven model (2011, 2015).[36]

While accepting and building on this analysis, our book argues that we need to look beyond 'abstracted' financial structures of FDI if we are to understand how Irish land, infrastructure, and resources have been produced for foreign capital. Beyond tax regimes, what has been underestimated is the extent to which the Irish state has created the environmental and infrastructural conditions for these companies to operate and profit in Ireland – what we call Ireland's 'postcolonial ecological regime', building on Deckard's theorisation of a 'neoliberal ecological regime' (2016). While neoliberalism has structured the financialisation of Ireland and its tendency to double-down on this development model, this is not a strategy that arose in a vacuum. Rather, Ireland experimented with strategies of market-led development at a relatively early stage, making it an outlier both in Europe and in relation to other postcolonial developmental states (O'Hearn 1989). With this in mind, we argue that land, ecology, and the infrastructures that mediate these are crucial to understanding the spatial politics of Ireland's FDI-led developmental model, especially amid the tech industries' monopolistic enterprises. This is surfacing most clearly today in negotiations about energy and digital infrastructures, specifically projects designated as essential for datafication and 'green' transitions.

Ireland's development across colonial and postcolonial periods has always involved the careful orientation of 'environmental' factors towards the capitalist world system – understood as the management and governance of land, infrastructure, and resources.[37] Across historical periods, 'nature' has been organised for different political projects and class interests. This is an important intervention because within mainstream green discourse today, organisations such as Bord na Móna, with their history in extensive peat extraction, are cast as villains, or at the very least compromised actors in the eco-modernisation of the country. From an anti-colonial perspective, however, the development of Ireland's bogs in the mid-20th century can be read as a partial and incomplete project of energy decolonisation. 'Environmental' from this perspective is not limited to conservation of habitats or species, but encompasses a more materialist understanding of state-mediated development within, or against, the imperialist world system.

Dependency and the Irish semi-periphery

In 1986, Raymond Crotty, one of Ireland's few dependency-inspired economists, wrote: 'The evident failure of Ireland's economy must be viewed in the context of Third World underdevelopment' (11).[38] Building on work he had developed throughout the 1970s, Crotty's analysis of what he termed 'colonial capitalism' outlined how the subordination of the Irish (agricultural) economy to Britain, particularly from the 19th century, offered a clear case of the 'development of underdevelopment'. Paralleling the historical analysis of dependency thinkers such as Theotônio Dos Santos in Latin America, Crotty plotted how structural features of Ireland's dependent economy persisted after formal independence – leaking value via foreign-owned industries and continued dependence on British markets, and explaining Ireland's ballooning national debt, high unemployment, and mass emigration in the late 1980s. At around the same time, sociologist Denis O'Hearn in a similar vein argued that Ireland was a classic case of dependency: 25 years of foreign-owned, export-led industrialisation had produced little economic growth and increased inequality. O'Hearn was pushing back against the growing dominance of modernisation theory, which saw universal application of liberal capitalist institutions as a means of spreading and securing global development. On the eve of Francis Fukuyama's infamous 'end of history' essay, modernisation theory looked to the apparent success of East Asian economies as evidence of 'convergence' between national economies in the world system. Defending the ongoing significance of dependency theory, O'Hearn, like Crotty, asserted that Ireland's role in the Atlantic economy remained a subordinate one, transferring value to US multinationals while failing to chart a path towards anything like sovereign development. For Crotty and O'Hearn, Ireland's economic underdevelopment offered a critical riposte to theories of economic convergence, revealing the core structural contradiction of imperial capitalism: the maintenance of inequality between core and (semi-)peripheries.

Connected to this economic analysis in Ireland was a vibrant new field of environmental sociology that was responding to a rise in environmental social movements. Rather than taking its lead from currents of European, middle-class, and urban-based environmentalism, the Irish scene was energised by rural community-based campaigns objecting to the siting of toxic chemical and pharmaceutical facilities. Environmental sociologists connected these anti-toxics campaigns to a longer history of rural, peripheral, and land-based politics in Ireland. By framing these struggles in terms of uneven development, this work also pushed back against a tendency that sought to place Ireland within a modernisation paradigm, 'catching up' with its European counterparts. While not explicitly articulating their work through world-systems or dependency theory, critical scholars in Ireland situated environmental conflicts within broader debates over modernisation, development, and Ireland's place within the global economy.[39]

Our analysis of monopoly tech and eco-modernity in Ireland is inspired by these now marginalised intellectual currents. Ireland's ascendance to one of the world's wealthiest countries measured by GDP per capita does not discount the usefulness of dependency theory.[40] Rather it demonstrates the deepening of Ireland's role as a semi-periphery, enabling super concentration of profits at a world-scale. These critical perspectives also allow us to see how internal socio-ecological contradictions are inseparable from Ireland's dependent position within an evolving capitalist world system. Dependency, according to Samir Amin, explained the inability of the formerly colonial developmental states to leverage indigenous assets towards effective integration into a global capital without 'leaking' value – and this was in large part due to the tendency of local elites to concede to capitalist influences and, at an amplified level, the institutionalisation of measures designed in the image of such imperfect integration (Amin 1976, 1990). As the postcolonial middle class became 'more central to peripheral accumulation, becoming the basis of import-substitution industrialisation and an enlarged internal market' (Ajl 2021a, 84), these nations were faced with the turbulence of a world system premised upon extraction from the periphery to the core and the structural dependence of peripheral states on core imports in technology and expertise.[41] This was not just formed on new relationships emerging in the world economy, but enduring structures of dependency that persisted whether colonial or postcolonial in character due to the imperial basis of the world system and, in a somewhat new development, the violence of US hegemony: 'beyond the natural unsettledness of the sea of economic development, the gales of US violence buffeted such states as soon as they set out. In the face of such storms, the peripheral bourgeoisie mostly accepted "compradorization"' (Ajl 2021a, 85).

Specific discussions of dependency theory in Ireland have typically been secondary to understandings of developmental and post-developmental phases of the postcolonial Irish state, and even then, the recourse to coloniality is reduced to a phasal shift in the management of Ireland (see Boylan and McDonough 1998). Much less has been theorised in terms of the endurance and continuity of, for example, land management and governance, as well as the inheritance of expertise and class structures from the colonial era and the persistent dependencies that remain in postcolonial contexts subject to integration within a (US-dominated) capitalist world system.[42] Throughout this book, we illustrate how Ireland's FDI-led postcolonial ecological regime dictates the terms by which the Irish state mediates environmental contradictions of capitalist growth, whether towards overtly toxic and extractive industries or apparently more benign activities emerging to support 'sustainability'.

This surfaces most clearly today in negotiations across energy and digital infrastructures, specifically projects designated as essential for datafication and 'green' transitions. More recent green political economy offers a corrective to the missing ecological dimensions in the analysis of Ireland's developmental model within the capitalist world ecology (Moore 2015). Deckard expresses this better when she writes that

> Ireland has played a significant role in the emergence of different cycles of systemic accumulation as a laboratory for new forms of

expropriation, from sixteenth-century plantation to twenty-first century neoliberal austerity. However, this role must be understood not only in terms of Ireland's socio-economic relation to the world-economy, but of Ireland's function in the world-ecology. (2016)

In this analysis, what happens in Ireland does not only have implications for Ireland, but also offers instructive apertures for understanding world ecology more broadly. This is not just because Irish state policies enable certain forms of extractive and polluting enterprise with planetary implications, but because experiments in capitalist eco-modernity are made possible here – from the construction of enclosed data/energy infrastructural campuses to peatland carbon mapping (Chapters 4–6). As we suggest throughout the book, these experiments in neoliberal statecraft and industrial technoscience have produced a transnationally mobile and influential comprador class of industrialists and technicians, who pass seamlessly through a revolving door connecting the state, commercial semi-states, and private/FDI sectors.

Our decision to turn to dependency theory does not happen in a vacuum. A range of thinkers have rejuvenated this perspective in recent years to account for the foundationally technological and ecological imbalances that continue to structure exchanges and power relations in the capitalist world system, in ways that force us to re-orientate climate debates towards their territorial implications.[43] But while there has been significant resurgence in the concept of dependency in ecological theory and debates, especially in relation to eco-modernity and various iterations of green grabbing, these dynamics of economic (and ecological) dependency have not been considered widely in studies of digital systems and the growth of AI in particular.[44] With current jostling for position on a global stage for AI dominance and investment, Ireland has clearly become a strategic site for embedding these technologies in the 'Western' semi-periphery – a readymade sink for the dependent technologies of data centres for US operations in Europe. This locks Ireland in technologically to some of the most basic and unsophisticated functions of US monopoly tech – its concentration elsewhere is supported by its technological operations here, and the managing of ecologies towards their function. Ireland becomes a party in not only its own dependency, but also in both facilitating monopoly tech and undermining technological development in the Global South, with all of the consequences for planetary ecological justice which that implies.[45] It is here that Ireland's inability to develop domestic AI capacity, while at the same time inserting AI infrastructure into public agendas at all levels of society, makes sense in the apparently paradoxical context of its data centre energy saturation.[46] To remain a dependent engine of US tech growth, infrastructures and green policies need to be shaped in its image.[47] Contesting eco-modernity from Ireland thus contributes an important perspective amid the unfolding contradictions of digitalisation and decarbonisation at a planetary scale: we are already seeing these contradictions play out sharply across Ireland's postcolonial infrastructures and ecologies, and it has presented both challenges and opportunities for movements orientated towards internationalist environmental justice.

Contesting eco-modernity from a green tech laboratory

In this final section, we want to show how the emerging contours and infrastructures of eco-modernity at a global (and planetary) scale can be better understood by examining it through Ireland. In the intensified expansion and development of FDI-led infrastructure towards green, digital transition in Ireland, we argue that Ireland has become what we call a 'green tech laboratory': a place through which the contradictions of capitalist growth are not only ecologically managed, but tested and innovated to secure future profitability and accumulation.

The figure of the 'laboratory' is one of the central heuristics that we return to throughout the book to explain this dynamic across history. Ireland is frequently referred to as the 'colonial laboratory' through which British statecraft was experimented upon through the 'corpus vile' of the island and its people, from mapping and surveying, to experimentation with free market trade policies, to tactics of counter-insurgency developed in the cauldron of the NI conflict.[48] While Ireland's colonial experience was (and remains) different from more extreme implementations of these strategies by the British state later,[49] there are nonetheless concrete instantiations wherein the experimental mindset evidenced by colonial administrators in Ireland clearly forged templates by which to govern and manage people and environments across the imperial peripheries.

The idea of Ireland as a colonial laboratory has been widely discussed and contested in Irish history.[50] In fact, revisionist historians of the 20th century have used Ireland's unique role as both subjects of and active, if junior, partners in the empire to ideologically whitewash the history of British colonisation in Ireland. The has not only resulted in a distancing of contemporary Irish society from its embeddedness in a trajectory from a colonial to a partitioned and ostensibly partially 'decolonised' island, but a liberal re-imagining of the terms by which Ireland interacts with the world system.[51] Aside from a brief couple of decades in which Ireland sought to partially break from economic dependence on Britain (see Chapter 2), the newly independent southern state eventually evolved towards postcolonial dependency – and the associated regimes of knowledge, infrastructure, and ecological relationships that could support it. From the 1950s, Ireland once again became a place of developmental experimentation. This time, however, it was for the statecraft of FDI-led development and the facilitation of multinationals, the main vectors of US-led imperialist monopoly capitalism. Crucially, the degree to which Ireland was able to become a modern colonial laboratory amid its bogs, fields, rivers, and coastlines was in large part due to its enduring peripherality – and this is something that was repurposed by the developmental strategies of the Republic. The Industrial Development Authority (IDA), for example, which was largely responsible for institutionalising the model of 'industrialisation by invitation', has long advertised Ireland as a wild, green place to do business, instrumentalising colonial stereotypes towards developmental imperatives (Brodie forthcoming). Ireland's position at the 'edge' of Europe, recently, has provided fodder for any number of state development agencies to advertise Irish businesses as worthy of multinational investment and partnership.[52] This peripherality, a frontier for the development of new forms of profit and extraction via experimental governance and technoscience, was one of the core values of the state as it developed an FDI-led development model from the 1950s.

Unlike other (post)colonial countries which developed various forms of 'resource nationalism' surrounding signature minerals and extractive economies, Ireland has developed what we might refer to as an 'FDI nationalism' that both acknowledges the structural importance of multinational companies in its economy and development strategies while also emphasising the uniquely Irish character of the 'ground game' that has brought this into being. In 2020, the IDA's CEO called FDI a 'contact sport' (Irwin-Hunt 2020), emphasising the challenges of attracting investors to Ireland when travel and regular business was disrupted. Sport metaphors abound, especially within the data centre industry, our entry point into these politics of state developmentalism and its inseparability from the private sector and its lobby groups.[53]

At the annual Data Centres Ireland conference in Dublin, sponsored by lobby groups such as Host in Ireland, the 2024 iteration featured Host in Ireland founder Garry Connolly on a panel referring to the role of all of his colleagues in the 'FDI game'. While everyone in the room working in the data centre industry were competitors across their different companies, they all were proud to 'wear the green jersey' across the world when attracting multinational partnerships and investments into Ireland, a clear and rousing illustration of the ground game of FDI nationalism. The members of the panels, which included the Irish head of multinational colocation data centre provider Equinix, Peter Lantry, made clear reference to their connections to the state, and especially the semi-state energy sector. Lantry himself is a former Eirgrid man, the semi-state grid operator. Mark Foley, the former CEO of Eirgrid and now a private consultant for the wind energy industry, was present, and gave a talk. BnM was there to promote its new energy projects for data centre partnerships. Barry Lowry, the Irish Government's Chief Information Officer, was the keynote speaker. The moving portrait of the revolving door between the state and corporate entities, whether multinational or in the business of partnering with and supporting multinationals, was rendered with overwhelming clarity by the conversations and attitudes of those in the room. This was comprador capitalism in a distilled form – and expressed through overt collaboration between multinational technology companies and Irish state agencies, especially those involved in energy.

But, the scene also describes a landscape of experimental governance motivated by FDI-led development. These are spaces of knowledge exchange, supported by organisations such as the IDA and Enterprise Ireland, to develop 'innovation' and partnerships that will support the state development model. This is why these spaces become such important elements of our analysis, as they provide longitudinal insights into how industry orthodoxies (and anxieties) form as time passes. For example: in 2023, almost the entirety of the programme was devoted to 'sustainability' and 'green technologies', with companies scrambling to develop solutions to the energy problems they were exacerbating. Lantry, also in attendance that year, while acknowledging the importance of sourcing decarbonised energy, also warned his colleagues against over-committing to infrastructural development – getting classified as 'utilities' would be disastrous for the autonomy of the industry and its ability to operate free from state scrutiny (Brodie 2024). Data centre companies, he said, were enthusiastic about developing and adopting sustainable solutions, and just needed the state to step out of the way. If regulation continued at pace, referencing the 'de facto moratorium' on new grid connections implemented by Eirgrid in 2022, there would be a mass exodus of FDI. He would later go to the national press with this warning, heralding a potential 'techxit' (Leonard 2024).

The 2024 Data Centres Ireland programme was largely focussed on threats to FDI and the challenges faced by AI for infrastructural provision and economic development more broadly. Amid the acknowledged mainstreaming of data centre critique and the recognition of their importance in instantiating monopoly tech in Ireland, Lantry changed his tune: maybe it was actually time to do something more transformative, and work with the state, considering the centrality of digital infrastructure in the contemporary economy and the inescapability of growing energy usage. He said that the state needed a new Ardnacrusha – the massive hydroelectric dam developed by the early Free State in the 1920s, one of the most significant postcolonial developmental projects in history at this stage (Mercier 2021).[54] However, while the Shannon Hydroelectric Scheme was about providing a public energy utility for citizens in the state and developing industries across Ireland, Lantry's argument was that such a large-scale electricity generation project, funded by the state, could provide for the electricity needs of exploding data centre growth, ushering in a new green, digital era of Irish prosperity.

While the delusional, monopoly techno-solutionism at play here is easy to call out, what is more interesting is that the imaginary of such a project is not about decarbonising Ireland. It is about developing electricity as a commodity – something to profit from, by selling electrons to multinationals and allowing them to process them via data-driven services (Brodie 2024).[55] This is thus not only about datafication – it represents an emerging ideology of decarbonised electrification *via* digitalisation, whereby electricity is evacuated of its public provision as a utility. These industry-led narratives are strong and worryingly central to state strategy. As the example of the Eirgrid engineer speaking in our class demonstrates, and as our research for the last six years has shown, the degree to which these discourses transfer from the industry to the state, and vice versa, is exceptional.

What is important to emphasise at this stage is that *history* is important to how these industrial narratives take shape. Garry Connolly is an impressive orator, and a master of branding history as a series of events that inevitably leads to and morally supports the activities of the data centre industry in supporting the 'sustainable' rise of digital capital. His lectures and seminars to data centre industry professionals frequently take the form of a pop history lesson. Take his example in a webinar we attended in 2022: that Ireland went from a 'spud' to a 'chip' economy in the late 20th century (Connolly 2022; see also Chapter 3). His identification of a real dependence on agricultural trade and land usage transitioning towards technology manufacturing from the mid-20th century to the Celtic Tiger (1990s–2000s) is not necessarily incorrect. However, his description of its origins and consequences are more troublesome: that Ireland needed to leverage the commodification of its land and infrastructure, harnessing electrons and data-driven innovation to export, just like it harnessed soil ecologies towards potatoes (Brodie 2024). This history intentionally elides the deep inequalities of Ireland's agrarian economy, its industrial adaptation in a necessarily subservient role to global enterprise, and the amplifying contradictions of dependency on multinational investment in an otherwise underdeveloped infrastructural landscape. In a way that isn't far off the academic strains of historical revisionism discussed above, these industrial narratives tell a history of Ireland through the lens of FDI as the only true means of national development. Our history needs to push against that.

Throughout this book, we thus demonstrate how the elision of (post) colonial histories also arise in the state narratives designed to support FDI-led development, considering them through the postcolonial ecological regime and its contested origins out of the imperial ecologies of the British state. The role of historiography in and through public institutions is thus a central part of our analysis – not only in the form of state developmental narratives and promotion, but also the everyday, lived historical situation of knowledge within public institutions (including higher education, which later chapters will detail). At the same time, however, this historical orientation of institutions involved in FDI simultaneously masks an anti-democratic, future-driven ethos – this is about retroactively positioning these companies as central to rather than problematic for Ireland's sustainable infrastructural development. This is a crucial part of the green tech laboratory – and only by understanding the powerful sway and common-sensical reproduction of FDI as the crux of development across state, semi-state, and civil society institutions can the apparently irrational contradictions of FDI nationalism make sense in an era of decarbonisation. This is especially the case through infrastructural and ecological management, by which we witness a creeping privatisation across both of these areas in and through 'green' policies ostensibly designed to channel the technologies and expertise of digital cloud providers into decarbonisation strategies that will eventually provide the spoils of 'development' (see Chapters 4–5).

Within the future-driven, speculative thinking of the energy transition, monopoly tech is given exceptional purchase in what green, digital transitions actually look like. These companies do so by emphasising the necessity of such technological expertise and investment in emerging infrastructure at a time of urgent large-scale transformation. But, despite the pop revisionism from industry, these are 'unproven' technologies – representing speculative hypotheses not (actually) towards how tech can help, but how these companies can profit from state imperatives towards decarbonised service provision. This backdoor privatisation and amplified exploitation is thus enabled by a system that thrives on experiment, whereby the infrastructures and ecologies of Ireland become a green tech laboratory for multinational development of the ongoing energy transition.

But our argument is less about privatisation, and more fundamentally about the positioning of the Irish state and the industrial interests represented by a comprador class that is fundamentally aligned with FDI-led state development policy. The 'green jersey' worn by the data centre business figures around the world is outfitted by the IDA; but while it is about drawing in investment for development and 'jobs', it is also about lining pockets. The argument about promoting Irish capacities, from human capital to fixed capital (for example, infrastructure), is about paradoxically ensuring that the investment relation, especially with regards to high-tech industries, *remains a dependent one*. Rather than developing and overtly investing in 'indigenous' capacity in the area of digital business,[56] it is fundamentally about orientating the entire ecosystem around multinationals. This structural dependence on monopoly tech is the overt result of compradorisation, which we can see at multiple points in the state–civil society nexus, from the data centre industry to the university to the mining industry to the halls of government. It is about securing a partially beneficiary position in these economic systems, even if that locks in dependency.

Our contribution to this debate, of course, extends beyond Ireland. The place of monopoly tech in the eco-modern transformations of green capitalism has been under-theorised, and one of our main contributions in this book is to link discussions surrounding the infrastructural expansion of digital technologies such as AI to the wider discussions and struggles around eco-socialism, anti-imperialist degrowth, and 'just transitions'. Many degrowth-orientated environmental movements against large-scale, top-down projects of climate transition – especially struggles against green extractivism and green grabbing in the Global South, Indigenous territories, and European peripheries – have been accused of 'anti-modern' sentiments, and, at worst, of 'NIMBYism' against development and technology, especially by those on the eco-modernist left.[57]

But we shouldn't short circuit such contested politics to reductive positions of pro- or anti-technology – or 'anti-modernity' for that matter.[58] As Kai Heron argues, left eco-modernism rests on a version of the 'fetter thesis' that supposes that the capitalist forces of production, the technologies of 'progress', can be re-directed towards eco-socialist ends through a socialisation of ownership, a revolution in the *relations* of production (2024). This position ignores how capitalism's 'metabolic control' over ecology also *produces* desolation, 'undermining rather than laying the groundwork for communism' (Heron 2024). In so doing, it enables eco-modernists to come to, at best, a bad faith conclusion about the progressive role of capitalist technological development in forging an ecologically viable, justice-oriented transition. As Heron argues, paraphrasing Marx's theorisation of agricultural soil exhaustion in Ireland as a core feature of colonialism's hold on the island:

> Capitalism, in other words, leads to the unevenly distributed ruination of the worker and non-human nature … It is not that the forces and relations of production are coming into contradiction – though this can happen – it is that the totality of capitalist social relations also come into contradiction with, and ruin, or cannibalize its social and ecological basis. (2024)

Ajay Singh Chaudhary similarly uses the example of Amazon's supply chains as an example of something that cannot be reorientated back towards a project of socialist planning and development by virtue of exploitative, extractive, and what Chaudhary calls 'exhaustive' structures of production and valorisation (2024). Such observations have long been bread and butter to Marxist thinkers in the Global South, as it is from the concrete question of how to develop (technologies, infrastructures, agricultural systems) from the periphery, liberated from the imperative of global capital, that the non-neutrality of technology becomes obvious.[59]

This is a key point in the navigation of monopoly tech amid the frozen horizon of eco-modernity: simply taking over the forces of production is not an option due to the fundamentally exploitative relations that dictate contemporary capitalism's world-spanning supply chains. Heron, and anti-imperialist critics such as Ajl (2023) and Hickel (2021; Hickel et al 2022), identify left eco-modernism's blindspot in the basic structure of unequal (ecological) exchange between core and periphery, presenting an insurmountable wall for any truly anti-imperialist, post-capitalist project for reshaping socio-ecological relations, especially if oriented within a single nation-state.[60] We need left visions of *different* regimes of sovereign but solidaristic development that do not look like or carry forward what monopoly tech has wrought, democratising production in order to remake supply chains and infrastructures through more careful socio-ecological planning and coordination – an anti-imperialist social metabolism that accounts for, and replaces, the role of monopoly tech in shaping (and foreclosing) collective futures and aims for planetary justice.

In this sense, we cannot begin any eco-socialist programme with the premise that 'data centres are necessary'.[61] Yes, cloud computing has enabled conveniences and efficiencies, much like FDI has brought certain forms of modern 'prosperity' to (some) people in Ireland. But we have to remember that the access and distribution of electronic information is possible under other, alternative systems, meaning we have to ask eco-modernists: What technologies do people need, how can they make peoples' lives better, and how are they provided?[62] Returning to historical 'modernities' is instructive, in particular experimental, unfinished projects of Third World socialist modernity that exploded in the 1950s and 1960s. Anti-colonial thinkers and revolutionaries from Frantz Fanon to Sylvia Wynter, Amílcar Cabral to Ibrahim Illawi, emphasised that world decolonisation meant going beyond European modernity and 'civilisation', an emancipatory impulse that took on material force when rooted in the practical reworking of relations to land and ecological relationships (Bresnihan and Millner 2023). As Ajl points out, Amin's early theories in the 1950s–1960s, in confluence with other dependency thinkers at the time, were grappling with the imperative to industrialise and 'modernise' production, which inevitably came with ecological consequences when linking in with a capitalist world system premised on value extraction from the peripheries. Without seriously grappling with the question of how agrarian and industrial development in the peripheries could 'delink' ecological value from the capitalist world market,[63] production would continue to 'pummel' ecology in unsustainable ways (Ajl 2021a).[64] As we discuss in Chapter 2, Ireland's own imperfect experiments with 'decolonial modernity' in the 1940s–1950s through peat-driven energy, though inheriting colonial logics and ideologies of progress, represent efforts to socially plan and foster different forms of modern life

– organised not according to the colonial imperative of value extraction, or the profit motive of private capital, but *an idea* of the common good and social development. That this project was unecological, exclusive, and insufficiently radical does not mean we should wholly dismiss the decolonial aspiration that gave rise to it.

We are not interested in reconstructing or, worse, idealising a grand narrative wherein the 'modernising' Irish state neatly transitioned from an under-developed postcolonial territory to a 'modern' nation-state in any naive or crass way. Rather, the project of modernisation was always confronting problems and contradictions in and through a negotiation with 'traditional' Irish life that could never be removed from its relation to the 'modern'. If the colonial project is also always one of modernisation, but modernisation for *some* and not for others (and what that looks like geographically), then the structure of modernity has long shaped Ireland's landscapes, ecologies, and economies. To perform a political ecology of the Irish state and its relationships to monopoly tech, one must understand the structural transition from a colonial political ecology to one inevitably navigating the agential remnants of these existing structures. Adopting this historically materialist approach also allows us to trace a long history of subaltern, or alter-modern, opposition in Ireland, centred on those disenfranchised by subsequent and overlapping periods and projects of Irish modernity – from the 17th century to the present day. James Connolly, in his treatise *Labour in Irish History*, ends his foreword with recourse to the cultural maintenance of what we would call coloniality in the 'Irish propertied classes' which became 'more English than the English' (1910). He continues, 'attempting to depict the attitude of the dispossessed masses of the Irish people in the great crisis of modern Irish history, may justly be looked upon as part of the literature of the Gaelic revival' (1910). In this sense, understanding earlier points of social, political, environmental, and cultural transition – as we do in this book – is essential for articulating a politics of contestation that accounts for the structural imbalances of modern Irish life in the shadow of monopoly tech capital.

Throughout the book, we focus on moments of tension and contestation – where modernity clashes with its discontents, as well as where it forms itself. What Dilip Gaonkar claims emerge as 'life-worlds' in the study of the subaltern everyday life supposedly underlying modernity (1999), and decolonial and Indigenous thinkers have theorised at length and frequently through the lens of colonial infrastructure and modern state-making (Spice 2018; Curley 2021), are 'submerged' by the projects of a top-down modernity (Gómez-Barris 2017), but new and insurgent formations arise and are forged in the cauldron of 'development'.[65] This ambivalence is part of what we want to confront and in some cases recover as a resource for contemporary Irish theorising of (and contestation around) capitalist eco-modernity.

INTRODUCTION

Structure of the book

We have spent this Introduction situating Ireland both in its specificity as well as within broader debates and histories concerning modernity, colonialism, imperial capitalism, and eco-modernity. But this is a book about Ireland, and the ways in which digital capitalism and the 'green transition' have historically aligned here. We are using all of these frameworks and ideas from other places in order to think about Ireland – and this is not only because of their critical import. It is also to make it clear that Ireland's experience is instructive for burgeoning struggles surrounding monopoly tech's eco-modernity elsewhere. It also more concretely and robustly situates Ireland within these global networks, and highlights the complex forms of dependency and complicity that have arisen here over the past hundred or so years. As this Introduction has made clear, we are also drawing from a deep well of knowledge and historical research about Ireland specifically, in Irish studies and Irish history, as well as researchers on the early modern world and the circulations of empire that would shape the contemporary world system as we still know it. In the coming chapters, we will develop these ideas further through our indebtedness to anti-, de-, and postcolonial – and finally, anti-imperialist – environmental thought in Ireland and beyond. These thinkers are the primary cultivators of the radical alternatives to an unjust eco-modernity that we want to contest as much as analyse.

As we have already stated, then, this is not an exhaustive history or even geography.[66] Rather, we have situated readers at this stage upon the ground of our own collaboration and ways of thinking about eco-modernity and the green, digital transition in contemporary Ireland, which will deepen throughout the coming chapters. One of the motivations for writing this book has been to situate these extremely present and pressing issues – as we write, data centres remain the most significant electricity users on the Irish grid (21 per cent in 2023) – within longer histories of industrial development in Ireland. This is because we are frustrated by the crises-thinking and presentism that has dominated data centre discourse and discourses about new and digital media more generally, especially with the advent of AI. We have to acknowledge that these are unprecedented times, and that the rate of 'innovation' and change in digital media systems are essentially without historical antecedent. Nonetheless, even this common-sensical acknowledgement comes with a potentially problematic, and at least compromised, sense of the role of digital media in our contemporary lives and environmental futures. We must also then understand that the alignment of digitalisation with the urgency of decarbonisation is a strategic one, which places digital media at the centre of our climate and environmental futures in a way that, ecologically, requires immensely more complex and critical conceptual frameworks for disrupting. In historicising these developments in Ireland, we are not only crafting our own frameworks, but also pointing towards places where the logics of monopoly tech eco-modernity are already being disrupted and challenged – and potentially alternative formations are already emerging.

One of the enduring problems of our work in this area remains how to situate Ireland's colonial, anti-colonial, postcolonial, neocolonial, and decolonial pasts, presents, and futures in its complexity. We have attempted to lay the groundwork above, but we acknowledge that these remain unresolved and in themselves contested. The far right's appropriation of the language of 'colonisation' and 'plantation' by inward migrants to Ireland speaks to ongoing battlegrounds of these histories within Irish 'identity', especially when directed towards nativist and supremacist positions. The language of 'anti-colonial' environmental politics is one that has been sparingly used by activists in Ireland in recent memory. The association of contemporary anti-colonial politics in Ireland with the paramilitary republicanism in the Occupied Six Counties of the North is off-putting for many, which speaks to the unfortunate distancing of politics in the South from what has been the most enduring leftist, anti-imperialist movement on the island for at least the last 150 years. However, while we do not claim to express a Republican position in this book, we might call our orientation an 'anti-imperialist eco-socialism', which points towards the intensive and extensive politics required to develop a clearly emancipatory position in the midst of complex changes in global capitalism being experienced in, and experimented through, Ireland today. This is not just about socialising production; rather, it is about transforming relationships to technology and land that ensures the expansion of collective human–non-human flourishing far beyond the borders of this island.

But to enact such transformations, as we will emphasise repeatedly throughout the book, we must historically position them. The first three chapters of the book do this most explicitly. In tracing somewhat of a 'prehistory' of the cloud in Ireland (Hu 2015), they trace the energetic dimensions of technological development in Ireland through three infrastructural transformations. Together, these chapters tell a story of Ireland's situation in the capitalist world ecology – one that continues to have significant implications for industrialisation led by monopoly tech.

Chapter 1, 'Energetic Mediation and Imperial Geographies', introduces Ireland's links to global imperialist networks and resistance through an early test-bed of imperial telecommunications: Marconi's 'technological marvel' of long-distance radio transmission. Established in 1905 deep in the west of Ireland, Marconi chose this point due to the uninterrupted ocean between it and a paired station in Newfoundland, Canada, across the Atlantic. Representing the imperial and migratory geographies that stretched from post-famine rural Ireland to the 'New World', Marconi chose these 'remote' locations to place his stations across the colonised world, from Hawai'i to

South Africa. However, what was striking about the Marconi station in Connemara was its particular entanglement with the local ecology. Distanced communication required, and still requires, huge amounts of energy. His station had a 300 kW generator on site to power the facility, along with a 15,000 V battery in the condenser station, and it was all so loud that to listen to the actual transmission the operator needed to be in a building hundreds of yards away from the machinery itself. Uniquely, the generator was powered by hand-cut local turf, transported across a proprietary railway built on the bogs. The uncanniness of this extremely high-tech facility built in a rural area only decades ago decimated by famine and outward migration was not lost on contemporary commentators – locals would watch the sparks flying from the radio masts at night like a lightshow, and modernist luminaries such as James Joyce made long trips to the facility to report on it. Unpacking these complex political and environmental prehistories of Ireland's privately energised telecommunications infrastructures, this chapter unravels the threads of corporate and state management of infrastructure and the environment within a changing imperial world system. Marconi abandoned the project in 1925, scared off by its capture and partial destruction by anti-Treaty IRA forces during the Irish Civil War. As the Irish state began to navigate a new terrain of formal, but compromised, decolonisation, planners necessarily navigated the partial ruins and spatial imaginaries of imperial infrastructure still remaining on the island.

Chapter 2, 'Bog Modernity and Energy Decolonisation', takes us deeper into the national politics of Ireland's peat reserves and complicates the ideas of 'modernity' and 'decolonisation' as they could be observed through the industrialisation of peat extraction and rural electrification in Ireland in the mid-20th century. Ireland has not typically been considered a 'resource-rich' country, and unlike many postcolonial states, did not struggle with the 'resource-curse' of valuable mineral or fuel reserves. However, arguably Ireland's most prominent extractive landscape remains its peat boglands. In the mid-20th century, the early Irish state industrialised the process of turf-cutting and burning in large-scale power plants, electrifying the nation and building the carbon-intensive, industrial modernity in the boggy Irish midlands that had somehow 'skipped' most of the country. While these projects of modernisation were driven by a sincere desire to incorporate rural areas into state infrastructure, they inherited environmental relationships – as well as urban/rural divides – pioneered by British colonial surveys and administration. This chapter demonstrates that the development of the Irish economy, and its infrastructural supports, were centred upon a metabolic relationship between energy and the bogs that needed to make land legible and valuable for development, a prehistory which continues to impact the emerging 'green' economy today during the ostensible 'just transition' away from fossil fuels. Within these logics, which made 'public' investments but still enclosed the bogs in particular ways for exploitation, existing forms of commonage and customary rights that had governed the bogs as alternative landscapes for centuries became 'traditional' and even 'regressive' against the progressive arc of modernity. This terrain of imperfect decolonisation, which promoted resource nationalism around peat, set the stage for resource privatisation and green extractivism within contemporary green transformations.

Chapter 3, 'Data Centre Land', builds on the ways that the emerging relationships of bog development in Chapter 2 operate in parallel to new extractive relationships formed across the late 20th century via FDI. After internal divisions and differentiations in the Irish state led to an eventual consensus about the developmental value of FDI, the decline of the public works-style development in energy represented an epochal shift in how the value of places in Ireland was integrated into environmental and industrial policy decisions. Land comes to be leveraged for FDI, inserted into global flows of value, and in this way FDI became the core feature of Ireland's development strategies. This is the origin of 'data centre land' as we know it – the establishment of a 'postcolonial ecological regime' whereby the contradictions of multinational growth would come to be mediated via Irish institutions and ecologies.

The last three chapters of the book bring us closer to the present, arguing that these prehistories demonstrate how the historical trajectory 'from the bog to the cloud' is a story of overlapping projects and transitions in the developmental narratives of the Irish state. Chapter 4, 'Atmosphere Meets Cloud', contends that Ireland's signature renewable 'resource' is wind, a product of a blustery North Atlantic climate which has also, by popular promotional discourses, contributed to the attraction of data centres by naturally 'cooling' servers, thus using less energy. But this provisioning of FDI via such an energy-intensive infrastructure has led to complicated energy relationships, as monopoly tech companies have become more involved in emerging energy regimes. These have seen different relationships between data centres and the bogs take shape – including wind farms providing electricity offsets for multinational tech companies and the planned construction of Bord na Móna Eco-Energy Parks pairing renewable electricity generation with data centres. The messy and entangled environmental politics where these projects arise show us that objections to the extractive shape of eco-modernity are necessarily intertwined between digital and energy politics, even in places apparently far from the sites of development of data infrastructures.

Chapter 5, 'The Value of a Bog', unpacks emerging forms of technological valuation of bogs for carbon markets. The preservation of intact, raised bog in Ireland has an interesting history that parallels developments in global conservation science and activism since the 1970s. Where previously bog conservation efforts were largely undertaken by small but highly committed voluntary community groups, now public and private entities are interested in the ecosystem services provided by re-wetted bogs – particularly water and carbon services. While the restoration of peatlands is crucial, the involvement of tech companies in the mediation and funding of these climate-centred projects is being enabled by the public research arms of universities, demonstrating the spread of FDI-led developmentalism through different public institutions. The eco-modern desire to map carbon sequestration potentials of peatlands in Ireland through cloud and AI platforms is paired with the idea to use it as a test-bed to transplant strategies elsewhere for the mapping of financialised carbon credits. At the same time, the situated, careful knowledge work of community conservation groups and citizen science networks are attuned to much longer temporal scales and registers of bog repair – which, while containing their own contradictions, are important to recover as an alternative to large-scale, digitalised mapping.

Chapter 6, 'Land, Extractivism, and Anti-Imperialist Endurances', opens by describing new 'green' extractive frontiers opening up across Ireland: earth mining for 'critical minerals' deemed essential for decarbonisation. Extending arguments laid down in preceding chapters, we identify the continuities and discontinuities between how these extractive activities have operated in the past and how they are operating today, especially in terms of environmental dispossession and struggle. We loop back to the beginning of the book to highlight and expand on the meaning and politics of decolonisation and anti-extractivism in the struggle against the eco-modernity of monopoly tech on the island of Ireland. Only by recognising and supporting struggles against extraction in Ireland and globally, with deep historical understanding of how these infrastructures and the struggles around them have taken shape, can a truly anti-imperialist environmental politics take shape with reference to the island of Ireland.

We conclude by returning to the stakes of the struggles that continue to shape the island of Ireland. If empire is still the determining factor of the development strategies and environmental politics on the island, then how do we orientate ourselves, both at home and abroad? Taking inspiration from current movements that model anti-imperialist engagements with tech and ecology, we demonstrate how the imaginary of 'development' remains a central and often-marginalised battleground for struggles against the eco-modernity of monopoly tech. If the postcolonial ecological regime has formed as a way to ensure Ireland's facilitative role for multinationals in the capitalist world system, the role of monopoly tech companies in the developmental futures of the state as it currently exists is essentially indisputable. We are told time and time again that if the government steps out of line, following through on commitments that might spite the US or regulate multinational investment, these companies will just leave, and in doing so tank the economy. Positioned from Ireland, we can see how important it is to orientate our politics against these companies, while not necessarily falling to the 'anti-modern' allegations of mainstream environmentalists. We must show that a different form of development is possible, one that rests on the achievement of anti-imperialist, democratic environmental principles and the public provision of infrastructure. Imagining an Ireland in this image, we can contest eco-modernity from Ireland, by disrupting our role as facilitators of empire and centring struggles around land, ecology, and infrastructure as avenues for anti-imperialist action.

1

Energetic Mediation and Imperial Geographies

Imperial innovation

> Today, Derrigimlagh seems an unlikely setting for cutting-edge innovation on an enormous scale. However its location and natural resources were key factors in making Marconi's achievements possible.
> (Derrigimlagh tourist site information board)

It is summer 2022, and we are taking a bus from the city of Galway out to Clifden, a small but popular town in the Connemara Gaeltacht (Irish-speaking region). Characteristic of the west of Ireland, the slow, meandering bus travels on a narrow N road inland, stopping at dozens of seemingly random points along the way, picking up women carrying groceries, workmen getting from one roadworks site to another, and tourists in places such as Oughterard. This is a national bus service, but it has the rhythm of rural Ireland – timetables are not as useful as chatting to the person waiting beside you. And it's good to make friends, in case the bus doesn't show up at all.

Our ultimate destination is Derrigimlagh Bog, just outside Clifden, and the site of the first regular transatlantic radio transmission service, built by Italian radio 'pioneer' Guglielmo Marconi in the early 1900s. Along the route, we see the jagged landscape of Connemara, divided by stone walls and fences, the land cut in unpredictable patterns by decades of turf-cutting and often grazed to the peat bed by sheep. Occasionally, evidence of the former railway that ran from Galway to Clifden makes itself visible in the landscape, a line memorialised by colonial tourism memorabilia in a disused museum in the former station building in Clifden. Like most of Ireland's colonial railways, this one was dismantled long ago, with only scattered ruins and elevated embankments marking its former pathways. Many roads still follow these routes.

Figure 1.1: Scenes from the ruined foundations of the Marconi installation, with sheep grazing and cutaway scars visible in background. A production still from *Do Sheep Dream of Electric Ruins?*, directed by Matt Parker (Audiogamma, 2025).

Source: Courtesy of Matt Parker

From Clifden, there is no regular bus service out to Derrigimlagh, which is several kilometres outside town. It's a sunny day, so we walk. It is some trek, but road signs – for tourists – supplement older, more practical signage, pointing the way along winding country roads, augmented by incomplete Google Maps directions.

Upon arrival, we are greeted by the first of a series of carefully designed information boards. Black and white images of moustachioed men in suits and industrial machinery are coupled with text explaining that this was the site of a most unlikely technological innovation. It does seem unlikely. Looking out over the bog landscape there are just a few grazing sheep (Figure 1.1), and a bicycle tour group taking a short break during their longer journey along the coast. We continue walking on the gravel path through the bog, appreciating tell-tale signs of an active turf-cutting culture – newly cut sods drying in the wind, elsewhere piled high and covered in flapping plastic tarp. Further along, a blurry image of turf stacks taken over a hundred years ago appears on one of the information boards (Figure 1.2). Marconi's technological feat required these same peat reserves to fire the generator that powered the station's electrical signals.

Figure 1.2: The Marconi Station, Derrigimlagh Bog, County Galway, with stacks of drying turf

Source: VIE Magazine

We quickly learn that this was more than a radio transmission centre. It was a community that grew over 20 years. Engineers brought in for their technical expertise lived here on the bog. They went to the social club to play cards and look at the stars. They fished in the artificial lake. They formed a football team and played against local teams. The Chief Engineer had his own tennis court – captured in a single photo that doesn't tell us how often weather conditions would allow for a game. We imagine a still day on the bog in 1912, the electrical hum of the generator mixed with the plick-plock of a tennis ball.

With the bicyclists having moved on, we appear to be the only ones caught in a sudden squall, a risk warned of by locals when walking in the bogs. The irony is not lost on us. It is these same climatic components of the location – the cold, blustery Irish weather – that would be among the conditions bringing multinational data centres to the country about a hundred years later, similarly extraterrestrial installations of technological, energetic ingenuity servicing the expansion of global capital. After getting pelted by rain whipping violently across the bog, we find refuge in a small weather shelter clearly built for this purpose. Luckily we brought layers, otherwise it would be a freezing trudge back to Clifden.

This chapter writes a 'prehistory of the (Irish) cloud' (Hu 2015) and the politics and economy that led to the construction, operation, and later destruction and decommissioning of Marconi's Derrigimlagh radio facility. It situates the durable relationalities instantiated by Marconi in Connemara within an ongoing history of energetic mediation and development in and through Irish peatlands. At this site in the west of Ireland, we see not only a historical precursor to the forms of imperial communication and resource-use that arguably still structure the global politics of digital media infrastructures. We also see how logics of 'improvement', the liberal civilising project of empire innovated through the Irish bogs, have modelled the forms of developmentalism that continue to treat land and populations as 'problems' to be solved via foreign capital, technical governance, and scientific innovation. We do not, however, make a facile connection between this moment of imperial wireless and the contemporary politics of monopoly tech operating in Ireland and expanding across the world. This is not a uniform process, and it looks differently depending on where infrastructure is built and technologies employed. This chapter demonstrates, rather, how the imbalances of modernity are reproduced across different eras and ecological contexts in ways that are instructive to current logics and practices of eco-modernity. These are about spatial – and cultural – politics that enrol people, land, and materials in the service of capital accumulation, albeit across different vectors and modes of production.

Expanding on formative studies in media studies, critical geography, and political ecology, our analysis of the energetic, technologically mediated relations of modernity goes beyond materialising and tracing particular energetic networks. It also concerns the politics and practices of remembering and historicising infrastructure and technological change. The history we trace here uncovers, of course, that the imagined 'ethereality' of radio, much like the 'cloud' a century later, was built on the violent upheaval of empire and its aftermaths, as well as within a fraught and contested context of anti-colonial struggle. We argue that by excavating the materiality of energetic mediation, we can recover alternative histories and formulations of this energetic technology – as a tool of empire and, as a result, a site of anti-colonial struggle – in order to ground our wider interrogation of Ireland's political ecologies of data and energy.

One of our aims in this chapter is to 'follow the infrastructures of empire', as Deborah Cowen describes her methodology for tracing the financial materialism of the Canadian settler colony (2019). Doing so helps us to understand how imperialist histories continue to act upon the future. We apply such a methodology directly to the political ecologies and resource regimes of energetic mediation in and through the Derrigimlagh bog complex. Here, we need to go back to pre-Famine Ireland to understand how certain land-based colonial logics became entangled in and through the energetic and communicative capacities of radio technology. What this tells us about Ireland's eco-modern imaginary – both historically, and in its re-narrativisation in contemporary discourses – reveals subterranean politics of (under-)development. These politics continue to resonate more than a century after formal independence, representing the profound stakes of historicising Ireland's energy transition within an infrastructural landscape of imperfect (and abandoned) decolonisation.

Technology, improvement, and colonial modernity

Marconi was not the first enterprising individual who tried to bring a version of modernity to Connemara. Alexander Nimmo, a Scottish surveyor and engineer, had first come over to Ireland to assist in the work of the Bog Commission in 1811. The Bog Commission had been set up in 1809 'to enquire into the nature and extent of the several bogs in Ireland and the practicability of draining and cultivating them' (Horner 2019). The context was Britain's ongoing involvement in the Napoleonic Wars. France had succeeded in undermining Britain's supply of hemp and flax (largely imported from Russia), which was, among other things, essential for making Britain's Naval sails (Horner 2005). A plan to drain the larger bogs of Ireland and develop hemp production resulted in the Bog Commission – an ambitious four-year project involving nine engineers, 20 surveyors, and dozens of labourers, mapping and surveying the bogs across parts of the south and west of the country.

The work resulted in four reports and 50 maps, but the end of the Napoleonic Wars removed any immediate urgency to act on the findings. Ireland's colonial status ensured that indigenous development, such as the draining of bogs, would always be subject to the vagaries of British geopolitical and economic interest. The Bog Commissioners had also concluded that any large-scale drainage of the bogs would be more expensive and labour-intensive than first imagined. Lack of clarity around ownership of land, and suspicions from local populations to any kind of developments that might adversely affect their use of the bogs for turf fuel, were added obstacles – early signs of the contested, on-the-ground politics that have recurred ever since. Nothing would come of the Bog Commission work until the South of Ireland gained independence more than one hundred years later.

Nimmo's own work focussed first on the bogs of Kerry and then Galway. His report on Connemara was completed in 1814. He was to spend the next 20 years in Ireland developing imperial logistical infrastructure – ports, harbours, bridges, and roads. In 1822, he was appointed engineer to the Western District (Wilkins 2016). This position was created by the 'Act for the Employment of the Poor in certain Districts of Ireland', a British Government response to the Famine of that year – a prelude to what would occur 25 years later during An Gorta Mór (The Great Hunger). The Government Act sought to initiate public works in the poorest and least developed parts of the country; namely, counties Galway, Leitrim, Mayo, Roscommon, and Sligo. Separate from this official work, Nimmo directed his will to improve through personal ventures, the main one being the founding of Roundstone village in South Connemara. His own intention was to create a 'tolerable fishing village' on land he took a lease on. This was at once a private financial investment, to raise rents from his property, as well as an extension of the wider colonial, civilising mission. The model of the enterprising individual bringing 'improvement' to the natives was thus not unique to Marconi – the civilising engineer has long been embedded in colonial practice.

An Gorta Mór (1845–49) created 2 million Irish refugees, many of them not making it to a final destination, with the most extreme clearances occurring in the west.[1] Over 100,000 emigrated to North America in 1847 alone, following routes that Marconi's wireless transmissions would 50 years later. Those who remained 'inhabited desolation' (Robinson 2012). Connemara, a vast region of bog and mountain, was sold as a single estate of 200,000 acres in 1872 to London brewer Richard Berridge for £230,000 – nearly a quarter of a million acres at just under a pound an acre. When put up for sale by the London Law Life Insurance Society in 1849, the vendors had described the estate as having vast potential, just lacking in capital investment:

> It is impossible for the mind of man to conceive anything necessary but capital, and a judicious application of it, for rendering this vast Property fertile beyond a parallel, that this Estate does not contain within itself; facilities for Draining, the formation of Roads, inland Navigation, abundance of lime, sea-weed for manure, valuable kelp shores, innumerable beautiful sites for Buildings, and the soil generally might be designated, to use a homely phrase, as one vast dung-heap. (Quoted in Robinson 2012, vii)

The Estate was purchased for sporting purposes and the Berridges built a number of fishing lodges. Connemara became a recreational haunt for super-wealthy industrialists who built their own fortunes off the extractive imperial economy (Williams 2022 [1944]). For everyone else, the choice was the emigrant ship from Galway, road to Dublin (then England), or the workhouse in Clifden. As David Nally argues, the Famine thus presented 'an unforeseen opportunity to ratchet up already "developmentalist" attitudes about regenerating Irish society' (2008, 716).

In Connemara as elsewhere across the island, after the Famine, a shift to grasslands for cattle meant less land for tillage and tenant farmers. By 1880, sporadic violence against landlords and cattle cohered into organised rural revolt, principally through the Land League, set up in Mayo, the neighbouring county to Galway, in 1879. The demand was to end landlordism and give land to the people who worked it. As with anti-colonial struggles across the world, the land question and peasant mobilisation became the primary social force behind the national struggle.

The British sought to contain the radical elements of the land agitation movement through limited land reform. The 1881 Land Act established the Land Commission, responsible for assisting tenant land purchase from landlords. In 1891, 'congested districts' were designated, largely in the west. Baseline reports carried out by the Congested Districts Board (CDB) commissioners recorded that 75 per cent of the population in some districts of Connemara were classified as 'very poor' (Freeman 1943), subsisting on 2-acre holdings, rotating potatoes and oats, with access to common hill pastures and turbary rights for cutting turf. Speaking in 1902 in the British House of Commons, William Lundon, Irish Nationalist MP for Limerick, the county south of Galway, described the situation:

> We have been emigrating and emigrated until the life blood has been almost drained out of us, and those who remain at home are no better off; nay, they are much worse off, because it is the fine young men and young women who have gone away, and the poor old people who are left behind to eke out a miserable existence on their bits of land or to die in the workhouses and fill each turn a pauper's grave. (UK Parliament, nd)

Despite the effective mobilisation of the Land League and the Irish Nationalist Party under Charles Stewart Parnell, the colonial administration did not offer much in terms of material development. While the CDB promised rural development in the form of forestry; breeding of livestock and poultry; sale of seed oats and potatoes; amalgamation of small holdings; fishing; weaving and spinning; and other local industries, these only ever arrived in the form of charitable gestures or occasionally enterprising landlords – always limited by an inability to imagine or allow Irish sovereign development.

This history of the agrarian economy of Connemara in the 19th and 20th centuries is instructive in that it echoes durable relations to 'under-developed' places across the colonial and postcolonial eras in Ireland. The paternalistic 'civilising' mission of landlords and colonial administrators treats local relations to place – and bog ecologies – as problems to be solved by injections of capital and limited, conditional programmes of social welfare and charity. But colonial capital's mechanisms of profitability are fundamentally extractive – so while these places were overtly victimised by imperial political economy in the form of the Famine, even the apparent 'improvement' imperatives designed to terraform Irish bogs for modern life carried extractive relations, with local interests subordinated in service of colonial objectives.

Marconi in Éireann: imperial wireless

This is the context for the arrival of the Marconi station in Derrigimlagh in 1907. As scholars of the dynamic relationship between waste/value within capitalist accumulation strategies have made clear (Wenzel 2019), we must understand the material and ideological processes that *produce* certain places and people as waste/d and in need of 'improvement' via capital investment and new rounds of accumulation. The governmental technologies of improvement are supplemented by the physical technologies of technoscientific mastery required to make places productive for capital. This is a long history that traverses the colonial and postcolonial state: the abandonment of people and ecologies to the vagaries of foreign capital, under the premise of 'development', injected with minimal democratic consultation. In the intervening years, these policies intensified through the forges of industrial modernity represented by industrialists and 'innovators' such as Marconi.

In 1897, with the help of wealthy relatives, Marconi founded the Wireless Telegraph and Signal Company, changing the name to Marconi Wireless Telegraph Company Limited three years later. Marconi was the 'inventor' of wireless telegraphy, expanding the range of radio communication through a series of patented technologies, which meant that anyone who would use or develop the technology would be doing so through his intellectual property. This was effectively a monopoly on radio technology at a time of its expanding application. At this time, the commercial application of wireless communications was not broadcasting, which came to be predominant in the 20th century before wireless computing and digital communications. Rather, Marconi sought to develop applications for sale to industrialists and large merchant companies operating complex international supply chains, as well as imperial powers, who faced the challenge of governing and rendering productive vast new territories often far from centres of power, manufacturing, and consumption. Reading *The Marconigraph*, the company's commercial periodical, what is most striking in many accounts is not that the early applications of wireless data are so removed from today, but that their ambitions for remote commerce, surveillance, and real-time action more *closely* mirror today's wireless applications than the 20th-century broadcasting business model (O'Dwyer, nd). These technologies not only connected discrete locations, putting a 'girdle around the world' as the magazine once promised,[2] but also coordinated movement in ways that were fundamentally about supply chain control.

Marconi's radio technology was thus developed in the crucible of early 20th-century imperialism. While European powers had been engaged in colonial and imperial projects for centuries, including in and through Ireland, the last decades of the 19th century saw an intensification of the struggle for resources, territories, and markets across the world. Between 1876 and 1914, colonial possessions increased by over 50 per cent for the major powers, three of which had no overseas colonies in 1876 (Germany, the US, and Japan). As Lenin argued in his seminal 1917 text *Imperialism, the Highest Stage of Capitalism*, this partitioning of the world by European and US empires into a system of dependent and semi-dependent colonies was inseparable from the simultaneous transition of capitalism from free competition to monopoly (Lenin 1963 [1917]). Lenin writes that colonial policy and imperialism in earlier stages of capitalism are essentially different from what he describes as the 'highest stage of capitalism' in the early 20th century. The principal difference being the domination of monopolies whose aim was to capture *all* the sources of raw materials so as to deprive their rivals of the opportunity to compete.[3] This was manifested in and through the development and deployment of infrastructure: in the preface to the French and German editions of the pamphlet, Lenin uses the example of railways to outline the interplay between finance capital, monopoly capital, and colonial policy. Railways are at once the materialisation and conduit of basic monopolistic industries (coal, iron, and steel) and financed by banks interested in opening up new markets. And while they are justified as part of a civilising enterprise, of modern progress, they are in fact an instrument for 'oppressing a *thousand million* people (in the colonies and semi-colonies) … as well as the wage-slaves of capital in the "civilised" countries' (Lenin 2024, 126). The late 19th-century development of the railway reveals the true character of capitalism: not free and democratic competition between small proprietors, but a world-system dominated by a handful of industrial and financial monopolies and imperial powers.

Imperial capitalism involves the production (and management) of colonial peripheries and hinterlands. What for Marconi was just the strategic location of the west of Ireland mapped its place within a geography of empire that produced remote imaginations of what would later be classified as 'rural' areas, far from the technological and industrial concentrations of urban metropoles. These were simultaneously produced as both wastelands and productive zones, in the sense that they could not become one (productive) without being classified as the other (wastelands), conditioning demarcated landscapes for value extraction (Rasmussen and Lund 2018). As the above history narrates, his station built in Derrigimlagh Bog became operational little more than half a century removed from the 'clearances' of the Famine, predicated on mass death and migration. In contemporary accounts, this facility was meant to connect this impoverished, remote location to the world via the technological marvel of radio, delivered by a free market pioneer.

As the stark contrast between the abjection of the Famine and the technological advance of radio demonstrates, the colonial ideology of 'remoteness' masks the violent materiality of imperial presence – the coevality of over- and under-development. Reports and descriptions of Marconi's Derrigimlagh site, and any existing photograph, conjure a science fiction scenario of stark, confounding contrasts.[4] The facility entangled the traditional landscapes and cultures of the region, including the subsistence practice of turf-cutting for fuel, with the scale of an anachronistic modernity that apparently has still evaded rural Ireland. Contemporaneous reports emphasise the loud, sparking conductivity of the facility, which could reportedly be seen across the bog – including by residents in Clifden, who were kept at a safe distance to avoid signal interference by trees and other buildings. Quoting a British Imperial Resources Bureau report from 1921, the Derrigimlagh tourist information trail informs us that the site burned 5,000–6,000 tonnes of dried sod turf per annum, this all cut by hand by locals only recently generationally removed from the traumas of the Famine. This cut, dried, and burnt soil from the bog provided the thermal energy to fling garbled signals across the Atlantean ether to the 'New World'. This is imperial ecology.[5]

Many in the environmental humanities have confronted these materialisms of energy and modernity, especially from a historical framework. Cara New Daggett, for example, has demonstrated that the technoscientific ideologies of energy were premised on the gendered, colonial rationalities of Enlightenment thermodynamics, and demonstrated early examples of rendering work machinic in the interests of imperial markets (2019). Brent Ryan Bellamy and Jeff Diamanti similarly unravel the importance of historical materialism as a methodology for articulating the ecological dynamics of capital and work in energy regimes (2018), taking an important academic stance within an unfolding turn to a more depoliticised 'materialism' in the humanities that we discussed in the book's introduction. More recently, Anne Pasek, Cindy Lin, Zane Griffin Talley Cooper, and Jordan Kinder have developed such ideas to show how media technologies are *essentially* energetic, from the physical and atmospheric labours of human and wind power to deliver paper messages to the electrical telegraph to the AI model, requiring reorientation of our conceptual tools to account for what this means in the political ecology of media (2023).[6] Together, such scholars recognise not only the *materiality* of energy within socio-economic systems, but also the importance of *materialism* as a frame of analysis to understand the socio-ecological dynamics employed as well as sustained by media.[7]

We are inspired by these thinkers, as our own ability to connect digital infrastructure, energy, and the emerging contours of eco-modernity in Ireland would not be possible without such formative work. However, standing on Irish ground with political investment in the movements and struggles for liberation in this place, we're less interested in the legacy of Marconi as an innovator and harnesser of thermal and atmospheric energies. Rather, we want to demonstrate how this prehistory of energy modernity affects a critique of empire that we see at the centre of our own critique of eco-modern transitions centred on tech-led growth and innovation. After all, as Daggett and others make clear, energy, the politics of work, and industrial production are inseparable from how the physical circulations of empire were laid down and established. How does the imperial project of monopoly radio technology, enacted in and through a colonial ideology of improvement, demonstrate the durable formations of imperial ecology that would pervade later transitions? And how was this project and its ideologies contested and disrupted? How can these contestations be read within a critique of the energetics of imperial power?

Wireless improvement

The history of de-development in Connemara created an accidental point of synergy for Marconi's operations, especially in the eyes of colonial governance. The intertwining of a strengthening imperial 'free market' which required the subordination of colonial territories to capital was thus the primary policy for the management of land and population, a market which would come to be organised by emerging networks of global communication. By the time Marconi arrived, the ground was set for a free market saviour of an apparently abandoned region – what we might call today 'underserved' or 'under-developed'.

To be clear, the purpose of the transmission stations was Marconi's commercial strategy as embedded and supported by imperial powers – whatever the secondary effects of their operation, including 'improvement'. Its purpose was not to develop a region, a potential promoted far more by colonial state authorities (and later Irish state revisions for touristic narratives) than Marconi himself.[8] Location, as a discursive and geographical mechanism for imperial activity, envisions a dot on the map as it charts an effective circulatory pathway across points (whether through cables or ether). Other elements of local economies and ecologies must be considered, of course, but only insofar as they can either be exploited or need to be smoothed over for efficiencies. In this context, benefits for local workers and economies were secondary to the scalar ambition of wireless communications.

At another scale, Marconi's wireless technology also promised to elevate global communication above the messy particularities of place and ecology, a promise that continues to drive ideological and metaphorical promotion of digital communications and innovation today – through the 'cloud'. Similarly, to harness the power of 'ether', radio had to produce and tame heat to generate electrical power and signals. Like the earlier heralding of space-time conquest by wired telegraphy, Marconi's stations promised to overcome the tyranny of wires with ethereal circulations of communicative matter – accomplishing for oceanic what the telegraph had accomplished for terrestrial space. Radio transmission's 'immateriality' was also conceived in the context of the carbon-polluted atmospherics of industrial cities. Ether was not only not-wires, it was also not-smoke. Wireless telegraphy was not just emerging as a response to the material intransigence and costs of wired communications systems, but also the 'smoggy' externalities emerging from the forges of industrial modernity more generally.[9] However, this perception ignores the energetic materiality of radio transmission itself, which required significant quantities of carbon fuel extraction and burning, generating exhausts associated with combusting it. Radio was thus both smoke and wires, but only at its individual sites of receiving and transmission, as the material abstraction across points was achieved by information's transport through the air.

Thus, even as wireless did away with some kinds of material resources and infrastructures for transport and communication, other resources and infrastructures became necessary – in particular, the quantities of energy required to shoot a message over the Atlantic, harnessed and electrified, on the Irish end of the signal, via turf cut from the bog (see Figure 1.3). Take this vivid description in *The Daily Mail* from 1907, subtitled 'A Wireless Thunderstorm', which resolutely positions the 'technological marvel' of radiotelegraphy within its material operation while promoting its affective and circulatory atmospherics:

> An entire room is given up to strange sheets of steel, which are hung from roof to floor, like washing on a line, until only narrow alleys are left. Queer brown earthenware jars, like old-fashioned receptacles, and all manner of outlandish electrical apparatus now confront the visitor. The plates are for acting as a reservoir to store electrical energy. The jars are transformers. The engineer gave a few directions to his assistant, who, seated before an ordinary Morse telegraph instrument in the operating room, placed a telephone headpiece to his ears, and began to fumble with the key, hastily bidding me to stuff cotton wool in my ears and don a pair of blue-glass spectacles. The engineer beckoned me to the connection room on the floor above, which is equipped

Figure 1.3: The Marconi Station, Derrigimlagh Bog, County Galway

Source: Robert French

with a medley of strange electrical contrivances. The use of the cotton-wool and smoked glasses became at once startlingly apparent. From the 'interrupter' instrument corresponding exactly in duration to the assistant's touch of the key below, came three blinding flashes of blue-white flame, followed by a short flash, and then three more short flashes. The two side-mouths of the instrument likewise spout eye-blinding flame of the same colour and intensity. Simultaneously, the discharger, a few feet across the room, emitted similar blinding flames, and there came a wearing, tearing boom like the deep bass of some gigantic organ, but immeasurably cruder and louder. The duration of each note again corresponded exactly with the assistant's dot or dash on the instrument below. This was the electrical discharger, which sends oscillating electrical currents from the building into the aerial wires outside. These at once begin to set up vibrations of the ether, which in loops and waves travel with inconceivable rapidity across the sea.[10]

Marconi's 'ethereal' communications were material and resource-intensive, requiring not only the jars and cotton wool devices mentioned above, but also a 300 kW turf-fired generator, a 15,000 V battery, powered by up to 6,000 tons of turf extracted on site per year, as well as supplementary coal shipped into the small port in Clifden town (to be transported via Marconi's proprietary railway). This turf was seasonally cut and transported by 140 seasonal turf-cutters from the local area, whose artisanal knowledge of this practice was key to the viability of the station.

By historical reports, the employment made Clifden a jewel of Connemara, and people were able to stay and work, not necessarily having to leave for other colonies to seek opportunities (Sexton 2005). This is hugely significant in the historical perception and development of the area – even though arguably, 'improvements' to infrastructure prior to the Famine had already developed the town relative to surrounding areas. But by successfully employing the resources of this place towards the installation of a profitable (if experimental) technological enterprise, this novel vision of 'improvement' was achieved via energetic industrial capitalism. Thus, while promoted as a site of industrial 'success' at different points in history, the way in which colonial modernity was brought to Connemara was incredibly partial – yet it was presented then, and remembered now, as universal.

Energetic mediation thus provides a framework through which to understand the infrastructural site, the 'landing point' of distanced communication, as an aperture towards wider analysis of imperial ecology. The consolidation of this strategy of improvement-by-innovation comes at a point in the development of energetic modernity where the infrastructuring of electricity and utility delivery was not only the imaginative horizon, but also was being planned and negotiated by states and engineers, beyond transport and mobility.

Undoubtedly, movement prior to Marconi's signals and the telegraph cable required the harnessing and use of energy – whether from the 'flow' of wind captured by sails which moved ships, or the combustion of coal to power steamships and trains. But what the Marconi signal represents is the imaginative obliteration of space by fossil-fuelled electricity, infrastructurally located in the peripheries of empire. In electrifying and supplementing the basis of communicative technologies of trade, technological modernity was prepared for further upscaling through this spatial extensivity and intensification of monopoly capitalism. Stations such as Marconi's formed the geographical groundwork for how imperial supply chains would continue to map the gaps and imbalances of the systems themselves, albeit within a regime of ostensibly liberal technological development.

With the first radio transmission from Derrigimlagh to Nova Scotia in 1907, the intersecting projects of colonial modernity and imperial capitalism thus manifested in the west of Ireland. The harnessed energy and communication it enabled formed an experimental template for the sorts of rural relations that would sustain Irish 'modernity' both pre- and post-formal independence.

Competing narratives

As we explain in the Introduction, anti-colonial thinking in Ireland has continually mobilised against apparently 'neutral' revisionist histories of economic relationships between Ireland and England, as well as to empire more broadly.[11] One aspect of the revisionist project over the past few decades has been integrated into state developmentalist narratives about how modern technologies should be understood as a universal, neutral 'good', necessary for modern progress and oftentimes delivered by external influences and expertise, ingeniously secured and supported by Ireland's people and environment. This 'natural' dependency has structured mainstream thinking on the possibilities of Irish modernity across history. But while such conceptions present a limited, colonial view of modernity, the role of 'modernist' Irish culture and thinking has been debated extensively, especially literary modernism and its specific cultural address of colonial and postcolonial modernity.[12] With this in mind, we ask: how have the anachronisms and contradictions of Irish modernity continued to take shape technologically and, specifically, developmentally across urban and rural orientations?[13] The cultural analytic remains instructive, especially as the specific position of imperial technology and development in the national narrative remains under contestation.

Let's take an example. Famously, quintessential Irish literary modernist James Joyce came to visit Derrigimlagh in 1912. He cycled out to the site from Galway via Clifden with the intention of writing an article for the

Piccolo della Sera newspaper in Trieste. The Italian-Irish connection was clearly of interest (Sexton 2005), but it is hard to imagine that for Joyce, like many others, the aesthetic allure of this cutting-edge technology located in an Irish bog was not the main draw. After cycling all that way, however, Ireland's great modernist was dismissed. What Joyce learnt was that the Marconi station was not just a technological achievement, but also a closely guarded imperial and commercial technology, encountering the brute imperial force behind technological modernity.[14] As you might imagine a military compound, the site was highly secure and securitised, closed to the public, and a British military installation during WWI. The soldiers' station was strategically positioned to have a panoramic view of the surrounding bogs in case any soldiers from whatever force (Irish Republican or German) came to attack the station by land. This fusing of imperial geopolitics and proprietary capitalism in the architecture of the compound breaks with the still dominant, modernist narrative of a supposed universal technology.

The resonance between this installation and the hyper-secure, monopoly tech data centres of contemporary Ireland speaks for itself. However, we also want to emphasise that this is not a direct and unilinear narrative – from empire to monopoly tech capital. Rather, these remain instructive sites of discursive contestation about the material politics of media infrastructures and their centrality in capitalist political ecologies. The stakes of 'modernity' across different registers become much clearer once one realises that there are multiple and overlapping 'modernities' (Gaonkar 1999), each with their own specific internal logics and orientations.

This is not to say that the prevailing, 'hegemonic' frame of modernity does not remain uniquely powerful in shaping public discourses, especially within the mobilisation of national 'culture' towards development. In 2014, Bord Fáilte invested nearly a million euro in the construction of an 'enhanced visitor experience' at the Derrigimlagh site.[15] The site valorises a version of revisionist narratives about Irish 'progress' in the British Empire amid chronic backwardness and under-development, while espousing an apparently paradoxical recourse to the unique traditions and ecologies of turf-cutting and conservation occurring in the surrounding Special Area of Conservation (SAC).[16] However, these ideologically construct an 'Irish' modernity that uniquely rests upon the ingenious utilisation of apparently limited or wasted resources such as peat, with innovation progressing Ireland as an important technological site in the world. Such narratives elide how for Marconi and his company the site and its location were primarily functional, with no sense of what it may signify in the future. Derrigimlagh was a temporary investment in a strategic location, largely experimental in its function, and one that became waste as soon as it was no longer economically viable in the troubled and fledgling Free State – the entire site was sold for scrap in 1925.

The state tourism narrative represented at the site glosses over the anti-colonial struggles mounting through the 1910s, within which radio (and Connemara) played a particularly important role. Among the most significant uses of Marconi's wireless technology came on 24 April 1916, when Irish republican rebels in the General Post Office (GPO) gave the 'first' radio broadcast in Europe.[17] Their hope was that their message would reach the US and be reported in the American press, mobilising Irish-American sympathies and support in the face of British military repression. Marconi's radio station in Clifden was taken off the air by the authorities but the message still managed to cross the Atlantic via the British telegraph station in Valentia, County Kerry. The telegraph operators, Tim and Eugene Ring, were both sympathetic to the nationalist cause and had been contacted by Padraig Pearse to cable a coded message to John Devoy, leader of Clan na Gael, the American wing of the Republican movement in New York, once the rebels sent word from Dublin. The coded message: 'Mother operated on successfully today in Dublin. Signed Kathleen' (RTÉ nd). It's a reminder that these stations were manned, that there was labour involved, and that there were political sympathies and potentialities in the operation and repurposing of imperial infrastructures towards anti-colonial ends.

Nonetheless, contemporaneous commentaries on the broadcast from the GPO and even its later consideration have emphasised its 'illegality', and the perils of mass media technologies for propaganda and misinformation, predicting the potent and persistent criminalisation of anti-colonial activities in Ireland and elsewhere. As staunch revisionist Conor Cruise O'Brien would proclaim, 'Broadcasting was conceived in sin. It is a child of wrath. There is no knowing what it may not get up to' (quoted in Sexton 2005, 101).[18] Such a fearful tenor towards the political appropriation of imperial technologies by revolutionary movements would become commonplace among liberal commentators over the coming decades.

The 1916 Easter Rising galvanised a mass, nationalist movement in Ireland, leading to the War of Independence that lasted for two years, between 1919 and 1921. It was one of the first national liberation struggles of the 20th century and it was successful insofar as popular mobilisation and guerrilla tactics forced the British Empire to the negotiating table. The resulting Anglo-Irish Treaty did not deliver on the ideals and promise of the 1916 Proclamation; partition meant that even limited dominion status granted to the 26-county Southern Free State did not extend to the six counties in the North of the country. Though the Dáil ratified the Treaty by a small margin, the Irish Republican Army (IRA) membership was split and Civil War ensued, lasting until May 1923. Those who rejected the Treaty adhered most closely to the social and political commitments of the Irish Republic and yet were quickly labelled the 'Irregulars' – a term first coined by Piaras

Béaslaí, Director of Communications of the Free State during the Civil War, and made compulsory for newspapers.

During the Civil War, Clifden was the final stronghold of the 'Irregular' anti-Treaty forces against the new Free State Army. Understanding that Marconi's station could be used to foster communication between the British Royal Navy and Free State Army, it was taken and occupied by the Irregulars in 1922. These anti-Treaty forces also destroyed his station in Crookhaven that same year, for the same reasons. Given that a few years earlier, British soldiers had been stationed at Derrigimlagh to protect the transmission site, it shouldn't come as a surprise that it would be a target of anti-colonial forces. And yet, reporting at the time from national and local newspapers toeing the Free State line, described the intentional sabotage done to the Derrigimlagh station as the work of 'degenerates' and 'acts of vandalism' that brought discredit and dishonour on the name of Irishmen (Irish Independent 1925). In all these pieces, the 'senseless vandalism' is juxtaposed with the numbers employed at the station, the fact that Marconi's investment put Ireland on the map of world science, and that the technologies did 'priceless good' in the world (Offaly Independent 1922). One paper described the actions of the 'Irregulars' as an attempt to 'cut Ireland off from civilisation' (Tuam Herald 1922). The Irish Independent (1925) was even more sensationalist, and overtly spoke to the association of science with progress, efficiency, and even 'public good', and republicanism with backwardness:

> Wireless, like most other sciences in use in war, developed rapidly, and it was [illegible] on experimenting with [illegible] transmitting apparatus at Clifden at the end of 1919 that messages could be transmitted across the Atlantic with this apparatus, using only about one-twentieth of the power hitherto employed. This would have resulted in the cheapening of the rates for messages and would have considerably benefited the public. ... Alas, the hand of the incendiary has laid to waste some of the greatest inventions of modern science, but it is hoped that this latest act of wanton destruction will not result in severing the connection with this country of a great scientist, with whom we are proud to claim kinship.

As Chapters 3, 4, and 5 will show, this language would not be out of place in the demonisation of environmental objectors against multinationals in the late 20th and early 21st centuries, especially with regards to the 'efficiencies' gained by monopoly tech's cloud data centres. Even in these early days, allegations of radical republicanism served as a moderating force for civilisational, capitalist politics.

Trying to parse historical facts from Free State propaganda is difficult but we do know that while the anti-Treaty forces in Clifden did enough to prevent the Derrigimlagh radio service from operating, they did not inflict substantial damage. The final transmission from Marconi's station was in fact a transmission from the Free State Army, informing command that they'd retaken the town and the station from the Irregulars. A letter written by Marconi himself shortly after the station had been occupied, and published in an Irish newspaper, also suggests that the damage was minimal and, in his own words, 'the company hoped to have it back working soon' (Offaly Independent 1922). And yet, in 1925 the company took the decision to relocate operations to Ongar in Essex. The site was scrapped and left to ruin. This move to England had already been mentioned in the press in 1922, just before the anti-Treaty forces occupied the station (Offaly Independent 1922). It was clearly an economic decision, but this did not stop the Irish media pouncing on the anti-Treaty republicans again, blaming the loss, including 'hundreds of jobs', on the Civil War sabotage (Irish Independent, 1925). We can already see with the Marconi station how the extraterrestrial character of this early greenfield economic development works: as soon as it ceases to be profitable, capital leaves, and takes its technology with it. What is more interesting is how responsibility for the failure to attract, or keep, mobile capital is blamed on local factors, domestic failings, and, in this case, subversive politics. The persistence of this colonial imaginary of development in rural Ireland is part of what drew us to this site in the first place.

Contemporary and subsequent interpretations of the 1916 radio transmission from the GPO and the sabotage of the Marconi station during the Civil War demonstrate an important point, one that resurfaces in how 'green', digital technologies are represented and narrated in Ireland today. The criticism of the irrational, anti-civilisational activities of anti-colonialism reflects a version of 'anti-Luddite' commentary today, which deliberately conflates justified attacks on for-profit, capitalist technologies with hatred of technology in general.[19] At best, we get a reformist agenda that posits 'excesses' of digital capitalism (carbon emissions, deteriorating mental health, concentration of power) as discrete and manageable aspects of an otherwise sustainable system. What these commentaries share is rejection of a supposed *politicisation* of technology – how could you be against such a 'marvel of world science', as one Irish newspaper described wireless radio? Despite all the evidence to the contrary, the 'normal' functioning of imperial wireless is assumed to be apolitical, without partiality or interest. Folded into this universalising praise of technology is the logic of improvement which, as we have outlined above, positions the tech entrepreneur as the only means of imagining development in an area such as Connemara, tied up in the promise of technological progress via the private harnessing of energy towards capitalist telecommunication.

There is a startling similarity in the way that Free State media reports on the 'hundreds' of jobs lost by the closure of the Derrigimlagh station and the way contemporary Irish media reproduces figures about employment and investment from US tech companies (see Chapter 4). In both cases, such figures obscure more than they reveal – not just forms and relations of work, but possibilities for *different* trajectories of development. In the decades after independence, we will see how state development could operate differently, even as stubborn assumptions and patterns of power remained and later deepened over time.

Conclusion

The events narrated in this chapter only precede the establishment of the Wireless Telegraphy Bill and broadcasting politics in the Free State in 1926 by a few years, which were overtly built in response to ongoing British influence (specifically in the form of radio signals and the messages they carried) but used as a tool of 'independent' nation-building – however compromised and unfinished. These politics of self-sufficiency, by which nationally produced radio signals were soon permeating the Irish atmosphere, from Dublin to Achill (Horgan 2001, 18), were to be matched by similar experiments in self-determination and domestic industrial development across the early years of partitioned Ireland.

At the same time, such projects are also instructive as to the incompleteness and barriers to decolonisation: while the peat industry would draw its expertise from the Soviet Union and act as a small theatre in Ireland's re-alignment with the US later on (as the next chapter shows), broadcasting was premised upon inherited and paternalistic tendencies from Britain, modelled after and subordinate to the BBC, as well as containing strict censorship after 1929 and, famously, being outwardly antagonistic towards political leftism in the mainstream. Paradoxically, it was this modern technology of connectivity and 'progress' which would continue to tether Ireland to a conservative, imperial past tinged with Catholic influence. The bogs, on the other hand, long (and still) associated with a muddy backwardness, were the fuel for 'modernisation' by which these territories of the rural became the precondition for industrial and technological development – even, later in the century, a landscape of export-led industrialisation, which required a robust bank of modern infrastructure to support multinationals. These diverging stories of energy independence and social conservatism will be the foundation of the next chapter, where we trace the development of the bogs as a site of converging and diverging political visions about how Ireland would develop post-'independence'.

This chapter raises preliminary questions that will be central to the remainder of our study: What is the purpose of 'modern' technological infrastructure, and how is this negotiated through local and national territories within a capitalist world system? We can see early examples of how the ideology of imperial technology presented opposition as not only acting against progress and the 'best interests' of areas determined by colonial administrators, but also as actively criminal and irrational. As later chapters will argue, the institutionalisation of these forms of undemocratic governance are not continuous or without contestation – especially as they relate to the shifting formations and frontiers of 'modernity' across colonial and postcolonial regimes of land and ecological management. The next chapter will dive deeper into that history, and introduce the ways that Ireland's contemporary multinational infrastructure landscape has arisen as a result of postcolonial developmental politics – and, in particular, the resource management of energetic modernisation.

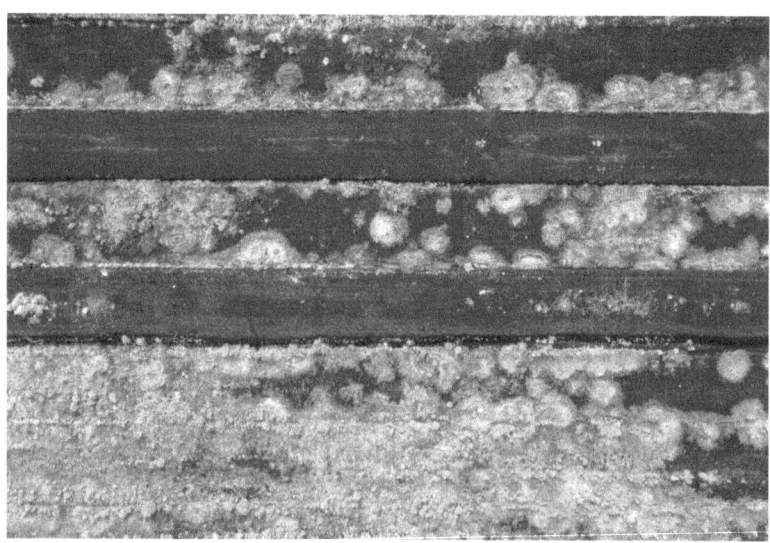

2

Bog Modernity and Energy Decolonisation

Peat-fired progress

There are no complete reproductions of Seán Keating's mural exhibited as part of the Irish Pavilion at the World Fair in New York City in 1939. Photos exist, however, documenting the mural being painted on a series of panels joined to a large wooden structure (Figure 2.1). The painters working in the foreground are the same size as the figures they are depicting. They wear similar clothes and adopt similar postures because the figures in the mural are artists too, as well as engineers and scientists. The distinction between the mural and real life is blurred. This probably would have pleased Seán Keating whose realist, romantic paintings had been part of the making of the new Irish state since the War of Independence.

The mural was a showcase of how far Ireland had come in 20 years – not just from former colony to sovereign nation, but a country that was at the forefront of modern technology and design. At the heart of this vision of modern Ireland was the Ardnacrusha hydroelectric dam. Keating was intimate with this totemic energy infrastructure having spent much of the years 1926 and 1927 on site in County Clare documenting the project. He describes one of his paintings from that period, 'Night Candles Are Burnt Out' (1928), as 'depicting the transition of Ireland from a country of ancient stagnation to a state of freedom and progress'. The Shannon Scheme would produce enough energy to power the country, spurring the world's first national energy utility, the Electricity Supply Board (ESB), and the rural electrification scheme.

In the mural, below the image of the power station, is a small propeller plane clearly marked 'Aer Lingus Teoranta'. Founded in 1936, the state airline company began with short flights between Dublin and Bristol. There are horses whose significance is not clear, a copse of trees, a woman with a bunch of tulips, and a modernist building that looks unfinished. In

Figure 2.1: Seán Keating, mural for Irish Pavilion, World's Fair, New York, 1939

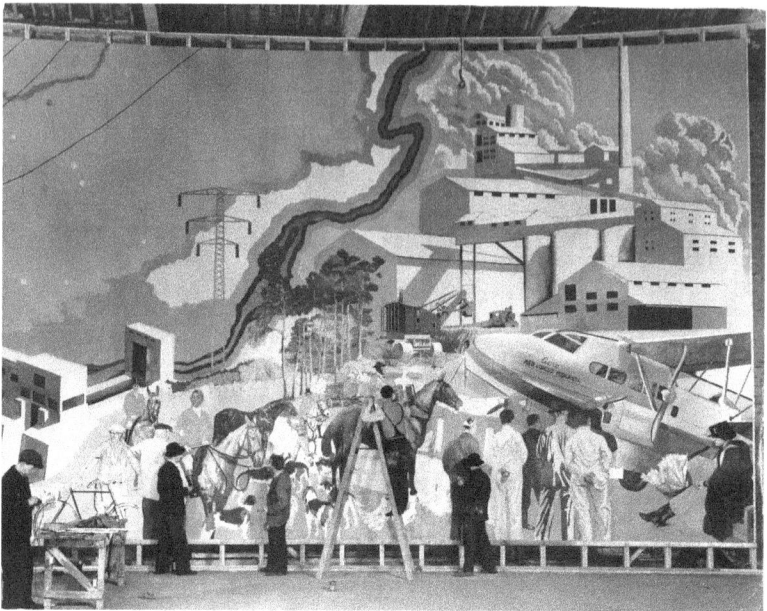

Source: Black and white original, Keating Papers Private Collection, with kind permission, private owner

the middle of the mural is a mechanised sod peat digger lifting cut peat into waiting railway carts. The digger represents the new national peat industry led by the Turf Development Board. Set up in 1933 under the new Fianna Fáil Government,[1] the Turf Development Board would evolve into Bord na Móna (BnM) in 1946. Led by Todd Andrews, a veteran of the War of Independence and anti-Treaty ('irregular') Republican, BnM set about transforming Ireland's peatlands into an energetic resource capable of powering the country's development and breaking reliance on imported British coal.

The theme of the World Fair in 1939 was 'the world of tomorrow'. For the Irish Pavilion, emphasis on a bright, new future had particular significance. Michael Scott, still a relatively young architect, designed Ireland's pavilion: a shamrock-shaped building made from steel, concrete, and glass that was awarded best building in show by an international jury. At this time, the fusing of the old and the new, the making of a distinctly Irish modernity, was still open and ambitious.

Ireland has not typically been considered a 'resource-rich' country, and unlike many postcolonial states, did not struggle with the 'resource-curse' of valuable mineral or fuel reserves post-independence. Its primary value, from a colonial perspective, was always its land – acting as a breadbasket, the pervasiveness and extent of the Irish bogs continually frustrated colonial administrators, who saw these inaccessible and infertile landscapes as fodder for 'improvement', both of the local Irish who lived on and by them as well as the soggy soil itself (Ruuskanen 2018). The extractive political economy centred on Ireland during the colonial era, as Marx and Engels long ago observed, was one of land and soil. The value was to be drawn from enclosing land and making it profitable, whether by extracting rents or producing food for the English granary. Technological 'innovation' in Ireland was most frequently tied up in the mastery of land and population towards colonial designs.

In the mid 20th century, arguably Ireland's most prominent extractive landscape became its peat boglands. From the 1930s, the fledgling Irish state industrialised the process of 'turf-cutting' and burning in large-scale power plants, electrifying the nation and building the carbon-intensive, industrial modernity in the boggy Irish midlands that had somehow 'skipped' most of the country. In the west, in counties such as Donegal, Mayo, Galway, Clare, and Kerry, where turf extraction and its generation of energy were not as overtly profitable at this scale, BnM still developed smaller power plants and extraction operations alongside the ESB, with the remit of not only electrifying but also providing regional development opportunities. While these projects of modernisation were driven by a sincere desire to incorporate rural areas into state infrastructure and provide 'modern' amenities, they inherited environmental relationships pioneered by British colonial surveys and administration.

As we argue, however, while enacting environmentally damaging relationships to peatlands by which these carbon-laden landscapes could be made legible and mastered for the benefit of the nation, this imperfect strategy of state-led decolonisation *via* energy represents a useful exception within the history of development in Ireland. Through the establishment of public bodies charged with delinking from neocolonial dependency and promoting domestic industrialisation, the Free State and, after 1937, Republic of Ireland built the infrastructure for powering a national grid through thermal power generated by burning peat. To do so, they not only produced the conditions for a supply chain – from extraction to transport to burning to the distribution of electricity – but also supported the construction of modern amenities and living standards for thousands of workers across the country.

As we introduced in Chapter 1, peat was (and remains) narrativised as a uniquely Irish resource, with the historical association between mostly rural bogs and the reserves of traditional Irish culture.[2] Thus, it was also a strategic cultural landscape by which to build a national infrastructure across an otherwise divided and internally differentiated territory. At the same time, making the bogs legible and available for development required methods of modern technoscientific management and mediation. This incorporated expertise from the Soviet Union, for example, as well as the inheritance of colonial-era plans and technologies. Wrapped up within the development of the bogs were also the contradictions of national progress in a polarised world system, particularly after World War II (WWII). Bound to ideologies of modernisation and the technoscientific transformation of land as a tool for modernising communities and ways of life, the development of the bogs also laid the groundwork for the kinds of 'green' development of peatlands unfolding today. By promoting a publicly orientated resource nationalism around peat, the Irish state paradoxically set the stage for resource privatisation and green extractivism within contemporary eco-modernisation. This is due to the governing and technological mechanisms by which land would become a resource-bank for the development of the nation, in whatever image that became – from Sean Keating's Celtic modernism to Sean Lemass' model of foreign direct investment (FDI)-dependent modernisation.[3] Like other postcolonial states, the 'national' project remained central to premises of development across both protectionist and free market policies, under whatever internal and external pressures.

This chapter examines the construction of this national project of electrification via turf to unravel some of the specificities of Ireland's developmental land use across the 20th century. The history we cover is only 30 years, from roughly 1930 to 1960, but in this relatively short space of time we can trace a fundamental shift from domestic industrialisation and state-driven development to a primarily FDI-led developmental paradigm from the late 1950s. As Denis O'Hearn (1990) has argued extensively, this represented decisions made and conflicts held between different factions of the state and industry and visions for the future of Irish economic policy in dynamic relation to a shifting world system. In the process of breaking reliance on Britain and facing the punitive economic discipline imposed, Ireland was left at the behest of the emerging polarities of the US, Europe, and the so-called Second and Third Worlds battling for developmental funding, international position, and the vagaries of self-determination within these dominant structural paradigms. The decolonisation of the Irish republic contains a compromise with empire – one that was not inevitable, but whose core contradictions within a 'modernising' 20th-century nation-state remain instructive of the infrastructural inequalities, gaps, and bottlenecks of a 21st-century Ireland undergoing an eco-modern transformation.

From colonial improvement to national development

The project of 'wiring' the countryside has been key to postcolonial infrastructural development, from telegraph to railways to electricity (Duffy 2011). In Ireland, the Rural Electrification Scheme is central to national infrastructural narratives (Shiel 2003). A state-wide endeavour from the 1940s (albeit with its origins in the 1920s), the scheme enrolled supposedly all territories of Ireland (at least the South) into a national grid service. Such large-scale, national infrastructural projects carry explicit ideas of 'progress' and 'prosperity' as they enable the growth of modern amenities enabled by electricity – from electric lighting to television and radio. In this way, the project of a decolonised modernity in Ireland was also one intimately connected to European ideological projects – interpreting civilisational imperatives in and through a state still forging its distinct relationship with external factors and influences. Trawling through the ESB online archives, the titles of their promotional documentaries from the 1950s to the 1990s tell a story of connecting the countryside and modernising the ways of life there through the everyday integration of advanced technologies, oftentimes explicitly acknowledging the risks of 'backwardness'. Take *Power for Progress* from 1955, which tells the history of the ESB and concludes with what almost reads like a warning: 'our prosperity depends on progress and progress depends on power'.[4]

As the Marconi station in Connemara clearly illustrates, the question of 'infrastructure for who?' – and through what ideologies of progress and development – remains central. What were the presumptions behind the state providing the infrastructural conditions for technological modernity, harnessed in and through rural ecologies? The answers are less clear when it comes to a postcolonial state than for Marconi's imperial endeavours. Modernisation theory in Irish history is most strongly associated with historical revisionism, and often sympathetic towards the market orientations of imperial liberals and reformers.[5] Such theories inherit paternalistic attitudes towards progress, whereby the teleological march of modernity across territories can be perceived as a relatively linear process of technological development and mastery, wherein, for example, policies that were designed to 'improve' rural Ireland under British rule contributed to an eventual transformation of ways of life and modes of production in these places. The real process of 'modernisation' in the early Irish state was premised upon a mobilisation of Ireland's rural geographies and cultures towards nation-building by a class of state industrialists. Returning to the development of the bogs can help us distinguish the continuities and discontinuities between colonial improvement projects and the national-sovereign projects that took place between the 1930s and 1960s.

In 1910, John Purser Griffith, a civil engineer trained at Trinity College Dublin, had privately purchased Turraun bog and associated property in County Offaly. Like Marconi before him, Griffith was another 'peat entrepreneur' who had chosen to invest personally in experiments with electricity generation from peat. A colonial administrator involved with the Leinster Carbonising Company, a regional enterprise that provided carbon for street lighting, Griffith sought to industrialise this process, extracting the carbon from harvested peat in Offaly and transporting it to Dublin via the Royal Canal, a key colonial transport infrastructure. In 1917, just one year after the Easter Rising and two years before the outbreak of the War of Independence, the Department of Scientific and Industrial Research in Ireland set up a committee to 'enquire into and consider the experience already gained in Ireland in respect of the winning, preparation, and use of peat for fuel, and for other purposes' (Andrews 1952). The Chairman of the Committee was Griffith. The Committee recommended the purchase of a bog capable of producing 100,000 tons of dried peat per annum, the construction of an electric power station using the peat, and the building of villages for workers in the vicinity of the bog. The report was effectively shelved, like many before it. But by 1924, two years after independence in the South, Griffith had established one of the earliest machine peat operations in Ireland in his privately incorporated Turraun bog, complete with overhead electric cables, cutting machines, and a moss peat plant driven by electricity.

The prospect of peat industrialisation was picked up again by the state in 1934 when Todd Andrews, the managing director of the newly established Turf Development Board, visited Griffith's enterprise to better understand what was possible in the area of turf-powered electricity generation. He later wrote in his memoir: 'My first visit to Turraun was a kind of epiphany to me. I saw there *in parvo* what BnM was to become in time' (Andrews 2001). Twenty years after that visit to Turraun, Andrews gave a presentation to the Statistical and Social Enquiry Society of Ireland entitled 'Some Precursors of Bord Na Móna'. In the paper he gives generous praise to those individuals, including Griffith, whose work was vital for the post-independence development of the bogs. Individuals, he writes, who were 'characterised by abundance of public spirit' but whose 'endeavours were dissipated in the unpropitious social, economic and political climate of their times'. He goes on: 'with an alien Government there would be no hope of profitable exploitation of Ireland's very limited natural resources' (Andrews 1952).

Andrews' political outlook shares much with other anti-colonial and nationalist figures who took up the mantle of governing newly independent nations after flag independence. He was not a socialist but he was a Republican, and part of the incumbent Fianna Fáil Government that had come to power in 1932 with the support of small farmers and workers frustrated at the laissez-faire policies carried out by the Cumann na Gael Government in the first decade after independence. Fianna Fáil's policies included stopping payment of land annuities to England (for lands acquired by the state from English landlords), increased land redistribution to support small farmers, large-scale public housing schemes, and economic protectionism. The Control of Manufacturers Act (1932) made it mandatory that all new production facilities would be at least 51 per cent Irish-owned (Breen and Dorgan 2013). This programme of import-substituting industrialisation (ISI), with high levels of tariff protection, was initially quite successful. Between 1931 and 1938, industrial production grew by nearly 50 per cent and industrial employment rose by 57,000, with the sectoral composition broadening out to include clothing, footwear, and engineering (O'Hearn 1990).

Fianna Fáil's decision to stop paying land annuities was brought about by an effective, rural popular campaign spearheaded by Republican socialist Peadar O'Donnell (O'Donnell 2017). The land annuities campaign re-articulated the land question and the national question, not only challenging the idea of financial compensation to England for land taken during colonisation but also igniting the Economic War (1932–38), which compelled the new Fianna Fáil Government into an economic policy of national self-sufficiency and development. Tariffs on British coal were met by tariffs on Irish beef, providing an impetus for the development of Ireland's domestic peat energy resources, as well as weakening Ireland's dependency on agricultural exports to Britain.[6] It was this dependency, Fianna Fáil argued, that continued to 'fetter' Ireland's sovereign development. In 1933, Fianna Fáil's Land Act reconstituted the Land Commission, giving it greater powers for compulsory acquisition of lands and expropriation of purchased farms. This 'threat to proprietorial security', as the opposition described it, was about advancing the task of breaking up large landed estates, redistributing land and migrating families from areas of marginal land in congested, western districts to better farming land in the midlands. For a time at least, the newly empowered Land Commission appeared to offer the sorts of radical agrarian reform, led by the state, that had been demanded by small farmers and landless labourers since the 1880s: by 1937, almost 353,000 acres of untenanted land were divided among 25,802 allottees (Dooley 2004).[7]

In colonial Ireland, any improvements in the land, including the bogs, had been dependent on isolated, individual efforts and charity.[8] This resulted in much moralising about Irish fecklessness and obdurance – the failure of schemes to adequately improve productivity was always a *native* problem. In fact, it became a key justification for continued colonial control – what would happen if the natives were in charge? For Andrews, and many others of his generation, formal independence offered a chance for Ireland to prove itself as not only capable of managing its own affairs but also of far exceeding what had been possible under English rule. His praise of individuals such as Griffith, or the Bog Commissioners before him, was really a means of attacking the system of colonial rule – a system of political and economic dependency that had prevented the development of Ireland's industry and people. From the 1930s, the expansion of infrastructural services, such as turf-powered electricity and telecommunications, was buoyed by this republican ideal and ongoing struggle for self-determination.

But what was this vision of national development? To what extent did it inherit or challenge colonial relationships to bog 'wastelands' and the logic of improvement? The simple answer is that it inherited a lot. At its base, the vision was about realising at scale the plans and individual projects that had been laid out by former colonial administrators. The maps made by the British Bog Commission (1809–14) were literally dusted off and used in the early plans of the Turf Development Board.[9] Turraun became the model of what each future bog scheme was to become in the midlands. Andrews writes himself in his memoirs that before he headed up the Turf Development Board, his only knowledge of the bogs was as something backward and undeveloped. He describes the large-scale draining and burning of the bogs as a 'crusade', marking Ireland's bid for real independence (from England) (Andrews 2001). And yet, his crusade also inherited 'imperial eyes', as Mary Louise Pratt calls it (1992), at least when it came to ecology – a way of seeing the bogs as 'wasteland' and 'desert', without value beyond the resources they contained, peat fuel to power Ireland's progress and modernisation. While this way of seeing the bogs contained residues of coloniality, what changed was the organisation of the state and the political project of republican nation-building it embodied.

Economic compulsion and the challenge of sovereign development

Compared with the modern feat of engineering that was Ardnacrusha hydroelectric dam, at the time of its construction the largest hydroelectric dam in the world, the traditional practice of turf-cutting and open-hearth fires was perceived as laborious and primitive, a legacy of colonial era backwardness. When the Turf Development Board was established in 1934, the volume of hand-won turf had halved from what it had been in the early 1920s (Clarke 2010).[10] When Seán Lemass, Fianna Fáil Minister for Industry and Commerce, brought the Turf Use and Development Bill before the Dáil in 1936, looking to promote the production and use of turf, one Fine Gael TD said: 'I never thought that the day would come in this country when a Bill would be introduced into our Parliament purporting to solve unemployment by turning the people's eyes to the bogs of Ireland' (Dáil Éireann 1936). These ideas, repeated throughout the Dáil debates at the time, reflect both the colonial legacy of seeing bogs as wastelands and, more importantly, a refusal to imagine domestic industry and development in rural Ireland beyond export-led agriculture.

It is important to recognise how ambitious the idea of a turf-powered energy industry was at this time. In the 1930s, turf was entirely cut by hand, largely for domestic (home) use but also for sale in rural towns and to a lesser extent cities such as Cork and Dublin. Cooperatives functioned to share the costs of transport and sale by rail and road; getting the turf from bogs to hearths was not simple or cheap. Coal was the predominant household fuel, and the vast majority of this coal was imported from Britain with infrastructure and logistics to support it – it is still possible to see the coal hatches outside Victorian-era houses, making for easy deposits of what was a dirty but efficient fuel. Sods of turf, on the other hand, were bigger, more awkward, and didn't fit so well in smaller grates. Thus, while Government support in 1934 and 1935 for turf cooperatives was successful in boosting production and employment, over half the cut turf was left unsold due to the lack of a market (Clarke 2010).

Propelled to power by a resurgent population of smaller farmers and workers, Fianna Fáil's mandate in 1932 was to return to the promise of the 1916 Proclamation of the Republic; namely, social equality and the 'unfettered control of Irish destinies'. The 1936 Turf Bill was thus part of a raft of new measures brought in by the new Government, marking greater state intervention in the economy and an active effort to develop productive forces endogenously, breaking historical dependency on Britain. To begin with, the Turf Bill compelled coal merchants to sell a certain proportion of turf for every 2 cubic tonnes of coal. Referring to the language of 'compulsion', John O'Sullivan, a Fine Gael (conservative) TD quipped: 'Having regard to all the compulsory powers which they are seeking, they will probably finish up by compelling the people to eat the turf and burn the beef' (Dáil Éireann 1936). O'Sullivan was referring to the protectionist tariffs (and subsequent trade war with Britain) introduced by the Fianna Fáil Government in 1932.[11] Reducing coal imports by supporting turf sales was thus not only an imposition for coal merchants but to those bigger economic interests: the grazier farmers and Britain. W.T. Cosgrave, leader of Fine Gael, argued that the 1936 Bill was 'an interference with the citizen's ordinary right to purchase whatever commodity he requires' (Dáil Éireann 1936). The national media aligned with Cosgrave's position, raising the 'spectre of socialism' (Dáil Éireann 1936). The furore over the Turf Bill highlights both the internal and external challenges to even a minimal break with dependency on the British economy. Central to this was the comprador class of Irish politicians and economic interests (graziers, middlemen, and, in this case, coal merchants) committed to protecting the (neocolonial) status quo.

In 1937, the Turf Board submitted a request to the Department of Industry and Commerce for an experimental scheme for establishing large-scale, mechanised peat production in North Mayo. This was in response to the Kirkintilloch tragedy, whereby ten young men and children from Achill Island in Mayo were killed in a fire in Scotland after fleeing miserable conditions at home to work as seasonal labourers harvesting potatoes. The Turf Development Board made clear to the government that any investment in North Mayo would not generate revenues for the state but would *develop* the area, providing employment and infrastructures where they were severely lacking. Significantly, the Board also appealed to the ESB, the other state-owned energy company responsible for generating electricity, which was from the beginning resistant to developing peat as a primary energy source.

Even between state institutions, different political interests and factions vied for supremacy as Ireland's national energy transition advanced.[12]

During WWII, fuel was in short supply as coal from Britain was effectively halted, highlighting the strategic value of local turf fuel. The Government pushed for increased turf production, including the large-scale drainage of 24,000 acres of bog in Kildare, producing 600,000 tonnes of turf in the period to its ending in 1947 (Clarke 2010). After the War, with the Turf Development Act in 1946, the Turf Development Board became Bord na Móna, a new semi-state company with the authority and resources to develop more bogs, more power stations, and more briquette factories. Supported by US grant aid via the Marshall Plan, the experimental plans and frustrated visions of the 1930s became feasible through the concerted efforts of state-supported industry and technoscience.

In 1950, Ireland's first turf-powered electricity generating station opened in Portarlington, County Laois – the largest peat-fired power station in Western Europe at the time (Figure 2.2). To mark the event, a short film was commissioned by the ESB and produced by British Pathé (1950). The film opens with a camera panning across a flat, bog landscape, dotted with small mounds of drying sod turf. A young man appears walking with a donkey and cart. He describes how lucky he is to live in such a lovely land. The music changes tone as the young man then explains how three of his family's best fields have been taken over by the government to build a new power station. At this point the power station, with its dominating cooling tower, comes into view and the music reaches a foreboding crescendo. We are led to believe that this modern development is negative, something that has been imposed on a humble farming family. But the narrator then speaks of his fascination with the power plant and his desire to get inside it. The young man leaves his thatched cottage to take up work, first as a seasonal worker manually lifting turf onto the waiting railway carts, then as an apprentice at the power station, before working his way up to become a plant engineer. The film is a genre of filmmaking we don't see now. Intended to play in cinemas before the main showing, it was part-entertainment and part-propaganda for the still new Irish Republic. It is also remarkable for the juxtaposition of two different Irelands: one represented by the young man with his donkey, cart, and thatched cottage; and the other, a modern future represented by the sprawling scale of the power station, with its industrial architecture and automated machinery transforming turf into electricity.

BnM was employing cutting-edge technology imported from Germany, Finland, and Russia, adapted by Irish engineers to Irish conditions. Between 1950 and 1957, the BnM research station, called the Experimental Station, based in Newbridge, County Kildare, recruited new engineering and agricultural science graduates, including future managing director Eddie O'Connor (see Chapter 3). Under the direction of Andrews, the

Figure 2.2: ESB power station at Portarlington, County Laois, 1950

Source: National Library of Ireland

Experimental Station compiled a library of international research on peat with the aim of learning everything there was about peat and its exploitation. In 1947, BnM had joined the Society for Cultural Relations with the USSR to obtain technical publications. In 1950, a monthly list was sent out to BnM engineers and managers with all new research papers available on request. As this international work and expertise developed, it was not surprising that BnM would host the first International Peat Symposium in 1954, with delegates from 15 countries presenting 54 technical papers covering everything from peat winning to utilisation (Clarke 2010).

Further west, the Oweninny bog complex in Bellacorick, County Mayo, just north of Marconi's radio station, began development in 1952. It took ten years for the power station to open, powered by peat cut from the nearby bog. It was a herculean task, with hundreds of labourers and Irish trained engineers working to 'tame a wilderness'.[13] The draining of this remote, rain-sodden bog and its conversion into electricity for rural homes and industries was 'ludicrous' from the start, as one engineer employed described it. When the Bellacorick power station finally opened in 1963, a celebratory dance was hosted in Crossmolina town hall (Loftus and Laffey 2015). The *Western People* newspaper declared it the 'event of the century', noting that 50 years earlier, the realisation of such a project would have been more unlikely than an independent Irish state. A writer for the *Irish Independent* spoke of the strange mingling of myth, magic, and modernity in the bogs of North Mayo. Eighty people were employed in the power station, three hundred on the bog. The impact on the area was enormous. The population of Crossmolina doubled in five years. Tradespeople were doing better business than ever, supplying the well-paid workers; clubrooms were packed and television sets brought in for entertainment. Unemployment seemed a thing of the past, at least for this part of the west of Ireland. The *Western People* praised the Government for transforming the 'once deserted Mayo boglands', opening the way for further industrial expansion. The same year, the Imperial Hotel in Ballina sold for a high price and the Moy River Drainage Scheme was underway. There was an air of economic buoyancy and hope for the future.

For Andrews, as many other Irish Republicans, the west of Ireland was the clearest evidence of colonial de-development. 'To Hell or to Connacht' was Cromwell's infamous line during the Act for the Settlement of 1652, an early colonial acknowledgement of ethnic cleansing which has remained an anti-colonial sticking point in Irish popular lexicon: send the Catholics west and trap them between the plantations and the sea.[14] As outlined in Chapter 1, the Great Hunger had seen off much of the western population to graves or the migrant ship, but still people endured. If an independent Irish state could develop these impoverished parts of the country, places that colonial administrators had failed so miserably in the past, then it would be the ultimate statement of Irish self-determination and development. This republican vision held true for the midland bogs, but it was more emotive when exported to the west. Four other turf-powered stations were developed by the Irish state along the west coast of Ireland in the late 1950s and 1960s: in Gweedore, County Donegal; Screebe, Connemara; Miltown Malbay, County Clare; and Cahirciveen, County Kerry. These were developed to create demand for hand-won turf and to generate jobs and electricity in under-developed areas. As Seán Lemass told the Dáil in 1952, the purpose was 'more of a social one, than an economic one' (Dáil Éireann 1952). Bellacorick never made a surplus, and periods of bad weather ensured the peat supplied was often too wet for power generation.

The fascination with the technological marvels of these power stations, particularly their enormous cooling towers, is resonant with the arrival of Marconi's 'science fiction' radio station in the heart of Connemara. The difference is the scale and purpose of these projects. Marconi's facility was a private, entrepreneurial venture designed for commercial gain and imperial interests. It provided very few 'local' jobs beyond seasonal work for turf-cutters. BnM's peat-powered development projects, in contrast, filled boarding houses, trained and paid employees, and generated electricity for homes, farms, and factories. These are not insignificant differences when we think about the particularity of mid-20th-century bog modernity – however much the memory of these carbon-intensive infrastructures may be tainted by the 'brown' industrial legacy of extraction and emissions. Why is Marconi's station commemorated so vividly as the site of a modern technological feat, the beginning of wireless radio communication, whereas these BnM's installations are not? None of these power stations are still in operation, but there are also no tourist trails or major artistic commemorations to them.

The next section considers how these alternative politics and promises of national and rural modernity[15] in the image of public provision and social planning were developed and later marginalised through the state. Uninterrogated assumptions linking technological innovation with global modernity sideline more salient questions: What forms of development was technology enabling? Where and for whom were these technologies deployed, and, as we look to the present, by what specific means are they designed and implemented? The competition of multiple potential visions demonstrates how modernity, and its relationships to ecology and social life, was and remains a site of contestation in constructing viable futures.

Rural modernity and its discontents

In 1936, Todd Andrews and colleagues visited Germany and Russia to learn more about their respective peat industries. At the time, Weismoor in Northern Germany was the showpiece of the German turf industry and a tourist attraction for residents of Bremen and Hamburg. They would come to wander around the large glasshouses that were heated with surplus heat from the turf-powered station. Exotic plants and produce were grown in these glasshouses. Andrews describes going to lunch with the bog manager and being taken aback by the opulence of his house (Andrews 2001). Open plan, it consisted of at least four reception rooms, parquet floors covered with thick rugs, and warmed by a domestic central heating system – something Andrews had never encountered.

For Andrews, this demonstrated that turf and bogs could be the source of modern ways of living if only the proper infrastructures and planning were put in place. As he moved around Germany and the Low Countries, he observed the well laid-out villages and towns, the neat and comfortable houses, all provided for those who worked the bogs and land. 'I made up my mind then', he writes, 'that if ever I had the opportunity, I would recognise as a priority the value of maintaining a decent environment for people at work' (Andrews 2001). Andrews wanted to create new social conditions in the midlands and west where the workforce required for the peat industry was located.

The development of the peat industry after WWII was an experiment in social planning, as much as an experiment in resource extraction and energy production. The Turf Development Act of 1950 authorised BnM to go beyond exploiting turf reserves, including providing direct housing for workers (Figure 2.3). No other semi-state body built houses for its workers, before or since.[16] Public housing was ordinarily under the remit of the local authorities. Between 1950 and 1960, nearly 600 houses were built across the midlands to house BnM workers. Funded in part by conditional US grant aid via the Marshall Plan, these houses were found in six distinct village schemes, ranging between 8 and 160 houses. The budget for the housing schemes was high – £1,000 per house – and they were built to the highest contemporary building standards. Andrews had some difficulty getting this through Government, with a Fine Gael minister initially insisting that it was 'un-Irish' to have rural houses clustered together, and that individual cottages should be scattered throughout the bogs.

All of the housing schemes were designed by the architect and planner Frank Gibney, who was influenced by the Beaux Artes school of modernist urban planning and the Garden City Movement with its underlying aesthetic borrowed from the Arts and Craft Movement. His vision and practice reflects these eclectic experiences: Catholic and conservative, but also modernist, experimental, and international.[17] This peculiar mash-up of styles and values

Figure 2.3: A layout plan of Cloontuskert by Frank Gibney (1905–78) for BnM housing, Cloontuskert, County Roscommon (circa 1952)

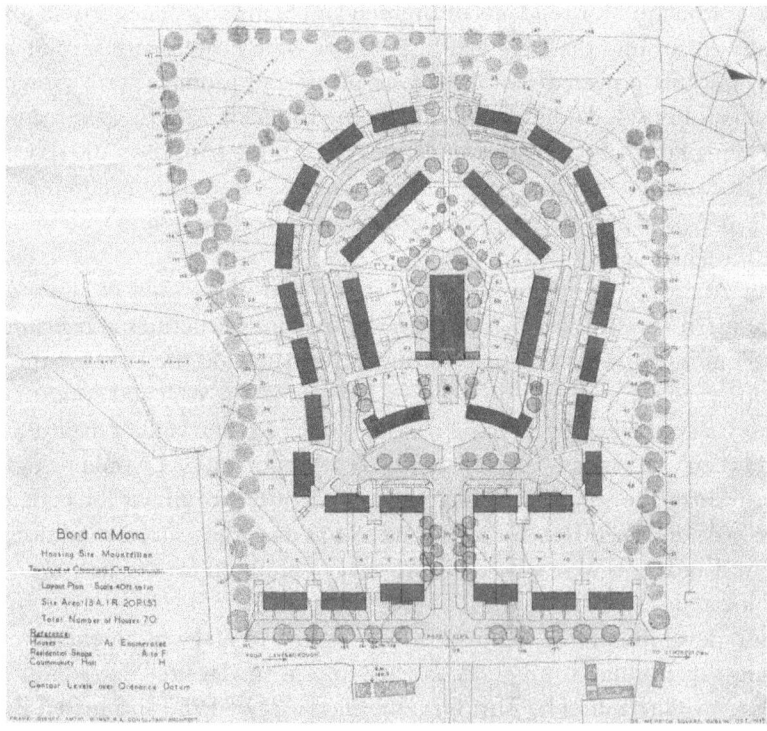

Source: Frank Gibney Collection, Irish Architectural Archive

is perhaps most evident in his national and town-planning schemes. The six housing schemes designed by Frank Gibney exhibit some of his proto-eco-modern features on a smaller scale. Radial designs, green space, central location for a church or community hall, children's playgrounds, sports facilities, even space for drying clothes. In one scheme, workers' allotments run parallel to the terraced houses, marking a green strip between the inner and outer perimeter of the village. While most of the village schemes were built on the outskirts of existing towns, it is clear that Gibney envisioned them as having a degree of autonomy and self-sufficiency.

In a national plan from 1944, Gibney presents the island of Ireland as an 'amputated body', with high-pressure extremes concentrated in the two eastern cities of Belfast and Dublin, draining vitality from the rest of the country (Figure 2.4). At once a critique of colonial extraction, partition of the island, and continued rural de-development, Gibney's vision of a more 'wholesome' Ireland combines familiar political and cultural themes of the day. In his utopian Ireland of tomorrow, a new capital city would be located on the shores of Lough Ree (between midland counties Westmeath and Longford), an Irish Brasilia, connected to a radiating network of regional, planned towns by high-capacity radial routes. Wind farms, tidal energy, as well as turf and coal, would power this future Ireland, re-balancing the country through urban and rural industrialisation. Gibney produced similarly ambitious plans for 25 Irish cities and towns between 1940 and 1950, none of which came to fruition.

These national plans, however abandoned, represent crucial elements of the foreclosed promises of an Irish 'resource nationalism' premised on the unique characteristics of the island's landscapes. Such plans contain a critique of existing and persisting forms of coloniality and rural extractivism – by which, in the view of contemporary critics of (neo-)extractivismo in Latin American decolonial thought, represents a key ongoing factor in the treatment of rural areas as territories for dispossessive removal of resources (Svampa 2019; Arboleda 2020; Riofrancos 2020). Instead, in Andrews' and Gibney's visions of rural Ireland, we see an Ireland utilising its resources and distributing them evenly among its primarily rural geographies – an early eco-modernity, in other words, looked something like a rural modernity, one that re-invested the surplus value and social utility of resource extraction within the country, rather than exporting materials and value to existing productive 'metropoles' that had characterised the colonial regime.

Andrews wanted a specific kind of rural modernity, and he saw this vision best realised through Gibney's BnM villages. 'They represent', he wrote, 'the fulfilment of a process aimed at industrialising a rural population while at the same time improving rather than disrupting its environment' (Andrews 2001, 204). But none of Gibney's housing schemes were completed as planned.

Figure 2.4: Stress Diagrams of Ireland, Framework for an Irish National Plan

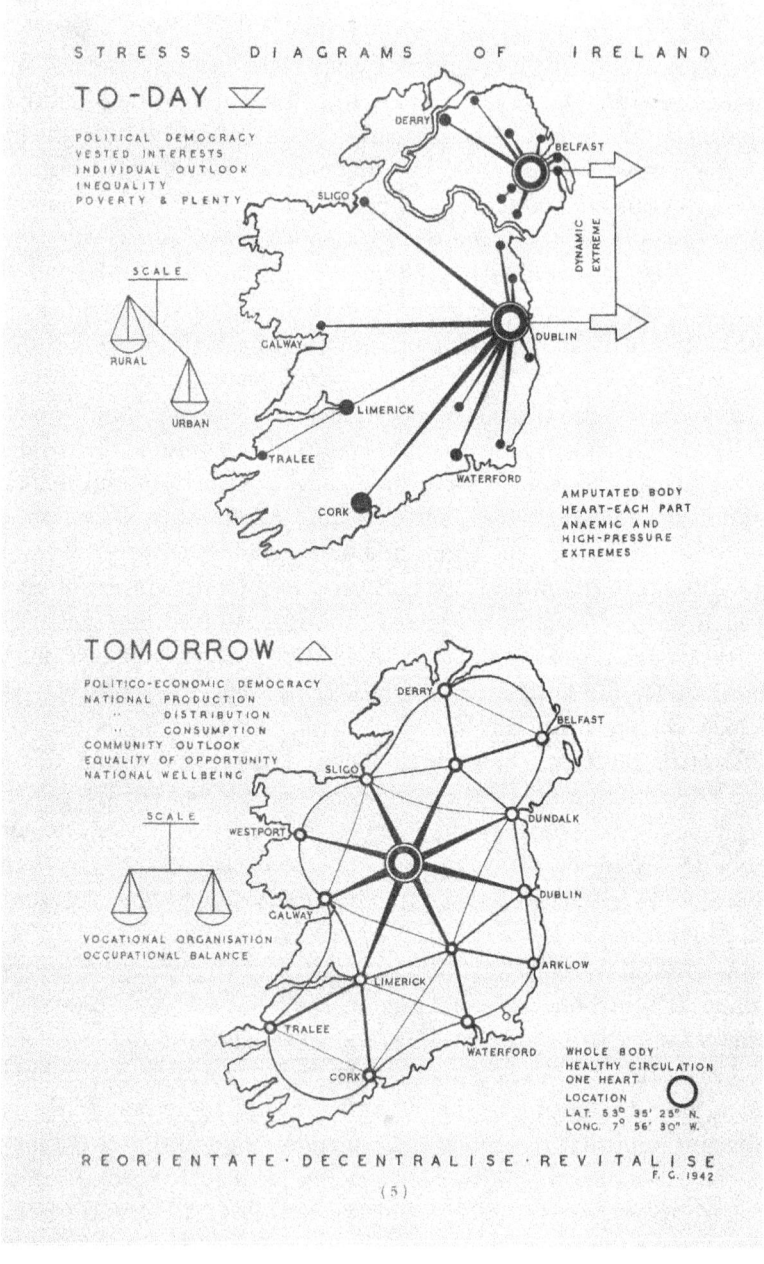

Source: Frank Gibney, Dublin, 1943, p 5

While they stand today as impressive monuments to an ambitious vision of national development, they also stand as reminders of how constrained and partial this vision was in practice. Six planned villages housed a small proportion of BnM workers, and failed to adequately cater for the needs and desires of the newly 'modern' citizenry that lived in them. In the 1960s, it was not churches that these communities came asking for, or even handball courts and allotments, but the schools that were never built and bus services to give them some distance from the claustrophobic confines of working and living in such close proximity. There were sports teams and pubs but, beyond this, opportunities for socialisation were limited. That may have suited some, but for others, the desire to get away and experience something different was strong. This passed on to the next generation who were encouraged to gain an education and advance to better things again.

While provided with some basic infrastructures and services, the plight of peat workers mirrored that of emerging rural- and agrarian-based movements also emerging in the mid-20th century. With small farmers continuing to struggle and landless labourers unable to access land, including the children of farmers, the chronic under-development of rural Ireland continued throughout the 1940s and 1950s. The Land Commission had broken up some untenanted estates and re-distributed land but the viability of the 'small family farm' was about much more than owning a 20-hectare piece of land, and ultimately the agrarian economy remained deeply linked to British export markets. Emigration was still exceptionally high, with half a million leaving the country between 1945 and 1960. After the War, land agitation erupted again, with a new farmer's party forming in 1957. Lia Fáil (named after the 'Stone of Destiny') was a minor nationalist party founded by one Father Fahy, who had been associated with the populist agrarian movements in the 1930s. Offering an early insight into the ambivalence of agrarian politics, and the strange fusions of national mythology and social reform, Lia Fáil sought to reconstruct Irish land use along the lines of the ancient Brehon law, raise an army to defeat the British Empire, and make emigration illegal (Madden 2012).

In 1965, Peadar O'Donnell, the Republican socialist who had spearheaded the anti-annuities campaign in the 1920s, wrote a pamphlet entitled *The Role of Industrial Workers in the Problems of the West*. He didn't mention the industrial workers now employed in Bellacorick, Oweninny, or the many other industrial bog projects. His focus was on the 'uneconomic' small farmer and what could be done to stop the 'dispersal' of the west. So-called 'peasant proprietorship', or the transfer of land from landlords to Irish tenant farmers, had done little to alter the unequal agricultural economy of Ireland that still prioritised large graziers and cattle exports to Britain. Rather than highlighting Gibney's worker villages, O'Donnell pointed to the work of Father McDyer in Glencolumbkille, who helped organise the community to build their own community hall, piped water systems, roads and pressure the ESB to bring rural electrification to the area. As was more often the case throughout rural Ireland, the infrastructures of modern life were not brought from on high, but were built from local initiative and labour, often spearheaded by the parish priest, an unelected authority. With electricity and water, Glencolumbkille soon had a vegetable processing plant (set up with the support of the state-owned Irish Sugar Company), knitting cooperatives, and a tweed factory. In 1967, the Glencolumbkille Folk Village was opened by Minister Erskine Childers, with three thatched cottages built and furnished by local people. This was a different kind of industry, appealing to visitors from the US whose remittances were one of the few sources of income that allowed people to remain on the western seaboard. The Glencolumbkille example highlights the contradictions and micro-struggles over development in the west – the active role of the state (when pushed), the centrality of a mobilised population, the links between agricultural production and industrialisation, and the possibilities for alternative forms of development that neither conform to 'tradition' or 'modernity'.

O'Donnell was writing at a critical point in Irish postcolonial development, when the 'threat of betrayal of the whole tradition of the national struggle', as O'Donnell (1965) put it, loomed large. These stark warnings do not tally with the 'boom time' declared by *The Western People* in Crossmolina. Bellacorick may have been the largest industrial development west of the Shannon but it couldn't solve the deep-rooted problems of 'uneconomic' farming, lack of broader industrial development, and emigration (Healy 1988). The problem of the west was the haemorrhaging of its people, demonstrating vividly the challenge of breaking with colonial patterns of dependency and uneven development.

With the shift in economic policy from the late 1950s, agriculture was put on a new footing. The small, family farm was no longer the benchmark of agricultural progress. Instead, 'development farmers' were encouraged: those able to attain certain levels of agricultural productivity. Such farmers tended to be those already with access to capital and resources, rather than those most in need of state support and access to land. From the 1950s, foreign ownership of land also became more prevalent, including investors speculating on land assets. In 1960, Erskine Childers, then Minister for Land, defended the purchase of two estates in County Carlow of 1,600 acres and 2,000 acres by a British syndicate: 'We cannot play a full part in the modern world, cannot attract tourism, new technical skills, or industrial capital, unless we take a sane commonsense view of landownership' (quoted in Dooley 2004, 184). This did not prevent boycotts of the Carlow estates in question, including re-prints of the 1916 Proclamation of the Irish Republic hung along the roads with 'We declare the right of the people of Ireland to the ownership of Ireland' underlined. Even the

Irish Times questioned the extent of foreign ownership of land, pointing out that Ireland was the only country in Europe allowing unrestricted purchase of land by foreigners (Dooley 2004). The pressure counted to some degree – what became known as the Carlow Land War resulted in the Land Commission buying back the estates in 1960, dividing 300 acres between local farmers, and establishing a new state agricultural research centre on the rest.

In 1965, new legislation was passed providing the Land Commission with powers to approve of all foreign purchases of land. This did little to quell the discontent, and in 1968 a new national organisation was founded: the National Land League. As the name suggests, the Land League explicitly referenced the much longer history of agrarian agitation and organising stretching back before independence.[18] The Land League sought to counter the depopulation of rural areas, with demands for renewed state support for small, peasant farmers. It sought to protect small farmers against big farmer consolidation (especially with entry to the European Economic Community (EEC)) and big-monied interests and investors speculating on land (RTÉ 1983). They had branches all over the country and claimed 12,000 members. They demanded that the Land Commission fulfil its promise: ensuring the viability of small farms by breaking up large estates, the provision of subsidies (away from big farmers), and the setting up of voluntary farming cooperatives. They were inspired by the civil rights movement in the North and organised with trade unions and the cooperative movement.

We can link the unfinished project, or promise, of land redistribution and reform with the unfinished project of rural industrialisation represented by BnM. Just as rural electrification was unequal and incomplete for much of its rollout, the Gibney estates became articulations of a partial and imperfect vision of rural planning and the management of communities at the behest of particular resource economies. The towns were developed as a kind of pilot project that never took off – unlike later experiments in export-processing and tourism, that utilised the land and 'cultural' resources of rural Ireland towards attracting foreign dollars to a cash-strapped state. Resonantly, while the post-developmental state began to crystallise its strategies of FDI from the late-1950s onwards, parts of the mainland were only connected to the national grid in 1978 (Black Valley, County Kerry). Islands such as the Aran Islands and Inisbofin were not connected until the late 1990s, and islands such as Tory in County Donegal are still powered by ESB diesel generators. This absence of material development in rural parts of the country highlights the durable imbalances represented in and through infrastructural investment. And while alternative visions were present, shifts in national developmental ideology were soon to become instrumentalised through these same landscapes and imbalances.

Postcolonial modernity to post-developmental ambitions

In his 2021 book, *We Don't Know Ourselves*, the writer and journalist Fintan O'Toole documents how his own life parallels the entry of Ireland into the 'modern' world – at first, economic modernisation and then, lagging behind, social and cultural modernisation. The hinge point in this story comes in 1958, the year he was born, and just a few years after the opening of Portarlington power station, with the publication of T.K. Whitaker's white paper, simply called *Economic Development*. Whitaker was secretary of the Department of Finance and is often credited as the person who set Ireland on course towards an open economy and receptive host to FDI ever since. For O'Toole, the period after 1958 is read as a kind of thaw, the slow disintegration of an Ireland dominated by a conservative social and economic class and a Catholic state that had extinguished the radical currents of republican, feminist, and workerist movements that had brought about independence.

O'Toole's modernisation narrative is one of the founding myths of Ireland's subsequent economic success story at the end of the 20th century, and aligns with a dominant strand of Irish history that runs parallel to historical revisionism and its fear of an 'unfinished' revolution haunting the national project. The story begins with the failure of Ireland's import-substitution model – characterised by projects such as peat industrialisation to reduce dependence on British coal – arguing that such projects were part and parcel of a narrow, nationalist ideology imposed by the conservative Fianna Fáil Government. The absence of robust domestic industrialisation, high unemployment, and mass emigration in the 1950s appear to prove this failure. Far-sighted bureaucrats, such as Whitaker, recognised the problem and steered Ireland on a new path of export-oriented industrialisation and liberalisation, carrying out what sociologist Denis O'Hearn anoints a 'peaceful revolution from above' (O'Hearn 1990, 8).

O'Hearn pulls this story apart by showing how Ireland's efforts to delink from Britain were compromised from the beginning, in large part due to continued attempts by the British to sabotage the new regime. But the postcolonial state was also insufficiently radical, hampered by a comprador class reluctant to relinquish its inherited privileges. The Cumman Na Gael Government that governed throughout the 1920s was more than happy to maintain existing economic (dependent) relations with Britain, reflecting in particular the interests of large grazier farmers and their middlemen (McCabe 2011). When Fianna Fáil came to power in 1932, riding a resurgent wave of republican, anti-colonial, and popular-agrarian social movements, there was a partial break with this comprador political elite. But, as the Republican socialist Peadar O'Donnell wrote in 1933, 'Great good will exist inside

Fianna Fáil leadership. When they fail it will be that good men can no more use the machinery of a capitalist state to serve the needs of the mass of the people than did small-bad men' (1933). Compradorisation would not escape Fianna Fáil leadership in the end.

Despite protectionist interventions and select state-owned enterprises, such as BnM, basic structural relations of dependency with Britain were left unchecked, including the maintaining of currency parity with the British pound (this lasted until the 1970s).[19] Coupled with this conservative monetary policy, the private banks retained considerable power across this period, refusing to release the credit that might have stimulated domestic industry and farming. National protectionism was also limited by the size of the domestic market and the fact that there was nothing to stop Irish capitalists – benefitting from state protectionism – from shifting their surplus outside the country, rather than investing in productivity gains. 'Private enterprise in our retarded economy was a policy of make-believe', as Peadar O'Donnell put it (2017, 120). Any encroachment on private enterprise was resisted not only by Irish capitalists, but also a conservative civil service largely inherited from the colonial era (O'Hearn 1990) – while there were some notable exceptions in new industrial sectors (such as BnM), there was no nationalisation of private industry in Ireland. As many other newly independent countries would soon discover, national modernisation via a limited strategy of import-substitution underestimated the continued drain of surplus to external capital, as well as the difficulty of stimulating domestic markets and demand.[20]

After WWII, Britain was on the wane and the US was on the rise. The US seized on the opportunity of rebuilding Europe after the devastation of the War both as means to create new European markets for US goods and a way to buttress against the rise of Communism. US Marshall Aid did flow into Ireland from 1948 through the Economic Recovery Program (ERP), though initially it seemed Ireland might be left out due to its neutral position during the War and its high level of under-development (O'Hearn 1990). The money that did come was largely in the form of loans, not grants, and came with significant strings attached: structural adjustment *avant le lettre*. Some of this money went to capital funds for semi-states, including BnM, as well as delivering on other social policies such as the building of hospitals and housing. But the focus of US aid was on encouraging industrial production for export. Negotiations had been underway for some time about what would make Ireland 'aid-worthy'. For the US, this included the end of protectionism, opening up the Irish economy to free trade, particularly with Europe (and thus beginning the US policy of using Ireland as a platform into more protected European markets). In 1948, despite objections from the Finance Department, Ireland joined the Organisation for European Economic Co-operation (OEEC), which ended protectionism.[21] A year later, in 1949, the Industrial Development Authority (IDA) was established with strong guidance from the US. Initially open to different possibilities, including the nationalisation of strategic industries, the IDA would soon establish itself as the primary vehicle for incentivising export-orientated, foreign-owned industrial investment. Finance was provided to non-domestic companies by the government in the form of grants for factories, machinery, low-cost electricity, and tax relief on profits – initially a 50 per cent tax relief on export earnings for the first five years, this was extended to 100 per cent in the early 1950s.[22]

The role of the US in shaping Ireland's economic departure after 1958 should not be underestimated, with old patterns of unequal exchange quickly re-establishing themselves. After WWII, US imports into Ireland continued to grow and Ireland needed dollars to pay for them. The US suggested, among other things, that US corporations should be given access to Irish minerals in order to raise the country's dollar earnings (see Chapter 6). US advisers even encouraged Ireland to follow the model of Puerto Rico: as a dominion of the US, Puerto Rico had attracted light industry from the US to the Caribbean through tax incentives in the 1940s.

Hinting at the ideology of postcolonial state development that was to come, the consolidation of economic ties with the US (and Europe) was framed at the time by Irish politicians as a form of decolonisation: breaking away from Britain by entering into new forms of US-dominated dependency, however much those bonds aligned with the newly dominant imperial power (with strong diasporic connections among its population, reflecting and predicting the cultural dimensions that would come with this neocolonial relationship). But some at least in the Department of Industry and Commerce understood the broader implications of these policy shifts, posing the question of 'whether there is any point at which we shall be forced to choose between European cooperation on the one hand and the development of our own country on the other' (quoted in O'Hearn 1990, 23).

The basic details of Ireland's shift from a nationalist, protectionist import-substitution development model to an export-led, foreign-dominated post-developmental model is not particularly novel or distinct – though it is significant that Ireland's shift was happening at almost the exact same time as dozens of former colonies across the Global South were just embarking on their own efforts at sovereign (often protectionist) development post-independence. However, the speed and extent of Ireland's shift *is* notable.[23] O'Hearn identifies three distinguishing characteristics that will become important as we trace the origins of the 'economic miracle' of the 1990s Celtic Tiger years in Chapter 3. First, radical free trade in large part brought about under duress from US and European integration post-WWII; because of Ireland's proximity to 'core' economies, Ireland's pivot to free trade was much faster and more sudden than in many other developing countries.

Second, radical free enterprise, which was not a massive departure from the previous phase of development – despite exceptions such as BnM, the Irish state never seriously contemplated nationalising strategic industries. Third, foreign industrial domination, which is to say that the new Irish regime was not about creating linkages between foreign and domestic industry. Rather, foreign industry was perceived as a replacement to domestic industry (O'Hearn 1989). O'Hearn quotes the Irish Minister for Industry and Commerce in the Dáil from 1958: 'we aim to convince [US industrialists] that Ireland is the best possible location because of its attitude to private enterprise … the more profits they make the better we will like it' (1989, 581).

In revisionist historical accounts, the 1950s is seen as the beginning of the end of Ireland's futile efforts at national self-sufficiency. But this is not just a shift in economic policy. Ireland's entry on to the 'modern' stage, as O'Toole put it (2021), is just as often dated to the visit of President JFK in 1962 as it is to Whitaker's new Economic Program. JFK's speech to the Dáil – recently repurposed by the Irish wind industry lobby, promoting a new kind of resource nationalism centred on multinational-led wind development (see Chapter 4) – appeals to Ireland's quest for self-determination and progress, even as his very presence augurs the entrenching of renewed dependency.

What is less well remembered is that two years earlier, in 1960, Kwame Nkrumah, prime minister of newly independent Ghana, came to Ireland on an official visit. Speaking to a packed meeting of the Irish United Nations Association at Dublin's Shelbourne Hotel, he paid tribute to 'those Irish leaders of the last century who realised that the struggle of Ireland for independence was not the struggle of one country alone, but part of a world movement for freedom' (quoted in O'Sullivan 2018, 1). The anti-colonial movements spreading throughout Africa were a manifestation of the same struggle the Irish had been through, and with it the dream of a future beyond colonisation and European imperialism. Five years later, in 1965, Nkrumah would write his seminal *Neo-colonialism, the Last Stage of Imperialism*, outlining the methods and forms through which former European powers and the US re-asserted their control of nominally independent countries: 'The essence of neo-colonialism is that the State which is subject to it is, in theory, independent and has all the outward trappings of international sovereignty. In reality its economic system and thus its political policy is directed from outside' (Nkrumah 1966, ix). The wages and conflicts of the anti-colonial fringes of the Irish republic versus the conservative cultural nationalism of the dominant state forces developed strongly in line with cultural forces that were shifting, roughly, from the colonial 'modernity' of European empires to the globalised, postmodern empire of US-led capital and the burgeoning economic power of the EEC.

Fianna Fáil's Frank Aiken was Minister for Foreign Affairs throughout most of the 1950s and 1960s, and was vocal in expressing Ireland's solidarity with newly independent former colonies and anti-colonial struggles on the international stage. Aiken had also been a key driver of the early peat industry in the 1930s. In 1957, Aiken came under strong criticism from Fine Gael opposition, the Church, as well as mainstream media for positions he took up on behalf of the Irish Government at the United Nations (UN) General Assembly. Aiken gave Irish support to the proposed withdrawal of Russian and US forces in Europe, as well as support for a resolution on the inclusion of China as a member of the UN. The opposition claimed that these actions went against the interests of Ireland – economic interests blended with the fiercely anti-communist position of the Catholic Church, and entangled with US interests. At a time when Ireland was courting US advice and investment, and the tide of explicitly nationalised sovereign development was starting to recede, Fine Gael TD Declan Costello had this to say about Frank Aiken's policy of non-alignment at the UN:

> Does it help us to secure our economic interest by making these fatuous observations which can have no effect other than a disturbing one of our friends? Does this entice anybody or make them more amenable to come to us and help us here if we take up that attitude, when we act in an independent and, I may say, irresponsible fashion? We have offended our friends and comforted our enemies. (Dáil Éireann 1957)

Aiken's response was that as an independent country, it was a betrayal of neutrality to align with one side over another, regardless of the short-term economic interests. Aiken was committed to the idea that the UN was an institutional platform that could be used to advance peace and non-proliferation in a context when militarism was escalating and Cold War positions hardening. These disagreements over foreign policy are significant because they capture the interplay of Ireland's shifting economic policy (towards US and European integration) and its geopolitical alignment, particularly as this pertains to the world-historical struggle for decolonisation across what was then called the 'Third World'. These dynamics are surfacing once again as Ireland is caught between historic and ongoing support for the Palestinian people, and US-EU support for Israeli apartheid and genocide (see Conclusion).

Understanding the geopolitical and economic origins of Ireland's reintegration into the capitalist world system after WWII can help us to better understand the stakes of Ireland's multinational-led digital and energy transitions today, and the importance of centring Ireland's anti-colonial history of non-alignment and active neutrality within our environmental movements and politics. The impetus to re-link with the capitalist world system, albeit under different economic conditions, was premised upon factions in the state cosying up to US economic interests and employing a geopolitical position at the periphery of Europe. Signalling this new era of strategic openness, the 'world's first free trade zone' for tax-reduced global manufacturing and shipment of goods was established in Shannon, County Clare, in the west of Ireland in 1959. The Shannon Free Zone was established as a tax-free export-processing zone – a roughly 2-km^2 territory where producers could locate manufacturing activities with exceptional status.[24] Harking back to days of colonial entrepreneurialism, this innovation in 'regional development' was pioneered by Brendan O'Regan, a businessman who had travelled to the US under the Marshall Aid Plan and first developed his vision of a 'duty free' area at the airport in 1947 (Callanan 2000),[25] taking advantage of the transatlantic flow of largely Irish-American tourists coming back to visit the old country. In a resonant example of pairing cultural with economic attraction, the Shannon Free Zone instantiated a durable logic of US capital flowing over the Atlantic through Ireland – with some of it, as the story goes, sticking around and providing the wealth base for regional development.

A story that captures the turning tide of postcolonial national development in this period relates to Frank Gibney. In the early 1960s, he was invited to design housing developments for employees of the Shannon Free Zone. The initial phase consisted of 136 houses and was completed in 1963, but a larger, much more ambitious town was also planned, called 'Project X'. As Fergal McCabe outlines in his book, this was set to be the first entirely planned town in Ireland since the 17th-century plantation towns (2018). It was a dream project for Gibney, who put his predictably grand visions of a Garden City-inspired town to paper. But his plans were not adopted. The Department of Local Government, who made the call, claimed Gibney's firm didn't have the capacity to deliver the development and that foreign consultants were required – the tender was given to Frederick Rogerson, based in the UK. In 2012, when Clare County Council prepared a new plan for the Shannon area, it concluded that Rogerson's development had 'no sense of place … or where the town centre is located' (McCabe 2018).

Gibney wrote an extensive memo documenting this process, reflecting how much the decision affected him. In the final pages he quotes, with irony, a line from a Seán Lemass speech given in November 1959: 'The future of Ireland is ours to make. We are not now or ever, prepared to admit that any people on earth are our betters. We are determined that nobody will get in front of us in working our new plans and applying new ideas for national projects' (quoted in McCabe 2018). Whether Lemass meant these words in earnest or not, a shift was underway, as the limited but still ambitious plans for national development and rural modernity were being hitched to global capital and US-EU geopolitical and economic integration.

Conclusion: The durability of modern progress

We opened this chapter with a description of Séan Keating's mural at the World Fair in New York. The mural represented the hope and ambition of an independent, modern Irish Republic. The fair closed in 1940 and with the War in Europe raging, many of the exhibits and pavilions were destroyed. The Irish state was given the option to bring Séan Keating's mural home (for the cost of $300) but refused. Whether this was because there were more important things to focus on, or whether the Government had little interest in monumental artistic visions of the future, it is hard not to read the incident as a fable for the new Irish Republic, the closing down of alternative futures before they could even take root.

Postcolonial theorist Joe Cleary refers to 1920–60 as 'de Valera's Ireland', an era that is almost universally perceived as negative, a byword for 'soul-killing Catholic nationalist traditionalism', economic austerity, and sexual puritanism (2007). It is true that the radical feminist, worker, and anti-imperialist elements of Irish republicanism were aggressively crushed during and after the Civil War, with the first decade of independence marked by a socially conservative, economically liberal Cumman na Gael Government. But Fianna Fáil's populist programme from its election in 1932 was driven by a resurgent republicanism, rooted particularly in the revival of the land question as it pertained to economic independence and decolonisation. This spurred a policy of economic nationalism and limited social redistribution. Fianna Fáil ultimately could not deliver on the promise of delinking from Britain, the economy continued to leak value, and the country remained chronically under-developed. Coupled with the entrenchment of Catholic conservatism and the further crushing of radical republican, feminist, and socialist cultures, it is easy to see how this period of Irish history can be dismissed as the 'dark ages'.

But there is more to it. Quoting Frederic Jameson, Cleary writes that every strong moment of rupture with an old order requires powerful disassociation of the present from the past, a project of historical revisionism central to any counter-revolutionary transition. For 'modern Ireland' to emerge, in other words, 'it had first to create "de Valera's Ireland" that would be its repudiated antithesis' (2007, 8). 'De Valera's Ireland' was not just a creation of post-1960s 'Lemass's Ireland', but also a necessary condition for it. In any modernist account of history, the crossing of a new threshold into 'modernity' requires that the past is relegated to a pejorative, the contested visions and potential alternative paths steamrolled into a catch-all of entrenched tradition, social inertia, and political naivety. In Ireland, the years before 1960 are either characterised by an inward-looking national culture, austere economic policy, and an imaginary of rural Ireland as the repository of the true Gaelic spirit; or, the grand modernist infrastructure projects such as Ardnacrusha and the draining of the bogs are seen as reflections of a nationalist ideology of progress that implemented universalist engineering schemes on distinct environments and rural places, ushering in a modern Ireland at the expense of what came before. The ambitious national energy projects undertaken by the state from the 1930s are easily transformed into artefacts of a well-intentioned but ultimately moribund anti-colonial nationalism. Driven by a compromised republicanism, these state-led development projects and their alternative technoscientific alignments are now often cast as evidence of a persistent idealism (rather than pragmatism) in Irish political life – one that asserted national independence against its best interests (that is, continued economic subordination to England). In truth, these two perspectives, and others between them, are part of the same revisionist historiographical tradition – one that settles for a linear, liberal, and frequently depoliticised view of history, rather than engaging with fundamental antagonisms and contradictions that represent Ireland's shifting position at a global scale.

As the history of the 20th century has demonstrated, ambitions of sovereign national development in the wake of formal decolonisation have everywhere been blocked by internal and external forces. BnM was sabotaged from its inception, even coming under criticism from the ESB, forced as it was to purchase less efficient peat fuel from its sister semi-state. Turf granted some degree of economic sovereignty – it also enabled rural industrialisation and modernisation. But a policy of national protectionism without a radical re-organisation of production and consumption and rupture with economic dependency on England (including sovereign control over banking and currency) could not overturn development deficits and, ultimately, the pressures of US and European geopolitical and economic interests. From the 1970s, entry into the EEC, and by extension the liberalisation of the state, further undermined the viability of state-owned energy industries. By the end of the 1980s, this postcolonial development trajectory would converge with the expansion of US FDI, particularly in the tech sector, to launch the Celtic Tiger. This era of structural transition is the focus of Chapter 3.

3

Data Centre Land

A postcolonial ecological regime

We are driving on the coast, among the blanket peatlands of North Mayo. These peatlands have been accumulating carbon in their anaerobic muck for millennia, quietly depositing the environmental and cultural memory of these places in semi-aqueous soil. An eeriness saturates the landscape. It may seem cliché, but we are going back in time – at least, becoming acutely aware of the history of this place, transported to different moments and sites of conflict that awaken our senses to the entangled pasts and futures of land, energy, and technology.

We start in Rossport, where 83 km offshore, the Corrib gas field was 'discovered' in 1996. After having already granted exploration licences in the early 1990s, the British multinational oil and gas company Shell was granted permission to exploit the field and build an onshore refinery by the early 2000s. The Shell to Sea campaign formed in direct opposition to the project, which mobilised local protestors and wider national and international solidarity groups (Figure 3.1). The campaign connected with those who had been affected by Shell's developments in the Niger Delta, and a solidarity mural of the martyred Ken Saro-Wiwa was painted. The message was clear: this pipeline will harm this community, and is connected to wider extractive practices by multinationals, supported by the Irish state and its foreign direct investment (FDI) policies. Most in the area considered this an untenable and unjust project, and we can still see the famous Shell-to-Sea mural on a cottage in the middle of a field.

We keep driving from Rossport, east along the coast. Humans have settled in this place for 5,000 years, with some of the earliest evidence of Neolithic agriculture in Europe preserved beneath the bog in the Céide Fields complex, first 'uncovered' by a domestic turf-cutter in the 1930s. About 20 km inland from the Céide Fields was the Bellacorick bog complex, where Bord na Móna (BnM) and the Electricity Supply Board (ESB) ran industrial turf extraction and power generation facilities from

Figure 3.1: Worker Solidarity Movement sticker protesting Gardaí repression of the Shell to Sea campaign in Rossport, County Mayo

Source: Flickr user jaqian

the 1950s, discontinued in 2003 (and the power station demolished in 2007). Today on the cutaway, BnM and the ESB have partnered on another energy venture – the 172 MW, 61-turbine installation Oweninny Wind Farm. The Siemens and Nordex turbines tip out at 176 m high, towering above the surrounding bogs. The scale is sometimes astonishing – one wonders how neolithic farmers, in their worship of celestial and atmospheric patterns, would react to such structures.

A few kilometres further north, nestled amid scenic strands and a small bay, is the town of Killala. We stop to photograph the beach, with wind turbines towering in the background, and to have a quick pint and a meal. Most people know Killala as the place where General Humbert arrived with 1,000 French soldiers in 1798 to help liberate Ireland from the English. Not so well known is the fact that it was also the site of one of the first major multinational investments in Ireland in the early 1970s. The Asahi chemical complex was at the time the largest foreign investment by a Japanese company anywhere in the world. It came to a newly zoned industrial park located just above the small town, with the state providing water infrastructure to the otherwise under-developed area. Providing hundreds of local jobs and economic development to the area until its unceremonious closure in 1997, the building now stands in ruin (Figure 3.2).

Now, 30 years later, the gutted factory floor and the surrounding industrial area have been planned for redevelopment as a site for renewable energy and a data centre.[1] Surrounded by plantation forestry, such a facility will deliver eco-modern promise to this de-industrialised space, taking advantage of the nearby fibre-optic cable landing which is situated just across the road – so the story goes. With so much information travelling underneath the sand and bogs surrounding, as well as the existing industrial infrastructure, why not take advantage of this resource? We just need investment, and a new dedicated supply of electricity, to

Figure 3.2: Ruins of the Asahi chemical plant in Killala, County Mayo

Source: Photograph by Patrick Bresnihan, 2022

do so. Many in the area consider this potentially positive, if done right, promising a renewed dream of sustainable industrial development through multinational investment and eco-modern technology.

This chapter turns our attention to the industrial ecology of what world systems and dependency theorists would refer to as the 'post-developmental' and 'semi-peripheral' Irish state (O'Hearn 2001a). The period we focus on roughly spans 1970–2000, as Ireland navigated its place within the emerging global landscape of high-tech manufacturing and services – in doing so, leveraging its landscapes towards the activities of FDI. There has long been an apocryphal assumption that contemporary rural Ireland has been spared modernity, rather being subject to chronic under-development. Such a lack of robust and widespread sovereign industrialisation has indicated to many, from cultural theorists to political economists, that Ireland faced a unique hurdle in the 1980s–1990s – how to make the leap from an under-developed, agrarian nation-state to a post-industrial, postmodern global economy?[2] As the prior chapters and this opening vignette make clear, the 'resource base' of Ireland has long been its land – and the financial structures that the state developed to accommodate multinational companies were made possible through their location on Irish soil. But one often-marginalised element of this equation is infrastructure – required to technically mediate between local ecological conditions and the specific operations of these companies. In this chapter, we unravel the prehistory of how Ireland's contemporary infrastructures have developed to meet the needs of multinational tech companies – the engines of 'digitalisation' – and, in turn, have become central to the contradictions of 'green' growth.

As we have carried out the research for this book over the years and spoken at events, we were frequently asked what appears to be a simple question: why are there so many data centres in Ireland? As researchers from different disciplines, this question formed the basis of our work together. United by interest in the environmental politics of data and renewable energy in Ireland in the late 2010s, we were familiar with the basic premise: Ireland had a climate that was amenable, as well as a business and tax environment that suited data centres' and their operators' unique infrastructural needs (Brodie 2020a). In these arguments, the conditions cited above made Ireland singularly attractive – these 'climatic' resources, from business to atmospheric climate, were effectively leveraged to draw in extraordinary investment. Since the 2007–08 financial crisis especially, the Irish state was hungry for large-scale investment, and the presence of the tech industry was so entrenched that the progression of digital infrastructure here seemed a relatively straightforward solution (Brodie 2021). In addition, multinational tech and Ireland's climate commitments appeared, in the popular press at least, to represent potential mutual benefits in the form of sustainability and energy partnerships (Chapter 4). From a basic perspective, even among mainstream environmentalists, this all appeared common-sensical: why not use what we have – multinational tech and abundant wind energy – to provide green development and jobs?

However, these politics go much deeper than a post-crisis entrenchment of monopoly tech, which began to concentrate with the growth in smart and data-driven technologies since the late 2000s. These developments were part of much longer historical processes, and elided the durable forms of infrastructural under-development and unequal ecological exchange occurring in and through Ireland. As Chapter 2 introduces, the country's gamble with enabling multinationals to 'organise nature' in Ireland (Deckard 2016) was in response to a burgeoning US economic empire, grafted onto existing and unresolved ecological formations left over from Ireland's incomplete decolonisation. While BnM and other commercial semi-states such as Coillte continued to operate as state-owned enterprises through the period traced in this chapter, the landscape was changing. All industrial activities responded in kind to these global shifts that interfaced with localised transformations at the intersections of capital, national development, and the environment.

We are interested in how the logic of FDI-led development becomes not only infrastructuralised, but also permeated through common-sensical, everyday operations of the state – and especially its management of environmental contradictions. This is part of the transition in Ireland from the 'developmental' to the 'post-developmental' state, terminology more frequently used to refer to industrialising states in, for example, East Asia in the 1980s (Ong 2006). If the developmental state was characterised by import-substitution and capital investment such as the energy and resource development of BnM, the post-developmental state is one which wagers developmental ambitions on the market-led operations of multinational companies and their spin-off benefits (O'Hearn 2000; Ó Riain 2004).[3] The transition from the developmental to the post-developmental state is one not only of compromise, but also the active engineering of an environment designed to provide development by and for FDI. Caught between rising US hegemony and European integration, it came to be that there was 'no alternative'.

'Data centre land', as we jokingly rebrand Ireland's post-developmental era, is thus a scene that must be staged first as part of a longer prehistory of the data centre phenomenon. It is a story of global shifts, enterprising semi-states, comprador governance, rural/urban transformation, infrastructural (under-) development, and land and resource management. In this chapter, preparing for the final three chapters' focus on much more present (and future) wages of eco-modernity, we shift from a deeper historical timeline across the colonial and postcolonial eras to a reckoning with a 'postcolonial' Ireland that was also global, European, and post-developmental in its treatment of FDI as the primary resource of economic activity. This would have transformative and ongoing effects on the resource base of Ireland's future development, including the current eco-modern transitions pairing digitalisation (whose industrial prehistory we can glimpse in this period) with decarbonisation – a planetary imperative under the remit of monopoly tech.

Neoliberalism with Irish characteristics

In 1980, a third of the Irish workforce was employed in the public sector, public debt was 15 per cent of GDP, unemployment was at 20 per cent, and emigration was averaging at 1 per cent of the population. Denis O'Hearn, writing in 1989, argued that Ireland was a classic case of dependency: 'slow growth and inequality caused by foreign penetration' (O'Hearn 1989, 593). Despite 25 years of export-led, foreign-dominated industrial policy, Ireland was in a deep economic depression. Raymond Crotty also argued at this time that 60 years of independence had brought about minimal 'progress', similar to other contexts of postcolonial under-development and indebtedness.[4]

Within the space of a decade, however, Ireland transformed from an economic basket case to an economic miracle in the form of the 'Celtic Tiger' of the 1990s, advertised the world over as a poster child of liberal globalisation. How did Ireland emerge so strongly from a turbulent 1970s–1980s in the world economy, to rise to such exceptional prosperity during the 1990s? This is not just a story of 'end of history' neoliberalism played out in one country. It is about 'neoliberalism with Irish characteristics',[5] a revolution carried out on the back of a postcolonial state that had been actively changing its role in the capitalist world system since the 1950s.

As we have sketched out in the previous chapter, the fundamental re-orientation of the Irish economy away from a policy of state developmentalism towards new forms of US (and EEC) dependency had been underway for some decades before the 1980s. In some sense, Ireland's wholesale shift from import substitution to export-led foreign domination over this period gave it an advantage when global capital became footloose and the world economy opened up. Within Ireland, the public debt crisis also provoked a more focussed and intensive strategy of institutional transformation, in spite of well-documented apprehension about the FDI strategy's perceived lack of success from hired think tanks and factions within the state, captured by the influential Telesis Report in 1982.[6] One of the clearest manifestations of FDI institutionalisation comes via the creation and reform of semi-state companies that owned and managed land and infrastructural assets. More commonly referred to in the UK and elsewhere as 'QUANGOS' (or 'quasi-NGOs'), such state-owned, commercial bodies in Ireland are one unique inheritance of UK-governing tactics, with over 800 semi-states operating in Ireland in

2016.⁷ These semi-states came into their own in the 1980s, playing a crucial role in the post-developmental Irish state. They effectively mediated relations between territory (land) and FDI, whereby infrastructure became a tool of industrial facilitation beyond mere 'privatisation'.⁸ Commercial semi-states are an institutional tool for internalising market logics within the state: if the semi-state's statutory function is to increase revenue from state-owned assets, then public interest becomes synonymous with profitability.⁹

In this chapter, we start by zooming in on the institutional transformations happening in BnM between 1987 and 1997, not only to keep the thread of energy politics, but also to demonstrate the strange non-event of neoliberal transition in Ireland. Why was the decimation of the peat industry in the late 1980s not met with more labour opposition? How did the transformation of BnM into a new entity, orientated towards narrowly commercial (rather than social) ends, not generate more political debate?

After the 1973 oil shock, BnM was tasked to expand peat production – national self-reliance again surfacing, this time triggered by the efforts of Arab states in the Middle East to assert their independence from US influence. The Third Development Programme, as it was called, extended BnM's ownership, drainage, and extraction of peatlands, but also resulted in increased debt – the cost of the new programme was estimated at £20,000,000 (Clarke 2010). Whereas the previous two Development Plans had been financed by the General Exchequer, with low-cost, flexible loans, the Third Development Plan was financed externally, through private financial institutions such as the European Investment Bank and the World Bank. BnM challenged this, pointing to the risks of using short-term loans for long-term projects, but by the mid-1970s, post-Bretton Woods, it was no longer government policy to finance national energy development directly. BnM's fate was now tied into international financial markets and fluctuating interest rates, as well as global energy markets. In 1974, BnM's debt was £19 million. By 1984, just as oil was becoming cheaper relative to peat, and debt was more expensive to service, BnM's debt rose to £172 million (Clarke 2010).

The same debt-driven dynamic that crippled Third World countries in the 1980s played out in Ireland, with a debt-dependency spiral both exacerbated and treated by market-led policies (Crotty 1977). Without the economic foundations of a welfare state built through wartime mobilisation and a strong industrial labour base, Ireland had always been more dependent on transnational capital, leaving it more exposed when crises hit. Semi-states, with their significant land and infrastructural assets inherited from a brief period of state-led developmentalism, were forced to respond to a rapidly re-structuring world system that would see the evolution of a new relationship between the Irish state, territory, and foreign capital. What became clear in the mid-1980s was that Todd Andrews' vision of BnM as a sovereign organ for developing Ireland's bogs was again subordinated to external (neocolonial) political and economic forces. For those tasked with ushering in this neoliberal transition, however, the key force 'fettering' Ireland's development was not transnational capital but the 'dead hand' of state administration.

Eddie O'Connor was appointed as CEO of BnM in 1987. His biography parallels the emergence of a new post-developmental, 'post-nationalist' (Republic of) Ireland: he was awarded a degree in chemical engineering in 1970 from University College Dublin (UCD), the same year Ireland entered into formal negotiations with the EEC and just as the 'Troubles' had begun in the North. O'Connor represented a new generation of the Irish comprador class that entered the ranks of the Irish semi-states in the 1970s, a decade marked by economic downturn and transformation.[10] He moved from the ESB to BnM, becoming CEO at a particularly difficult time. We were 'prisoners of history', he would later say, meaning the decisions made throughout the 1970s had led to indebtedness, declining profits, and low morale (Scéal na Móna 1994).[11] They were also prisoners of ascendant neoliberal globalisation in which competition meant everything. For O'Connor, this was an opportunity. 'Bord na Móna is in a race to the future', he said in an interview at the time, 'to be first with new products, to be best, and to create the future rules of competition in order to grow and develop' (Scéal na Móna 1994, 6).

Borrowing from the production model of Finland's peat company Vapo, which contracted local farmers to harvest peat rather than directly employing workers, O'Connor was convinced that profitability in the industry depended on making remuneration dependent on results – the more output, the more pay. These changes were controversial and negotiations with the unions took place throughout 1988–89. Brendan Halligan, the union representative on the board of the company, was in favour of the changes, arguing that 'profits were no more than a measure of efficiency' and, crucially, were essential to BnM delivering its social mandate in the midlands (Clarke 2010, 237). In other words, the end goals remained unchanged; all that was being proposed was a change in management, or the means to get there. This is the magic of neoliberalism – always presenting the problem as technical, the product of out-dated modes of operating, rather than any political disagreement.

In just two years, O'Connor halved the workforce in BnM without any significant labour pushback.[12] Compare this with the UK, where Thatcherism and the closure of the mines resulted in near civil war. The peat industry was nothing in size to the UK coal industry, but there was also a different political culture. In Ireland, autonomy and self-sufficiency (aka entrepreneurialism in the neoliberal lexicon) is more the Irish norm in the absence of a strong welfare state. The desire for individual freedom (in the face of an oppressive Church and sclerotic state bureaucracy) was easily articulated with ascendant market logic, and the corporatist 'social partnership' model, a strike-moderating bargain between labour, the state, and employers, was in full effect after 1987. For all the housing estates and rural industrialisation efforts, the midlands and rural Ireland more broadly were still under-serviced, without basic transport infrastructure or schools. Until Eddie O'Connor took over it was assumed by some workers that the industry would close entirely – the ESB had been closing turf-fuelled power stations and it was thought the most suitable bogs had already been exploited. The children of peat industry workers had new ambitions, now accessing free third-level education designed to produce workers for growing pharmaceutical and tech sectors. Workers that took redundancy received generous packages, enough to build their own houses. They went on to get work in the budding construction industry or engineering services for new industrial facilities such as Intel (more below) that were cropping up on the fringes of 'bog country'.[13]

As well as driving competition in the workplace, O'Connor also pushed the internationalisation of BnM. We have seen how under Todd Andrews, the peat industry was a means for Ireland to develop relationships with Russia and Germany – sharing expertise in the productive development of bogs. For O'Connor, the international focus was all about developing markets for new products (or undermining labour). He established the Irish Peat Board (IPB) Global Consultancy Service in 1989 to sell engineering and peat expertise abroad.[14] Clients included countries in Eastern Europe, Indonesia, Central Africa, and Cuba. The shift from a non-aligned internationalism to selling services to Third World and post-socialist countries is emblematic of Ireland's active entry into the re-structured world capitalist system of the early 1990s. It is also worth pointing out that the accumulation of this expertise, the making of this particular asset, was the result of state development and investment from the 1930s geared towards a domestic energy industry (not international markets). This was in stark contrast to the FDI-led R&D model contemporaneously being pioneered by the Industrial Development Authority (IDA), as we discuss in the next section.

Internationalisation also meant tapping into the diaspora, particularly in the US. In 1994, to promote a natural peat and wax fire log, a festival was hosted by BnM in New York called 'Beat on the Peat' (Scéal na Móna 1995). Forty-ft containers were used to transport sod peat to Yonkers, then reconstructed into a 150-ft facebank on site. Visitors could use the traditional Sléan to play at cutting turf or visit a showpiece of traditional Irish village life complete with a wake, poitín-making, and traditional cooking. Thirty thousand people attended over the weekend and it was deemed such a success that it also ran the following year. The Scéal na Móna editorial writes: 'for like practically everything else, nostalgia is a commodity nowadays that can be sold' (Scéal na Móna 1995). 'Bord na Móna' kept its name – as it does today – to maintain its association with Ireland, bogs, and even national development. But in every other aspect, the company underwent a 'passive revolution from above',[15] particularly in this period, as it responded to economic crises and popular pressures that surfaced sharply in the 1980s. Compradors such as O'Connor were vital in negotiating this transition, establishing Ireland's place within a rapidly liberalising, globalising, and Europeanising world system. To do this meant fusing the particularities of postcolonial Ireland with the forces of global capital.

O'Connor was forced to resign from BnM in 1996 due to controversy over £66,000 in 'unvouched expenses'. He went on to found a private renewable energy company, Airtricity, which launched his subsequent career as CEO of one of the largest renewable energy companies in the world. This subsequent success in a period of globalising Celtic Tiger Ireland has ensured he is remembered as a 'man before his time' who was undermined by inept civil servants and overly prescriptive state bodies (Cooper 2008). One Labour TD later stated in the Dáil that O'Connor had 'turned Bord na Móna around' and that instead of getting a bonus, as he would have in the private sector, 'he was hounded from office and his good name dragged through the mud' (quoted in Collins 2024).

O'Connor did turn BnM around – from its origins in state developmentalism towards a market-focussed, commercial company competing internationally. This wasn't his work alone – and we don't want to suggest that O'Connor or the transformation BnM underwent was unique, especially in neoliberalising Ireland, as state organisations and arm's-length bodies had to adapt to the tides of debt and financialisation rocking the economic boat. In little more than a decade, BnM had moved from responsibility for the national peat industry to competing with foreign-owned energy companies in the Irish electricity generation market.[16] This shift – largely driven by liberalising competition rules brought in as part of EU integration – effectively eroded the state's direct role in managing the energy sector. But BnM continued to carry significant debt that, perhaps counter-intuitively, resulted in the state buying £120 million equity in the company as part of the 1998 Turf Development Act. Rather than this resulting in an enhanced public remit, the trade-off was exactly the opposite: under the Act, the company was divided into three separate subsidiary companies authorised to engage in the full range of commercial practices, specifically entering into joint ventures and equity partnerships. Their remit was now to generate returns for shareholders, the main one being the Irish state. The 1998 Act carried through the neoliberal revolution from above that would allow the company to be 'nimble' and 'innovative' in the new world of uncertain, global competition.

The debates in the Irish Dáil over the drafting of the 1998 Act are instructive for understanding how this rupture in the form and function of BnM took place with such little opposition (Turf Development Bill Deb 1997). The history of BnM is referred to repeatedly. Tributes are paid by government ministers to Todd Andrews for his 'ideal of pure public service'. Fianna Fáil minister Brian Lenihan goes so far as to say there has always been 'a strong

Marxist strain in our [Fianna Fáil] political thinking'. He makes the case that competition and commercial success are not, however, antithetical to public purpose, and that when BnM was established in 1946 it was never only to provide a social function. It had always been tied to 'economic performance', he declares. From this perspective, the 1998 Act is simply a means of *modernising* BnM, providing it 'with a legal structure that will allow its business to develop along normal, modern commercial lines' (Turf Development Bill Deb 1997).

What is erased in this brazen revisionism is that the 'economy' is not ahistorical or neutral. As Andrews made clear in his speech in 1956, referenced in the previous chapter, no amount of enthusiasm on the part of enterprising individuals could have resulted in the development of Ireland's bogs under colonial administration. He understood, at least, that the economy consisted of conflicting class and (neo)colonial interests. This meant that sovereign development in a republic required the assertion of political power. It is ironic that during the Dáil debates in 1997, a Mayo TD used his speaking time not to debate the Act but to ask the minister about the future of Bellacorick power station, a base of development and employment in North Mayo that would have been unthinkable under the constraints of 'normal, modern commercial lines'. Todd Andrews was already turning in his grave.

Ireland's postcolonial ecological regime

The above history is instructive about the development of a logic that was arising at a particular point in time and across different, if sometimes overlapping, state bodies and profit-making organisations. These shifts institutionalised forms of knowledge and expertise that would become the signature factors in the Irish state's developmental strategies leading into the Celtic Tiger. In this section, we focus on the ecological character of Ireland's neoliberal transition: beyond the declining industrialisation of peatlands and the transformations that would arise through this, from local politics to the energy system, what were the other conditions that were put into place, and capitalised upon, from an ecological perspective? The narrative, as we are arguing, is not simply that Ireland opened up the floodgates to FDI at the right time, which was afforded by certain ecological relations and contradictions. Rather, the manipulation and mediation of environmental factors – including land, resources, and infrastructure – was instrumental to FDI-led development and the work of state officials and semi-state bodies from the late 1980s.[17] Again, the historical conjuncture is significant, with growing public awareness and corporate 'responsibility' for the environment entering into the mainstream of policy making and business strategy (Bresnihan and Millner 2023).

It is here that dependency theorists and the figure of the comprador help illuminate the structures that would emerge in and beyond the state over the next decades to facilitate FDI companies. Conor McCabe (2015) is one of the few Irish scholars to use the figure of the comprador to better understand the specific, (post)colonial social formation of Irish capitalism. He traces a throughline between the middlemen who profited from Ireland's export-oriented cattle industry both pre- and post-independence, from 'gombeen men' to the new comprador class that emerged from the 1960s onwards to service transnational capital (2011). This class became especially important within the financially arcane accounting and management systems of FDI-driven state organisations. As others theorise, the transition from developmental to post-developmental states – for example, the shift from experimental export-led industrialisation to a full-scale FDI-led model – involves the leakage of value from such states via multinational extraction (Mezzadra and Neilson 2019). This is often, as suggested by Max Ajl (2021a), premised upon the technological development and expertise of foreign capital – what assets are put up for sale, how is the local labour force disciplined, and where does that value accumulate? We can see at this time the origins of the premise that 'spin-off' and 'ripple' effects of such investment will produce benefits – 'modernisation' in the newer terms of neoliberalism – in the absence of direct investment in public infrastructure and welfare. As the logic would advance, and amplify in and through the economic circumstances of the 1980s, such investment becomes mediated by the private sector and, in a more advanced way, by multinationals.

As we suggest in the Introduction, there is a minimal – but important – intellectual tradition of dependency theory in Ireland. Debates about Ireland's postcolonial development were especially lively in the 1980s and 1990s – specifically, in intellectual response to revisionist debates circulating in public discourses regarding the character of Ireland's social and economic transformations.[18] Of particular interest is the field of rural sociology, concentrating Marxist analyses on the question of Ireland's contested 'modernisation' with regards to the ecological consequences of Ireland's FDI industrialisation strategy (Tovey 1993; Leonard 2008). The background to this was the surfacing of place-based but networked rural and peri-urban environmental campaigns objecting to the siting of toxic pharmaceutical and chemical facilities. These environmental conflicts were thus a key locus through which discussions about Ireland's modernisation were being worked out.

In 1993, the sociologist Hilary Tovey made a distinction between 'two versions of development and modernity' that were finding expression at the time through two forms of environmentalism: 'official' environmentalism and 'populist' environmentalism (1993). For Tovey, official environmentalism was predominantly urban-based and consisted of NGOs and professional experts (including academics) whose principal concerns were heritage and conservation. Important for our argument, official environmentalism rested on assumptions about Ireland's path towards modernisation: that growing environmental awareness was either a response to new forms of industrial development previously absent from the country, or the result of modern cultural norms and values entering the country since 'opening up' in the 1980s.[19] 'Official environmentalism posits Irish "backwardness" and "traditionalism" against British and international "modernity"' (1993, 419), she writes. In this framing, Ireland lags behind other European 'core' countries due to deficits in the Irish political system and wider society. Instead of criticising state development policy, the focus of official environmental discourse were the 'irrationalities' of traditional Irish politics and culture (Allen 2004).[20] In identifying key features of Irish society (rural, nationalist, agricultural) as the main obstacles to environmental progress, official environmentalism even tends towards a form of authoritarianism, expressed as a frustration with 'overly democratic' ways of getting things done. This frustration with more dialogic, democratic forms of governance results, Tovey argues, in a greater emphasis on technocratic, top-down environmental management.

Critical commentary on the development of Irish capitalism from the 1980s emphasises, understandably, the emergence of Ireland as a tax haven and the specific role afforded by a new comprador class of accountants, lawyers, and financial consultants (Boyle and Allen 2021; McCabe 2011). But Ireland's land, resources, and infrastructures were also being leveraged for FDI in distinct ways that required other forms of expertise and mediation that acted to mitigate and head off disruption. Applying these forms of state mediation and 'compradorisation' to environmental (and infrastructural) management in the post-developmental state, we theorise this as Ireland's 'postcolonial ecological regime'[21]. Importantly, the lens of the postcolonial ecological regime re-casts the periodisation of Ireland's data centre boom as emerging from a much longer period of postcolonial development within the post-WWII capitalist world system.

Tovey's analysis of official environmentalism is helpful in this regard. Environmental experts did not emerge from nowhere. They too were beneficiaries – or products – of state investment in education for science and technology from the 1960s. Across different fields – engineering, architecture, planning, applied science – this generation was well positioned to design and advance environmental technologies, standards, and protocols in Ireland. As the 1992 Rio Earth Summit made clear, environmental questions were no longer peripheral to policy making or to multinational corporations who sought to take advantage of new opportunities in green technologies and eco-markets (Bresnihan and Millner 2023). In Ireland, where environmental contradictions were mounting from the export-oriented agricultural sector and the activities of multinational corporations,[22] there was growing demand for state mechanisms to mediate (but not interfere with the core basis of) these pressures. There were untapped opportunities here, in a world where everything needed to be turned to competitive advantage. Over the next three decades, the leveraging of Ireland's environmental conditions for FDI would become an industry in itself.

Focussing on infrastructure and the ecological, we thus aim to displace a somewhat limiting emphasis on the Celtic Tiger's economic success story. In mainstream accounts, Ireland uniformly attracted investment in particular strategic sectors – namely, pharmaceuticals, technology, and financial services – as a coordinated financial 'gamble' that paid off and enabled Ireland to 'catch up' to so-called developed economies. In this narrative, modernisation came about due to the successful gaming of the world system. These accounts, especially due to focus on Ireland's soaring GDP in the 1990s–2000s and the subsequently violent financial crash in 2007–08,[23] have tended to privilege neoliberalism as an 'invisible ideology' brought in from elsewhere (O'Callaghan et al 2015), emphasising the structural importance of global finance to, for example, the property sector, which arguably drove the most severe aspects of the financial crisis.[24] However, in focussing too intently on the rupture of the financial crisis following the exceptional growth of the 1990s, this framing elides two things: (1) the infrastructural conditions put into place by the state and semi-state bodies to support FDI, and (2) the epochal shifts happening in high-tech industries and their alignment with the structural forces coalescing around 'green' transitions since the 1990s–2000s. This had already given rise to an exceptionally high concentration of tech industries pre-financial crisis – Amazon Web Services (AWS), for example, launched its first infrastructure region outside the US in Ireland in 2007. How do we explain this beyond orthodox (FDI nationalist) accounts of competitive advantage and ingenuity?

Ireland was not entirely subordinate to changing global conditions in the 1980s, due to mainstream enthusiasm for 'Europeanisation', already strong economic links with the US, and the growing consensus among successive governments towards an FDI-led model of economic development. Existing structural conditions navigated during postcolonialism had laid the groundwork for a state that was *exceptionally* receptive to offshored value production. Earlier experiments with emerging production and financial processes, such as the Shannon Free Zone, already demonstrate a kind of precociousness on the part of the Irish state. As Ó Riain points out with regards to the IDA's development in the 1970s, the facilitation of tech and pharma multinationals was a result of intensive research into market trends and the promotional work of IDA officials to attract this investment in a competitive global market (Ó Riain 2004, 76) (Figure 3.3). While even the IDA would acknowledge that a large part of its work is promotion – and contemporaneous advertisements evidencing its engagement with revisionist discourses, such as one ad proclaiming that 'Ireland skipping the industrial revolution' was a good thing for its industrial future, show its savvy in mobilising history – this has materially shaped the use and development of

Figure 3.3: 1980s advertisement from the IDA, indicating to US investors Ireland's competitive tax advantages amid other European economies

Source: Finfacts Ireland

Irish land and infrastructure since the 1960s. Beyond selling Irish people, labour, and culture in a receptive way in relation to national character, this promotional work also promises material support in the form of land, pollution sinks, water, energy, buildings, and machinery.[25]

While many, including ourselves, have focussed extensively on the role of the big tech multinationals in Ireland and the specificity of their sourcing of electrical power and water for data centre infrastructure, these processes require a longer perspective of the instrumentalisation of Ireland's infrastructural resources and strategic 'location' towards private operations. A pertinent example is the Asahi synthetic fibre plant in Killala, Mayo, established in 1977 and operating until 1997. As John Healy narrates the story of the Japanese multinational locating there:

> [t]he proposal was welcomed with open arms, and everything was done to smooth the path. A 400-acre site for the plant was secured; Mayo County Council rushed through a €1.6 million water-supply scheme to provide the plant with the 20 million gallons of water it needed per day; and efforts to recruit 500 workers, most of them from the area, swung into action. (2018)

The involvement of the IDA and the county council in the build-out of significant amounts of water infrastructure to supply its facilities stands in stark contrast to water provision for the rest of the region, where group water schemes have represented a kind of community-based solution to those otherwise lacking state utilities (Bresnihan et al 2021) – a common experience of under-development in rural Ireland, where these FDI-for-development strategies have mixed infrastructural results.[26]

Documenting these different industrial activities is important not just because it offers a way to analyse Ireland's postcolonial ecological regime, responding to changes in the capitalist world system, but because it demonstrates how the urban/rural character of these processes and the production of rural peripheries as 'sacrifice zones' for Ireland's (eco-)modernisation continue to form the fault lines of ecological and infrastructural inequality across the island (Horrigan 2021). These are the conditions under which Ireland participates in an unequal system of global exchange: the model of state development facilitates the financial operations of multinational industries by providing land and infrastructure, absorbing some of their global profits reaped in exploitative and extractive manners in Ireland and elsewhere. At the same time, rural areas are unevenly materially and ideologically incorporated into industrial 'progress'.

Intel in Ireland and multinational tech infrastructure

As we have illustrated, Ireland's developmental strategies have not remained static over the last 60 years, and the FDI model in particular has faced internal frictions and debates at different points in time, whether internal dissent from the Department of Finance in the 1950s (O'Hearn 1990), the specific contentions surrounding the role of the IDA (Barry and Ó Fathartaigh 2015), or, later, in the Telesis Report in 1982, which questioned mounting dependence on FDI overall. Nonetheless, the 1980s would remain a key period of crystallisation for the IDA's and other semi-state companies' activities in securing the conditions for continued multinational growth. Much writing has been devoted to the 1987 establishment of the

International Financial Services Centre (IFSC) and Ireland's facilitation of offshored finance through tax incentives (O'Boyle and Allen 2021). Key here is the oft-perceived shift from manufacturing to 'services' in the Global North, with the offshoring of manufacturing to the Global South. There is thus a misapprehension that a drift to services in the 1990s marked a rupture in the productive basis of FDI – especially with regards to high-tech industries. From the end of the 1970s, IDA policy certainly shifted away from manufacturing, which was already dependent upon state grants due to higher labour costs in Ireland, and these sectors were progressively lost to parts of the Global South even with state investment and infrastructural provision. The basic developmental imperative of jobs was subsidised by the state, specifically in high-tech computer industries, so by financially incentivising the computer industries, 'the IDA bought economic tigerhood' (O'Hearn 2000, 74). A growing service economy perhaps masked that state attention and investment had always been focussed on capital-intensive rather than necessarily labour-intensive industrial activity.

But at the same time, the country presented other advantages for companies investing in high-tech enterprises and specifically computerisation – this gave it advantages as a site of capital- rather than labour-intensive industries. As O'Hearn details, '[t]he dominance of foreign industry, especially US-owned electronics companies, intensified after Ireland entered the EU (then EEC) in 1973: the country became an export platform for US companies seeking access to the European market' (2000, 72). Just two years after the establishment of the IFSC, the same FDI-driven incentives would see the IDA land its whale: Intel's first manufacturing facility in Europe, to be built on the site of a former stud farm in County Kildare. This came three decades after the pithy opening lines of a US industrial report on Ireland that proclaimed: 'In the Irish economy, cattle is king' (Barry and Ó Fathartaigh nd). Chips – and later bits – would come to stand in for cattle in this industrial narrative by which even rural Ireland could be 'modernised' via high-tech investment.[27]

Intel forms a crucial origin story in these FDI-led developmental narratives.[28] This 'coup' for the post-developmental state is heralded as an early template for Ireland's strategy of attracting – and keeping – multinationals on the island through the 1990s–2000s. As Barry O'Leary, chief executive of IDA Ireland, reflected in 2013, 'Intel was a step change because of the scale. It would require massive buildings, and massive infrastructure' (quoted in Lillington 2013), meaning that it would need significant infrastructural support and grants to locate in Ireland in the first place to scale up operations. Seen at the time as a risky endeavour due to the stagnation of the 1980s, the IDA was able to leverage financial and infrastructural incentives to not only draw in Intel's operations, but also effectively deploy strategies such as university training partnerships to demonstrate added value to Irish society.

But why did Intel choose Leixlip?[29] Reasons usually listed include: state investment in infrastructure (for example, water supply); available land and other infrastructure (for example, roadways); state incentives for manufacturing jobs; absorbed construction jobs lost in nearby 'peat country'; and the geopolitics of investment, as worries about 'fortress Europe' in the 1980s led to US companies looking for platforms into the integrated market (RTÉ 1990). Within all this, Intel saw the opportunity to develop *Intel* infrastructure – the plant is its own infrastructural installation, organising many inputs as well as surrounding land use and management (Explore Intel nd). Additionally, as with similar industrial operations, planning encircles and accommodates these infrastructural changes – largely, in suburban plants, driving further infrastructure:

> Intel says that local authorities first proposed to build an interchange linking a highway to its factory in Leixlip, 16 kilometers west of Dublin, in 1995. But work on it started only about a month ago. … Intel was first attracted to Ireland in 1990 by its surplus of engineers and an abundant power supply. (Pringle 2001)

The Intel facility specifically became a template for future investment in the tech sector (Lillington 2013) – enabling companies to scale up the infrastructure required for discrete operations (starting from manufacturing, extending into wider management, services, and other portfolios). Intel also became deeply embedded in the Irish R&D environment, with partnerships and memoranda of understandings with multiple Irish higher education institutions (HEIs). This also embeds Intel and multinational capital into public agendas and imperatives around research and innovation more broadly (Collins and Pontikakis 2006). It also, crucially, offers lucrative tax benefits – as a minister confirmed in 2024 suggesting the state and the IDA's continued courting of Intel investment, the plant would receive these R&D tax credits along with other potential financial incentives (Connelly 2024).

Reports from the time of the initial investment demonstrate a state policy logic that sees buy-in from these companies as public investment in industrial development (RTÉ 1989). The jobs promise 'return' for the state, as tax-payer money – rather than going into infrastructure – goes into snagging multinationals.[30] This logic extends far beyond the tax incentives or even the provisioning of land and other basic infrastructural services. As mentioned already, 'the Irish educational system was gradually re-oriented to the employment needs of information-technology and other knowledge economy sectors. In the case of Intel, the curriculum at Irish technology institutes was reshaped to match the company's specialist needs, and Intel would absorb these graduates every year' (Lillington 2013). This large-scale state investment into Intel – with the core idea that such investment would feed back into Irish society, even somewhat unevenly – was a robust and widespread strategy. By the end of the 1980s, the IDA was buying jobs from tech companies, including an estimated IR£100,000 paid per job 'created' by the Intel facility. By 1998, 'Ireland was the world's second largest exporter of software behind the United States', with software accounting for 12 per cent of the country's exports (O'Hearn 2000, 74).

With such a scale of investment, Intel would also become an influential factor in lobbying for industry-friendly policy and infrastructure into the 1990s – including vocal support for FDI-focussed infrastructural investment in spite of the dotcom downturn in the early 2000s. When the lobby group ICT Ireland was formed in the early 2000s, John McGowan, the VP and GM of Intel Ireland, was its first president. A report in the *Irish Times* in 2001, for example, platformed McGowan to express the grievances of the technology FDI sector:

> Lack of infrastructure and how it impacts on the quality of life is another critical problem, according to Mr McGowan … 'If people get frustrated and their lives are being impacted by having to drive into the city or Leixlip and fight traffic, it undermines the whole enjoyment of going to work and it makes them more likely to jump ship.' … Concern over the ESB's ability to supply the necessary amount of electricity to the high-tech sector has forced Intel to consider building its own onsite combined heat and power plant. … However, to build the necessary level of infrastructure to support investment and maintain competitiveness may require a change in culture. … 'We have a significant issue in Ireland in that the time it takes to get infrastructure put in place is very, very long by international standards', he says. … It took eight months for Intel to get full planning permission for its $2.2-billion expansion last year. In contrast, permission for an Intel plant in Hudson, Massachusetts, took just 30 days. … 'Ireland does have the advantage of being very democratic and the whole process is transparent here', says Mr McGowan. … 'But when I sit as a businessman and I compare with other countries who have higher standards of planning – they seem to get through the process much quicker and that gives them an advantage.' (The Irish Times 2001)

Echoing Tovey's observation about the 'excess' of democracy in Irish planning and governance, the speed of the processes through which FDI gains access to Irish resources is a recurring issue that must be taken up by a state if it is to appease multinational investors. In response to this excess of democracy, Intel became interested in building its own parallel infrastructures – including looking into sourcing its own electricity as early as 2003 through on-site combined heat and power, recognising the challenges of energy supply on the public grid and emerging sustainability scenarios (Fingleton White 2003).[31]

Rather than slowing down resource-intensive activities, Intel has become more infrastructurally intensive over time. For example, Intel's approved expansion plan in Kildare quadrupled its energy supply, to account for 7–9 per cent of national electricity demand when it is built, equivalent to four times as much power as Galway city uses (Melia 2019).[32] Eirgrid and the ESB agreed to foot 50 per cent of the bill for the €30–40 million project (O'Halloran 2019). Similarly, stalled plans to build a €1.2 billion, 160-km water pipeline to bring water from the Shannon to the Greater Dublin Region have been strongly supported by the IDA (MacNamee 2024), eager to ensure that Ireland's water infrastructure can support water-intensive FDI operations such as those at Intel – which, crucially, requires immense quantities of ultra-clean fresh water for its manufacturing process.[33] The significance of this is not just the quantity of energy or water, but that it requires physical infrastructures to be built by publicly owned utilities to bring resources to the plant. It also suggests that as Intel's flexible manufacturing develops, there is less need for a human workforce – more energy typically means more automation. In other words, the expansion of the facility is not about local or regional development in terms of jobs, but about access to public/private infrastructures, cheap utilities, and low corporate tax rates.

We have to remember that these investments are not necessarily permanent. In the early 2000s, when Ireland experienced acutely the global dotcom crash, there were rumblings in the press that Intel and other technology multinationals would sour on Ireland. Reasons cited were soaring housing costs and strained infrastructure – not only electricity supply for industrial operations, but under-developed roads and transit that made the country difficult to do business at the scale these companies presented.[34] Nonetheless, proposals from the press and policy makers – led by the dictates of these multinationals – were to invest in infrastructure and policies that would *keep these companies here*, meaning that such state investment was directed towards the needs of the private sector. This has re-emerged recently, including in language explicitly about keeping 'big employers' in regions such as Kildare by ensuring the infrastructure is up to capacity (O'Connor 2024). These slow, sideways moves towards privatisation – whereby the idea that companies such as Intel should just do it themselves becomes common-sensical to relieve burdens on the state – can be identified at very particular moments in time, and, we should be clear, are related to global economic shifts and not in any way inevitable.

Thus, similar to contemporary industry-led debates about the state's inability to develop infrastructure to support the growth of data centres, the discourses surrounding the tech downturn in the late 1990s–early 2000s were in large part laying the blame on the Irish state for its failure to address infrastructural challenges – challenges exacerbated by the extreme growth of multinational activities:

> 'it has lost its competitiveness with other locations', says Mr. Riley, arguing that Ireland's power, water and waste-management systems, as well as its road network, are now substandard. Intel, which employs more than 3,000 staff directly in Ireland, is still planning to open a $2.2 billion (2.56 billion euros) factory here in the second quarter of 2003, but Mr. Riley said the infrastructure problems could affect future investment decisions. (Pringle 2001)

Descriptions of issues surrounding Intel and other industrial plants in Ireland also reflect a durable discourse of peripheralisation and backwardness associated with non-modern imaginaries of Ireland. 'Historically', said Bill Riley, spokesman for Intel in Ireland, 'our country does not execute what we plan to execute at a reasonable speed' (quoted in Pringle 2001).

Microsoft offers another illustrative example, having opened a small manufacturing facility in 1985 and shifting over time from production to services in Ireland. When the dotcom boom was occurring the late 1990s, discussions around Ireland's lack of telecoms connectivity and internet speed were already paramount:

> In 1997, Microsoft decided against locating its Microsoft Service Network project, codenamed 'Mirror', in Ireland because of inadequate telecommunications infrastructure at the time. The UK already had the necessary telehousing facilities. … But that warning served to drive investment in such infrastructure in the interim. (Irish Independent 2000)

Such investment in infrastructure would form a later basis for Ireland's attraction of hyperscale computing just a decade later (Microsoft's first 20 MW data centre in Ireland went online in 2009). Architecture scholar John McLaughlin remembers that Ireland directly invested in transatlantic cable infrastructure in the late 1990s as well to receive a stake in European broadband connectivity, but the investment was washed out in the dotcom crash (2015). In the diversified terrestrial telecoms environment, companies such as Eir, the ESB, Vodafone, and others manage and control fibre-optic and broadband connectivity, much of which has been centred on the T50 fibre-optic cable route surrounding Dublin (supplemented by ESB dark fibre in the mid-2010s). The public-private development of this infrastructure, as with elsewhere (Duarte 2017; Ali 2021), is promoted as enabling business connectivity – and especially in Ireland, as an attractive and high-capacity infrastructural conduit to plug servers into.

Ó Riain focusses his studies of these industries on software manufacturing – the packaging and export of discs, mostly located in Ireland as a platform to the European economy (2004). As shifts in these industries led to virtualisation – via extensive and infrastructural digitalisation, especially in the 2000s – the base of Ireland required computing power in order to shift operations to the cloud. Ireland remains an export hub for these computing services; the only difference is that the service provided is no longer packaging of software, or its development, but the provision of 'cloud' infrastructure.

The combined centrality of R&D and software, in and through this environment, was infrastructuralised and, in a logical way, raises contradictions for the basic intensity of its resource demands (and lack of jobs) in the increasing flexibilisation of production. As the burgeoning 'knowledge economy' (Preston et al 2009) needed infrastructure, a development model premised on the development and utilisation of Irish human capital by moulding the economy towards FDI, never grappled with the (imbalanced) infrastructural landscape this would create. When faced with initial questions about the infrastructural viability of intensive FDI development performed at scale, recommendations from 'independent' consultations advocated for reducing resource consumption and promoting efficiency. Industry actors, on the other hand, blamed the Irish state for not successfully deploying the infrastructure they would need for increasingly flexible modes of production. The story of Ireland's becoming 'data centre land' is thus not only one of the expansion of computing for smart technologies, but also, crucially, the policy of industrialising FDI operations into Ireland's infrastructural (and ecological) basis.

Thus, while tax and financial incentives have a huge impact on the location of industrial activities in Ireland, they are part of a more diverse toolkit of state strategies that have enrolled not only ecological conditions, but also infrastructural resources and technical expertise towards multinational production. This comes with significant ecological implications. It is not that financial management is somehow discrete from ecological management. Rather, the bringing of FDI has always been an ecological prospect, one requiring immense infrastructural build-out, land, resources, and public investment from state bodies for viability. From the state's vantage point, then, the form of environmental management that it offers – mediating the contradictions of multinational growth and accumulation, as the next section will outline in more detail – is to act as a kind of territorial sink for the most resource-intensive aspects of their technological and infrastructural operations. What it gets in return is the jobs, tax take, and 'ripple effects' of such investment in localised contexts – which, however tenuous, remains a strong, and naturalised, incentive for the state to continue to provide these conditions.

Thus, what monopoly tech companies such as AWS, Google, and Meta, along with the already-existing foothold held by Apple,[35] Intel, and Microsoft, took advantage of after the 2007–08 financial crisis was not necessarily just available land and tax regimes amplified by the dictates of austerity and renewed dependency. It was also a state that was already particularly responsive to the environmental and infrastructural contradictions raised by multinationals' accelerating demand for what Jason Moore refers to as 'cheap nature' amid compounding digital growth and its need for 'cloud' computation at scale.

Infrastructural under-development and amplifying contradictions

In this final section, we will lay the conceptual groundwork for analysing how the state has adapted to mediate the relationship between FDI and the contradictions that arise when it 'hits the ground' (Mezzadra and Neilson 2019), especially in the form of environmental conflicts. This is becoming especially pertinent with the emergence of the industrial policy paradigm of 'digitalisation and decarbonisation', 'twin transitions' increasingly promoted as inseparable and symbiotic factors in the development of green industry in a landscape of pervasive data-driven capitalism, led by big tech multinationals. Here, it is useful to return to Tovey's discussion of populist versus official environmentalism.

If official environmentalism implicitly supported Irish state economic policy, populist environmentalism carried a strong and pointed critique of the model of development pursued by the Irish state – a fundamental disconnect that, unfortunately, has widened, laying the groundwork for the often reactionary politics of rural contestation today. Populist environmentalism as Tovey identified it was fundamentally a discourse of peripherality, drawing on historical critiques of de-development and colonialism, particularly in rural regions (see Chapter 6). With shifting realities and growing success of multinational-led development, populist environmental campaigning began to respond more directly and materially to interventions by manufacturing and extractive enterprises in peripheralised parts of the country. Detailed by Robert Allen in his 2004 book *No Global: The People of Ireland vs. the Multinationals*, these 'anti-toxics' movements were among the most profound expressions of environmental disaffection against the FDI state.

The experiences of 'anti-toxics' campaigns are instructive as to how the IDA had instituted a regime by which infrastructure and land were freely provided for companies deciding to locate here. Allen focuses in on the case of Raybestos Manhattan, who decided to build in Cork in the 1970s. Attracted there in part by the deep harbour, the company was seeking to alleviate financial difficulties due to the wave of environmental regulations that had been introduced in the US in the early 1970s. The other main appeal of Cork was access to efficient, cheap, and long-term methods for disposal of toxic waste by-products. According to Susan Baker, the IDA was aware of this and saw that one of the keys to attracting such companies into the Cork Harbour area would be the provision of a state-monitored toxic dump (Baker 1987). After huge and coalitional community opposition – leading to outright conflict between the police and the local community in 1978 as Raybestos trucks attempted to use a state-mandated dump for their toxic waste (RTÉ 1978) – Raybestos Manhattan pulled its Cork-based operations in 1980.[36]

Ireland was also becoming a hub for mining in the 1970s, an industry that was one of the first successful experiments with FDI-led development – and a much more obvious site of environmental harm as well as overt multinational exploitation of resources, which saw (sees) robust contestation around the country (Regan and Walsh 1976; also Chapter 6). As well as growing 'public' concern about the environment, then, it was the success of place-based movements in materially obstructing the state's FDI-led policy that drove the need for a new regime of environmental governance to support continued multinational expansion.

A key institutional response regarding state management of technical and environmental contradictions of multinational operations was the setting up of the Environmental Protection Agency (EPA) in 1993. The EPA effectively translated contentious political debates about the FDI-led model of development (and agricultural intensification) into the technical domain of a supposedly neutral state body tasked with setting and monitoring 'justifiable' quantities of pollution towards development (Taylor 1998). We see something similar with the role that An Bord Pleanála plays within planning, or the Commission for Regulation of Utilities (CRU) plays within the water and energy systems: state strategy has been able to inoculate itself against any challenge to the basic model of FDI-led development by containing controversies and opposition within narrowly defined, highly technical, and administrative systems. Institutionalising 'allowable' amounts of pollution served to contain public concerns within the technical domain of measurable environmental pollutants, risk, and harm (see Horrigan 2021). Thus, as particular state institutions stepped in to mediate the relationship between multinational companies, the environment, and civil society, there arose a knowledge elite licensed by the state that could determine how environments, and environmental contestation, came to be known, regulated, and governed. The state's gamble was that contradictions could be resolved by technocratic planning – setting up a planning system to mediate potential issues while promoting technical solutions to amplifying environmental contradictions. McCabe's analysis of Ireland's financial system demonstrates the role of the comprador in technically managing financial contradictions of FDI tax avoidance (2022). Through the postcolonial ecological regime, we propose a distinct but ultimately complementary function of the Irish comprador class: to construct and organise environments-for-FDI and technocratically contain environmental opposition to FDI-led development.[37]

One of the enduring consequences of this form of environmental management has been the displacing of contested politics into the realm of planning. The planning system has become the terrain of official environmentalism and its common-sensical recourse to the necessity of FDI, versus the place-based, anti-progressive 'irrationalities' of localised objections. The dismissal of complaints about development as base NIMBYism ('Not In My Back Yard') is a common tactic of mainstream discourses promoting infrastructural development, and this has become particularly evident with the transition to renewable energy, as the next chapter will detail. However, it has currency across the sectors and activities constituting multinational investment.[38] With the state constantly having to mediate now between these 'pesky' delays which enrage the industry, and the reality of its FDI-dependent strategy of development, one of the primary mechanisms of pre-planning processes and the social engineering of acceptance for this development model is about containing dissent. In extreme cases, this has also meant introducing legislation to 'streamline' planning processes by reducing the ability to object to projects. With companies getting stuck in the weeds, and the technocratic decision-making procedures favouring their activities against the NIMBYs, the overall result is the deepening of the conditions that informed Tovey's autocratic warning all the way back in 1993.

Contestations and controversies around Intel's water management at the Leixlip site, for example, while subject to negative rulings against the company, have also seen widespread public relations campaigns – both by the company itself, and by state partners such as the IDA and the National Parks and Wildlife Service (NPWS) – enacted through environmental partnerships. Beyond well-established water hoarding and pollution controversies in Ireland and elsewhere, the company, as of 2023, utilised the equivalent of 264 Olympic-sized swimming pools of water directly from the Liffey in Dublin every year (The Irish Times 2023). In this vein, Intel has invested in water-offsetting projects in Wicklow bogs – part of its efforts to be 'net water positive' globally – managing contradictions via environmental technologies and accounting (see Chapter 5).[39] Crucially, this project is a public partnership with the NPWS. As we explore in Chapter 5, these projects don't just have local implications – they produce commercially valuable knowledge and institutional practice to be exported elsewhere. Ireland becomes a laboratory *because* of the heightened contradictions that exist here and the experimental attitude of the state to address them.

Across these different sites, the state and its semi-state organs propose technical responses to the material contradictions brought about by the state's own economic development strategies. At the heart of these contested politics is a question about development – development, but for whom? These debates have been progressively sidelined and silenced as Celtic Tiger economic success appeared to resolve any questions about Ireland's modernisation through the successful facilitation of large multinationals such as Intel. Parallel to this was the dominance of the social partnership model over labour mobilisation, which, arguably, crystallised environmental and infrastructural contestation around this model of development as a primary site of anti-establishment political organisation in the country. It is these fault lines that have returned again in the context of Ireland's green transition, with division between rural communities and urban-based elites central. This political geography has been a feature of Irish society across colonial and postcolonial periods – indeed, this spatial class division characterises core/periphery divisions in other former colonies as rural territories were typically sites of resource extraction and urban areas the sites of mercantile and political power (Leonard 2008). We turn to these debates in the remaining three chapters as we analyse how these environmental geographies map onto the current landscape of monopoly tech-led green, digital transition.

Conclusion

While this chapter has shown how the IDA and other Irish semi-states come to manage resources and ecologies *for* multinational accumulation, this shift in state developmental strategy needs to be understood on its own terms as a form of sovereign industrialisation. Key to remember is that this strategy has its origins, still, within the long-suffering promise of national development, especially from the legacy of Fianna Fáil. This wasn't just about opening up the economy – it was foundationally about modernisation via development, however compromised in its relationship to the national struggle. We have to understand ongoing desires for development in and through FDI – which often seem extremely counter-intuitive, and even irrational – within this continuum. Whether or not they have directly experienced FDI-led development, communities around the country often still see multinational investment as a potential source of prosperity in ways that make the recognition of neocolonial dynamics not as strong motivators of political activity today. This is why a data centre in the ruins of industry in Killala, surrounded by otherwise unpopular extractive enterprise, becomes a popular prospect: it fulfils a promise of development otherwise unavailable, via large-scale investment and the potential of new infrastructure.

But this is, at best, a compromised mode of development, one that more deeply entrenches Ireland as a territorial sink for managing contradictions in the capitalist world ecology, funnelling accumulation offshore and, in some cases, into the pockets of a few enterprising industrialists. As the next chapter will describe in detail, this regime of FDI has been carefully branded and managed by a comprador class within the Irish state and its aligned industries (for example, boosterism, lobby groups, semi-states). Their argument is the basis of 'FDI nationalism' – that the tax take and capital investment arising from FDI represents a reliable base for Irish economic development, even if requiring immense buy-in and infrastructural development by the state. As Crotty argues, similar to later developmental revisionism that we will discuss in the next chapter, the idea was that the grazier cattle pasture was replaced by the capital-intensive plant in post-developmental Ireland (1977). Without the large-scale investments in industry by multinationals in Ireland, and the 'spin-offs' that these provide, there would be no 'economic miracle' and the remarkable prosperity that Ireland has ostensibly enjoyed since the 1990s. This branding of Ireland as an enthusiastic collaborator in global capitalism, which comes with complex wages of Whiteness and empire (Cook 2024), is part of the 'resource-making' regime of this particular formation (Bridge 2011; Kama 2020). But it is not just branding and promotion by the IDA and other semi-states. Ireland's recently established sovereign wealth fund is drawn from corporation tax takes, which are exceptionally high in spite of the exceptionally low corporation tax rate. The size of this wealth fund is comparable in scale to sovereign wealth funds held by oil- and gas-producing nations, the bank vault of FDI nationalism – indicating not just the scale but also the function of FDI within Ireland's political ecology.[40]

Since the 1970s, while every jurisdiction has had to compete for mobile, transnational capital, in Ireland, the dependence on this model of development has led to the intensifying of a situation whereby FDI becomes an essential rather than an additional part of the national development strategy. Private multinational investment and expertise are tethered into core infrastructures. Now, when industry solutions become necessary, the state must step in to politically and financially support these solutions. We argue that this arises as a logical development of the postcolonial ecological regime: the organisation of Ireland's ecologies *towards* enabling an extractive relationship of multinationals to Irish territory.[41] This is not something that arises in the vacuum of a global marketplace, but rather is the result of the emergence of a set of logics and institutional common sense that can be traced to the evolution of a comprador state over the past 60 years.

Thus the problem with FDI nationalism is that it rests upon the exploitation of land and infrastructure that has scarcely ever been situated in a 'public' regime of ownership. The 'neoliberal' process of privatisation in Ireland has thus never been simply about selling public assets, but rather the wholesale development of state-owned infrastructures, land, and resources *for* multinationals. Just as Lenin once opined that the map of colonial railways visualised the resource-extractive gaze of imperial power, so too do infrastructures formed in the image of multinational interests form the image of a profoundly compromised developmental strategy dominated by transnational monopoly capital.

What does this shaping of Ireland's infrastructural connectivity in the image of multinational capital do for the political orientations of the state – especially as they arise between the revolving doors of state and FDI capital? What is a resource nationalism that rests upon a resource that disappears if foreign enterprise decides to jump ship? This is not peat, gold, copper, lithium, or even wind – this is a different resource regime entirely, and it is one that manages *other* resources for the profit of multinationals. While this produces beneficial effects for some, increases the wealth base of the nation, and excludes and/or pollutes others, we return to the idea that tax evasion through Ireland is framed as in fact a public good – and the FDI model 'sacrosanct' (McCabe 2022). This presents irresolvable contradictions for the other forms of evasion and abandonment that such privatised regimes represent.

This chapter demonstrates that Ireland's FDI-led strategies are thus intricately tied up in energy, ecology, land, and resource management in ways that have not been as deeply theorised or analysed as its financial implications. Common refrains about Ireland's neoliberal governing powers and structures since the 1990s do not fully capture the stakes and endurances of the industrial and infrastructural histories that preceded and laid the groundwork for contemporary Irish politics in the postcolonial era. This is where the more material, specifically ecological, lens for understanding Ireland's FDI-led development since the 1970s is so important, especially in identifying how a new comprador class came to mediate and manage Ireland's ecologies and infrastructure for the shifting accumulation strategies of global capital. The intersection of BnM and the comprador represent a key point of orientation – the comprador, in such an organisation, is not the financial consultant or accountant but a figure such as Eddie O'Connor, who was able to instigate a process by which the hard-won legacies of peat resource nationalism could be converted into novel commercial assets for 'Ireland Incorporated' in a liberalising (and 'greening') world capitalist system.

As we document in the next three chapters, this process was not a one-off event and requires ongoing, active, and committed investment on the part of government and state institutions: 'data centre land' is still under construction, and contestation. This is because Ireland's postcolonial ecological regime was never just about permitting resource extraction or industrial pollution. It is about producing environments-as-resources and landscapes-for-extraction, legitimising these uses against those who object, including within current green initiatives. The next chapter will articulate some of the specific ways in which the postcolonial ecological regime has evolved through the infrastructural demands of big tech's cloud computing, for the policy paradigm of the 'twin transitions' of 'digitalisation and decarbonisation'.

4

Atmosphere Meets Cloud

Wind-blown clouds

We are driving through the borderlands between counties Donegal and Tyrone, in the north-west of Ireland, on our way to the Meenbog wind farm (Figure 4.1). This was the site of a 2020 peatslide, reportedly caused by the construction of a 'floating' access road for the installation and maintenance of turbines. A video of the peatslide posted on Twitter by a passing hillwalker shows trees and boulders floating on rafts of peat drifting down the hillside.[1] Eighteen months earlier, Amazon Web Services (AWS) had announced that it was entering into a corporate power purchase agreement (CPPA) with the facility's owner. This was proudly heralded in the media as a clear sign of the tech multinational's commitment to climate action.

To get to Meenbog, we follow the Barnesmore Gap. Today, what appears as a passageway for infrastructure across the rugged Bluestack Mountains was carved by glaciers about 13,000 years ago. Sphagnum moss, the 'bog-builder', along with the wet climate, has decomposed and created uneven layers of peat over the bedrock. It is this soil formation that characterises the bogs as a resource, beginning with its recognition as a fuel source after the clearance of the woodlands. Large swathes of blanket bogs in Ireland are still beholden to ancient, commons-based turbary rights of local residents, or the right to use certain plots of land for domestic turf-cutting. Driving across the western countryside, we can see the extent of this still-lively culture of energy. Veins of drainage ditches, excavation lines, and stacks of dried peat made by turf-cutters are visible for miles across many of these landscapes, with typically few permanent dwellings. This semi-subsistence energy economy takes place alongside wind farms, sprawling evergreen plantations, and industrial-scale cutaway sites. The interlocking degradation of small- and large-scale energy continues to damage the integrity of active bogs, and while 'new' resources such as wind are valued as greener

Figure 4.1: Driving in County Donegal on small country roads through a 'resource-scape' dominated by Sitke spruce plantations and wind turbines

Source: Photograph by Patrick Bresnihan, 2021

Figure 4.2: The base of a wind turbine at Meenbog, County Donegal, stabilised on cement and gravel, dug out from the bog, in 2021

Source: Photograph by Patrick Bresnihan, 2021

alternatives they still require significant damage and excavation of peat for construction (Figure 4.2).

We stop by the 'official' entrance to the Meenbog site, taking photos of the signs indicating that the facility is off-limits to all but builders and turf-cutters. The signs warn of 'deep peat' as trucks and vans dart to and fro between the hills and the gravel access roads. We feel unwelcome (and surveilled), and head on our way. After criss-crossing the border multiple times, through farmland and conifer plantations on a continuous road alongside the border-marking Mourne Beg River, we are eventually able to get a phone signal and contact Donal, a local wind farm objector. We meet him on the side of the road, and quickly realise that we are being informally vetted. Donal asks us if we have the proper footwear to walk the bog. We do not, but we're okay with getting our boots wet.

Describing our journey across multiple border points that day, Donal was amused, and happy to tell us about his own experiences. In the 1970s and 1980s, when the 'Troubles' flared in the North and along the border, small rural access roads across the Mourne Beg River were blockaded or demolished to funnel traffic into military customs checkpoints. Communities which for centuries had existed across this colonial border found themselves only illegally or inconveniently connected via limited, harrowing, and militarised rural crossings. Later, Donal showed us objection letters to proposed wind farms in the area. They frequently referred to the conflict and its permanent scars awakened by the tension and sense of helplessness around the new energy developments. Even the vocabulary of the place was heavy with history – Donal frequently referred to the wind turbines 'occupying the land'.

Our friend takes us to the Tyrone side of the border, parking in the ruins of a recently clear-felled industrial conifer plantation. Walking through it, partially reclaimed by the bog, was the quickest path to get to the construction site in Donegal, on a neighbour's land. The neighbour's commercial agreement to allow turbines on his land was controversial in the area. Many were overtly opposed to the development, and saw individuals agreeing to the construction as either opportunists working against the greater good of the community, or as unfortunate victims of tricks being played by the backers of this multinational project. The company had allegedly employed former combatants in the door-knocking campaign to get signatures on the project.

We can't walk for more than 5 minutes without Donal stopping to tell a story or point something out: where his grandparents lived before and after they emigrated to the US at the end of the 19th century; how they used to light a fire to get cousins from around to come help with the harvest; deaths of young relatives from treatable diseases and malnourishment; 'misery bridge', so-called because it was the bridge that emigrants passed never to return. His knowledge of the bog was deep – coverage that indicated wetness and should be avoided, plants with medicinal properties, edible roots and dyes that could be extracted. The bog had been his playground since he could remember, he told us. For Donal, this was no wasteland, nor simple repository of resources.

After crossing the pines and a few small streams, we come to a barbed wire fence, which Donal masterfully teaches us how to jump without injuring ourselves. We realise only then that the plan was all along for some light trespassing to see the site of the peatslide. Throughout the day, we transgress borders and property lines, across industrial woodlands, private pasture, enclosed peatlands, and the border itself, all land that may have once fallen under commonage, and could certainly be imagined as 'public' under different circumstances.

As the prior chapter narrates, the shift from a developmental regime with ambitions towards energy and resource independence to a post-developmental regime dependent upon foreign direct investment (FDI) introduced new contradictions into the Irish ecological landscape. Already burdened by the history of colonial exploitation and under-development, the formations of the comprador state adapted to manage the emerging harms and imbalances produced by the intensified presence of multinational capital on the island. This is the landscape of 'data centre land' – and the stage for Ireland's role in the planetary emergence of the green digital transition.

In the ever-expanding landscapes of the 'fourth industrial revolution' driven by 'digitalisation', 'smartness', and 'green' technologies (Schwab 2016; IEA 2017), cloud giants such as Amazon Web Services (AWS), Google, and Microsoft are taking on a sizeable role in the transformation of Ireland's energy systems, and in the global extractive landscapes required to supply them.[2] How does digital technology work to distance and mediate the extractive impacts and contradictions of FDI, as described by the 'postcolonial ecological regime' in the first three chapters? And how does this demonstrate a basic structure and function of monopoly tech's mobilisation in Ireland? These questions are explored across these final three chapters of the book. This chapter expands on the unfolding implications of the capitalist ecology of digital data and 'green' energy as it is taking shape within what we argue is Ireland's 'green tech laboratory'.

This is not only an assessment of the politics of 'digitalisation and decarbonisation' – the 'twin transition'[3] – in its Global Northern context of capitalist ecological modernisation. As we argue, this is intricately related to Ireland's ongoing and deepening structures of dependency and specifically the state's facilitation and management of capital's mounting contradictions. In an assessment of the continuing purchase of the 'agrarian question' in

2012, the editors of *Agrarian South* argue that the re-articulation of imperial power through monopoly-finance capital is increasingly enacted through 'green' policymaking that recognises (and superficially addresses) the 'historical responsibility of the industrialized North in the destruction of the atmosphere'. At the same time, with the emergence of green capitalism formed along existing lines of dependency and exploitation, the adaptation of largely northern power centres has meant increasing 'monopolization and depletion of natural resources and *atmospheric space*' (Agrarian South 2012, 6, our emphasis).[4] Thus, the ongoing structure of dependency in the capitalist world system means that 'sustainable' modernisation centred on Global North productive capacities, utilising and unevenly developing Global South resources, deepens unequal ecological exchange to sustain growth. This is key to critiques of coalescing green/digital extractivism, which includes the resource politics of atmospheric exploitation (Brodie 2024; Dunlap et al 2024). As atmospheric energies coalesce with the intensive operations of 'the cloud' in Ireland (Brodie 2020a), these climatic politics are necessarily navigating monopoly tech's increasing reliance on Ireland's public energy systems and their attempts to mould them towards digital accumulation. As prior chapters have suggested, this is being enabled by a state with vested interest in ensuring public infrastructure serves the interests of multinational capital; in this case, 'green' tech that has captured the eco-modern visions of mainstream environmental action and policy by mobilising green, digital transition. These potentials are heralded even by climate commentators, who frequently concede that data centres, and the monopoly tech companies that own this infrastructure specifically, are 'essential' to sustainability and have a central role to play in environmental futures. However, this is an eco-modern imaginary that needs to be robustly challenged – by emplacing it within a history of industrial technoscience that mobilises ecology towards capital accumulation.

The industrial changes to boglands in Ireland come along with incentives to move to renewable energy sources for the Irish grid, already powered by wind farms (roughly 35 per cent of grid supply) that dot the rural landscape. This form of energy is often literally sat on boglands where turf would formerly have been harvested.[5] Despite these very material consequences, wind farms and other renewables are seen as more atmospheric, drawing the climatic movements of weather – notably, Ireland's notorious wind – into the country's energy assemblage, and thus the political economy of the business climate. Wind, like the 'cloud', is imagined as ethereal and innocent – much like Marconi's imperial wireless assumed the dematerialisation of communications via technology. Rather than spewing particle-heavy smoke into the atmosphere, the eco-modernist aesthetic of wind energy pictures sleek technology harnessing invisible atmospheric currents. This green resource will power Ireland's digital industrial ambitions deep into the future, as the story goes.

These modes of modernising the bogs mark a continuity with the historical labour of making the bogs 'productive' by state administrators. But unlike earlier forms of resource nationalism represented by Bord na Móna's (BnM) industrialisation of the bogs, the emerging forms of resource nationalism represented by the increasing interconnections between wind and digital industries are dictated by the transnational and neocolonial forces of 'climate finance' and its regimes of privatisation. These emerging 'resources' – of wind, data, and climate harnessed for green modes of production – contain different ecological and discursive possibilities. The future of human life depends on a transition away from fossil fuels. But rather than making abundant, common energies such as wind or solar public (Howe 2011),[6] their futures are short-circuited into the privatised supply chains and techno-solutions of corporations across energy and tech (Howe 2014; Günel 2019). It is within this landscape that we analyse the unfolding infrastructural politics of wind and data in Ireland.

As political stakes intensify, Ireland has again become a test bed where infrastructural technologies and governance are innovated. The fundamental limit point, however, is Ireland's faltering infrastructure – pointing to a key, irresolvable contradiction at the heart of the postcolonial ecological regime. If multinational companies are provided basic infrastructure without investment in wider public provision – which has been the modus operandi for decades now – what happens when growth outstrips functionality, and the state loses its ability to provide both minimum public services and maximum facilitation for these companies? It is clear that the state's solution is not to slow down growth or scare off these companies. Rather, it is to enable these companies to sustain their own operations without the burden of the public system amid decarbonisation imperatives. FDI-led provision and use of Ireland's infrastructure was always about extracting value via territorial management, and today this is tied to the 'sustainable' operations of large-scale renewable energy. Data centres have become a way to operationalise a renewable energy future centred on the trade and efficiency of digital technology companies. Ireland's FDI strategies have laid the conditions for this to play out in extremely unequal and imbalanced ways, which allows us to see what monopoly tech's eco-modern imaginaries actually look like when put into action.

Resource regimes of wind and data

The first commercial wind farm in Ireland began generating electricity in 1992, the year of the Rio de Janeiro Earth Summit, the formalisation of the United Nations Framework Convention on Climate Change, and the setting up of the European Environment Agency. A reminder that the early 1990s was not just a time of neoliberal global restructuring, it was also a moment that climate change arrived on the political agenda. Eddie O'Connor personified this conjuncture (Chapter 3),[7] driving the development of the first wind farm on cutaway bog formerly designated for fossil fuel extraction in the Oweninny bog complex in northern County Mayo. There wouldn't be another wind farm built in Ireland for over a decade, and O'Connor would resign from BnM a couple of years later, founding Airtricity (now SSE Airtricity) in 1995, Ireland's first commercial renewable energy company. Using his background and connections from the Electricity Supply Board (ESB) and BnM, he set up wind farms in Ireland, the UK, and North America. In 2007, Airtricity sold its assets, netting O'Connor €50 million, much of which he invested into a new company, Mainstream Renewable Power, now one of the largest renewable energy companies in the world, with wind and solar farms in Europe, Latin America, Africa, and the Asia Pacific region (Collins 2024).[8]

The story of Ireland's first wind farm and the personal trajectory of O'Connor as a global energy entrepreneur reaffirms the place of Ireland as a proving ground for new capitalist ventures. Signalling a shift in energy resources (peat to wind), the Bellacorick wind farm also marks a new political economy (and ecology) of energy in Ireland. The wind farm was financed with EU money and involved Danish and German shareholders investing in a new holding company, Renewable Energy Ireland Ltd. BnM had shares in this company, but its main asset was the land on which the turbines were built. This early experiment in Ireland's energy transition shows the outlines of what was to come: state–private partnerships that enclosed public land and atmospheric commons into a financialised, for-profit energy transition. The only local involvement in the wind farm was the voluntary, community-run Oweninny social club, which organised tourist visits to the wind farm, tea and homemade cakes, and walks over the Nephin Beg mountain range. The new resource regime provided very few new jobs and no access to the physical, energetic benefits of the wind farm for the local area. This was about the substitution of electricity on a national scale, whereby the benefits of such sustainability would come more clearly and fully at a later point of achievement.

Though largely ignored in the more recent periodisation of the 'energy transition', the Bellacorick wind farm also shows that there is a longer history of decarbonisation – from fossil fuels to lower-carbon sources, from peat to wind – where the groundwork for the present green, digital transition was laid. The Bellacorick wind farm also coincided with the arrival of Intel and the expansion of companies such as Microsoft in the Irish landscape. On the surface, these events do not appear connected. However, they are the harbingers of what are today labelled digitalisation and decarbonisation, and it is in their gradual convergence – literally and discursively – that we can begin to map Ireland's data/energy landscape. Over the last decade, impetus has been gathering around tech energy demands, semi-state companies with land-holdings, and renewable energy developers. Ireland's green tech future converges around the resource frontiers of wind and data.

In a short film produced in 2016 by the Irish Wind Energy Association, a lobby group for private wind energy developers, a recording of John F. Kennedy's speech to the Irish parliament in 1963 is cut with emotive music and images of contemporary Ireland.[9] Kennedy describes Ireland's successful journey towards becoming a modern, developed country since independence in 1922, as an isolated, rural house is suddenly lit up, followed by Dublin's docklands – today, home of the International Financial Services Centre (IFSC) and 'Silicon Docks' hosting the Europe, Middle East, and Africa (EMEA) headquarters of many US tech multinationals. In Kennedy style, the speech goes on to call for more to be done, bigger dreams, and bolder futures. Reference to global responsibilities coincides with an image of power plants pumping out CO_2 emissions. The eyes of Irish children reflect waves crashing and electricity pylons. At last we see a horizon of wind turbines as a young boy plays in the foreground. The film ends by asking why Ireland imports 85 per cent of its energy when it is surrounded by an energy resource that could grant energy independence.

Kennedy's prophetic speech in 1963, it turns out, was about Ireland's new struggle for (energy) independence as part of a global mission towards clean, green, renewable energy. This compelling 'salvation' story of renewable electricity powering the developing green nation (Weston 2012) has been given fresh impetus by the war in Ukraine, rising energy prices, and the growing demand for energy by the tech industry. As Ireland's energy grid creaks, and household bills soar, a chorus of media commentators and experts promise that Ireland can be the 'Saudi Arabia of green energy' with its abundant offshore wind resources.[10] All that is needed, the advocates claim, is a more active state capable of enabling private investment and building out the necessary infrastructure, supply chains, and security apparatuses to support a new large-scale green energy industry.

In policy, media, and academic discourses, wind and data are posed as new 'frontiers' for valorisation. Wind is seen as an abundant, immaterial, sustainable resource that just needs to be 'harvested' through technological intervention. Traditional definitions of the 'frontier' have always imagined (and constructed) a site of 'bountiful emptiness', 'empty but full' (Bridge 2001), that needs to be tamed by civilisation. At the same time, the 'raw resource' of big data has generated a source of value that needs to be 'mined' through modes of computational optimisation (via platforms, algorithms, analytics, or the like) (Mezzadra and Neilson 2019). This neocolonial epistemology relies, as always, on an occlusive logic of extraction that paints over the productive forces at the heart of the contemporary tech economy, and its multifarious actors, locations, and social and labour practices (Couldry and Mejias 2019). Industry-led arguments have long been at the forefront of the promotional politics of environmental issues, especially in the data centre industry (Carruth 2014). They are driving the infrastructural build-out of new energy infrastructures at a time of immense monopoly tech power – and the growing centrality of cloud providers to industrial operations in a variety of sectors. This has shaped Irish state (and semi-state) policy, as monopoly tech also becomes a source of 'critical' investment, resources, and infrastructure.

Thus, cutting across the high-tech green energy landscape are multiple points of friction and contestation, as often-contradictory policy aims of energy security, decarbonisation, and (FDI-led) economic growth are inflected through the provision (or not) of infrastructure. As we argued in the previous chapter, these are precisely the conditions that are mediated in Ireland by industry-led, commercial semi-states such as the Industrial Development Authority (IDA), BnM, and Eirgrid (see below). These comprador formations ensure the continued strategy of infrastructural build-out and publicly subsidised incentives to bring multinational industry into the country, whether brown or green, at the expense of other social and environmental objectives. State investments in the infrastructure to facilitate multinational capital have produced a profoundly uneven and anachronistic society, one inextricable from Ireland's postcolonial condition, and these patterns and logics are now intensifying through the infrastructural nexus of data and energy.

A laboratory of clouds and wind

The postcolonial regime of FDI-led development blurs the distinction between the state and private sector. The commercial logic of semi-states, such as BnM, captures this non-distinction perfectly:[11] Ireland's neoliberal transition was never one of a public welfare state eroded by market forces, but rather a comprador state that actively made 'public' resources and infrastructures in the image of multinational corporations. In the context of the green, digital transition, Eirgrid, the semi-state with responsibility for the energy grid, takes on a particularly significant role.

Eirgrid was established in 2000 in response to EU energy and competition directives aimed at stimulating market-led efficiencies in the energy sector. A key obstacle to EU liberalisation of the sector was existing state 'monopolies' – not just in energy but across all essential services (water, energy, telecommunications). In the energy sector, this led to the 'unbundling' of energy generation, distribution, and retail to prevent 'anti-competitive' practices within the sector. The ESB and BnM were (further) fragmented into distinct commercial divisions competing in an open market for state tenders, while responsibility for the transmission grid passed to Eirgrid. This grid (which includes large-voltage transmission and smaller-voltage distribution networks) amounts to approximately 6,500 km of overhead line and underground cable, as well as more than 100 bulk substations. While the ESB owns the physical assets, Eirgrid oversees the energy generation market and connections for large energy users.

Between upgrading the grid to account for significant, projected increases in wind and solar energy, and supplying the growing energy needs of data centres, Eirgrid has come under increased scrutiny. What is clear, now, is that data centres are overwhelming the Irish electricity grid. The Central Statistics Office (CSO) reports that data centres in 2023 utilised 21 per cent of Ireland's electricity, rising steadily from 14 per cent in 2021 and 18 per cent in 2022 (CSO 2024). This is expected in different estimates to rise to 28 per cent or 32 per cent by 2026 (IEA 2024). While the Republic's electricity use rose by 20 per cent, 80 per cent of that was driven by data centre growth. These numbers are stark, especially in comparison with other countries. The closest in terms of direct, national-scale electricity usage of data centres in Europe are the Netherlands (5.2 per cent), Luxembourg (4.8 per cent), and Denmark (4.5 per cent) (Kamiya and Bertoldi 2024), two out of three of whom have implemented data centre control measures to manage these demands – along with additional measures to incentivise 'green' data centre growth. The wider situation has meant that Ireland has begun importing greater quantities of electricity from Britain through the Moyle Interconnector between Scotland and NI, which has meant the energy flow on the island has been primarily North to South through three interconnectors linking Northern and Southern grids. Ireland's electricity mix is dependent upon these external energy flows, across a precarious and incompletely connected all-island grid. This importation of energy, and the expanded use of natural gas as a transition fuel, is primarily being driven by the growth of data centres.[12]

The pressure on Ireland's energy security became so acute that Eirgrid, following a recommendation from the Commission for Regulation of Utilities (CRU) (2021), introduced a de facto moratorium on new data centre connections in the Dublin region in 2021, demonstrating how arm's-length and semi-state bodies have come to mediate the amplifying environmental contradictions of the FDI regime. The CRU recommendations detail how data centres should provide their own on-site energy, enter corporate power purchase agreements (CPPAs) for alternative energy, and/or locate outside Dublin, which introduces the possibility of rural 'energy parks' run on circular data/energy pathways.[13] Since the moratorium, lobbying and public relations campaigns from the industry and beyond have intensified, as lobbying and promotional apparatuses of tech multinationals have privileged access to Irish public discourse and, often, direct access to decision makers.

In December 2021, for example, just months after the moratorium was announced, Host in Ireland, a major data centre industry group, organised a webinar entitled 'Empowering Change: The Challenges and Opportunities for Ireland's Decarbonised Grid' (Host in Ireland 2021). Moderated by Gary Connolly, founder of Host, other speakers were Mark Foley, then-CEO of Eirgrid;[14] Noel Cuniffe, CEO of Wind Energy Ireland (WEI), the industry group for wind energy, and formerly employee of Eirgrid; and Brian Ó

Gallachóir, Professor of Energy Engineering and Director of the Science Foundation Ireland (SFI)-funded MaREI Centre. The session began with projected data centre energy growth, estimated at 30–50 per cent of total energy on the grid by 2030. Rather than challenging this colossal energy use, the focus of the webinar was how to meet this challenge while also meeting Ireland's climate obligations and energy security. Foley, representing the state-owned grid, referred to data centres as 'good energy citizens who were playing their part in the decarbonisation of the grid'. He made it clear, as he has done on a number of other public occasions, that EirGrid supported the growth of an industry that was essential to Ireland's 'social fabric'. He assured the audience that EirGrid was, in his words, 'working hand in glove' with the industry to ensure solutions could be found.

In November 2023, Peter Lantry, MD of Equinix in Ireland, wrote an opinion piece in a national newspaper, arguing that curbs on data centre growth threatened 'modern life' in a digital society as we know it (Lantry 2023).[15] Receiving other national coverage, he asserted that '[d]ata centre operators are collectively working to become the solution to our squeezed grid while also having a positive impact on our national carbon reduction goals' (quoted in O'Halloran 2024). Lantry was making the case that data centres were not just a lynchpin of Ireland's FDI-dependent economy, providing vital digital functions for society – they were also essential to Ireland's decarbonisation efforts. How could this be? By providing flexible demand services for when the grid is constrained: switching from the grid to on-site gas generators 'when dinners are being made, children's baths are being run, and central heating switched on', as Lantry put it (2023); by storing excess wind and solar energy, a particular challenge in Ireland where potential wind energy far outstrips what the grid can manage; through district heating schemes that can transform waste heat from data centres into home heating; and by financing wind and solar generation through CPPAs. Here, Lantry maps out some ways that data centre facilities are positioning themselves as essential grid infrastructure – not just providing digital services, but energy services. Mirroring the visits of Todd Andrews to glasshouses in Germany, marvelling at the technological affordances of peat to support modern industrialisation, Lantry promotes the same vision for digitalisation as the engine for decarbonised development. Only this time, rather than houses and steady jobs, we are promised digital services and profits beyond Andrews' wildest dreams (or perhaps nightmares).

Lantry's media intervention came one week after the annual Data Centres Ireland industry conference in 2023, which has been held annually in Dublin since 2010, and where he made the astonishing argument that it didn't matter how much electricity data centres used, as long as it came from renewable sources. Such arguments, made to rooms full of CEOs, industry leaders, facility managers, and politicians, lay the groundwork for how tech-led energy transitions are being promoted in the press and the halls of government. The Data Centres Ireland Conference in particular is not only a showcase of new products and services offered for and by data storage providers, it is also a place of exchange, collaboration, and regulatory discussion.[16] The 2023 conference featured Fine Gael Minister for Enterprise, Trade and Employment Simon Coveney as the keynote speaker. Visiting these industry events clarifies how extensive and connected the data centre industry is – not just data centre operators but engineering, security, construction, energy providers, and semi-states with land banks, all eager to sell their services, amid decision makers and lobbyists sharing coffees and even free pints (after 4 pm). This is what Host in Ireland describes as the digital ecosystem, operating in equilibrium, internally and in relation to the global landscape, as long as these different actors across the public and private sectors continue to cooperate.[17]

In February 2024, three months after the 2023 Data Centres Ireland conference, Engineers Ireland, a representative body for professional engineers in Ireland, issued a statement that the moratorium on data centres was undermining the state's 2030 climate targets (Allen 2024). The reasoning was that large tech companies had the financial muscle to invest in new wind and solar projects, and without it, investment in the sector would drop off. Companies such as AWS, along with representatives of companies such as Lantry (with Equinix), have put out statements threatening a 'techxit' if curbs on connection remain.[18] The lobbying situation has become so obvious that even conservative national newspaper *The Irish Times* admonished these companies' influence in infrastructural decision making, specifically referencing an AWS public tantrum about increasing regulation (The Irish Times 2024).

In August 2024, it was revealed that Eirgrid, in its own words, had been 'continually asked' about the likelihood of new connection agreements in the Dublin region (Foxe 2024). A briefing from Eirgrid warned of a potential 'mass exodus' of large data centres if the uncertainty around connections continued, again reported in the national press. Economists and individuals such as Lantry hop on these shifting discourses to further hammer industry agendas of deregulation and, in the most extreme cases, complete industry independence from public oversight (McWilliams 2024; Pollock 2024). We see clearly in these politics, which play out in public fora, how promotional and infrastructural dimensions of ongoing green, digital growth occur in tandem – overlapping logics of multinational extractivism and neoliberal climate action require both discursive and technical mechanisms to lay the groundwork for continued growth (Brodie 2024).[19]

We have, then, a familiar scenario: the grid is overburdened, decarbonisation targets unmet due to a history of under-development, and lack of investment in public infrastructure and renewable energy. State development strategy further enables private, energy-intensive infrastructures to locate here, hoping they can provide the technological solutions needed, with an industrial landscape completely saturated by decisions supporting FDI-led infrastructural investment.[20] Beyond pure FDI facilitation, as prior chapters argue, Ireland has become a laboratory for resolving unfolding contradictions of green, digital growth, as the practical limits of growth are experienced within a constrained environment and open economy.

With this landscape of practical infrastructural limits and frontiers in full view now, we can see why tech companies have found such fruitful ground for experiments with emerging energy regimes in Ireland. These companies need more than R&D; they need infrastructure through which to enact their projects. Google has for years been working publicly on generation- and grid-responsive computing at its facilities as part of its decarbonisation strategies – as far back as 2020, Google was promising that its data centres would 'now work harder when the sun shines and wind blows' (Radovanovic 2020). Microsoft's data centres in Ireland specifically have tested projects with industry partner Eaton geared towards grid flexibility via on-site energy storage and uninterruptible power supply (UPS) mechanisms (Roach 2022), which would both 'unlock the value of the data centre' for grid services towards reducing excess emissions via grid-responsive battery storage (Eaton nd). These experiments with and through the Irish grid were heralded as a success, which can now be exported across Microsoft's data centre fleet.

While promised and promoted as a 'service' towards sustainable and resilient grids, these partnerships are inseparable from the profit imperative of these companies. Take Microsoft's grid flexibility partnership with Eaton: while the Microsoft article promoting the project does not explicitly mention the potential profitability of providing these services for a fee (Roach 2022), Eaton is less evasive in selling the battle-tested product to other data centre providers. 'There's money lying on the floor of your data centre … and all you need to do is pick it up', says their promotional video for the UPS solutions product.[21] This explicitly positions Ireland's facilitating role as monopoly tech's infrastructural laboratory – providing infrastructural support to test and innovate products that will further enable monopoly tech integration into public service provision.

Microsoft is responsible for 30 per cent of Ireland's CPPAs, agreements promised to be the most significant (and 'subsidy free') contributor of new renewable energy to the grid in the future. It is hard to establish whether these CPPAs are providing 'additionality' (that is, would the wind farm have been built anyway) on the grid. What is clear is that renewable energy capacity financed through CPPAs is nowhere near equivalent to existing or planned use of data centres.[22] Further, they allow monopoly tech to lock in energy prices at low, agreed-upon rates for extended periods of time.[23] Promotion of monopoly tech and data centres as essential components of Ireland's decarbonisation, despite colossal energy-use, illustrates the techno-optimism at the heart of eco-modernist ideology and policy. These techno-solutions are derived from industry itself, creating new commercial opportunities within a virtuous 'circular economy' of 'green' growth. Much of this expertise is being developed in and through the data centre sector, with investment in programmes at higher education institutions (HEIs) and partnerships with researchers and state bodies. This hand-in-glove relationship, developed in and through FDI strategies unpacked in prior chapters, has expansive consequences for how wages of data and energy are being articulated in and through infrastructure, but also land – specifically, peatlands. In the remainder of this chapter, we show the sites where these regimes are being shaped and tested, specifically through extractive frontiers and supposedly 'post-extractive' landscape of the 'just transition' in the midlands.

Wind extractivism at the Irish frontier

While theories of unequal ecological exchange and the Marxist dynamic of 'metabolic rift' have tried to account for environmental imbalance at a global scale (Foster and Holleman 2014), what this means in the Irish semi-periphery, and the internal regional variations and geopolitical borders of Ireland, requires deeper analysis[24] – especially when it comes to technical management of the current energy transition. Wind farms, like data centres, are built along existing networks and pathways of extractive affordances, from planning to environmental regulation (Figure 4.3). Often assembled along the border and/or on otherwise undeveloped bog landscapes, they must be built on land that is suitable – in the case of bogs, areas seen as 'wastelands' good for nothing else[25] – and at least marginally linked via existing infrastructure to transport enormous turbines for installation and electrical cables to distribute electricity to substations, storage, and the grid. Where these networks do not already exist (and often even where they do), they must be fashioned through enormously transformative and disruptive means. Thus, the distributed networks within which wind farms take part, far from 'undergirding' the everyday life of locals in rural Ireland as dominant industry imaginaries of (usually privatised) energy infrastructure argue,[26] have tended to disrupt or visibly bypass them, whether roads closed or expanded only for large lorry transport, massive wind turbines, substations to process and move energy, the overhead pylons and underground cables transporting energy elsewhere, or fibre-optic cables underfoot bringing data to and from Dublin and the oceanic cable connections on the west and north coasts.

AWS and similar companies have privileged access to green capabilities and other utilities, which takes on particularly stark relevance in places such as the border region described in this chapter's introduction. Many communities in areas cloud companies are drawing energy from do not have reliable access to a variety of different infrastructural resources (whether roads, railways, telecommunications, electricity, or water) (Brodie 2023). Able to pay for 'green'

Figure 4.3: Homemade sign in County Donegal

Source: Photograph by Patrick Bresnihan, 2021

credentials through contracts and offsets while continuing to use enormous amounts of resources for profit, multinationals are lauded for pioneering renewable transitions, at the same time that eco-austerity is promoted as a necessary adaptation for 'consumers'. The large-scale, high-tech infrastructures of renewables and monopoly tech exist in stark contrast to the forms of underdevelopment that still characterise some of the country and the types of shared responsibility assumed within planetary transitions, especially in the border region – whether via poverty, with one in four people 'at risk' in the border region in 2017 (CSO 2019); fuel and energy poverty, where border counties and rural areas in general are significantly more affected than urban areas, although nearly 30 per cent of the population was 'energy poor' in winter 2023 (Pillai et al 2022; Threshold nd); lack of broadband access, where the border region has the lowest fixed broadband penetration of any Irish region at a mere 77 per cent (compared with 92 per cent in Dublin) (CSO 2022); or other (dis)connectivity to reliable infrastructural utilities such as water and waste disposal.

Zooming in on our case study from the start of the chapter, the Finn Valley Wind Action Group (FVWAG) surrounding Meenbog has been lodging complaints and objections against local wind farm developments since at least 2015. In 2019, while planning was still underway for Meenbog, AWS and then-Taoiseach Leo Varadkar announced publicly that the company would buy 100 per cent of the projected 91 MW of energy produced by the wind farm, another step towards fulfilling its pledge to 100 per cent renewable energy use. Locals were 'baffled' to hear that AWS was involved in the project

(Kiernan 2019), especially after so much controversy, and coming from the mouth of no less than the Taoiseach of Ireland, paving the way for approval before any had been democratically reached. As Varadkar swooned:

> AWS's investment in renewable projects in Ireland illustrates their continued commitment to adding clean energy to the grid and it will make a positive contribution to Ireland's renewable energy goals. As a significant employer in Ireland, it is very encouraging to see Amazon taking a lead on this issue. We look forward to continuing to work with Amazon as we strive to make Ireland a leader on renewable energy. (Quoted in Day One Team 2019)

To the knowledge of 'blindsided' members of the FVWAG that we spoke with, AWS officials had not directly engaged in any public hearing or consultation with local communities, signifying that AWS' 'investment' was a contract with another corporation, not in service of local or even wider environmental interests. This sense of climate responsibility is one that is entangled in planetary extractivism that applies calculative rationalities of carbon accounting and 'net zero' to abstracted landscapes hundreds of kilometres from sites of decision making.

In early June 2022, it was announced that Planree Limited, a subsidiary of Invis Energy in charge of the Meenbog Project, would pay a meagre €1,500 fine for damages as well as legal costs for the investigation into the peatslide. Local authorities on either side of the border would be in charge of remediation of the river, which in 2021 was designated by the Environmental Protection Agency (EPA) as one of the two worst-polluted waterways in Ireland, with major damage to an EU-protected fishery (Scanlon 2021). The price put on such catastrophic damage was €1,500. In the vein of this type of accounting, one can think about the carbon credits lost in the peatslide, or the value lost within the fishery, and still understand that €1,500 – even by their metrics – is insulting to all forms and ways of life involved. At a local district meeting, reported by Ireland Live, there was outrage and even confusion at the figure:

> Cathaoirleach Cllr Patrick McGowan said everyone was shocked by the small fine. 'The fine seemed to be absolutely ridiculous. Can you find out what range is this fine in, is it the lower end or the higher end of the scale?' He added it seemed unfair a fine of €1,500 was issued for damage to a whole mountain and river yet the council could not clear out the bridges at Clady, Stranorlar, or Castlefin for fear of being fined for interfering with the environment. (Duffy 2022a)

The same PR machine that worked hard to associate AWS with Meenbog wind farm in terms of climate commitments worked equally hard to distance the tech company from harmful consequences linked to its development. AWS will get cheap renewable energy for the foreseeable future from a wind farm in Donegal, where few residents wanted it, even fewer will experience any form of measurable value from it, and where an active bog and fishery have been irreparably damaged across two functionally separate countries. The Loughs Agency will administer remediation works for the next 'number of years', through phased restoration, likely paid for by its own public accounts (Afloat 2021), as turbines continue to go up around the damaged bog.

A 2022 update to the Donegal County Development Plan continued to include all non-designated land as 'open to consideration' for wind development. This decision was supported by Norwegian renewable energy giant Statkraft, who also consult for the data centre industry.[27] The company argued in a submission that general statements about landslide susceptibility should not preclude submissions for wind development:

> The (Geological Survey of Ireland [GSI]) mapping is a high-level approach that does not reflect the actual susceptibility of a landslide occurrence with respect to any proposed or ongoing activity in any particular area. Additionally, this approach does not take into account if, historically, there has been no recorded landslide events in a given area. As a result, there are large areas with some level of landslide susceptibility within which there are no recordings of landslide events. (Quoted in Tobin Consulting Engineers 2023)[28]

Oddly enough, Statkraft here advocates for more locally attuned and less overarching territorial designations for development as long as it means it will be able to continue developing wind farms. This revised development plan was perceived as a 'slap in the face for local democracy' by a local Sinn Féin councillor, as for many residents in this particular corner of the Irish borderlands (Duffy 2022b). From their perspective, these towering turbines are not a mark of a renewable future, but a destructive monument to eco-modernity that inherits its world-eating desires of earlier forms of techno-colonial capitalism – leaving them behind once the attention has turned away and the energy (and what it powers) has become infrastructurally invisible to everyone else. The collapse of an ecosystem at the Donegal/Tyrone border is perceived as a necessary sacrifice to progress dictated by the calculative rationalities of eco-modern growth.

What is important about the Meenbog peatslide is that it demonstrates that capitalism *produces* rather than *affects* ecologies at its frontiers. The event of a peatslide is something that demonstrates catastrophic disruption to an ecology, to be sure. But it represents a durable logic and material consequence of capitalist modernity by which processes of 'improvement' and development *shape* ecological conditions into resources and landscapes through which value could be generated. As we discuss in the next chapter, risks associated with large-scale developments on peatlands becomes a new frontier for (state-funded) scientific enquiry and technical adjustment. The secondary effects of such disasters are of little to no consequence in profit-making equations: ultimately, they become problems to be managed more efficiently and more profitably. The state puts the conditions in place that enable these extractive epistemologies, *mediating* capitalist relations to produce more effective extraction.

The landscape of wind extractivism goes beyond these more direct interactions with local objection and friction, which represent spectacular and often 'eventful' interactions between multinational capital and its discontents.[29] The frontier of 'energy intensive modernity' (Szeman and Boyer 2017) is also a place for direct experimentation within the green, digital transition. An example from 2017 stands out as a precursor to later attempts to create closed loop, 'moebius strips' between wind and data industries.[30] Microsoft entered its first CPPA in Ireland with GE for a wind farm in Kerry. This agreement would not only supply Microsoft with 37 MW of electricity credited towards its ongoing data centre growth in the Dublin region (Microsoft News Centre 2017) – it would also serve as a test bed for Microsoft software integration into wind farm management, optimising the harnessing of wind by greater meteorological precision managed towards demand-side fluctuations. This experiment at the site of generation, employing Microsoft cloud technologies towards the more efficient capture and distribution of wind energy on the grid, does not have to be deployed for the public benefit. In fact, it represents an early attempt to commercially exploit the growing partnerships between data and energy providers. What begins to coalesce is an eco-modern infrastructural future dependent upon the efficient – and profitable – deployment of decarbonised, digitalised energy systems, as well as closed-loop mechanisms by which the messiness of the public energy transition can be disrupted and bypassed for direct private intervention.

Energy park as future

The above section demonstrates how the uneven geographies of the energy transition are shaped by the prevalence and expansion of digital infrastructures. Even on an island the size of Ireland, distinct environmental conditions, political cultures, and developmental histories ensure that state policy and global capital hit the ground differently.[31] For tech multinationals assessing jurisdictions capable of hosting and supplying their infrastructural needs, this unavoidable messiness of place is an inconvenience that needs mediating,[32] even in this supposedly atmospheric phase of capitalism. These atmospheric resource regimes are far from completed, and require state facilitation to make them viable. Historically, multinationals investing in Ireland have relied on the Irish state to develop infrastructures for their operations. But the scale of energy demand from cloud storage providers is over-stretching the state's capacity, forcing these companies to more directly control their supply chains via infrastructure.

CPPAs were fully introduced in 2019, with government plans expecting these private energy contracts to meet 15 per cent of new electricity demand by 2030. The logic is simple: the state is constrained in terms of its own capacity to financially support private wind energy generation in a competitive energy market (Costello 2024), while tech companies, specifically, need to build towards their own net-zero aims. The overarching problem with CPPAs, as the Meenbog wind farm demonstrated, is that they involve a degree of separation between where the energy is generated and where it is supposedly used. As with all offsetting schemes, it is an abstraction, a form of financial and energy accounting that ultimately cannot escape local realities, such as unstable peat geology, histories of de-development, colonial borders in the north-west of Ireland, and chronic constraints on a public energy grid.

Hyperscalers such as AWS prefer to manage supply chains in-house, rather than navigating between local energy companies, grid operators, and public policy that may contradict their interests. CPPAs will continue to be a major pillar of the green, digital transition in Ireland, but we can see how the desire to contain and control these emerging relationships has pushed innovations in energy governance. Tech companies want to position their operations as integral to Ireland's energy transition without taking on any responsibility for public functions and accountability: how to act like a utility, without becoming a utility? This is a concern voiced in industry circles, recognising the cloud's centrality across multiple overlapping sectors.

One of the most recent innovations in this regard is the BnM Eco-Energy Park. Here the geography of the green, digital transition becomes bounded by a new spatial operation located not in the hinterlands of the north-west of Ireland, but the post-industrial midlands: BnM country. The idea for an Eco-Energy Park had been on the table since 2017, advertised as a pilot project for an FDI-led 'just transition' and effective use of BnM's huge post-extractive land banks. But it wasn't until May 2024 when the 'anchor tenant', AWS, was secured, that BnM made the official announcement. The Eco-Energy Park will be built across 3,000 hectares of BnM's land bank, crossing three different counties. The plan is to co-locate large, energy-intensive companies (that is, manufacturing, pharmaceutical, ICT) with renewable energy technologies. Across local authorities, semi-states, and within government, co-location has been the aim for some time – containing the 'twin transition' within eco-modern industrial zones.

The form of the Eco-Energy Park suits companies such as AWS who want to secure large supplies of 'clean' energy, while avoiding responsibilities for any utility functions and negative attention for their outsized energy use. Containing large energy users within specially designated zones, particularly on land with little other productive value, suits government and policy makers keen to show tech-dominated FDI that Ireland remains open for business, while quieting public concerns about energy security and climate targets. The Eco-Energy Park appears an elegant solution to mounting contradictions, and BnM has promised it has more in the pipeline. There has also been no visible local or public opposition to these projects despite the fact that they represent a radical reconfiguration of how energy governance operates in Ireland. Rather than financing individual energy projects that continue to supply the public grid, the Eco-Energy Park model proposes to separate energy generation and use from publicly mediated infrastructure and oversight. Similar to grid-flexibility mechanisms innovated by data centre providers, proposed 'Private Wires' to support such energy parks are similarly designed to 'unlock private sector resources' (Devine et al 2024) – however, in this case, to build *new* infrastructure outside of the direct remit of state investment and oversight, supplied with land and license by the commercial semi-state.

Experimental plans for Eco-Energy Parks run directly against the long-standing legal model for energy development. Under the 1927 Energy (Supply) Act, which established the ESB as the world's first national, public utility, it is not permitted to develop private electricity infrastructure. This provision was in direct response to 'the existing colonial mess of electricity companies, random wires and connections' that existed in the laissez-faire energy market prior to independence (Mercier 2023). The vision behind the ESB, and the state-led energy schemes of Ardnacrusha and BnM, was to electrify the country and power national development. Fast-forward to 2023, with pressure mounting from tech and wind energy industries, and the government launched a consultation on Private Wires. The briefing document states: 'It is recognised that there are currently numerous challenges in building electricity grid infrastructure, both in Ireland and internationally. As such and in order to accelerate the delivery of the electricity sector's climate targets we must examine the potential of off-grid opportunities, such as Private Wires' (Government of Ireland 2023). As we write in autumn 2024, it isn't yet clear who will own what in the Eco-Energy Park, nor how the use and flow of energy generated will be governed. What we know is that the consultation on Private Wires, dominated by industry lobbyists with an interest in 'off-grid opportunities', is occurring in tandem with developments such as the Eco-Energy Park, enabling large companies to '[build] their own infrastructure between generation and demand sites and [circumvent] the National Electricity Grid. By doing so, issues around grid constraint … are avoided' (Devine et al 2024).

Ironically, what is celebrated by BnM as progress towards an eco-modern green transition, appears more like the reactivation of a fragmented, colonial state which has a complete lack of interest in providing for its population in any kind of public way, as Sinéad Mercier has theorised in terms of the historical development of Ireland's energy infrastructure (2021). Rather than a collective future of energy abundance, the Eco-Energy Park represents a future of advanced enclosure: zones of excellent infrastructural provision provide for low-employment cloud storage facilities, while populated areas exist with artificial scarcity and broken infrastructures.

BnM's Eco-Energy Park crystallises the logic of Ireland's postcolonial ecological regime as it takes shape around the eco-modern green, digital transition. As we suggest through the Shannon Free Zone in Chapter 2, Ireland has a history of experimental developmental zones – a form of internal 'offshoring'. The CRU's recommendations, at least those adopted by Eirgrid, have set this in motion explicitly, encouraging companies to either source their own energy directly – connecting to gas networks and creating on-site power plants, in the case of at least 12 proposals across the island (including a 1 million square foot centre in Ennis, Clare, with its own 200-MW capacity gas generator onsite) – or locate in rural areas removed from grid constraints. Microsoft has already put in place a plan to build a 170-MW on-site power plant for its facilities outside Dublin (The Irish Times 2022), and New Fortress Energy, the US multinational behind the disastrous Shannon/Kerry LNG project, intends to build a connected data centre campus on 'more than 1,000 acres of land' in the area (Murray 2025).

Other similar or aligned projects to the BnM Eco-Energy Park have also been proposed at specially designated developmental sites in the midlands and beyond, demonstrating that the 'energy park' is becoming a durable model anchored by the prospect of multinational data centre investment. Offaly County Council partnered with Siemens to develop a report on the potential for data centre investment paired with renewables in 2023 (Siemens 2023). In Killala, boosters pitch a data/energy hub at the Asahi site through a data centre and 'renewable biomass' plant, marshalling the resources of the region into what is being clearly earmarked as a similar model supported by a data centre – in this case, a venture capital company called Avaio Capital.[33] The Eco-Energy Park, like these other projects, fits within this regime of FDI-based regional development: provide a template of land and infrastructure, and they will come. This means not simply a new infrastructural arrangement – as it is generally presented – but a new form of juridical rule (that is, different standards and regulations governing how energy is generated and used), premised on the generation of new industrial-scale energy infrastructure. It is thus also a new way of organising nature, transforming exhausted peatlands, as well as other post-industrial landscapes, into revenue-generating assets. We can only speculate, but these 'offshoring' experiments in green tech capitalism look set to intensify as Ireland's offshore marine sector develops.

In March 2024, the Irish Government launched its strategy for developing offshore renewable energy (Government of Ireland 2024b). Presented not only as a necessary response to climate change, Ireland's vast offshore exclusive economic zone promises to be the bedrock of 'green-tech industrialisation'. The spectacular mapping of offshore wind potential functions to encourage the further growth of data centres, positioning them as a practical necessity for transforming 'excess' atmospheric energy into commercial and exportable cloud services. Indeed, part of the promise of offshore renewable energy is that it escapes land-based social struggles and contradictions by building out spatially extensive infrastructures in 'empty' blue space. But, as with the north-west and the midlands, oceans are not 'empty'. Not only are there different, often competing social and economic uses, there are also complex and vulnerable ecosystems.[34] The expansion of offshore renewable energy will require marine enclosures on a new scale and in forms more akin to territorial property regimes, raising new questions about ownership of the ocean. Offshore energy installations will also require extensive onshore supply chains – from port expansions to battery storage.

The Irish state, supported by media and academic commentators, predictably frame these large-scale developments in terms of rural 'boosterism' and coastal regeneration despite little evidence that such projects will benefit these areas in the long term (Meek 2021). In its strategy, the government identifies a model of 'green industrial parks', citing the Ventspils Industrial Park in Latvia, which operates in a designated Freeport in order to promote 'Green Tech, Green Energy, and High Tech' (Port of Ventspils 2005). Consistent with the green tech laboratory, these parks are explicitly presented as means to achieve 'the co-location of renewable energy supply and demand, and in many cases these also serve as test beds for technological innovation' (Government of Ireland 2024b, 67). Already, Rosslare Europort in County Wexford has been designated a potential free zone as a means of stimulating the offshore energy industry in the south-west. This means it would be subject to exemptions on tax for imported, processed, and exported goods.

Just up the coast, in Arklow, County Wicklow, Echelon Data Centres was finally granted grid connection in September 2024 after months of negotiation with Eirgrid (RTÉ News 2024). In partnership with SSE Renewables, the company has promised to fund construction of a landing substation for a planned offshore wind park, which would directly connect and supply the data centre with renewable energy. It would also lock the company into landing that electricity on shore, representing the ways in which data infrastructure is increasingly central to the infrastructural territorialisation of such renewable energy developments.[35] Responding to the announcement, Taoiseach Micheál Martin said: 'This collaboration between renewable energy and tech will ensure that key decarbonisation targets contained in the Climate Action Plan are met *and is a model which could be rolled out in other communities across the country*' (Gorey 2020; emphasis added). Earlier in 2024, a private investment fund, Starwood Capital, bought a 50 per cent share in Echelon. Starwood is one of the world's largest private investment firms, with around $115 billion worth of assets. In 2023, it launched its first dedicated data centre fund, Starwood Digital Ventures, with the aim of growing its data centre portfolio, which it clearly identifies as a strategic growth area (Swinhoe 2024b, 2024c). In Arklow, a small fishing town on the south-east coast of Ireland, we see the coalescing of global finance, tech, and energy in new state-mediated arrangements. We can draw a direct line between these experiments and what, in 1986, Raymond Crotty described as Ireland's 'enclave industries': foreign-owned industries that benefited from price transfers, tax relief, land zoning, and other mechanisms evolved in and through unique partnerships between the state and multinational capital (Crotty 1986). In Ireland's fast advancing eco-modernisation, the 'industrial enclave' has become an 'energy park'.

Conclusion: Tech, eco-modernity, and the unjust transition

In this chapter, we have introduced the emerging landscape of the data infrastructural politics of eco-modernity as it is taking shape in Ireland. In the way that it is intensifying and expanding upon the existing infrastructural and resource landscapes of the country, it is also creating novel, experimental formations by which environmental futures are being forged. In this way, it extends from the past, but is also materially distinct: it is explicitly about 'green' transition, crafting a technoscientific consensus by which the environment, including the atmosphere, is rendered as services, and by which economic growth occurs without meaningful development, especially in rural areas. But as we argue, this builds upon an overlapping history by which the postcolonial ecological regime of multinational investment in Ireland, premised upon a robust neoliberal consensus, aligned with the planetary imperatives of 'green' transition in the early 1990s.

The way that these development paradigms are promoted also aligns with the marketing strategies of the Irish Government across the 2010s, which aestheticised 'development' in and through the eco-modern landscapes of clouds, wind, and polished, mess-free futures (see Brodie forthcoming). Take Google's Boland's Mill offices in the Docklands, in central Dublin, rebranded 'Boland's Quay' by the enterprising developers of the project in the late 2010s. In this mixed-use office development bought entirely by Google for its central Dublin headquarters, sprinkled throughout its marketing is the recognition of its history. Boland's Mill was not only a major industrial flour mill in Dublin's port hinterlands, it was also a command centre for the rebels of the 1916 Easter Rising, who held the top floor for several days, called 'the Outpost'.

In late summer 2024, we visited the Boland's Mill Google offices as part of a tour group with an academic conference. Rooms in the building have been renamed to honour chosen Revolutionaries,[36] and to match the industrial activities of these former port lands, today called 'Silicon Docks' because of the multinational tech headquarters in the area. Companies such as Google, the employees told us, were responsible for bringing prosperity to this former industrial wasteland, which had been plagued by dereliction prior to its 'regeneration'.[37] This area was only 'developed' in this way by private developers after major industrial remediation projects funded by government bodies, zoned and managed by the exceptional Dublin Docklands Development Authority (DDDA). The entire development is thus a microcosm of the postcolonial ecological regime: state bodies providing land, resolving and managing ecological contradictions, and facilitating development for multinational investment and capital accumulation. In the Outpost today, an event and visitor hosting space for the company, the decor cartoonishly illustrates this neoliberal revisionism. There is a colourful, unremarkable mural dominating the room: 'You can dream, so dream out loud.' The 'Google aesthetic' of smooth, colourful, simple surfaces brands the narrative that investment from the likes of Google is an unchallenged good, packaged at best as a mundanely inoffensive industrial revisionism for visiting clients.

Travel kilometres west, on a meandering bus route through south-western suburbs of the city, and you would arrive at the true productive centre of Google's activities in Ireland: its data centre campus in IDA's Grange Castle Business Park South. There, we see a different version of the Google aesthetic painted on the wall of one of its main data halls: a young girl, flying a kite in the wind, clouds above.[38] This mural heralds Google's role as a green energy citizen of Ireland. Computers hum when the wind blows and the sun shines. However, like the DDDA, this data centre campus is dependent upon state incentives and infrastructural conditions that brought it there – the carbon-intensive grid connections, water, roads, pavements, bus routes, and land that make computers run and get labourers there, and, most importantly, the IDA campus, which required Compulsory Purchase Orders to redevelop the surrounding area (Brodie forthcoming). Without these state mechanisms paving the way for smoother investment and development, such sites would have been too risky, too cost intensive. These risky investments require mediation by the state that put conditions in place for corporate profits.

CPPAs, ultimately, serve a similar function, as do any additional procedures by which the state will put into place the conditions for further infrastructural development by monopoly tech. These activities will not only continue to lock these companies – and their profit motives – into Ireland's 'green' futures, they also represent ways in which these companies can export technologies tested in and through these 'green' and 'brownfield' landscapes enabled and facilitated by the state and its semi-state organs, which 'enclave' such operations for multinational accumulation.

Move further west to Offaly, the 'hidden heartlands' of bog country, and you will encounter the sharper edge of eco-modern capitalism. Not far from the proposed Eco-Energy Park is Derrinlough briquette factory (Figure 4.4). Until it closed in April 2024, it was the last remaining briquette factory in Ireland. After dismissing the 62 workers, BnM put the building up for sale without consulting the union. An ad on Daft.ie described the property as a 44-acre site with 'former industrial buildings'. A campaign, led by former workers, union reps, and academics, proposed transforming it into a centre for green social and cooperative enterprises engaged in retrofitting and other essential energy transition work – particularly important in an area experiencing some of the highest levels of energy poverty and reliance on solid fuel heating. They cited the government's own Territorial Just Transition Plan (Government of Ireland 2022b), which identified the social, economic, and cultural value of the peat industry's heritage, particularly for the midlands. Fáilte Ireland has recently secured €68 million in EU Just Transition Funding to support regenerative tourism in the midlands. As part of this strategy, it identifies the potential for regenerating and repurposing industrial heritage assets. BnM did not respond to the campaign and the building, like others before it, has likely been stripped, its contents sold for scrap.

It says a lot that BnM, backed by the state, can hold up the Eco-Energy Park as an example of commitment to 'just transition', while letting factory workers go and ignoring calls for a fundamentally different, bottom-up transition. The enclave logic is so strong as to actively marginalise real, well-articulated ideas of people who experience these transitions as external procedures. To these directly affected people, without democratic input, green, digital transitions are clearly enacted by and for FDI activities that provide minimal, and unclear, benefits for rural communities. There is no illusion that profits are distributed locally. Employment, and profits, are centred in offices in Dublin and farther afield.

The infrastructural laboratory of Ireland's green, digital transition, in extension of earlier resource extraction and FDI dependence, is one that concerns struggles over land, livelihoods, and resources – whether land, wind, data, or water. This is what unfolding eco-modernity, and its profound imbalances, looks like in Ireland: the intensification of uneven development

Figure 4.4: Derrinlough Briquette Factory, County Offaly, just before closure in 2023

Source: Photograph by Sean Breithaupt

and peripheralisation, and the explosion of contradictions across more diverse sites across Ireland. As our analysis is keen to emphasise, these are not local issues, even if they are localised. They are contradictions that the Irish state has sought to manage and mediate for the expansion of monopoly tech activities both within and beyond Ireland, protecting Ireland's role as a landed service provider for imperial capital.

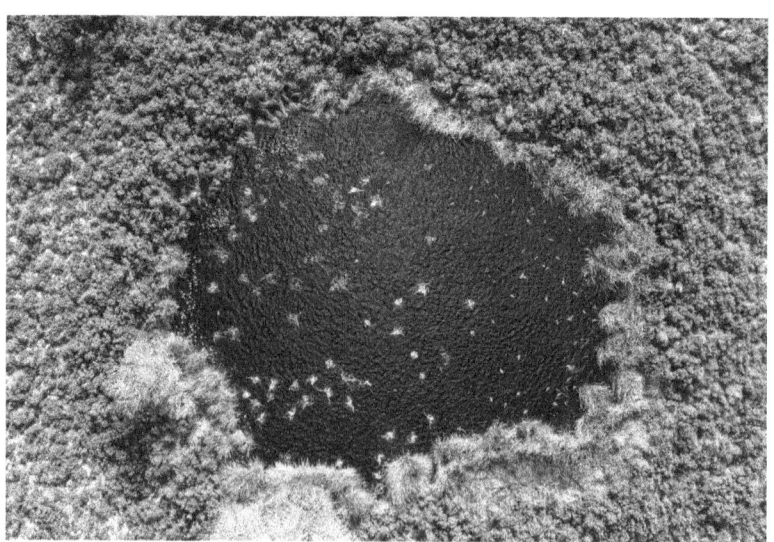

5

The Value of a Bog

Commercialising the carbon cycle (through technoscience)

We arrive in Abbeyleix, a small town in County Laois, in winter 2023. We are here to attend a conference, entitled 'Future of Ireland's Peatlands: Science, Engineering & a Just Transition', which promises to connect 'researchers, community groups, industry, state and semi-state agencies' to discuss 'how current and upcoming research can best address challenges faced by the peat sector'.[1] Convened by iCRAG, the Science Foundation Ireland (SFI) Research Centre in Applied Geosciences, the conference features speakers from multiple universities and research hubs, primarily drawn from the sciences as well as industry groups interested in the value and potential of peatlands for future enterprise.

Across a packed day of panel discussions and keynotes, and a poster display of maps, images, charts, statistics, and figures, all branded with public bodies such as iCRAG, SFI, National Parks and Wildlife Service (NPWS), and the Environmental Protection Agency (EPA) alongside private sector organisations, we are introduced to multiple digitally enabled regimes of dissecting peatlands across Ireland. Aerial radiometry, satellite imaging, environmental sensing, drone surveillance, GIS mapping, machine-learning, among other digital, technological innovations, are allowing scientists to better understand the unique ecologies and resources offered by peatlands, enabling policy makers and landowners to better harness them towards climate action. However, that action is buried in arcane and technocratic language. We hear terms such as 'ecosystem services', 'nature-based solutions', 'natural capital', 'emissions trading' thrown around by scientists in coldly neutral or even enthusiastic terms, with minimal explanation or reflection on why these images and graphs translate to these terms of interpretation. We think about the ways that such terminology pre-emptively encloses and dictates the terms by which climate action occurs: here is the evidence, presented in forensically scientific ways, for how a bog should become a carbon ledger. The why is conspicuously unspoken.

Being an event on the 'just transition', the science and industry speakers frequently heralded the importance of jobs for local communities, and social scientific perspectives in assessing and planning the future of peatlands. As this demographic, we don't have to be told that the social implications of peatland strategy are especially important to acknowledge in this room. Abbeyleix is Bord na Móna (BnM) country, and some attendees are members of communities whose livelihoods had once been defined by the presence of the peat industry in the area. However, while social impacts are cited tokenistically all day, there is a notable dearth of social scientists featured as speakers at the event – by our count, four in a full day featuring at least 24 individual speakers and presentations. This dearth of critical perspective on the 'just transition', a term first coined by trade unions to chart a just pathway towards decarbonisation amid widespread job loss, gives us pause. At least the event boasted a peatland tour given by the Abbeyleix Bog Project, a community initiative led by local residents and environmentalists. However, officially unacknowledged at the event was the history of the group, which had to fight BnM for access to the bog to re-wet it and 'bring it back to life' in the aftermath of extraction and development. As critical social scientists, we are acutely aware of this omission, and can't help but roll our eyes at any tokenistic mention of social science.

We come to the realisation that this room, like the data centres conference that we attend yearly, is largely designed to network and foster partnerships between public institutions and the private sector – environmental compradorisation. Whatever the importance placed on the transition's social dimensions, these can be equally captured under the umbrella of state-led transition – social scientists are brought there to study how to get communities 'on board' with already-decided regimes of climate action, and nothing more. Communities, like the bogs, must bring value to the green, digital transition – or else be left to waste and abandonment, dismissed as anti-progressive actors against the inevitable march of eco-modernity. Stuck between a rock and a hard place for funding and livelihood, with a small chance of doing some good in these communities by leveraging funding for public benefit, many well-meaning social scientists and scientists themselves get on board.

About 20 per cent of the surface of Ireland is covered in bog, including blanket bogs along the western coast and raised bogs in the midlands. Intact bogs are carbon sinks, vital to the global carbon cycle, storing carbon for millennia underneath. Drained bogs, however, are carbon sources, releasing substantial CO_2 from their carbon-rich environment to the atmosphere (Wilson et al

2022). It is estimated that there has been a 99 per cent loss of the original area of active raised bog in Ireland (Renou-Wilson et al 2011). And yet, the country still contains approximately 60 per cent of raised bog habitat in the EU (Renou-Wilson 2022), making Ireland a hotspot for climate mitigation efforts via peatlands. As well as preserving intact bogs, Ireland's 2023 Climate Action Plan (Government of Ireland 2024a) aims to rehabilitate 33,000 ha of exploited BnM peatlands and an additional 30,000 ha of non-BnM peatlands by 2025. This is the largest programme of bog rehabilitation in the state's history and appears an obvious step in the 'brown to green' industrial transition happening across Ireland's bogs. But the delivery of such an ambitious project, and its overall impact on carbon emissions, is not so clear. What does 'rehabilitation' actually mean and how will it happen? Whose interests does peatland climate mitigation serve? What (unintended) implications does this have for specific peatland communities, and land-use and climate services more generally?

Unlike decarbonisation via renewable energy, the potential value of bogs as carbon 'sinks' is relatively new, only coming to international and national policy prominence in the last decade or so. As a new frontier in climate governance, the role of peatland science and technology is particularly to the fore – mapping, measuring, and quantifying carbon emissions and potential carbon storage for different state and private actors. This chapter wades into this highly speculative field, to illuminate the uneven political ecologies of climate mitigation via bogs, being amplified by the digital datafication of knowledge regimes supported by monopoly tech.

Our argument builds on the previous chapter: Ireland's postcolonial ecological regime operationalises peatlands in the same way it operationalises wind energy or grid infrastructure. The task of transforming peatlands into carbon sinks places particular emphasis on the technoscientific labour and infrastructures required to do this. In this context, data-intensive computational systems and platforms have become more and more central to quantifying the carbon cycle (Pasek 2019; Buck 2022). What is particularly important about studying these dynamics in Ireland, then, is how the presence of monopoly tech – which, as we argue, has come to treat Ireland as a kind of 'green tech laboratory' for its operations – takes on a central role in the environmental futures of peatlands and climate mitigation more generally. This goes beyond their infrastructural power, and into more indirect forms of partnership and influence over research and policy agendas.

Take the landscape of climate action represented by the event in the opening vignette: many major projects are not only using digitally enabled tools, but are also designed around the testing and development of digital technologies to better understand the carbon cycle, in peatlands and beyond. Whether BnM using cloud services to manage real-time dashboards of rehabilitation schemes; the huge, multiple terabyte-scale platforms of the Microsoft, SFI, and Maynooth University partnership Terrain AI; or the machine-learning technologies being developed by the multi-institution Research Ireland (formerly SFI),[2] iCRAG, NPWS, and CeADAR project AI2Peat (which aims to create a platform for peatland stakeholders to register their own carbon calculabilities), the 'cloud' is being operationalised towards a global carbon accounting ledger.[3] Who, or what counts in such a ledger, and who is it made for? In supporting the calculative logic of 'net zero' and general offset regimes through expanded digital investment, the state deepens rather than resolves the contradictions of the 'extractive circuit' (Chaudhary 2024) – energy use continues to grow via data centres, enabled by new wind farms and carbon sinks, but embedded in a circuitry that supports further extractive growth.

While semi-states such as BnM evidently play a key role in the development of peatland climate mitigation, the focus of this chapter shifts towards Ireland's higher education system. Specifically, it assesses how publicly funded science has been operationalised *towards* the sustainability agendas of large-scale industry via partnership incentives, knowledge transfer, and, more recently, digital and AI technologies. Tech companies are uniquely positioned to avail of industry–university partnerships – as potential co-funders, infrastructure providers, and/or beneficiaries – effectively laundering their reputation through higher education institutional (HEI) imperatives to draw in funding and build 'impact' profiles. The 'public' and social responsibility demonstrated by monopoly tech's involvement in sustainability research, similar to other partnerships in innovation, act as a Trojan horse for more insidious forms of privatisation and, sometimes worse, the foreclosure of alternative pathways towards environmental justice. In this research environment, it has become difficult and unpopular to challenge the commercial orientation of knowledge production – similar to foreign direct investment (FDI) more broadly, these logics have become so entrenched that they feel impossible to challenge for rank-and-file researchers, forced instead to operate within the limited parameters offered by climate action and sustainability.[4]

In comparison with previous chapters' larger-scale infrastructural and industrial transformations, this chapter's partial detour into the political economy of the Irish university system may appear surprising. We are not the first to notice the structures of dependency that also shape Ireland's public research environment, in particular through the neoliberal confusion of economic with social benefit in the university sector.[5] However, what has become clear to us is that the knowledge frontiers of 'sustainable' (industrial) technoscience are as crucial to eco-modern transformation as the physical construction of wind farms and data centres. We align with media scholar Megan Wiessner's argument that 'computational articulations embed environmental knowledge politics in distributed industrial systems' (2024, 181), demonstrating how digital systems instantiate regimes of carbon calculability not only through technology, but also specific industrial incentives, applications, and research paradigms. As we argue, the calculabilities of 'net zero', a form of accounting that states regulate and corporations navigate, are being enabled and encouraged by Irish state developmental imperatives towards climate policy.[6] Intricately connected to the application and development of cloud-enabled digital technologies, this is another sphere of eco-modern transformation, one intricately related to – and supporting – wider infrastructural changes throughout this book.

Due to the structures of Ireland's public research funding policy, we observe how universities have become a site for not only promoting and building 'sustainable' technologies, strategies, and policies across the sciences and social sciences, but also have served as a tool for building and maintaining FDI-led growth. Like earlier moments in this book, this is due to decisions and policy changes that occurred at very particular points in time, and have become naturalised through successive governments and changes in economic activities, especially since the establishment of SFI in the late 1990s and early 2000s.[7] As historian John Walsh narrates, 'A new phase in the transformation of the Irish higher education system emerged from the late 1990s, characterised by sustained national and international pressures on HEIs to prioritise economic objectives', quoting an Organisation for Economic Co-operation (OECD) review in 2004 that proclaimed 'perhaps more strongly than anywhere else in Europe … tertiary education is a key driver for the [Irish] economy' (2018, 387). While in Chapter 3 we gesture towards how universities adapted to support the presence of companies like Intel and the broader FDI-led developmental model, in this chapter we show how companies, especially in the tech industry, have come to launder expertise and social responsibility through university and other public-funding partnerships in 'sustainable' technology. In this way, HEIs and other scientific organisations come to serve as another organ of the state in enabling and technologically managing the environmental contradictions of the FDI model. It is not just universities, but an environment of industrial technoscience under which HEIs are playing an increasingly significant role. Once again, we contextualise this in the history of the bogs – starting with the 'rediscovery' of the Irish bogs by Dutch naturalists in the 1970s.

Who cares about the bogs?

The semi-aqueous, anaerobic environments of living bogs carry ecological and cultural properties that historians, archaeologists, artists, and environmental scientists have long sought to demonstrate and defend. The cultural and ecological properties of living bogs are tied to the storage and preservation of cultural and environmental artefacts and traces. Until recently, the value of the bogs-as-storage referred to the potential treasure trove of cultural and environmental records that lay underground, including the famed 'bog bodies' preserved for centuries in the anaerobic muck. The Celtic Otherworld of Tír na nóg, or the Land of Eternal Youth, is associated with bogs, a place where time stands still, indicating the entanglement of scientific and cultural temporalities of the bogs. In spite of this recognised historical value, efforts to protect these records by ensuring appropriate archaeological surveying have been sidelined by the drive of large-scale industrial peat extraction in the 20th century, whereby turf-cutters have been the excavators of most major discoveries (Hitchcock 2019).

Since the 1970s, a small but committed community of environmentalists and ecologists have been instrumental in protecting and raising awareness about bogs in Ireland – linked in with transnational networks and expertise on wetlands that began around this time. In 1971, the International Convention on Wetlands was adopted in Ramsar, Iran, with the UK, France, and the Netherlands among the early signatories. It was the first global intergovernmental environmental agreement, establishing a framework for 'the conservation and wise use of wetlands and their resources' (Ramsar Convention nd). At this time, emphasis was on the unique habitats wetlands provided for migratory birds, and the threats posed by various forms of land reclamation. Following the Ramsar Convention, the Dutch Government established the first national Peatland Conservation Plan in 1974. This was designed to inventory, purchase, and restore peatlands, and it was the background for research being conducted in Ireland in 1978 by Dutch ecologist Matthijs Schouten.

When Schouten came to Ireland as a doctoral student, he was 'shocked' to find that (BnM) machines were still draining bogs and cutting peat on an industrial scale.[8] The lesson he brought from the Netherlands – a country that has overseen some of the most extensive land reclamation projects anywhere in the world – was that large-scale terraforming of precious wetlands should not be viewed as progress or development.[9] Schouten returned to the Netherlands and set up the Dutch Foundation for the Conservation of Irish Bogs (Stichting Tot Behoud Van de Ierse Venen), which campaigned to raise funds to purchase Irish peatlands – including by selling symbolic shares in Irish bogs to Dutch people. In 1982, the Irish Peatland Conservation Council (IPCC) was set up to carry out similar work in Ireland. By 1987, enough money had been raised to buy three Irish bogs in counties Kerry, Galway, and Westmeath. In an RTÉ news story covering the purchase, an Irish botanist and member of the IPCC tells the reporter that '[w]e as a nation have a very unhealthy attitude to conserving our bogs, and that even those living right beside the bog have little understanding of their value' (RTÉ 1987). In a ceremony laden with colonial baggage, Dutch Prince Bernhard officially handed over the deeds of Scragh Bog to Noel Treacy, Irish Minister of State: the bog, purchased by the Dutch for safekeeping, was now being graciously handed back to the ignorant Irish people.

This early episode in Irish peatland conservation is revealing of a green colonial discourse that permeates global environmental governance – 1987 was also the year that the Brundtland Commission Report was published, heralding a new era of 'sustainable development'. This framework recast the 'poverty' of so-called developing countries as not only a social and economic problem, but also an environmental one, as efforts to overcome poverty drove policies and practices that were destructive of ecosystems and resources (Sachs 1997).[10] Left out of such paternalistic, colonial narratives were the unequal structures of global trade and (neo)colonial development that had reduced countries across the Third World to plantation economies and crushing indebtedness (including Ireland) – structural factors that had been repeatedly challenged by anti-colonial thinkers from the so-called Third World since the 1970s (Bresnihan and Millner 2023). Within hegemonic narratives of sustainable development advanced by transnational organisations such as the United Nations Environment Programme (UNEP), the question of conservation was usually pitched *against* the possibility of sovereign industrial development. The Netherlands destroyed its peatlands to productively utilise land, a pathway implicitly now denied to developing countries under the guise of environmental conservation. The adoption of 'enlightened' European environmental perspectives against 'backward' national commitments would define the emerging ideology of 'official' environmentalism in Ireland (Tovey 1993).

Building on arguments from the previous chapter, the 1980s is also significant in terms of the neoliberal restructuring of the state. For peatland conservation campaigns in Ireland, the Irish state (especially BnM) was an environmental villain, supporting continued destruction of Ireland's peatlands at scale for energy. Here the peat-based energy regime of the mid-20th century is not just about the type of fuel, or energy system, but the ideological apparatus that it is inseparable from – in this case, residues of national, sovereign development and industrialisation. It is significant, then, that the IPCC (and other environmental NGOs) adopted a strategy of privately purchasing bogs to protect them from the state, rather than demanding *more* state intervention for the public good. From the beginning, environmental transition was premised on the retreat of the interventionist state and the proliferation of private actors (community organisations, NGOs, international donors, and private investors) operating in tandem with the market.

Amid these epochal shifts of the postcolonial ecological regime, tensions between peatland conservation and the social and economic use of peatlands have remained, most visibly in conflicts involving domestic and commercial turf-cutters. Beginning in the 1990s, Ireland was required under EU law to identify raised bogs for designation as Special Areas of Conservation (SACs) and implement rehabilitation measures on these sites. Between 1997 and 2002, 53 raised bog sites were identified as SACs and a further 75 raised bog sites as Natural Heritage Areas (NHAs) under the Wildlife (Amendment) Act 2000. The 53 SAC raised bogs required a prohibition on turf-cutting (and other potentially destructive activities). The problem was that these sites had been chosen without an understanding or any engagement with turf-cutters who had historic, customary rights to these bogs.[11] Conflicts between official conservation narratives and peat-based cultures and livelihoods reached a head in early 2012, when the Peatlands Forum was held in a hotel in Athlone, County Westmeath, in the heart of the midlands.[12]

Over the past decade since, there has been a gearshift in terms of scientific and state interest in Ireland's bogs – specifically, their function in climate mitigation strategies. This reflects international developments, where peatland rewetting is now widely advanced as a mitigation measure (see Global Peatlands Initiative 2019). The United Nations Framework Convention on Climate Change (UNFCCC) has recognised peatlands as a priority for action, with peatland rewetting and restoration identified as 'low-hanging fruit, and among the most cost-effective options for mitigating climate change' by Achim Steiner, Executive Director of the UNEP (quoted in Brahic 2007). Following this, the Irish Government's Climate Change Advisory Council stated in its annual review that '[t]he rewetting of drained peatlands is one of the most cost-effective measures supported by carbon tax revenue' (quoted in Renou-Wilson et al. 2022). In the context of net-zero pledges and commitments, peatlands are an 'easy win' in the battle to reduce emissions. Unlike forests, for example, which involve complex plant ecologies, conflicting social uses, and territorial communities, industrially drained peatlands are imagined as 'empty' wastelands, the reduction of emissions a simple, relatively cheap task of raising the water table.

Ireland's peatland rehabilitation programme was first announced in late 2020, on the cusp of BnM's rebranding as a climate solutions company – 'more than móna'. Funded through the EU's Recovery and Resilience Facility, €108 million was committed to rewet 80,000 acres of cutaway bog. Significantly, the announcement came with the claim that this would ensure 'the storage of 100m tonnes of carbon in perpetuity' (McGrath 2020). Where the notion of a pollution 'sink' evokes something negative, the notion of carbon 'storage' suggests the intentional design of infrastructure to keep something into the future. There is no doubt that living bogs offer some of the most effective forms of organic carbon capture and storage (Leifeld and Menichetti 2018), but in reality, the allure of 'containing' waste in natural 'infrastructures' is only ever that – a simplification and abstraction of complex processes that evade human-centred climate and ecological temporalities (Gabrys 2009). This is the challenge of net zero: to transform portions of land into stable, measurable 'containers' of carbon emissions. The Irish media thus report on how the carbon storage capacity of Ireland's bogs is greater than that of the Amazon rainforest (M. Donnelly 2024). Such abstract claims, originating in scientific research, are more than 'fun facts'. They are part of a broader discursive political economy orientated around climate speculation and fantasies of a global carbon ledger.

The functions of such discursive speculation are, in part, to displace action onto the future – enabling carbon-intensive 'business as usual' – but they also open a new frontier of carbon calculability, one that requires new forms of technoscientific mastery (and commercial opportunity) (Buck 2019).

While bog rewetting projects have happened since the 1990s, the emphasis was less on carbon accounting and more on ecological rehabilitation – easily observable and less constrained by the imperative of quantitative metrics. Measuring carbon fluxes in peatland soils is difficult, time-consuming, and costly. It requires physical infrastructures capable of monitoring carbon emissions across specific peatlands. In 2021, the government spent €2.7 million on the expansion of the National Agricultural Soil Carbon Observatory (NASCO), meaning that Ireland now has the highest density of agricultural flux tower installations per hectare in Europe. The data gathered from these instruments allows Ireland to participate in the EU ICOS (Integrated Carbon Observation System) network, an EU-wide research infrastructure that aims to build a 'consistent, sustained measurement network operating under exactly the same technical and scientific standards' (ICOS nd). Such research infrastructures are essential elements of transnational climate governance (Edwards 2010).

While state actors and private companies are enthusiastic about peatlands' climate mitigation potential, the emphasis on scale and standardisation is contradicted by peatland scientists who repeatedly stress that rewetting should be site-specific and sensitive to multiple factors – including temporality (Renou-Wilson et al 2019).[13] Uncertainty around peatland climate mitigation is intensified because activity happens underground and in far away futures; the volumetric space and long temporal lag of carbon sequestration makes peatlands more elusive to the carbon gaze than forests (Goldstein 2022). Critical scholars have demonstrated how the (political, social, and economic) problem of 'uncertainty' in climate mitigation is usually presented as a technical problem to be overcome through scientific expertise and consensus (Gifford 2020). Particularly in the context of neoliberal or market-led climate mitigation, the quest for certainty lies in the promise of abstracting specific qualities or functions (for example, carbon or water) from complex and situated ecologies, rendering them measurable, standardised, and fungible.[14]

Our contribution to discussions on scientific uncertainty and financial risk within climate mitigation is less about broadly neoliberal environmental governance or the construction of carbon markets. Our interest is in the role that monopoly tech is playing in these formations, enabled by (and deepening) Ireland's postcolonial ecological regime. As Holly Jean Buck articulates (2022), digital software, with cloud computing provided by powerful multinational companies, is required within the unfolding imaginary of carbon accounting and the securing of lucrative carbon credits via the de-risking and efficient verification of carbon commodities. Problems of remoteness, temporal lag, and uncertainty are, as the vision goes, reduced by the efficient application of digital technology and AI. Often marginal in critical literature on neoliberal climate governance (which focusses on marketisation and financialisation), the tech sector has thus identified commercial opportunities at the frontier of climate mitigation and carbon sequestration: the 'problem' of uncertainty becomes an opportunity, where data-intensive computational models and tools can be designed and applied. This demand is being met by a coalescence of Ireland's industry-led university research culture and the climate solutions offered by monopoly tech. As currently imagined by the most influential actors in this sphere, a robust public-private technology research ecosystem is the only way to achieve the large-scale infrastructural promise of deploying peatlands towards the transformative potential of eco-modernity, wherein 'net zero' enables growth by enlisting landscapes as a kind of infrastructure (Buck 2021).

University technoscience and the postcolonial ecological regime

The infrastructures required for global carbon accounting extend beyond field instruments and institutional standards. As the cloud comes to organise relations of innovation and efficiency across vast digital supply chains and diverse geographical calculations, data centres figure within the infrastructural formations of climate governance – after all, where is Microsoft's cloud platform on carbon storage hosted? As the 'political ecology of data' (Nost and Goldstein 2022) helps us understand, beyond analysing how datafication has affected the epistemological coordinates of science for climate action in terms of tools and fieldwork, these practices enlist distributed and multilayered technologies and infrastructures required to gather, harness, and utilise environmental data (and evidence for action).

A major but often elided player in this landscape is monopoly tech (Pasek 2019) and, more recently, its promises of AI-driven climate action (Nost 2024). Media scholar Mél Hogan (2018) identifies 'big data ecologies' by which monopoly tech companies organise environmental systems towards regimes of capital accumulation – from managing water and energy, to calculatively offsetting this across distributed land and territories. Anne Pasek (2019) has also articulated how carbon credits are 'fungibly mediated' through Microsoft's cloud but also, more importantly, its corporate strategies of identifying and certifying viable sources of carbon offsets. This landscape represents an emerging regime of technoscientific mastery driven and martialled by monopoly tech companies. In Ireland, this is enabled and incentivised by the state's climate action strategies – an intensified version of the postcolonial ecological regime applied to the distinct conditions of production assembled in the 'fourth industrial revolution'.

There is of course a long history of colonial science and technology being mobilised towards landscape mastery, especially in Ireland – see William Petty and the 'improvers', for example. Science and technology studies (STS) scholar Patrick Carroll (2006) theorises what he calls a proto-'data state' in colonial Ireland in the mid-1800s, wherein the tools of managing Irish territory and population depended upon sophisticated surveying and mapping techniques that formed an early data infrastructure for the management of Irish land. Sociologist Stephen Yearley (1995) points out that Ireland's scientific institutions during this time were hamstrung by the politics of imperial ascendancy: science was dominated by Anglo-Irish and British scientists and institutions, and while alternative initiatives such as what would later become the Royal Dublin Society (RDS) attempted to generate an 'Irish' culture of science, these were ultimately informed by the interests of the landed and/or ascendant classes disproportionately represented in Irish parliament – and who had become locally disempowered after the Acts of Union in 1800, united with British imperial institutions.

All this to say, scientific endeavour was dominated by the crown through the 19th century and until after partition. The story, here, gets more complicated; although, as Yearley narrates, '[t]he scientific estate in post-partition Ireland is seen to have moved from one kind of dependence – the nineteenth-century imperial condition – to another' (1995, 172). Walsh argues that higher education policy was terminally under-developed due to the ideological construction of the 'nation' under 'state formation, Gaelicisation, Catholic traditionalism, economic nationalism, and fiscal conservatism' (2018), meaning that the relations of universities and technical institutes with the state were stunted by a conservative national elite in 'de Valera's Ireland'. However, such narratives occlude the fact that alternative, if minor, circuits of knowledge exchange – orientated against or parallel to the emerging dominance of an export-led, US-orientated consensus of industrial development – also formed across the 20th century. As discussed in Chapter 2, for example, transnational networks of peat knowledge and expertise were constructed between Ireland, Germany, Finland, and the Soviet Union, between the 1930s and 1960s. Such an alternative internationalism cuts against the grain of Ireland's imperial networking, and is conveniently omitted from many mainstream histories.

Ireland's sharp pivot away from nationalised industrial development to a model of FDI-led development carried specific implications for higher education and R&D.[15] As revisionist narratives emphasise, Ireland 'learned its lessons' from republican insularity (and trade war with Britain), beginning to re-orientate science policy towards supporting 'invited' business within an otherwise under-developed research culture – beginning roughly in 1958 (Yearley 1995). From the 1970s, the Irish state invested in the education system to produce graduate engineers and technicians to meet growing demand from multinational computer and chemical manufacturing industries (van Egeraat and Jacobson 2004), heavily influenced by the Industrial Development Authority (IDA). Beyond providing an 'educated workforce', the IDA was also responding to changing industrial circumstances globally from the mid-1970s, 'by targeting foreign high-tech electronics firms for siting in Ireland to create a secure web of industry that might transform the Emerald Isle into a silicon Isle' (Jacobsen 1994, 110).[16] In 1978, the Department of Labour set up the Manpower Committee, intended as a forum for dialogue between the IDA and HEIs, quickly identifying a shortage in engineering and computing graduates (Walsh 2018, 268). This particular relationship between the development of an explicitly national workforce *for* FDI as a tool of economic modernisation speaks to developmental imperatives that were not the case in neighbouring countries such as England.

Additionally, in specific relation to science and research policy, Ireland adopted an economistic mindset towards science well before England, arguably foreshadowing later neoliberalisation in the university sector. Ireland caved to international pressure from the OECD as early as 1966 with the establishment of the National Science Council (NSC), whose allocated grants for science and industrialisation were defined in almost exclusively economic terms (Yearley 1995). By the time of the establishment of the National Board for Science and Technology (NBST) in the early 1970s, this language had fully entered the basic lexicon of science policy.[17] As Yearley quotes:

> In the recent history of Irish science – certainly from the very first meeting of the NSC – economic justifications have been pervasive, whereas the cultural defense of science (the idea that a civilized society just ought to perform scientific research or that science is diffusely beneficial to society) has made virtually no appearance. By the time of the NBST's draft national plan it had come to be stated that 'despite the contribution which S&T make to economic development S&T policies cannot stand alone and do not have a justification in and of themselves. Rather this justification arises from broader economic and social goals of government' (NBST 1983, 14). (Yearly 1995, 192–3)

This centrality of economic development in science policy from such an early stage is in the DNA of institutionalised Irish science – as much as it is also influenced by international flows of knowledge and capital.

Yearley shows that Ireland's economistic policies around science were exceptional even among similar European peripheries. However, while influenced by European initiatives, what connects Ireland more closely to other sovereign industrialisation strategies of postcolonial and otherwise dependent states is the intricate tethering of universities to the state's *developmental* imperative. This strategy was aimed at addressing perceived gaps in skills and expertise *necessary to achieving modernisation* via FDI-led industrialisation. By the late 1980s, investment in post-secondary skills-training through organisations such as Foras Áiseanna Saothair led to a unique situation whereby Ireland was spending 2 per cent of its GDP on labour market measures designed towards these sectors, double the OECD average through the 1990s (Kirby 2009, 5–6). However, as Seán Ó Riain (2004) points out, the Telesis Report in 1982 (see Chapter 3), which chastised the state strategy of depending exclusively upon FDI, also led to the further integration of university research clusters with local businesspeople and state officials as a way to support domestic economic growth alongside FDI. These national enterprise incentives, strategically cordoned off from FDI, were largely directed towards the burgeoning tech sector and skills in 'computer industries' – which would serve to further build and support the labour market base for high-tech industries favourable to a more 'developmental' project. But these parallel institutions were 'dwarfed' by the establishment of SFI in 2000, 'which channeled more money than ever before into university research, university-industry joint research, and institution-building' (Ó Riain 2004, 121).

SFI had its origins in a study by the Irish Government in 1998 called the Technology Foresight Reports. Expert panels made up of scientists, engineers, industrialists, and government officials assessed the Irish economy to identify how key sectors could evolve over the long term. They concluded that biotechnology and information and communications technology represented 'the engines of future growth in the global economy ... A world class research capability in selected niches of these two enabling technologies is an essential foundation for future growth' (SFI 2017). In response to the report, the Government established SFI in 2000 with an initial budget of €646 million under the banner of Forfás, a former state body in charge of assessing economic and industrial development needs in the state, aligned across enterprise and science policy.[18] The Oireachtas Bill establishing the statutory basis of SFI is the Industrial Development (Science Foundation Ireland) Act, which amends two prior successions of government Acts: the Industrial Development Acts 1986–98 and the Shannon Free Airport Development Company (Amendment) Act 1986. The first stated purpose of the Foundation, as referred to in the Bill, is to 'promote, develop and assist the carrying out of oriented basic research in strategic areas of scientific endeavour that concerns the future development and competitiveness of industry and enterprise in the State' (Government of Ireland 2003, Part 2, section 7.1.a). With enterprise and industrialisation in the organisation's charter, it worked to make HEIs more productive within this landscape – not least, motivated by a real need to support higher education and grow and maintain skills in Ireland – while at the same time correcting what was still seen as an under-developed domestic R&D culture, imbalanced towards the private/multinational sector.[19]

Like state organs developed to mediate multinationals and Irish territory, SFI was thus formed to mediate between science and industry, using the former to support the latter – and where the primary outcome is one of industrialisation and employment of knowledge generated in/through HEIs towards private enterprise.[20] The structural role of FDI makes the distinction between research in the public interest and research for industrial applications almost impossible – or at least, unpopular – to make in Ireland. This shows how universities act to deepen the relations found in the last two chapters: that FDI, somehow, becomes a public good.

Most importantly for this chapter, however, 'sustainability' and environmental partnerships have also become a central facet of this public imperative, especially as the 'twin transitions' of 'digitalisation and decarbonisation' are increasingly institutionalised through funding regimes and commercial partnerships. The twin transitions operate on the same logic as other industrially-led activities, courting the development and utilisation of additional, external expertise to enact (eco-)modernisation. Take CeADAR, for example: Ireland's 'Centre for Applied AI', this industry-focussed group offers 'a market-focused technology centre that drives the accelerated research, development, and deployment of AI and data analytics technology and innovation into businesses'. CeADAR is hosted *within* University College Dublin (UCD) but quasi-independent from it, supported by the IDA and Enterprise Ireland, offering a 'bridge between the worlds of applied research in AI and data analytics and their commercial deployment' (CeADAR nd). Many projects are focussed on how Ireland can act as a test bed for training AI and machine-learning systems to be applied to landscapes and ecologies beyond Ireland, indicating how research leverages Ireland's competitiveness and innovation to global sustainability marketplaces.[21] These activities require advanced and computationally intensive forms of research to manage the contradictions of growth amid fragile and turbulent ecological circumstances.

If the post-developmental strategies of Coillte, BnM, and the Electricity Supply Board (ESB) described in the prior chapters are about mobilising land, resources, and infrastructure for FDI, then SFI has done this for knowledge and labour; the infrastructures and resources of the university are martialled towards FDI. Bodies such as iCrag (formerly working with fossil fuel companies and more recently 'green' mining) and CeADAR serve as research-washing institutions for FDI industries with very real implications for how knowledge is developed – arm's-length bodies from the university with their own internal procedures and incentivisation for partnerships with the private sector, especially in the way that they operate across multiple institutions and with their own internal governance procedures.[22] As we outline below through peatland science, there are different ways that these bodies, intentionally or not, hijack climate action and critical research towards a status quo beholden to the limited outcomes of market-led sustainability accounting. The result is the slow, steady crystallisation of an eco-modernist consensus within the mainstream technoscience of climate action; performed, innovated, and legitimised in university-aligned organisations; and dictated by an enforced technical logic of capitalist sustainability. AI, privatised green energy, carbon offsetting, and mining are uncritically adopted, researched, and applied in universities with minimal regard for meaningful climate and environmental 'justice'. At its worst, this becomes a research-washing of extractive corporate activities with a 'green' tint.

Techno-solutionism and monopoly tech's field laboratory

The productivity of the bogs has historically relied on technical processes and infrastructures of drainage: creating firm ground from which to cultivate, extract, or build productive enterprise. Technoscientific understandings of peatlands designed to rewet and restore them rest on a reversal of these processes, but also inherit capitalist logics of value by justifying such activities in market terms. 'Sustainability' science more broadly, a policy promoting particular technoscientific divisions whereby human activity must dictate and manage 'nature' towards growth, has undoubtedly been the dominant paradigm of governing peatlands in Ireland for some time (Renou-Wilson et al 2011). The turn to seeing ecosystems and landscapes as 'service providers' is of course also not new – between catchment management, biodiversity conservation, and climate mitigation and adaptation, the potential socio-environmental and financial benefits of harnessing nature's bio-physical and geo-chemical properties have been widely identified within environmental governance since the 1990s (Carse 2012; Nelson and Bigger 2022). The task of making ecosystems legible requires considerable scientific and technical work to map, assess, value, monetise, and, ultimately, circulate an ecosystem service such as carbon sequestration (Dempsey and Robertson 2012). Private multinational tech companies, with their cloud technologies and platforms, are advancing as powerful actors in this space – as companies in the business of information, closely aligned with state industrial strategies, and managing mounting environmental contradictions along their supply chains. Here is a new fold in the green, digital transition in Ireland.

Take, for example, a project between NPWS and Intel, announced in 2021: this project 'restores' 60 hectares of degraded blanket bog in the Wicklow Mountains, just south of Dublin, with the potential to extend to the entire 400-hectare area. A novel 'public-private project collaboration' (Department of Housing, Local Government and Heritage 2023), it has been promoted by the Irish state in fora such as the European Peatlands Initiative hosted in Dublin in 2023, as a way to demonstrate how governments can leverage private partnerships towards publicly binding mandates of climate action. As the first industry investment in peatlands with the explicit aim of obtaining a verified natural capital credit, it has also been identified as a 'test-bed for composite credits combining water, carbon, biodiversity and community gain' (Peatland Finance Ireland 2021). At the same time, the restoration project serves a very concrete goal for Intel, a company known for excessive water usage and pollution in its microchip manufacturing (Chapter 3) – to contribute to its aims of 'net positive' water in Ireland and globally (Intel nd). Thus, by partnering with Intel in this process, the Irish state launders the ecological contradictions of monopoly tech growth in and through a public partnership research funding scheme – including by deploying state resources towards a goal that, while admirable in basic purported function, serves the interests of Intel's reputation and sustainability reporting without addressing *in situ* their impacts elsewhere.

These regimes of calculability are, however, not only about promotion and reputation – they act to produce new processes and products to support capital growth such as carbon and water credits. This new class of 'fictitious commodities' is not produced through the traditional, industrial labour process, but through a novel and complex assemblage of science, technology, and multiple non-state and financial intermediaries (Leonardi 2017), including cloud-enabled platforms, developed at public institutions. The Intel partnership described above is part of a pilot to develop how such crediting can be implemented through peatlands, a landscape still being formalised in this market.[23] It is in this context that we see the advent of digital technologies and tech companies – both technologically, and in terms of investment power – as providing potential solutions to the challenges facing policy makers, scientists, and NGOs in translating situated and complex ecosystems into information (Gabrys 2016). The emphasis on data-tech-as-solution to environmental problems stands as the obverse side of the environmental externalities produced by data – landscapes become silos for carbon and/as data to be recalled and made profitable, as ongoing capitalist growth requires emerging and networked infrastructures to store and manage these two aligned materials. To quote Pasek on what she refers to as the 'fungible' flows of data and carbon in planetary ecological ledgers: 'as with data, so with carbon' (2019).

The role of datafication in environmental relations is not commonly understood as a tool for accumulation within eco-modern capitalism, especially in its central importance in the realm of offsets.[24] This is not just about the specific political ecology of data, but about the institutional integration and normalisation of tech software in practices of data gathering, processing, and, eventually, decision making. For example, BnM uses Geographic Information System (GIS) software solutions from a company called ESRI Ireland (part of a multinational geo-mapping software group, ESRI Global) (McGowran 2022), depending on it for communication of peatland information to public stakeholders, from NPWS to government ministers. ESRI operates through 'strategic alliances' with technology partners – which include AWS, IBM, and Microsoft, who act as cloud providers in terms of both infrastructure and software/analytics solutions for the company (ESRI nd). These forms of industrial mediation and collaboration entrench private software into public governance. This is an issue frequently critiqued in other realms of geospatial governance such as smart cities, but rarely applied in terms of environmental privatisation.[25] The imperative of 'smartness' is both a technological and epistemological project of governance (Halpern and Mitchell 2022) – one that institutionalises regimes of digital efficiency supplied and supported by monopoly tech platforms within limited avenues of public, democratic participation.

Multinational tech companies (undoubtedly, mostly invested heavily in AI solutions and infrastructural support by this point) are involved, materially and discursively, in sustainability research projects in Ireland along these lines. Specifically in AI, the Terrain-AI project at Maynooth University, a partnership of Microsoft and SFI, has developed a petabyte-scale cloud-based platform for mapping and identifying carbon sequestration potentials within strategic 'green' landscapes including forests and peatlands (Terrain-AI 2024). The platform will generate a database as well as an actionable template for understanding and managing these landscapes across the planet.[26] Terrain-AI is also explicitly about Irish carbon budgeting and emissions: managing and offsetting those emissions through the platform until budget imbalances are corrected. Speaking to Microsoft's ambitions of a 'planetary computer',[27] the integration of petabyte-scale data and analytics into their cloud software leverages these advanced computing capabilities towards environmental certainty in both state and private offsetting regimes, testing capabilities in Ireland with the support and partnership of the university and SFI. Similarly, EPA-funded Smartbog, an AI and remote-sensing project for carbon sequestration using photographs to train a machine-learning system, promised to 'reboot the process of carbon capture by these ancient landscapes' (McGuinness 2023), associating bogs with a computing device for carbon storage.

Sharing some of the same personnel as Smartbog, the AI2Peat project responds to challenges of peatlands' remoteness and inaccessibility by applying remote sensing and other digital tools to leverage AI towards capturing and reducing CO_2 emissions (AI2Peat 2024). The project, funded by a consortium of public sector bodies, notably includes SFI, iCRAG, NPWS, and CeADAR. What the AI2Peat project offers to peatland science (and finance) is a means of combining and analysing a range of different data collected from drone surveys, satellites, earth observation, and on-the-ground measurements from citizen science projects. As a member of the project explains, '[a]rtificial intelligence technology can give us insights into the complex dynamics that are degrading our peatlands and represents an exciting new solution to the preservation of the environment for humans and animals alike' (Irish Tech News 2023). AI2Peat is about establishing and exporting *certainty* and eliminating *ambiguity* in the definition of peatlands, starting with the test bed of Ireland. Part of this is the process of monitoring and locking down carbon stores. But it also concerns lack of communication between stakeholders, and reducing a perceived transparency gap. Effective ecotype classification through a satellite imaging-trained neural network (Grappiolo et al 2024), for example, becomes essential to territorialising a crediting mechanism – with the science, mediated by AI, establishing and reducing the contingencies of that relationship.

These projects to 'smarten' the bog and apply AI to their climate solutions are primarily designed to remotely and computationally map carbon and water cycles to make up for oft-perceived data gaps in (time- and labour-intensive) field data (Renou-Wilson et al 2022; Habib and Connolly 2023). Within the current research 'ecosystem', while ostensibly supporting climate action and policy, commercialisation and efficiency are preconditions of many scientific-funding schemes. Peatlands' carbon-based ecologies need to be understood and leveraged quickly towards climate action and, more importantly, climate justice. However, these attempts are ultimately undermined by the epistemological underpinnings of the eco-modernist project represented by the language and practices of 'ecosystem services', 'nature-based solutions', and 'natural capital', which have roots in long histories promoting mastery of more-than-human ecologies by technoscientific measurement, representation, design, and engineering. The net product of these projects is the moulding of environments (and their calculability for) capital accumulation (Costanza et al 1997; Robertson 2006, 2012). AI-led efficiencies, as the story goes, reduce the need for 'boots on the ground' to actualise these visions.

But such solutions, however much funded as public research, need a market to be commercially viable; they need to prototype sustainable technologies and practices, and in some cases directly produce commodified goods and services. In peatlands, this will include facilitating data and technologies towards emerging markets of carbon crediting and offsets, which act as calculative mechanisms by which companies can continue to emit carbon while inching towards 'net zero' via investments in 'preserving' or 'restoring' carbon-laden landscapes such as peatlands (Buck 2019). The next section dives into the specificities of this global marketplace of carbon – whose emerging dominance serves to foreclose pathways towards more just peatland futures by forcing communities to court private finance for sustainability.

Governing for peatland carbon

Despite frequent debunking, the 'fantasy', even colonial imaginary, of carbon offsetting (and its waste economies) persists (Liboiron 2021; Mbaria 2023). These net zero-driven accounting schemes enable multinational corporations and Global North countries to continue burning carbon in one place while 'offsetting' these emissions with 'green' activity elsewhere, whether direct carbon capture, conservation, or other sustainability projects.[28] In effect, it is a political economy of planetary flows that calculatively enables ongoing growth: an eco-modernity supported by landscape carbon. Applying peatland science towards carbon mapping and management, commercially oriented projects of institutional technoscience promote this infrastructural function of landscape ecologies, instrumentalising the planet towards overarchingly unsustainable forms of capitalist activity. But such markets only emerge in response to institutional mechanisms. As Adrienne Buller shows, the commodification of carbon (and its valuation) only emerges as a result of climate targets (2022). As a result, regulatory approaches must balance ensuring the reliability and standardisation of such mechanisms with the viability of the market – and they need to organise landscapes towards their construction.

Peatland Finance Ireland (PFI) was established as a legal entity in 2022 with the overall goal of establishing a national financing system for peatland restoration. It is at once a clear example of the nebulous public/private, multi-scalar genre of contemporary climate governance and the ways peatland restoration in Ireland operates within the broader institutional logic of the postcolonial ecological regime. The lead organisations behind PFI are UCD, NPWS, European knowledge transfer service ERINN Innovation, and the UK-based Landscape Finance Lab, an organisation within the international conservation NGO World Wide Fund for Nature (WWF), founded in 2016 to 'test the best approaches for regenerating and attracting finance for landscapes at scale' (Landscape Finance Lab nd). PFI is part funded by the Irish Government (via NPWS) and part through the Natural Capital Financing Facility (NCFF), launched by the European Investment Bank in 2015 to provide financing for 'natural capital' projects (categorised as green infrastructure projects, payment for ecosystem services, biodiversity offsets, environmentally sustainable businesses, and nature-based solutions for adaptation to climate change). The NCFF is designed to demonstrate financial viability of natural capital projects to private investors; for example, peatland restoration projects that can demonstrate commercial revenue from the sale of peatland credits.

PFI emerges from a growing consensus within NGO, government, and private sectors that peatland restoration at scale depends on new models of 'blended' finance. PFI estimates that the cost of restoring Ireland's peatlands is more than €1 billion, with current sources of peatland finance 95 per cent state-dependent, with no expected return-on-investment. Establishing the 'conservation finance gap' has been the discursive foundation of market-based green finance for at least three decades, prompting a cascade of governmental interventions and schemes to bridge between conservation projects on the ground and institutional investors seeking returns – 'selling nature in order to save it' (McAfee 1999). In reality, despite the promise, self-financing conservation remains like 'the legendary Holy Grail … elusive' (Ferraro and Kiss 2002, 1719). PFI is public money chasing private money, or in its financial jargon: 'the support of the EIB will be fundamental in bridging the "capacity gap" … in providing concessional capital to catalyse the return-on-investment model to attract larger investors seeking higher returns' (PFI 2011, 2).

Up to now, the work carried out by PFI has been to scope out interest in and obstacles to the effective mobilisation of (private) peatland finance. While declaring it is about working with all stakeholders, a glance at the stakeholders consulted reveals a familiar list: Wind Energy Ireland (WEI), IBEC (Irish Business and Employers Association), Davy Stockbrokers[29] (Ireland's leading wealth management and investment banking services provider), major agri-food industries (including Nestlé), government departments, semi-state companies, Intel, international conservation NGOs, and the large EU-funded peatland research projects mentioned above. Amazon Ireland has publicly supported the initiative, as part of its own climate commitments (Amazon Team 2024). These industry actors want verification protocols and community acceptance, uncertainties that PFI is now addressing – effectively constructing a new supply chain for peatland credits that meets needs of industry seeking to offset carbon pollution and investors interested in low-risk, green financial products. This will require the development of an Irish 'peatland code', similar to those in other jurisdictions,[30] and a key investment metric. Such codes establish a standard for measuring and valuing emissions savings for different types of peatlands, at different stages of degradation or rehabilitation. As with carbon offsets attached to forestry projects, the challenge is in quantifying and verifying the emissions avoided from rewetting peatland and measuring the rate of carbon sequestration in recovering and actively conserved peatland.

The financialisation of carbon mitigation via peatlands is still in its infancy, and so we can only speculate. What we know is that scientific and financial uncertainty remain key stumbling blocks in the development of peatland restoration, and that projects such as PFI are deployed to rectify this. Monopoly tech comes into the picture through the promise of AI and machine learning, computationally intensive operations pitched as necessary for addressing the complex problems of climate mitigation in 'unruly' bog landscapes. Here then is the convergence of climate science, finance capital, and monopoly tech, mediated by the state. The significance of monopoly tech in this eco-modern formation is important because it helps us to understand the limitations of supposedly open-ended stakeholder engagement on peatland management and funding. Similar to the context of HEI research and engagement in peatlands, these dynamics help us to recognise how these market-dictated schemes exhaust energies, maintain the status quo, and fundamentally shrink the horizon of what else is possible.

In June 2023, we presented at a one-day event entitled 'Exploring finance and governance for community-led peatland restoration'. The symposium was organised by the Community Wetlands Forum (CWF), a grassroots network made up of 40 community groups involved in community-led wetland conservation. In the months preceding the symposium, some community groups had been approached by private companies interested in establishing voluntary carbon and water offsets for their clients – including major food and drink processors. The informality of these exchanges and the growing interest in peatland finance (including via the PFI scoping exercise which included the CWF) inspired the network to organise the event and learn more about the pitfalls and opportunities of private finance. Representatives from PFI, NPWS, BnM, and several of the third-level research projects on peatlands also spoke at the event. While there was no outright opposition to the ideas of natural capital and carbon offsets, conversations we had with participants in the CWF made it clear that there was scepticism about the motivation behind these schemes and private finance[31] – why else was the symposium held? Summing up this position, one member told us: 'My concern is with the tendency to exclude communities – or limiting their involvement to mere tokenism. But more importantly the absence of approaches to mobilising financial investment in peatlands which ensure communities reap their share of the financial benefits, and where public benefit trumps private sector profits.' Most of the active members of the CWF have been working in the area of rural community development and environmental conservation for years, long enough to know that these are not the priorities guiding the current drive to assign 'value' to peatland restoration. Despite the justified scepticism, there is little room to manoeuvre for these community groups. Understanding how this situation has come about is important in recognising the political stakes of the current moment – beyond an apparent choice of engaging or disengaging from peatland finance.

Contrast this limited aperture with the history of the Abbeyleix Bog Project mentioned at the beginning of the chapter. In 2000, a local action group called AREA (Abbeyleix Residents for Environment Action) organised a direct action to prevent BnM machines from accessing the bog to harvest horticultural moss. After years of negotiation, in 2009 BnM eventually agreed a 50-year lease with the local community to manage Abbeyleix for conservation and local amenity. Over the intervening years, Abbeyleix Bog

Project has become one of the best-known, widely cited examples of bog restoration in Ireland. Inheriting a 500-acre site of degraded raised bog, the community began blocking the drains, installing over 3,000 individual dams over 14 years. In 2020, an ecotope survey showed that the area of active raised bog habitat at Abbeyleix Bog had increased from 1.1 ha to 13.78 ha – in just over ten years. Largely through voluntary labour and fund-raising, a raised walkway has been installed and a coffee truck opened in the hotel car park adjacent to the bog. On its website, the project quotes English travel writer and farmer Arthur Young, who passed by Abbeyleix Bog in the late 1700s: 'I should apprehend this bog to be among the most improvable in the country.' The website clarifies, 'Young meant that more could be done to drain the land for other land uses … As you can see from the above data, we certainly feel the bog is most improvable in a different way!' (Abbeyleix Bog Project nd).

The Abbeyleix Bog Project emerges from an earlier phase of peatland restoration that was led by local communities, former BnM workers, and conservation groups – before carbon storage was identified as a potential new peatland frontier. In 1997, a conference was organised on the 'Future Use of the Cutaway Bogs'. John Feehan and Bernard Kaye, passionate voices on heritage and landscape, spoke about the value of letting the bogs go their own way.[32] They were speaking against a tide of commercial interests (including BnM) who wanted to reclaim the peatlands for agriculture or forestry, replicating centuries-old missions of making the bogs productive. 'This new land of the cutaway becomes available for "non-productive" purposes because it is considered not to have commercial agricultural or forestry potential', they write, 'by default in other words: it is no good for anything else'. In the interregnum between carbon modernity and today's eco-modernisation, Feehan and Kaye imagined instead a vast networked public wilderness. This bog wilderness was not understood through its embedded 'natural capital' or potential economic 'services', but in terms of relinquishing control – 'light-touch' ecological management, a far cry from heavily instrumented, computationally intensive mapping currently underway, driven by the imperatives of carbon calculability.[33]

Supported by early injections of EU funding and state welfare schemes, a couple of these early rewilding projects got off the ground. The most well known is Lough Boora, one of the first bog complexes to be developed by BnM and the first to be exhausted. As one of the first former industrial peat-cutting sites to undergo this kind of transition, the project received local, national, and EU funding. However, while successful in connecting arts, culture, and ecology towards peatland protection and restoration (Tipton 2010), this is also where the present ambivalence arises: after years of activism, organising, and unpaid labour, such community-led bog restoration projects are now the focus of attention and efforts at valorisation. Take the 2023 event narrated at the beginning of this chapter, hosted at Abbeyleix. In the world of de-risking and environmental, social, and governance (ESG) principles, community participation is as valuable as carbon sequestration, and not just because of the 'social licence' for offset schemes. A walk around Abbeyleix bog reveals a thoroughly instrumented peatland. Abbeyleix has already become a 'test-site' for developing knowledge about carbon sequestration, chosen as one of 15 'knowledge sites' for the EU Horizon WaterLands project, based on past success in restoration efforts (Meleisea 2022). UCD was the research partner in Ireland, working with 32 partners from 14 countries in the EU. Since then, Abbeyleix has received €75,000 from the Irish Government's Peatland Community Engagement Scheme to allow more engineering works to be implemented.

Abbeyleix is a good example of how 'citizen science' operates with institutional science: the Abbeyleix Technical Advisory Group (TAG) includes representatives from NPWS, BnM, the local council, and community members. There is nothing in these digital knowledge systems that precludes the combination of citizen science and satellite imagery, for example. From early on, those involved in the Abbeyleix Bog Project recognised the financial and technical constraints they were operating under. In 2015, the community identified the potential for external financing linked to carbon-offsetting schemes. Working on the margins of the state, like similar ENGOs, they are directed to the EU to compete for regional funding (rather than state funding) and often embrace a culture of DIY autonomy. This has produced a situation in which any sense of a public remit, or demand on the state to secure community and social benefits, is limited.

Understanding the origins (and non-inevitability) of this common sense helps us understand the awkwardness and discomfort at the CWF event. Once you assume that community-scale peatland restoration won't be supported financially by the state, there is little alternative but to look for alternative sources of funding. And waiting there is a growing host of actors, such as PFI, happy to enrol you into opaque networks of market-led carbon governance. This is not reducible to the 'retreat' of the state because, as we have outlined above, PFI is a state initiative, as are the SFI-funded research projects partnering with Abbeyleix and other peatland communities. The state is more active than ever, represented in multiple forms and state–private networks. By shining some light on these relationships, we want to illustrate the ever-receding back-end of commercially-led research that forms a part of the infrastructure of eco-modern privatisation. Here, the power inequalities and interests enabled by the state become clearer. It is through the *extensive* operations of these networks that less visible forms of capitalist accumulation take place – whether offsetting pollution from water- and carbon-intensive industries or refining climate services and products owned by monopoly tech.

The obvious problem with this is that so much of what stands behind PFI is obscured. As offsetting schemes have proven time and again, the power dynamics within market-based environmental accreditation schemes are not only opaque but also highly unequal. And unlike in 2000, when AREA blocked BnM machines and confronted the state and its extractive activities, there is no clear opponent anymore. On the surface, there is room for more community engagement: the logic of 'improvement' remains, just focussed on transforming the work of on-the-ground communities such as Abbeyleix into the value proposition of peatland standards and finance, enabled by and through large-scale investment and advanced digital technologies. Across the extensive relations that make up contemporary climate governance, what remains is an imperative to make peatlands productive for capital.

Conclusion

It has become popular in recent years for critical scholars to pay attention to the ways life coexists with the speculative and destructive ecologies of capital – political economic systems enrol places and subjugate rich emplaced relations, but other practices exist in the ruins and amid toxicity.[34] While important, we also need to understand that what coexists as subjugated to or alternative to capital is not always incommensurable with it. This is what anti-colonial and dependency thinkers alike have tried to articulate when dealing with developmental economies. It is about being direct and clear about how particular knowledge practices – and the political economies behind them – promote conditions that are amenable to capitalist development. How peatlands are becoming a novel land bank for green, digital capital requires a deep dive into the way public infrastructures surrounding peatlands are being transformed in the image of this emerging landscape, and the various actors that are existing in, alongside, or in antagonism with it. Whose interests can actually coexist, and what are the points at which other interests become a challenge to the existing structures – not only of knowledge, but also funding and the directionality of that knowledge across history?

The landscape of Irish research culture, as much as the types of conferences described in the opening vignette, is about building connections across science, industry, and communities, whereby publicly produced knowledge acts as a resource to support business activity and vaguely defined 'impact'. These environments are dominated by the ethos of what Gökçe Günel describes as 'technical adjustments' in climate thinking, or applied technoscientific rationalities that are 'imaginative and wide-ranging responses to global climate change and energy scarcity, which open up certain interventions (such as extending technological complexity) while foreclosing others (such as asking larger-scale moral, ethical, and political questions regarding how to live)' (2019). Tovey's model of 'official environmentalism' in Ireland (1993) has become rife with these climate-orientated technical solutions, with institutionally supported scientific experts technologically dissecting bogs with greater precision towards 'planetary' climate benefits with vaguely defined economic ends, especially at the local level. Well-meaning scientists and 'green' policy makers, including those represented at the 2023 peatlands event, are oftentimes more frustrated than sympathetic to the proliferating localised inequalities these relationships to the environment reproduce. To many of these experts, resistant communities do not know, understand, or care about the benefits of renewable technologies and green development strategies at whatever scale. While the importance of 'social science' and 'listening to communities' is always tokenistically acknowledged, it is primarily deployed as a tool to 'get communities on board' rather than design alternative policies and developmental strategies more democratically.

Two anecdotes from the event illustrate this most profoundly. The first is related to the wider extractive enterprises occurring on and through peatlands. Two scholars affiliated with the Geological Survey of Ireland (GSI), a state subsidiary of the Department of the Environment, Climate and Communications and also in charge of promoting the social benefits of extractive projects from minerals to wind to local communities for the green transition, gave a presentation about the conditions that led to the peatslide in Meenbog (see Chapter 4). Experts argued that the experts who had designed the process of designating landslide vulnerability had failed to account for the specificities of peat soil in their analyses prior to the peatslide, a soil described as 'like custard' and 'behaving more like water' than soil. This data gap, between experts in peatlands employed primarily in government offices and scientific institutions in Dublin, had arisen amid rampant development of wind farms and sitka spruce plantations, similarly transformative projects designed for extraction on poorly understood hydro-geological environments of peat blanket bogs in Ireland's western highlands. This data gap presented a new problem for experts to solve with more standardisation, digital sensing, remote monitoring, mapping, and of course funding from companies like Intel and SSE represented by research at the event. This data gap, however, is contradicted by planners' reports from as far back as 2015, which facilitated the eventual rejection of a 49-turbine plan on the site, indicating that this was an area of 'proven environmental sensitivity' and at a medium but 'tolerable' risk for peatslides (Corr 2020).

The second example is more direct. In the opening address, a senior member of iCRAG, when outlining the ethos behind the organisation's interest in the just transition, was enthusiastic about the new resource potentials offered by these landscapes. Amid what was widely acknowledged as a destruction of the bogs for fossil fuels and sovereign industrialisation across the 20th century, new resource frontiers were waiting underneath in the bedrock, activated by the push for onshore 'critical raw materials' in Europe: 'green' minerals were potentially awaiting exploration in the cutaway reserves to be exploited alongside carbon credit schemes in adjacent rewetted bogs.

These final examples demonstrate that the transformative infrastructures and frontiers of (green) capital continue to expand beyond apparent sites of data and energy infrastructural development, penetrating deeper into the earth and its atmosphere. Central to this expansion is the university, facilitated by and through funding bodies beholden to the commercial imperatives of the Irish state development model more broadly. This is not the result of some direct, intentional action on the part of most administrators and funders, let alone researchers and students. It is part of the continuing evolution of Irish public bodies towards the facilitation of FDI and commercial activity more broadly as a condition of existence. This did not start with austerity, but the groundwork was firmly established during the same periods of FDI-led industrialisation traced in prior chapters.

However, at the same time, we hope we have begun to demonstrate that the premises of development and viable, ecologically sound livelihoods for rural communities are central to building just futures – and at times, this means thinking with or reclaiming 'scale' from the relentless industrialisation of FDI. What, for example, would a vision of the state as a vehicle of development orientated directly towards the restoration of peatlands look like, rather than mediated through the common-sensical logics of FDI and multinational, eco-modern accumulation strategies? To build this alternative, the idea of peatland restoration, for example, would need to be aligned with apparently incommensurable aims such as de-alignment with global green development imperatives. In some senses, then, the virtue of the postcolonial ecological regime analytic is to show how connected and pervasive the FDI ideology is. We thus have to articulate sites of apparently disparate struggle as connected and needing to cohere into a real movement for eco-socialist development – whether this movement is focussed on land use, agriculture, energy, technology, housing, resource sovereignty, or something else. What would peatland restoration under an industrialisation paradigm such as the Turf Development Act look like (see Chapter 2)? Asking this question is not a nostalgic look backwards, but rather a question about the meaning and ongoing purchase of industrial development as a powerful political mobilising force. In the final chapter we will start to articulate the ways in which we need to reclaim scale in our thinking, and not cede it to the varied forces of regression and/or global capital. Alongside other regimes of knowing and valuing land and ecology, in the final chapter we demonstrate how 'anti-imperialist environmental justice' coalitions are beginning to form against the eco-modern premises of the green, digital transition.

6

Land, Extractivism, and Anti-Imperialist Environmentalism

Fighting extractivism

One Saturday in May 2023, about one hundred people gather in the Bee Park community centre in Manorhamilton, County Leitrim, in the north-west of Ireland. They are here to welcome and learn from three water protectors, Chas Jewett, Jeshua Estes, and Lewis GrassRope, visiting from the Lakota Nation (Figure 6.1). The visit has been organised by Making Relatives, a collective of water protectors in Ireland and North America, and supported by Friends of the Earth NI, Communities Against the Injustice of Mining (CAIM), the Derry Playhouse, and us – a group of researchers.

Before we hear from the three Indigenous visitors, speakers from three local campaigns tell us about what they are facing in Leitrim. Save Leitrim is a campaign resisting expansion of monoculture industrial forestry, which covers over 20 per cent of the county[1]; Treasure Leitrim is the most recent campaign group, organising to stop mining developments in the area; and Save Dough Mountain, opposing the construction of industrial wind turbines on sensitive, upland bogs in North Leitrim. We don't hear from Love Leitrim but they are of course mentioned – formed in 2011, they successfully organised with other local communities, activists, and environmental non-governmental organisations (ENGOs) to block proposed fracking across the country, resulting in a fracking ban in the Republic in 2017, one of the few places in the world to do so – a campaign which continues to be fought across the border in the North.

For most people outside Leitrim, the least-populated and 'poorest' county in Ireland, there isn't any obvious connection between forestry, mining, wind farms, and fracking. But for those living in Leitrim, the connections are impossible to ignore. For them, it is no accident that multiple toxic industrial activities, which bring very little employment

Figure 6.1: Chas Jewett, Jeshua Estes, and Lewis GrassRope, visiting from the Lakota Nation, at Greencastle Peoples Office, Sperrins, County Tyrone, 2023

Source: Photograph courtesy of V'Cenza Cirefice

or benefits to the area, are sited here. These are the familiar patterns of uneven development that have coursed through Leitrim's history since colonial times. It is easy for the water protectors from Lakota, who have themselves fought in multiple campaigns against toxic infrastructures, state marginalisation, and oppression, to find common ground with those attending.[2]

Sister Majella McCarron is also in attendance that day. On mission in Nigeria, she became a close friend and ally of Ken Saro-Wiwa, one of the Ogoni 9 executed for resisting the toxic operations of Royal Dutch Shell in the Niger Delta in the early 1990s. Shortly after his execution, Sister Majella returned to Ireland and became involved in the Shell to Sea Campaign in County Mayo, another western periphery, where Royal Dutch Shell was given permission to process gas onshore. Now in her 80s, Sister Majella is an Elder of the Irish environmental movement, whose presence in the Community Hall speaks to deep connections between what appear at first to be disparate sites and moments of land-based, environmental struggles.

The next day, we attend a ceremony in the Organic Centre in Rossinver. An oak sapling is planted in the shelter of a hawthorn and holly tree. A local man explains that the oak grows with the support of the two trees. Chas, Jeshua, and Lewis lead the ceremony, with song and a smoke ritual. It is incredibly moving, and some people cry. If yesterday connection was made through stories of shared suffering and resistance, today it is love of Place and affection for the Land.

After Leitrim, the delegation travel to the Sperrin Mountains in County Tyrone to learn about the decade-long campaign against Canadian company Dalradian's mega gold mining project. They also travel to Derry, visiting the Free Derry Palestinian solidarity mural on the Bogside. In the space of six short days, the Making Relatives Tour draws together many strands of land-based resistance and anti-colonial internationalism that links not only water protectors in Turtle Island and Ireland, but also struggles across the colonised world. As a visiting researcher from London says to us with naive surprise, 'you'd never have this kind of thing in England'.

This isn't the whole story though. In the Community Centre in Manorhamilton, a man hands out copies of The Irish Light, a far-right conspiracy newspaper linked to a sister publication in the UK. The Irish Light took off in the wake of COVID, propagandising about the 'globalist agenda' and the 'Great Reset'. Once the man is identified, he is quickly asked to leave and copies of the publication binned. But why would someone think that an event organised with Indigenous Water Protectors and community campaigns focussed on protecting land, water, and environment was a receptive place for spreading racist far-right conspiracies?

This gets us thinking about how much has changed since Chas first visited Ireland in 2017. It was just after the shutting down of the Standing Rock Camp, which had become a centre of gravity for the global climate justice movement. In Ireland, at the same time, there had been mass mobilisation against the proposed introduction of household water charges. This was a long-awaited act of popular resistance to years of austerity imposed in compliance with IMF–EU bailout conditions. It felt like a hopeful moment, with Chas speaking to communities around Ireland, connecting Indigenous with anti-privatisation water struggles.

One of the key elements of the water charges movement was the mobilisation of urban, working-class communities. As they blocked the installation of water metres and turned up to national demonstrations, protest signs proliferated, broadcasting the many communities that said 'no' to water charges. Today, these signs have returned. However, now they are also expressing 'no' to the housing of international protection applicants – those seeking asylum in Ireland. Protecting Irish water, or other national resources, is now just as likely to be linked with an exclusive ethno-nationalism as it is a liberatory, internationalist politics.

Of course, territorial, particularly national, resource politics is always rife with contradictions and exclusions. In Ireland, this is complicated by the fact that the country was colonised but also benefited from British colonialism and imperialism – Chas, Jeshua, and Lewis do not need to be told about the role of Irish settlers in the subjugation of Indigenous people. These contradictions cannot be whitewashed or resolved by appeals to empirical evidence. As Ireland's complex relationship with colonialism and empire surfaces in new and potent ways – from support for Palestine to anti-migrant racism – there is an urgent need to reclaim and re-articulate a tradition of Irish anti-colonialism, anti-imperialism, and Third World solidarity.

The previous chapter narrated and analysed the technical, knowledge-based processes by which the state enables deeper penetration of multinational tech capital into landscapes in Ireland – which commodify peatland carbon as a resource to be exploited through financial instruments of carbon crediting and the technoscientific calculations of emissions trading. Similar to our analysis of Ireland's decarbonisation and its growing relationship to the tech industry, this introduces knotty questions about the practices and directionalities of climate politics and the energy transition. We argue that by facilitating the operations of offsetting and waste management for multinational corporations through the 'postcolonial ecological regime', Ireland contributes to the global intensification of foundationally colonial regimes of knowing and valuing land and ecology (Liboiron 2021). In this way, Ireland continues to be a site where the contradictions of imperial ecology are managed through land, organising ecology towards the global accumulation of capital.

This chapter situates our analysis of this extractive regime towards a more obvious environmental 'villain': the mining industry. In particular, we use the mining industry to understand a final site where Ireland's model of foreign direct investment (FDI)-driven development has been adjusted to manage the contradictions of ongoing global economic growth within overt forms of extraction. It is not widely known that Ireland is a mining hub – unlike other countries in Europe, and correlated to its postcolonial development, Ireland 'opened up' for mining in the 1960s, as one of the early sites of FDI-led resource exploitation (Regan and Walsh 1976). While Ireland has long been a site of industrial mining activity and expertise – also related to organisations such as the Geological Society of Ireland (GSI) and Institute of Geologists Ireland (IGI) (GSI 2022), with strong, technical geological knowledge at some stages inherited from British mapping projects – it has not been viewed as a continuous aspect of Ireland's economic make-up (Murray 2024). As we mention early in the book, apart from its land-bank, Ireland has never been perceived as 'resource rich' by external forces – which has in some ways shielded it from the most overt forms of postcolonial extractivism. But in other ways, and due to particularities of its colonial partition, this has also left certain regions exposed to mining and toxicity in ways that are intensifying today. Ireland has become a 'key player' in the 'critical minerals' transition,[3] and this has included developing research infrastructure to legitimise the technoscience of mining – 'official environmentalism' repackaged as a tool for expanded 'green' extractivism.

This is less obviously related to monopoly tech than the activities covered in the last several chapters – where we connect the logics and technologies of tech companies to how the infrastructures of the postcolonial ecological regime have transformed to support climate action. But the growth of green, digital systems, shaped by the accumulation imperatives of monopoly tech, also drives the demand for raw materials under the discursive cover of 'greenness'. We need more wind/solar energy, and for that we need more land; we need more carbon in the ground, and for that we need more data; to achieve these things in tandem, we need more minerals.

The tech industry, however, has discursively distanced itself from mining – unlike energy or carbon sequestration.[4] It is worth reflecting on why that is. Activists and human rights groups have connected tech, energy, and mining in ways that are in some ways less clear, but in others, far more recognisable as environmental harms than other forms of monopoly tech-led eco-modernity. We can take the much-cited case brought by US human rights firm International Rights Advocates against Apple, Google, Dell, Microsoft, and Tesla in 2019 on behalf of families of children killed in the Congolese mining of cobalt, 'seeking damages for forced labour and further compensation for unjust enrichment, negligent supervision and intentional infliction of emotional distress' (Kelly 2019). This was a landmark case that was the first overt legal connection between tech companies and the source of their raw materials – a connection that up to this point has been primarily discursive (Stefanović 2024). The argument becomes one about the complicities of tech-driven growth in the extractive enterprises of green, digital capitalism as they are managed through intermediaries, rather than direct infrastructural and supply chain arrangements – ultimately, a question of who is responsible for ongoing ravages of imperial capitalism.

In this chapter, we unravel where these logics form and how they are enacted. Land is central, and mining clearly surfaces these politics – a key point when fighting against the abstractions of monopoly tech, datafication, and 'atmospheric capitalism' (Hughes 2021). By situating these discursive transitions within the political ecologies of FDI, we can identify that this is not somehow 'new', emerging out of thin air via novel technological innovation. The development paradigm remains the same, in support of extractive arrangements of technology and capital, and this is where we need to locate our horizon of struggle: the end of a capitalist world system dictated by the competitive regimes of the market, the imperialism of the US, and the growing dominance of monopoly tech. We cannot just replace fossil capital with green/digital capital, or 'dig our way to a just transition', as members of the GSI proposed in 2023 (McGrath et al 2023). Rather, a new orientation needs to be forged across environmental, anti-colonial, and anti-imperialist struggles and commitments.

This chapter also brings us closer to a conclusion, as we channel the book's insights through mining – and the history of the location and contestation of 'toxic' industries in rural Ireland – to articulate the basis of an anti-imperialist approach to monopoly tech. Such an approach requires unlearning (justified) reactive politics on the left to think ahead of and against monopoly tech. We draw on comradely debates among many scholars and activists in our orbit, in particular the work of Save our Sperrins, Communities Against the Injustice of Mining (CAIM), and the Making Relatives collective. The pathbreaking activism and scholarship coming from these groups has opened up new horizons of environmental struggle in Ireland, both activating existing anti-colonial solidarities while forging new ones through careful, principled, radical internationalist organising.[5]

Our contribution to these debates both within Ireland and beyond[6] is this: in situating monopoly tech and private renewable energy development as key drivers of this extraction, the centrality of anti-imperialist struggle must be orientated within (and against) the longer history of Ireland's dependency within the world system. This might mean re-awakening contested currents in Irish left thinking, including legacies of republicanism, which have historically developed the clearest anti-imperialist thinking on the island. This is not to cede environmental movements to only (left) nationalist currents. Rather, we want to recognise that enduring promise of sovereign national development, as a core dimension of even the postcolonial ecological regime, is a powerful political and democratic motivator, and one that movements orientated against technocratic green, digital transitions are uniquely poised to confront and mobilise. This chapter situates mineral extractivism and anti-extractivism, and anti-toxic campaigning more broadly, within these currents of left thinking – by way of opening up discussion about what the Irish left can do to wrest and build eco-socialist futures from the grip of monopoly tech's eco-modernity.

Mining Ireland

Ireland's first metals 'boom' came about in the 1960s due to coalescing factors, including tax measures for economic development, the role of the Industrial Development Authority (IDA) in attracting multinational companies to Ireland, and global demands for specific metals. In a sense, it was the first wave of the new FDI-led resource regime that would develop later through industrial manufacturing and, later again, financial and digital services. A 1957 Act granted tax exemptions for mining activity, leading to a rush of interest from Canadian and Swedish companies (McCabe 2011). The 1967 Finance Act extended tax exemption for a further 20-year period. By 1970 Ireland had the largest underground zinc mine in Europe, at Silvermines, County Tipperary; the largest-producing lead mine in Europe, at Tynagh, County Galway; one of the largest silver, copper, and mercury mines in the world, at Gortdrum, County Tipperary; and the world's most profitable Barytes deposit in County Sligo. In 1976, 4 per cent of Ireland's exports were metals and it was Europe's largest base metal producer (mostly lead, zinc, and copper) (Kearns 1976). But, as with neocolonial arrangements elsewhere, the value of these mineral resources largely accrued to North American and European mining companies and their shareholders via tax-free profits and minimal royalties (Resource Study Group 1972).[7] Nonetheless, in a place notorious for lacking in 'natural' resources beyond (sometimes) arable land, a propensity for mineral extraction was established: 'Ireland's mineral wealth is unsurpassed in Europe', read a byline in *The Economist* in 1974 (quoted in Regan and Walsh 1976).[8]

Today, we are seeing the next mining boom emerge around the global shift to green energy and smart technologies in the form of 'critical minerals' or 'critical raw materials' for clean energy and tech, such as lithium, nickel, cobalt, manganese, graphite, copper, aluminium, and rare earth elements. The policy language of 'critical raw materials' in the EU has aligned with its promised 'twin transitions' towards green and digital technology. In response, Ireland has added strategic designation to mineral deposits and their development to ensure their rapid exploitation amid protest and controversy:

> Today, Europe relies heavily on imports, often from a single third country, and recent crises have underlined EU strategic dependencies. Without joint and timely action, a well-functioning single market, resiliency and competitiveness, European industries and EU efforts to meet its climate and digital objectives are at risk. … The [EU Critical Raw Materials] Act [coming into force in Ireland] is a comprehensive response to these challenges. (Department of the Environment, Climate and Communications 2024)

Undoubtedly, one of the major implications for this is the erosion of democratic accountability towards 'green' development, as well as overt colonial legacies in the flattening, universalising language of resource exploitation for an expanding EU economy.

Ireland has actively sought to position itself as a potential 'hotspot' for critical minerals; as Lynda Sullivan has found, 27 per cent of the Republic of Ireland and 25 per cent of Northern Ireland are now concessioned for mining (2021). The Irish Government's Climate Action Plan identifies the necessity of increased mining on the island for the transition to a climate neutral economy. A 2024 RTÉ article, entitled 'EU critical materials rules could lead to new Irish mines', quotes Emer Blackwell of the IGI:

> Ireland is ahead of many countries in Europe with a mature and established mining industry, accompanied by comprehensive geological data and developed regulatory systems … Most have had limited mining experience in the last three decades compared to Ireland where mining has evolved since the 1960s. It's clear that Ireland can harness this experience to play a significant role in Europe's quest to secure the future supply of critical raw materials. (Quoted in Goodbody 2024)

This sums up the imaginary of Ireland in the supply chains of critical raw materials, especially with regards to its specific developmental strategies and position in the world economy. Ireland has evolved itself towards mineral extraction because of its specific development pathways since the 1960s. Major, core European economies in the late-20th century have tended to be reticent about intensive minerals extraction within their borders, at least beyond securing essential goods and supplies. The same protection does not hold for many of Europe's rural peripheries, and this is becoming starker by the day – from Ireland, to Portugal, to Spain, to Serbia.

Why is this the case? In literature on the 'resource curse' and underdevelopment, the argument is that the external development and exportation of 'surplus' to core imperial countries creates a durable relationship which implements basic dependencies (Patnaik and Patnaik 2021; Rodney 2022) – whether expertise, financing, or humanitarian aid. The depth of these dependencies and under- or de-development are of course different from Ireland to Serbia to Chile to the nations of Central Africa, as are degrees of ecological vulnerability and the ability to manage and remediate harm. However, the basic pattern holds across a spectrum of peripheralisation. From structural adjustment paradigms – which, in the case of the European PIIGS economies, included mandatory privatisation of state assets and resources – to classical regimes of imperial extraction, the exportation of harm from the core to support the exportation of value from peripheries remains fundamental.

That said, it is important to acknowledge why even a semi-peripheral country such as Ireland continues to support these primary extractive industries. The promise of modernisation *via* external investment remains the basic unifying factor. Over its postcolonial history, Ireland has enabled extensive exploitation of zinc and copper reserves, and has developed significant infrastructure and expertise in developing these resources (Murray 2024). The existing groundwork is seen as a continuing reason to facilitate extraction, this time to support EU measures towards digitalisation and decarbonisation, factoring in geopolitical manoeuvres surrounding sustainability and energy security. As Thea Riofrancos describes the situation with regards to lithium, crucial to digital technologies and 'clean' energy storage:

> First, Global North governments are promoting domestic lithium projects to enhance 'supply chain security'. Second, these same governments have committed to 'sustainably sourcing' lithium. Both phenomena are unexpected: harmful extraction is generally sited in the Global South, and sustainability rarely factors into interstate competition. (2023)

This landscape represents an emerging aspect of the green, digital transition: the shoring up of transparently extractive supply chains branded towards sustainability, whereby countries such as Ireland can support 'socially-necessary extraction' via more 'developed' ecological management strategies. The International Energy Agency (IEA) estimates that, to support decarbonised energy development, 'since 2010, the average amount of mineral resources needed for a new unit of power generation capacity has increased by 50% as the share of renewables in new investment has risen' (IEA 2022). Ongoing demand for these same minerals – such as lithium, copper, cobalt, and rare earth elements – comes from the need to power and manufacture digital devices and infrastructures. From a fossil-fuelled world to a simultaneously minerally intensive and 'atmospheric' green, digital capitalism, the extractive geographies of capital are multiplying rather than contracting.

This process has political, scientific, discursive, and material elements, and it gets to the core of our critique: that the eco-modern consensus inherits a foundationally colonial-extractive logic, premised on the continuation of unequal global exchange for 'sustainable' progress. The core aspect of dispossession at the heart of imperialist modernisation gets transferred into 'well-meaning' discussions of development, supported by technoscientific designation of territory for extraction. Territories can 'modernise', but only if they know what to do with their resources – which requires technology, expertise, and capital that Global Northern economies are happy to import, for the small price of the rights to extract materials and profits (Arboleda 2020). The World Economic Forum (WEF), for example, advocates critical raw materials as 'opportunities for green industrialization' in 'developing countries' (Botwright and Dabré 2024). The WEF references that the African continent contains 30 per cent of the world's mineral reserves. However, similar to arguments about wind and carbon sequestration, and all the way back to the basic ideas about FDI-led industrialisation in earlier chapters, the argument remains that 'expertise' must be brought from elsewhere: these countries can leverage their resources to 'catch up', but that requires importing knowledge via exploration and mining rights.

The mining industry has, for its part, turned towards its role as an 'enabler' of electrification and a 'clean energy future', a future that the Irish state is more than happy to facilitate. In 2024, the Irish Strategic Investment Fund, under the state National Treasury Management Agency, announced a €30 million commitment to the Irish Minerals Fund, a strategic partnership with South Africa/UK-based Lionhead Resources. With a focus on 'regional development' and alignment with climate-orientated business, and activating an acknowledged history of mining expertise, the Fund will 'seek minority investments in value-creating, ESG-responsible, high-quality metals and mining investments in the Republic of Ireland. The investment strategy will focus on ESG-responsible projects with proven mineral deposits, including zinc as the primary product, and strong social licenses in the community' (ISIF nd). Lionhead Resources, for its part, is focussed on 'investors in the minerals critical to a prosperous, clean energy future' (Lionhead Resources nd). The centrality of zinc, copper, and lithium in Ireland's resource extraction investments is a result of multiple overlapping state and corporate interests – which hinge primarily on their role in energy transition, although conspicuously not overtly referencing digitalisation.

In early 2021, two new prospecting licences were granted to Chinese and Canadian mining companies to explore the lithium reserves buried in granite in the Wicklow Mountains (The Hard Shoulder 2022). UK exploration company Technology Metals was similarly prospecting for lithium reserves in Leinster, selling its development rights to Australian company European Lithium in 2024.[9] This multinational land grab for elements is due not only to changing material requirements of technologies in energy and digital tech – these are not necessarily 'new' mineral requirements – but also the simultaneous resource intensity of emerging technologies themselves (International Energy Association 2022). Karelian Diamond Resources PLC announced in 2024 that it had 'discovered' copper, nickel, and platinum reserves while prospecting for diamonds in Fermanagh. Nickel and platinum are advocated as replacements for more damaging lithium exploitation in electric vehicle (EV) batteries, and platinum is used to mitigate emission waste. As certain minerals become more valuable, new resource frontiers are continually opened – making fights against extractivism a daunting prospect when depending upon reactive, localised campaigns.

As Daniel Macmillan Voskoboynik and Diego Andreucci recognise, the political dimensions of 'green' extractivism, and as we argue its relationships to monopoly tech, are as much discursive as material. Green extractivism takes shape through policies and research conducted under identifiable ideological umbrellas. Like 'critical infrastructure', 'critical minerals' are about streamlining the process of securing raw materials for top-down green transitions. These designations discursively set the agenda and conditions for a certain type of action, orientated towards maintaining the hegemony of private, multinational industrial development. This 'social engineering', as it is referred to regarding the mining industry, is both subtle and not so subtle, ranging from discursive campaigns in the local press and language from politicians, to overt counter-insurgency and violent policing (Dunlap and Riquito 2023).

One key vehicle for this is university research aligned with the scientific support of the industry. For example, iCRAG promoted a series called 'Writing the Earth', which connected with the Irish Writers Centre to promote funding for writers working across 'climate justice and geoscience' (iCRAG 2023b). Considering iCRAG's current industry partners, which include mining companies Trevali Mining Corporation, Black Angel Mining, Rio Tinto, and Greenfields Exploration,[10] along with fossil fuel companies (and Bord na Móna (BnM)), CAIM organised a boycott of the initiative, arguing that it provided 'social licence' via greenwashing to an industry attempting to reform its image towards green minerals. ISI and GSI regularly produce pamphlets and policy recommendations supporting expanded mining in Europe and Ireland, including a 2023 report entitled 'A More Diverse, Sustainable Supply of Critical Raw Materials in Europe', arguing that for Ireland to 'support' Europe's transition from 'brown to green', it needed to 'streamline its permitting process' and 'de-risk resource exploration finance', as well as commit to more effective social engineering:

> While due process is essential, opposition still arises from incomplete understanding of the environmental standards applicable to modern mining practices or an unwillingness to locate mines in certain localities or communities. Further collaboration and communication with all stakeholders, including local authorities, will be essential for understanding and acceptance of modern mining. (IGI nd 5)

Continuing on from the previous chapter, these extractive industries are in large part not only enabled by the state, but also supported by a public research ecosystem intended to develop Ireland's green ambitions – and this provides scientific and discursive cover for the ongoing ecological consequences of large-scale corporate mining. Beyond greenwashing, this is about constructing a vision of the world in the image of green capitalism. If the eco-modern consensus is about a twinned transition of economic growth decarbonisation and digitalisation, the expertise that comes along with managing the contradictions is crucial in terms of maintaining and scientifically legitimising the paradigm. Researchers effectively become mouthpieces of the industry, and propose its solutions as those that will ultimately, and effectively, support green, digital industrialisation.

We should be clear here, before we move on, that the entry of the mining industry into discourses of 'sustainability' and even environmental politics as a self-promoted protagonist is a novel, and transparently cynical, development[11] – more akin to the fossil fuel industry than monopoly tech, whose relatively recent development has roughly coincided with the rise of green capitalism. Mining is an industry known for exporting its most harmful practices of extraction and refinement to the Global South; an industry that is globally responsible for multitudes of human rights abuses and dispossessions. The dream of European planners to bring the industry under closer territorial scrutiny at the 'security–sustainability nexus' (Riofrancos 2023) is directly related to the regime of calculability within which monopoly tech intensifies the concentration of resources and accumulation *through* the promotion of greater infrastructural efficiency. Mining is only 'necessary' for climate action because climate action is reduced to a top-down framework of brute like-for-like substitution to enable digitally driven growth and capitalist accumulation – a form of eco-modernity that continues to produce winners and losers through the core-periphery relations of imperial capitalism.

Thus, we come to the crux of the contradictions of the green, digital transition: more than just data centres, wind farms, and carbon services, it is about securing mineral supply chains for electrification and its digital management. And it is through the struggle to secure these supply chains, extending from minerals to the manufacturing of chips, that imperial rivalries and geopolitical tensions are surfacing most acutely today. How do we continue to put pressure on these connections, while acknowledging that they are both hard to connect directly to the operations of monopoly tech in Ireland, and part of a wider logic of environmental governance and facilitation of FDI-led growth? As we argue in the next section, framing this only as a problem of 'extractivism' has its limitations – especially if we are to engage with the core problem of 'development' that brought mining to Ireland in the first place as a bellwether of the postcolonial ecological regime.

The limits of extractivism

As we emphasise in other chapters, digital media is functionally energetic – and electronic, depending upon the conductivity of metals to transmit information (Pasek et al 2023). From Marconi's radio to the iPhone, electronic media has required the marshalling of energy in and through material apparatuses, which extends from remote sites of generation to increasingly distributed electronic devices. It has become the central facet of monopoly tech strategies to secure these energetic apparatuses through control of infrastructure, as we trace in prior chapters. However, it is impossible to understand this without seeing how the core of these supply chains remain raw materials – something that the mining industry is quick to emphasise. In a 2024 article, the website Mining.com incredulously pointed out that NVIDIA, the primary chip provider for high-intensity AI computing, was valued higher than the 'entire listed mining industry', briefly overtaking Apple as the most valuable company in the world (Els 2024). However, as the article acknowledges, these companies have become exceptionally powerful based on their ability to marshal multiple material supply chains into electronic devices and their operation in production and communication. What makes digital media unique in this sense is how it multiplies and intensifies the regime of extraction across these various areas of activity, necessitating greater integrated operation of geographically distributed extractive supply chains (Brodie 2024).

'Extractivism' has been theorised extensively across disciplines and contexts as a material and epistemological strategy of the state and capital.[12] To anti-extractivist theorists and activists, it represents *the application of a logic of violent dispossession* of landscapes and peoples in resource-rich territories towards the ongoing accumulation of capital and, in particular, economic growth centred on powerful productive centres.[13] Discourses surrounding the growth and importance of mining, usually driven by the industry itself, argue for its economic benefits, employment opportunities, and fostering of 'independence', the latter characteristic making it especially attractive to elites and planners in postcolonial states. In Ireland, where FDI is an index of global capitalist growth compromised and managed through the state, speaks to the deepening of extractive logics in modes of governance centred on attracting multinational investment and/in infrastructure.

Developed most prominently by Latin American theorists and activists looking at mining and, later, forms of agrarian extractivism, the concept has been expanded, sometimes unhelpfully, to include an eclectic range of activities – from finance capital to data mining to renewable development. Scholars have spent a lot of time unpacking what exactly extractivism means in such a stretched context (Gago and Mezzadra 2017; Szeman and Wenzel 2021), addressing its analytical and practical utility at a time where global dynamics of capital appear to be intensifying via extractive relations. What extractivism identifies, and what makes it an important concept for the international left, is a continued directional imbalance that speaks to the *unequal global geographies and ecologies* of extraction that sustain contemporary imperial formations of capital. In this way, extractivism is a (globally) distributed rather than (nationally) concentrated phenomenon – one that makes it sometimes tricky to reconcile with the monopolistic and verticalised supply chains of multinational tech companies, who remain intentionally distanced from the sites and practices of mining and manufacturing that form the hardware of their operations.

But at the same time, there has perhaps never been more lively discussion surrounding extractivism as it operates within hegemonic formations of global capital from digital to energy industries – and especially in discourses of green extractivism, which Dunlap et al define as 'a system of extractive development that harnesses climate change and other socioecological crises as profit-generating and re-branding opportunities' (2024, 438). There is little doubt at this stage that green capitalism and its supporting variants – green colonialism, green grabbing, eco-imperialism[14] – is a branding exercise as much as a material transformation, and there has been a similarly diverse proliferation of critical theories to accompany these changes. However, as we have argued, capitalism branded green has implications for how nation-states adapt developmental strategies to accommodate these market and policy orientations, occurring within existing and durable geopolitical structures.

As capitalism is branded green, it has also become inextricable from modes of production heralded by the 'fourth industrial revolution', with Europe's 'security– sustainability nexus' (Riofrancos 2023) linked explicitly to 'smart' technologies in electrification and transport. As Martín Arboleda posits, it is not necessarily the types of extraction that change during this 'fourth machine age', rather it is the extensivity and networked character of extraction that feeds material components of networked devices. As he observes, with up to 30 metals contained in an iPhone, this '"one device" that has come to mediate even the most mundane activities of everyday urban life, then, puts us in relation of direct material intercourse with the networks of territorial infrastructures of the mining supply chain' (2020, 244). In that way, the same processes that source and build the iPhone are also those making the iPhone 'an instrument of extraction', which Arboleda theorises through the extractive relations of labour in 'smart' cities and surveillance capitalism (2020, 244–5). This 'explosion of the mine', that 'mine shafts and pits … are merely the starting point of an intricate system of generalized transnational intercourse that brings together ecosystems, workers, and cities, into a complex unity under the spatial division of labor', shows how the growth and automation of extraction in this fourth machine age are expanding in lock-step, but in geographically and ecologically uneven ways. Digital technology acts as a tool of not only efficiency, but also as a way to distance extractive impacts and contradictions from the actual activity of extraction – especially as digital efficiencies permeate extractive supply chains.[15]

But, as Arboleda acknowledges, the fallout of and modes of navigating this explosion is also massively geographically differentiated, which we emphasise when linking the operations of monopoly tech via the disarticulated distribution and concentration of data centres, wind farms, energy grids, research centres, and peatlands. By understanding global capitalism in its unfolding 'planetary' dimensions, in terms of the necessary coordination of materials across territories by multinational supply chains, we see how digital machinery permeates through these processes, opening new pathways towards efficiencies. This, however, is still related to basic structures of dependency, and the flow of technology from core to periphery, with materials and profits flowing in the opposite direction.

Thus, to make sense of this, we take cues on the political ecology of extractivism from Max Ajl's recent work.[16] He shares with Arboleda, us, and others an apprehension towards the overemphasis on the centrality of extractivism within contemporary capitalism. 'Extractivism', he writes, 'confuses a technical system – extraction of minerals like oil or under-processed agricultural riches – with a mode of accumulation' (2023). This confusion can result in a conflation of extractivism with capitalism, rather than identifying how extractivism relates to and operates within the capitalist world system. By placing the emphasis on extractive activities, and their adverse social and environmental impacts, the burden of political agency is placed on the Global South. 'Extractivismo', as Ajl points out, 'too often offers a political ecology without a geopolitics of development: eco-socialism in one country' (2023, 23). From this perspective, the failure of progressive governments to dismantle the extractive base of their dependent economies has been met with criticism by anti-extractivist activists and researchers – in particular, the critique of governments emerging from Latin America's 'pink tide', which in many cases sought to intensify such activities (as Arboleda also emphasises). What this amounts to is an anti-state anti-extractivism that opts instead for an internationalist left position that effectively seeks to by-pass the state, investing instead in an amorphous, transnational, or even internationalist, civil society as agent of change (Moyo and Yeros 2007, 174).[17]

Rather than jettisoning the national question, or dismissing dependency theory and the need for delinking from the imperialist world system, Ajl and others offer a textured and overtly anti-imperialist reading of the contradictions thrown up by national sovereign development and socialist construction in the Global South.[18] By foregrounding imperialism in an analysis of extractivism, the national question becomes central – as in, how does the country forge a just, sovereign path of development independent of the imperial core? This was the question animating socialist Third World thinkers such as Samir Amin from the 1950s, who were as critical of autarkic models of national development as they were of neocolonial economic arrangements that sought to deepen economic entanglements with the imperial core. For example, Walter Rodney emphasised that 'nationalisation' when performed within the 'international division of labour and the international allocation of resources could well mean that production is no more independent than if it had remained in the hands of foreign enterprises' (2022, 103). The detailed and nationally specific work of Third World Marxist thinkers such as Rodney, Amin, and Amílcar Cabral invites the further elaboration of their methods and perspectives, seeing the project of decolonial national sovereign development as unfinished rather than exhausted (Molinero and Pedregal 2024). In their work, we see that delinking from the world economy involves a more far-reaching, planned re-organisation of national production and markets, a progressive 'nationalisation' of the law of value. On this basis, any anti-imperialist, socialist transition *requires* nationalism as 'a necessary, but not sufficient, ideological force in the periphery' (Moyo and Yeros 2007, 173–4).

Since the 1980s, the shunning of the national (and agrarian) question has also quietened debate over the substance of an alternative development model. Resisting extractivism is crucial, but positing an effective, popular plan for social and economic development is another story - one that the left often fails to tell effectively. Once we engage with this concretely, we realise that transition to more sustainable, equitable models of development across the world will require some form of material extraction, perhaps more intensive in some places for a time. We also should realise that such scales of planning require a state capable of mobilising resources, labour, and popular support for projects, which does not also offload toxicity and environmental contradictions onto ever more marginalised and 'wasted' populations and ecologies. In such a model, decisions and value would be democratically centred on material needs and social benefits for such places. Questions related to such (eco)socialist construction are largely missing from debates on post-extractivism, an absence that belies the fact that such debates were rich and lively across the decolonising majority world in the 1960s and 1970s (Ajl 2023).[19] Returning to the opening vignette, the urgent danger of an anti-extractivist politics *without* a robust engagement with development as a potentially progressive force under alternative ecological circumstances opens space for more reactionary 'anti-modern' stances.

The constructive limits of extractivism as a framework for understanding the changing nature of Irish capitalism and eco-modernity within the world system are illustrated profoundly in County Mayo. Here, separated by 50 years, are two fundamentally different regimes of resource extraction that are rarely, if at all, distinguished as such. In 1996, the Corrib gas field was 'discovered' by a consortium of petroleum companies, including Enterprise Oil. It was the first commercial gas discovery in Ireland since 1973. The consortium planned to pipe the gas from the Corrib gas field and refine it onshore at Rossport, in North West Mayo. Under the licence agreement signed in 1993, the Irish state only received 25 per cent of revenue on any discoveries. This was significantly less than other European and North American countries, and less than the average across the Middle East and North Africa. As Amanda Slevin writes, Ireland appeared 'to have internalised the idea of natural resources as "free gifts" of nature to such an extent that it demands one of the lowest rates of government take in existence in exchange for the privatisation of its resources' (2016, 125).[20]

In 2002, Royal Dutch Shell bought out Enterprise Oil and proceeded with plans to build the refinery in Rossport. Community opposition grew as the state instituted compulsory purchase of lands for the pipeline. Local concerns about environmental and health risks were ignored. Protests reached a head in 2005 when five men from Rossport were arrested for refusing to obey a court injunction forbidding them from interfering with work undertaken by Shell on their land.[21] Across the country, pickets and boycotts of Shell filling stations broke out. Shell sites around Rossport were blockaded by the men's neighbours, preventing work. After years of planning reviews and delays due to unsafe design and construction on the part of Shell, the refinery finally began operating in 2015.

Less than 40 km from the Shell refinery is the Oweninny bog complex, which had been industrially mined for peat since the 1960s. The state-owned Bellacorick peat station, supplied by peat from Oweninny, was decommissioned in 2003, exactly 40 years since it was first opened as the 'event of the century', celebrated with a dance in Crossmolina town hall (see Chapter 2). When the cooling tower was demolished in 2007, more than 3,000 people came to pay respects. Brendan Delaney, Archive and Heritage Manager with the Electricity Supply Board (ESB), was one of the onlookers. 'For the local community it's nearly like attending the wake of a close friend', he said (quoted in Irish Independent 2007).

What is the difference between the extraction and refining of gas in the early 21st century, and the extraction and combustion of peat in the mid-20th century in the west of Ireland? Both developments engaged in the ecologically damaging removal of materials from the ground for the purpose of 'economic' and 'industrial development'. But from a *political* ecological perspective, the industrial peat extraction carried out by BnM bears little resemblance to the industrial gas extraction carried out by Shell at the turn of the 21st century. Barely miles apart, these resource-extracting projects must be understood within their wider, global (imperial) political and economic contexts. The development of the Oweninny bog complex can be seen as part of an incomplete project of delinking from energy dependence on Britain, a limited project of national sovereign development and industrialisation. The development of the Corrib gas refinery by a consortium of multinational oil companies, paying minimal revenue to the state, was, conversely, a symptom of Ireland's re-linking to the capitalist world system underway since the 1960s as part of FDI-led development. The contrast between the celebrations at the opening of Bellacorick power station in 1963, and the intense protests by local communities and the wider Shell to Sea Campaign in 2005, also gives some indication of the different class formations behind these widely divergent forms of state development. What Corrib represents, then, is not just the privatisation of energy resources, or a reliance on export-led extractive industries, but a more profound shift in Ireland's position within the world capitalist system, dominated by US (and EEC) interests and enabled by an internal comprador class.

Ajl's perspective is critical of the term extractivism in part because it blurs the distinction between these types of development (Riofrancos 2020). Below we aim to connect more recent waves of anti-extractivist environmental campaigns with a longer continuum of environmental movements on the island – specifically, anti-colonial and anti-imperialist environmental movements that led with the national and agrarian question. Earlier campaigns and political organisations were not just reacting against 'extractive' projects, but systemic de-development, recognising the need for a long-term strategy of sovereign, popular development for people throughout Ireland and abroad. In deliberately connecting these different eras and modalities of anti-colonial, land-based struggles in Ireland, we invite reflection on how earlier movements map onto global green, digital capitalism.

Anti-imperialist environmental politics

In this section we focus on the sites, subjects, and political cultures that have taken shape in response to Ireland's postcolonial ecological regime. A key argument we want to make in this section is that while the scholarly periodisation of rural environmental movements in Ireland usually dates from the 1980s anti-toxics movement (Allen 2004), earlier campaigns demanding the nationalisation of key sectors and more radical agrarian reform offer a way of highlighting the anti-colonial and anti-imperialist endurances of land-based protest politics on the island. While the forms of resistance that arise, and their political articulation, are diverse and often ambivalent, the continuity stems from a clear opposition to state development policy from the 1960s. Drawing again on Tovey's concept of 'populist environmentalism' (1993), these struggles and campaigns are rooted in grievances borne out of a sense that infrastructures and development policies are not for 'the people'. The ambivalence lies in a strain of conservatism that arises from place-based environmental politics, territorial and community-based identity, and anti-state sentiment. But when articulated from the left, this populism has generated an outward-looking perspective, the building of national coalitions, and networks with peripheral movements across the Global South that can offer lessons for potentially building on vibrant anti-extractivist organising in Ireland.

The Resource Study Group was begun by students in Trinity College Dublin in 1970 (Figure 6.2). They published pamphlets and short reports on the Irish state's policy around resource development, focussed on the role of multinational mining and petroleum corporations, and the minimal social and economic benefits that accrued to the Irish people through state concessions and tax arrangements. In 1973, the group developed into the Resource Protection Campaign (RPC), founded by the Communist Party of Ireland and Official Sinn Féin. The RPC described themselves as 'a non-political public education campaign which has as its main objective the development of State companies to explore for, produce and develop industries from our immense natural wealth' (Resource Protection Campaign 1975). One of the earliest campaigns was after the 1971 discovery of gas offshore in Kinsale, County Cork, with exclusive rights sold to the US-based Marathon oil company. As with the mining concessions in counties Galway and Tipperary, the Irish Government failed to secure control over the resource and could only command relatively nominal royalties on tax-free profits – payments to the state on Tynagh, Silvermines, and Tara Mines were as little as £1.7 million by 1973.

While an Irish state mining company and state oil company did technically exist, these are referred to by the RPC as 'paper holding companies', that ensure a minimal equity stake in resources otherwise licensed to and developed by multinationals – state ownership of resources is not the same as state development of those resources. In contrast, the RPC called for active state resource companies that would retain ownership and revenues from natural resources, enable the development of ancillary industries, provide employment, expand domestic markets, and ensure less pollution and environmental damage from extractive activities. Rather than mediate the extraction and development of resource deposits via multinational investment, with environmental protections and place considerations slapped on, the RPC's proposal was for the public reorientation of resource extraction. Alongside sector-specific state companies, the RPC also called for a state industrial board to work in concert with these companies, with powers to direct the investment patterns of public and private enterprise, and to carry out a 'degree of planning unheard of in the economic history of Ireland'.

Unsurprisingly, there is not much historical information available about the RPC. We know their campaign was supported by student and trade union movements, and that they established local branches in parts of Dublin and other major towns. What is significant in the context of this chapter, and book, is the analysis they offered of Ireland's postcolonial ecological regime and how this differs from contemporary anti-extractivist politics. Adopting an anti-imperialist dependency framework allowed them to not only identify the loss of direct revenue from concessions with multinational companies, but also the much more significant lost development opportunities and surplus value associated with expanding Ireland's industrial base through smelting and processing. As Ray Crotty diagnosed in the 1980s, the RPC also identified

Figure 6.2: Cartoon from Resources Study Group pamphlet (1970, 32)

how multinational companies were establishing 'enclave industries' that effectively meant taking advantage of domestic resources, infrastructures, low taxation, and access to EEC markets, while giving back little in terms of employment, industrial development or reduced dependence on high-cost imports. In a classic formulation of unequal exchange – what they call 'neocolonialism' (Figure 6.3) – the RPC articulates how multinational companies have no incentive to invest in capital-intensive processing plants in Ireland when they can export the raw or smelted metals to their existing plants (located in the US, Germany, France, or the UK). In turn, these processed products were sold back to Ireland at a higher cost, perpetuating the flow of surplus value from the (semi-)periphery to the core. The challenge presented by the RPC was not just for the state to retain ownership of natural resources, but to ensure that use, development, and value derived from production was retained in Ireland.

The importance of this dependency theory framework is highlighted by developments with Tara Mines in Navan. Tara Mines was an Irish company granted an exploration licence by the Irish Government in the 1950s. Significant zinc ore deposits were discovered in the 1960s. While these were owned by the state, Tara Mines was given the contract to develop the site with a minority ownership stake and royalties guaranteed to the state. The Government also ensured that zinc ore was smelted onsite, to retain the added value. However, in 1974, the company was taken over by a consortium of corporations: a South African-based Anglo-American company and two Canadian mining companies (Resource Protection Campaign 1975). Now foreign-owned, these companies controlled the zinc ore, the smelter, and access to the EEC. Because the Government were focussed on equity, royalties, and tax, they failed to appreciate the greater significance of what the RPC termed 'stage 3 development', or processing – in fact, tax relief on exports was an incentive for private mining companies to export smelted metals to the EEC. This experience was for the RPC evidence of why there needed to be active state control of resource development – not just ownership of resources licensed to private companies, but full ownership of the process to ensure that surplus value did not continue to leak out of the country.

In a 1975 pamphlet entitled *Ireland's Resources: The Case for State Control*, the RPC concludes by citing BnM as an example of a state-owned enterprise

Figure 6.3: Cartoon from Resources Study Group pamphlet (1970, 13)

that effectively developed national resources. As well as developing the resource through the acquisition and drainage of 130,000 acres of bog, the state company built turf-powered power stations, provided thousands of jobs, reduced the cost of energy, and was now able to export capacities in R&D to other countries. Unsurprisingly, the RPC does not mention the ecological destruction wrought by such large-scale industrial development, but this has less to do with a politics of socialist construction and national sovereign development than the comparative lack of ecological understanding and awareness of bogs and climate change in the 1970s.[22] However imperfect, the RPC represents a historical current of anti-imperialist environmental politics that did not demand the cessation of extractive activities – whether peat, zinc, or gas – but rather the re-organisation of extractive activities around broadly socialist, anti-imperialist goals of producing socially useful goods, improved lives for the majority, and convergence between core and periphery.

From the 1960s, Irish Republicanism was alert to the question of development via 'economic imperialism' in the South, even after most of its attention had turned to the North and the border through the mid-20th century. For example, Irish Republican Army (IRA) leader Cathal Goulding proclaimed after the ill-fated Border Campaign (1956–62) that 'the salesmen of imperialism aided by their native servants commenced a systematic takeover of Irish assets, a systematic speculation in Irish money, Irish manpower, Irish land. The Army guarded a frontier while the imperialists quietly entered by another and laid claim to Ireland' (quoted in Finn 2019, 30–1). The IRA was involved in attacks on foreign-owned properties during the 1960s and 70s, with allegations that Jack Lynch, Irish Taoiseach at the time, requested that newspapers would not publicise statements from the IRA regarding such actions. The fear was that if the IRA became associated with land redistribution, they would gain rural popularity, especially along the border (Dooley 2004).[23] The language of nationalisation, anti-imperialism, agrarian reform, and resistance to foreign domination took on new meanings and significance in the context of the anti-colonial, militant struggle in the six counties. Rather than igniting an all-island reckoning with the unfinished project of decolonisation, the 26-county Southern state worked to distance itself from the North, driving a wedge between the political cultures of the two jurisdictions (McVeigh and Rolston 2021).[24]

Commonly, rural environmental politics in Ireland is assumed to begin in the 1980s, with Ireland's anti-toxics movement aligned with the broader genesis of ecological social movements across Europe, which are frequently critiqued by mainstream commentators for 'anti-modern' positions towards development. The significance of stretching this genealogy back to the land agitation campaigns of the 1960s and the work of the RPC, and their explicit connections to Ireland's unfinished project of decolonisation, is that it allows us to construct a tradition of *anti-imperialist* environmental politics on the island – even in cases where these movements were not explicitly orientated as such. As Terence Dooley points out in his book on the land question post-partition, the rhetoric adopted by land campaigns in the 1950s and 1960s drew explicitly on the rhetoric of the 19th-century Land League and its promise of 'land for the people' (2004). The Carlow campaign (Chapter 2) contended that the demand for 'free sale', which had been central to the 19th-century Land League, was never intended to enable foreign syndicates with unlimited capital to buy up land against small farmers. Despite the reactionary nationalist elements, the simmering grievances articulated in the demand for more radical agrarian reform were rooted in the understanding of a project unfinished. The same can be applied to the RPC, whose anti-imperialist rhetoric was obviously more explicit given the political composition of the campaign, but nonetheless also pointed to the endurance of Ireland's economic peripheralisation in the world economy and the need to advance further in order to realise the ideals of the Republican, socialist project.

While demands of nationalisation and agrarian reform did not carry over into the 1980s, there are still links between these earlier forms of 'populist' environmentalism and the anti-toxics and anti-extractivist campaigns that emerged towards the end of the 20th century (Allen 2004; also Figure 6.4). At a basic level, they concern material objections to Ireland's FDI-led developmental strategy from the 1950s, which occurred at the expense

Figure 6.4: Sister Majella McCarron with members of Ogoni Solidarity Ireland at the annual Action from Ireland (Afri) Famine Walk in County Mayo, 1995

Source: Ken Saro Wiwa Archive

of 'progressive' currents of national development orientated towards modernisation for distributed social good. To be clear, we don't advocate a return to past (resource) nationalist politics – even if that was possible. Reclaiming the buried currents of anti-imperialist land agitation within a left paradigm – wresting the promise of 'resource nationalism' from the hands of compradors, eco-modernists, and the far right alike, while presenting an alternative to 'FDI nationalism' – is essential for any successful environmental justice movement on the island. This is not just wishful thinking. Despite the falling away of earlier, nationalist demands and movements, the resonances between rural environmental protests in Ireland and other former colonies have not disappeared, especially in terms of shared experiences and anti-imperialist solidarities that continue to mobilise political action in Ireland.

The locus of more recent environmental movements in Ireland has tended to be on the socially and ecologically destructive elements of toxic industrial and extractive activities – with local communities being the key protagonists, supported by ENGOs and other networks of environmental activists.[25] What has been missing in these disparate if networked campaigns is a vision, even desire, for a different kind of development, one that would necessitate at least some aspects of state power capable of challenging relations of dependency, and mobilising land and resources towards different ends. If earlier instantiations of anti-colonial environmental politics were still invested in the promise of development, and the stakes of such an ambitious project, then it is not apparent where the promise of an anti-extractivist politics lies – once an extractive project is stopped, then what? While contemporary anti-extractivist movements and campaigns in Ireland continue to carry the banner of anti-colonial internationalism, particularly in opposition to mining, this has sometimes shied away from an older tradition of liberation struggle that rested on popular claims on the state and forms of national development capable of breaking with imperialist relations of dependency and unequal exchange. It is hard to see how we can overcome monopoly tech eco-modernity delivered under the guises of the 'twin transition' without reclaiming elements of this tradition.

There is another, arguably more pressing reason to engage more seriously in the political articulation of grievances around extractivism, development, and the green transition. As alluded to in the opening vignette, and reflected in the historical forms of land agitation and resource nationalism, there is a constant danger of reactionary, nativist protectionism. Rural environmental struggles have always been politically ambivalent, and cannot be naively claimed as blanket 'anti-colonial' or even 'anti-imperialist' – whether articulated in terms of conservation, anti-development, anti-toxicity, or anti-extractivism. The same strains of popular mobilisation in relation to land and in response to the activities of global capitalism in Ireland are present across multiple different political orientations. In Athenry, County Galway, for example, Apple tried to develop an €850 million data centre facility in spite of incomplete Environmental Impact Assessments (EIAs), which found that the company's promised ability to supply the facility with 100 per cent renewable energy was untrue and that the EIA had only accounted for the energy usage of a fraction of its proposed development. Long-time residents, hopeful for the prosperity that such a project could bring in the face of an area largely abandoned by state projects, nonetheless supported the project and saw it as an environmentally responsible alternative to other industries, even articulating their support through anti-colonial history and continuity on the land (Brodie 2020b). It created division, and supporters became frustrated with the state and the planning process that allowed two environmental objectors to hold up the project until Apple finally withdrew. In this context, appeals to the extractive enterprise of monopoly tech and its expansion of toxic supply chains – from local to global effects – were less important than local support of a potentially lucrative global company perceived as bringing 'development' to the region.

In Ennis, County Clare, on the other hand, where a company called Art Data Centres has attempted to build a primarily natural gas-fired data centre facility, residents feel like they are becoming a sacrifice zone for extractive and polluting infrastructures because of the data centre and its movement through the technocratic planning process. The campaign Futureproof Clare against the Shannon Liquefied Natural Gas (LNG) project got involved and connected this local issue to planetary environmental justice and Ireland's binding climate targets. It is a similar story for rural wind energy politics across the board, where groups are united by opposition to forms of development that enable large-scale wind farms without meaningful provision of local services and benefits.

What unites these differing political campaigns is not only their location in areas, towns, and villages classified as 'rural', but also their relationship and articulation within the connected destinies of energy, technology, and development within the postcolonial ecological regime. If we as scholars and activists do not start to get involved in understanding and articulating how these contexts are materially aligned, from Cork to Leitrim to Galway to Antrim, alternative narratives and connections will be made and capitalised upon by much more nefarious actors – whether US multinationals and their lobbyists or the far right. This is a huge question to confront, but it is central to think about in terms of key issues of land politics, resource sovereignty, decolonisation, self-determination, and other difficult terms concerning Ireland's enduring place within imperial capitalist networks. If we can show that different struggles in Ireland are aligned, from climate justice to military neutrality, as ENGOs and activist groups are already doing these alignments can begin to chart a way forward in the face of apparently irresolvable environmental contradictions. Multinational capital, of course, is clear in its alignments and long-term planning – in the case of Ireland aligning themselves with supportive state and semi-state boosters, and often acting as an extended arm of US foreign policy. The left must be equally, if not substantially more proactive.

There are examples of successful campaigns waged against large-scale developments, such as in Cork in the 1970s, leading to Raybestos Manhattan pulling out of the area, or the anti-gold mining campaign on Croagh Patrick in the 1980s. But these are few and far between, and more often than not the romantic narrative of 'David versus Goliath' ends with exhausted and divided communities, unable to withstand the conjoined forces of the post-developmental Irish state and global capital (Slevin 2019). As outlined in Chapter 3, it was precisely the success of earlier anti-toxics campaigns that provoked novel environmental governance, including more prescriptive planning legislation deliberately aimed at undermining democratic participation and scrutiny. Given the narrowing of political options via institutional mechanisms in the postcolonial ecological regime, as well as the practical limits of anti-extractivist discourse against ostensibly 'green' projects, there needs to be other avenues for organising local grievances and articulating them within wider progressive visions of the future. Constructing an alternative vision of development is part of this process, where land reform and public ownership are non-negotiable. A hollow appeal to partial efforts of sovereign development in the mid-20th century is not what we are arguing for – but there are strains there of an anti-imperialist environmental politics that can be salvaged and should be amplified in the present. This is particularly true at this juncture, when Irish reunification and Ireland's position within a fracturing world system have become salient political questions across the island once again.

Conclusion

By ending the empirical chapters of this book with an analysis of mining and minerals as industries entrenched within Ireland's FDI-led developmental histories, its colonial legacies, and its contemporary ecological transformation towards green, digital transition, we are focussing on what is a clear, vibrant site of environmental opposition to the postcolonial ecological regime on the island. The mining industry is well known for its means to contain resistance, which V'cenza Cirefice has articulated extensively in her research with the Save Our Sperrins campaign against the Dalradian gold mine (Cirefice and Sullivan 2019; Cirefice 2021). But across the continuities in environmental campaigns that have arisen around mining and other 'toxic' industries in the postcolonial ecological regime, we notice a tendency towards (often necessarily) reactive, rural struggles against individual companies and global industries that are *enabled and facilitated by the state, North and South*, to exploit and extract resources for monopoly capital accumulation. What we are talking about is uneven development within the global economy, and a state development model designed to support that for its own benefit. What is perhaps backgrounded in our existing apprehension and support of these movements, however, is a more robust and systematic sense of how these individual campaigns map onto the world ecology. Peripheralised territories are always made to be zones of valorisation for entrenched systems of accumulation. How this is taking shape to support monopoly tech eco-modernity is our theatre of struggle against this ongoing expansion, in Ireland and beyond.

This chapter thus attempts to consolidate some of the book's earlier insights into the history of Irish developmentalism through the lens of extraction and extractivism. In particular, by looking at mineral extraction in Ireland exists in a clear and instructive continuum across early multinational investment in the 1960s–1970s to the 'green' minerals and wider forms of multinational, digital extractivism arising today. By narrating and analysing this history, we try to understand the legacy and ongoing purchase of anti-colonial land struggles within contemporary movements against green extractivism on the island. In doing so, what we emphasise is that the perceived 'anti-modern' stance of such movements reflects a response to a dominant regime of understanding land and ecology in Ireland, which relegates its management to the necessity of monopoly capital accumulation and expansion.

In analysing these campaigns, we want to emphasise that it is not just 'development' and 'progress' that is at stake within transitions from fossil fuels and polluting industries to supposedly more 'atmospheric' solutions via the cloud and renewable energy: these projects are happening in places that have experienced long histories of de-, under-, and over-development as enacted across what we call the postcolonial ecological regime. These include the simultaneous under-development of vital infrastructures, such as water provisioning, and the over-development of private, multinational industrial facilities and activities. These emplaced relations matter for understanding the chronic conditions extending across the last 50-plus years of Irish economic development (and rooted in longer colonial histories). Only by understanding this can we comprehend the kinds of political cultures that take shape. This is true whether discussing communities who overtly connect their grievances to a longer history of colonisation, postcolonial under-development, and networks of multinational capital – such as the case in the anti-mining campaigns forming around the CAIM network on the island – or anti-wind objectors who argue that the liveability and viability of their communities are being affected by these 'green' infrastructures. And beyond this, deeply analysing the histories and political cultures that motivate and provoke these struggles is an essential task for modelling an alternative future.

We argue that we should understand contestations against monopoly tech eco-modernity fuelled by expanded modes of extractivism through an anti-imperialist framework that borrows from earlier forms of land-based politics on the island. The common-sensical alignment of industrial development *with* multinational capital in the form of these and other industrial activities has been a state strategy for over half a century, meaning we need to realistically navigate the common sense that we have traced throughout this book as it has permeated through Ireland – much like the wider neoliberal common sense proposing the lack of alternatives to capitalism. One of the consequences of this strategy has been the conflation of the state with negative interventions, particularly in certain rural regions. This experience and feeling cannot be countered by abstract appeals to or fights against the 'state'; it must be about reclaiming aspects of the state and transforming institutions into a vehicle of popular transition, particularly as this relates to land reform and social control of production. Equally, large-scale visions of development, anti-imperialism, and translocal solidarity do not need to be opposed to one another. It just means reshaping the proposed horizon, from solidarity and struggle to an eco-socialist future orientated against green, digital capitalism. What we need to build is something that is specific to the current situation – not necessarily national liberation struggle, nor a localised David versus Goliath, but something with anti-colonial and anti-imperialist campaigns and histories as inspirations and allies, connecting town and country against the dependent arrangement of eco-modern transformation. This is a premise that we develop further in the Conclusion.

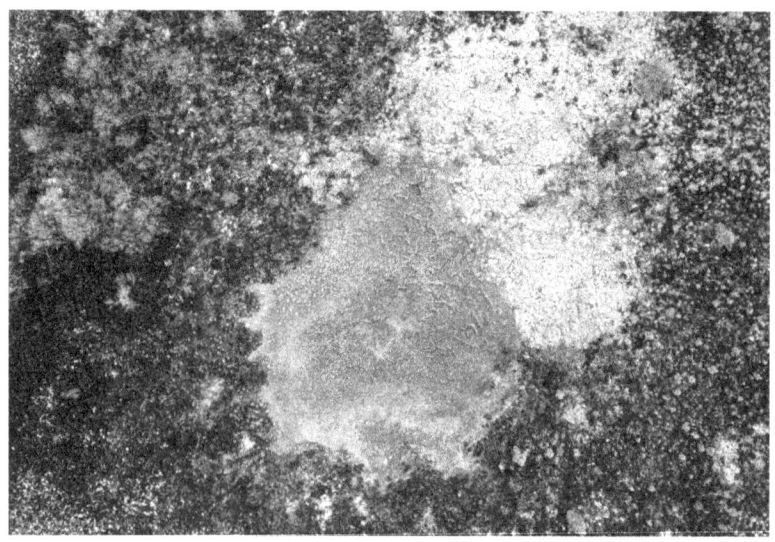

Conclusion

From the plough to the stars

Over the past two years, Ireland has gained a reputation as the 'most pro-Palestine country in Europe' following mass mobilisations against the genocide in Gaza since the 7 October 2023 uprising. This reputation is not unearned, and in fact rests on a much longer history of solidarity, especially among Republican communities in the North, who have long seen (and made) allies in the Palestinian anti-colonial struggle. However, the fierceness of this same support in the South has taken some politicians by surprise, and even centre-right Government parties Fine Gael and Fianna Fáil have been vocally critical of Israel, making Ireland an outlier in Europe. That said, Ireland's greatest complicity in the US-Israeli project is in its trade links, and despite the rhetoric from the ruling coalition, there has been zero real threat of sanctions.[1]

In November 2024, a report from The Ditch reveals that the US Ambassador had written directly to the Tánaiste (deputy Prime Minister) warning of 'consequences' if Ireland enacted the Occupied Territories Bill (OTB) (The Ditch Editors 2024). The proposed law, first brought forward in 2018, would ban and criminalise trade with companies operating in or from illegal settlements in occupied territories (as determined under international law) – in particular, Israeli settlements in Israeli-occupied Palestinian territories. Despite widespread popularity, and unanimous support across opposition parties, the Bill is once again 'sent for review' following the Ambassador's intervention. In her email, the Ambassador cited more than 1,000 US companies located in Ireland that would be adversely affected by the passing of the OTB. Though it may not seem significant, and it only demonstrates what many know to be the case: that this is an overt example of US imperialism working through Ireland.

Also in November, a coalition of groups including the Rosa Socialist Feminist Movement, University College Dublin BDS, and United against Racism organise a protest outside of the annual Irish Technology Industry Awards. The protest is held in support of 'No Tech for Apartheid', a growing global worker-led movement against the complicity of monopoly tech in the Israeli genocide and apartheid system. The event is sponsored by Fidelity Investments and recognises the contributions of Hewlett Packard, both BDS boycott targets for their support for the Israeli occupation. Along with a focus on Gaza and the Israeli military, protestors chant at attendees about the tech industry's complicity in human rights abuses surrounding mining materials for batteries in the Democratic Republic of the Congo (DRC). While sponsored by multinationals, the event is organised by IBEC-listed lobby group Technology Ireland. IBEC is the leading coalition of industry lobby groups in Ireland, and one of the primary civil society organs of Ireland's foreign direct investment (FDI)-led development model. The protest is thus orientated against state strategies that continue to facilitate these companies being in Ireland – packaged within a more overarching aim of ending Ireland's complicity in the murder and oppression of Palestinians and Congolese.

The day after the Irish Technology Awards action, there is a protest against the controversial Shannon Liquefied Natural Gas (LNG) terminal project, organised by the Climate Justice Coalition. This 'March for Global Climate Justice' is geared around three overlapping demands: End fossil fuels, Stop Shannon LNG, and End the Genocide – the latter focussed on getting the government to enact the OTB. Just before leaving government in late 2024, the Green Party supported a change in policy to allow Ireland to import fracked gas, reversing their previous commitment and angering environmental movements. New Fortress Energy, the company responsible for the proposed Shannon LNG, has also entered the data centre business to shore up its energy supply investments. But even in places where new gas infrastructure won't be directly tied to data centres, activist groups are pointing their fingers at data centres – including a group called Galway against Gas, who have made data centres the primary villain in their fight against a new gas plant in Tynagh. The protest by the Climate Justice Coalition is connecting all these dots: gas expansion, climate change, imperialist-backed genocide in Gaza, and the continued development of data centres and their disproportionate energy consumption. It's a hard narrative to capture, and the messaging around these connections is sometimes unclear, particularly to mainstream environmentalists.[2]

Soon after this protest, there is another demonstration planned, but this time more overtly against the specific infrastructures of tech in Ireland and their challenging of Ireland's climate goals. Friends of the Earth (FoE) Ireland, Extinction Rebellion (XR), Not Here Not Anywhere, and the Irish Palestinian Solidarity Campaign (IPSC) organise a protest against the annual Data Centres Ireland conference at the Royal Dublin Society (RDS), a relic of colonial Ireland as the name suggests. The conference, which we've attended before, is part of a global series organised by industry group Stepex and heavily supported by global data centre groups such as Uptime Institute. Also heavily represented are Irish-specific lobbying organisations across the data centre and energy sectors such as Host in Ireland (for Ireland-based companies), Cloud Infrastructure Ireland (the IBEC voice of the monopoly tech hyperscalers), Wind Energy Ireland, and the Irish Solar Energy Association. This time, the intent of the protest is to foreground the climate impacts of data centres in Ireland, for many of the reasons sketched throughout this book. A poster made by FoE shows an illustration of underground gas lines spewing emissions through the inner workings of a data centre, with the word 'toxic' integrated into the machinery. The slogan is: 'Stop the power grab! We demand a moratorium on data centres. Why is the Irish Government letting Big Tech burn our future for their profits?' While this message is clear, the presence of the IPSC is new. Inside the event, two protestors disrupt a keynote from Barry Lowry, the Irish Government's Chief Information Officer, with a banner protesting the role of Ireland's facilitation of these companies in the genocide in Gaza. Outside, Helen from the IPSC gives a speech calling out the role of Google, Amazon, and other tech companies headquartered in Ireland for developing software to further enable Israeli apartheid and genocide. Hurried guests pushed through the blockade, and inside, Gardaí pulled suspicious-looking characters from the crowd to prevent further disruption. The business of green, digital FDI was too important to be stopped by us 'loony lefties', as trolls on X are quick to call us.

The actions of Western powers since 7 October 2023 have thrown the violent operations of Western imperialism into sharp relief. Linking this explicitly to climate justice, the Colombian President, Gustavo Petro, said Gaza was a rehearsal for the future: 'Genocide and barbaric acts unleashed against the Palestinian people is what awaits those who are fleeing the south because of the climate crisis' (quoted in Fadul 2023). In different contexts, including Ireland, the question of complicity with genocide, and its implications for the future, have taken on new social and political significance. When we started writing this book, our main concern was to better understand why and how monopoly tech has such an over-sized role in Ireland's energy transition. But, as with the new convergences playing out in the protests outlined above, the framing of these questions has expanded and deepened over the past two years. In Ireland, the seemingly disparate set of antagonisms around climate justice, monopoly tech, and Irish alignment with US/EU imperialism, can be clearly articulated against a common cause: a comprador state, whose developmental policy manages the ecological contradictions of multinational capital as a tool for expanding empire. Whether articulated explicitly or not, new protest movements in Ireland are responding to an unfolding landscape of digitalisation and decarbonisation, whose futures are dictated by the visions and technologies of multinational corporations invested in deepening these contradictions towards the imperatives of capitalist growth.

As hopeful as these new convergences are, the movements described above remain small and far from a coherent platform or shared vision of what the alternative might look like. This is where we come up against the force of eco-modernity and its common-sense hold over our collective future. We frequently face the basic criticism, typically in bad faith, that we appear 'against' modernity in our critiques of monopoly tech and its expanding energy regimes. Critics ask: What about the ways that privately developed energy and telecommunications have improved the lives of some people, and how the promise of these forms of connection continue to be a horizon of possibility for many? What about the positive, beneficial applications of digital technologies? What about the lights in our homes, the video calls to our families, and the writing files in our Google Drive? Our responses to these questions tend to engage in a similar whataboutism: What about the uneven forms of connection, how out of reach these infrastructures are for public development, and the costs of that connection to people in the Global South facing the enduring toxicities and ruins of extraction? What about the anti-social, even genocidal, applications of AI technologies and related cloud storage infrastructures, including for furthering the extraction of fossil fuels? What about the forms of data extractivism and surveillance that disproportionately victimise racialised people and support apartheid regimes? What about the ongoing emissions of the growth that these systems demand, administered and profited on as they are by a select group of multinationals? This is only a partial list – a full detailing of the basic problems could go on for each of the final pages of this book. In professing the many contradictions arising from the multiplying 'externalities' of green, digital capitalism, we face the exhaustion[3] of fighting in defence of relations that are already permeated by the value relations of capital. We are beset on all sides by attempts to digitally terraform a planet with a system that depends upon sacrifice zones, war, and the accumulation of waste (Kadri 2023). In this book, we have looked at how one island and its two compromised states have supported this process by facilitating these contradictions – and in doing so, shown how the relations of coloniality and imperialism that shape this global system continue to depend upon peripheralised territories to support emerging regimes of green, digital growth.

But as we have also shown, where there is contradiction, there is also politics. While resistance is crucial to the fight for a better world, the struggles that arise in response to new extractive frontiers and infrastructural development are facing the challenge of responding to a rapidly shifting and intensifying global climate situation. In particular, the latter chapters of this book deal with the unfolding contradictions of monopoly tech and AI. Monopoly tech represents the growing hegemony of US imperial power in this latest iteration of a computational mode of production – 'data extractivism' or 'data colonialism' as framed by the tech-focussed left.[4] This iteration of capital has increasing interest in owning and controlling its infrastructural means of production and circulation, an interest that has seen the immense concentration of infrastructure in the hands of a few powerful companies.

This book has tried to coax this strand of thinking away from the tech reductionism of a particular brand of contemporary social science: one whose focus on emerging circumstances and the contours of 'innovation' can accidentally elide the historical durabilities of capitalism and colonialism, depending on sometimes broad-stroke simplifications of 'digital technology' and its role in the capitalist world system. This has recently resulted in the explosion of discourses surrounding the energy usage of AI, a focus almost exclusively concerned with climate action and climate targets. We see this becoming another side of the coin of facile techno-solutionism, which claims that AI can and should be a necessary tool of decarbonisation. The alignment of such tech reductionism with climate reductionism must be displaced by a robust account of the ecological politics of technological development as it has continuously been under contestation since the (coinciding) establishment of colonial power and the advent of large-scale industrialisation. Only with these understandings can the imperial dimensions of green, digital growth be meaningfully challenged.

Mainstream climate politics and 'action', informed overwhelmingly by institutional technoscience, is now the domain of 'official environmentalism' (Tovey 1993) – which, while sometimes well meaning, as Jesse Goldstein describes similarly scaled approaches to sustainability (2018), are frequently overtly antagonistic to fights for environmental justice at sites of ecological contradiction. Mainstream climate action centred on 'sustainable growth', supported by digital efficiencies, green energy, and net zero, continues to require 'externalities', and continues to lay waste to landscapes territorialised by the state and capital as unproductive, wilderness, or sometimes worse, 'critical' to these strategies. The Irish state, for its part, has overwhelmingly bought into this regime of climate action, institutionally structured by economic dependency and its unfolding consequences in emerging regimes of production. And this does not only reflect Ireland's acquiescence within the EU, where such technocratic policy finds its most durable expression. In fact, it may be the opposite, considering Ireland's frequent transgressions of EU climate and environmental policy, not to mention tax and competition guidelines. These transgressions are most frequently the result of its FDI-led development regime, supporting, for example, multinational companies who evade tax on the island, build wind farms in protected areas, or pollute local waterways through industrial run-off – the postcolonial ecological regime deployed not only to manage multinational growth, but also breaches of international compliance.

This book argues that Ireland's climate action accounts more for the economic imperatives of multinational facilitation than the legally binding imperatives of the EU, let alone climate justice in any existing version of eco-modern, green, digital transitions. This is due to Ireland's dependency within a US-dominated world system, and this FDI-led common sense pervades public institutions and civil society in a way that is hard to shake. Take the 2024 launch of University College Dublin (UCD)'s new 2030 strategy, an important roadmap for the island's largest university. Closing remarks were given by the Chair of the Governing Authority, Michael Beary, also the Irish Country Manager for Amazon Web Services (AWS), extolling the virtues of Irish universities' close relationships with industry. In subsequent points, he argued that Ireland needed to push against the 'headwinds' of economic nationalism and climate change by committing firmly to the FDI model to ensure that the country keeps moving forwards, and that UCD research could be at the forefront of ensuring that Ireland's infrastructure keeps up with the growth of AI as a central tool for its economic future. In 2025, with geopolitical uncertainty only deepening, the apparent need to cleave even closer to US interests – whether through commitments to buy US gas or further enable US tech infrastructure growth – has intensified in Ireland. As we trace throughout this book, eco-modernity here is looking more and more like monopoly tech's eco-modernity. Public good and ecological care are subordinated to and dependent upon the business strategies of multinationals – a model of 'development' that would not be out of place in the time of colonial improvers and gombeens.

At the same time, we have to acknowledge that the apparent decline of dependency theory from the 1990s to the 2010s is likely the result of the closing aperture of the nation-state as the platform for liberation – as much as it never went away as the territorial platform for the 'global' operations of multinationals. Historically, this elision of the unfinished and unresolved 'national question' in Ireland – explicitly tied to Ireland's position in global colonial and imperialist geographies – coincides also with the growing foothold of Irish revisionism. Both of these dynamics can be read simultaneously through the dip in critical diagnoses of imperialism as the structuring dynamic of world systems, and Irish society in particular. However, speaking with colleagues at an event in December 2024, following a lecture from anti-extractivist scholar Martín Arboleda, we realised that dependency theorists remained the sharpest critics of imperialism at a time when nation-state self-determination was coming under increasing attack from US imperialist intervention in the Global South in the 1970s. As emerging neoliberal, free market orthodoxies towards privatisation took shape and enacted their influence over territories and geopolitics, anti-imperialist thinking and activity – usually situated in specific national or sub-national contexts of resistance, building meaningful alternatives – came under fire. The 'end of history' narrative was supported by the end of imperialism in Western political economy and critical theory, displaced by breathless accounts of 'globalisation' and 'deterritorialisation' that in turn obscured the fact that the territorial influences of capital have become more powerful, if distributed, than ever.

Where does this leave us, then? We have sketched out the origins of this situation, which can tell us both about how Ireland has re-situated itself over the 20th and 21st centuries within a shifting world capitalist system, in relation to attempts to delink and restructure its dependencies based on changing imperial powers – and especially the rise of the US as the centre of the global economy. We have also attempted to articulate how this has specifically responded to the growing dominance of certain technology industry and energy regimes within this system, which Ireland has enthusiastically participated in and supported. It is impossible to understand Ireland's contemporary landscape without this history of coloniality and postcoloniality, and a strong comprehension of Ireland's ongoing partitioned state and incomplete decolonisation. The conflict in the North, the dominance of historical revisionism, and a populace in large part allergic to addressing the 'national question' in the late 20th century has long made the issue of Ireland's colonial past and present role within empire an unpopular and controversial debate.

However, it has re-emerged in the past decade, in part due to the global reckoning prompted by the Black Lives Matter uprisings in 2020, the emergence of the republican Sinn Féin as Ireland's biggest political party, and, more recently and horrifyingly, the genocide in Gaza and Israel's campaign of annexation in Palestine. This latter situation has awakened an anti-imperialist strand of the Irish left and even forced (nominal) condemnations from the centre-right Irish Government, the spineless comprador lapdogs of the US Empire. More radical, land-based strands of the environmental movement on the island have also taken up the mantle of the anti-colonial struggle, and we have drawn immense inspiration from the Save Our Sperrins campaign, Communities Against the Injustice of Mining (CAIM), and other movements forging internationalist alliances with anti-colonial peoples and campaigns around the world. These solidarities are also especially strong in the North, where republicanism and ongoing colonisation by the British state remain at the centre of liberatory politics. However we look at it, the ongoing struggle of the North for liberation and the end of partition needs to be central to any left political project on the island, and this goes especially for environmental campaigning that centres ecology and its management or protection.

On the other hand, however, the issue of 're-unification' has been taken up by regressive actors: both towards neoliberal and fascist ends. Since 'peace' in the North, it has been an underlying argument among 'liberal' unionists and industrialists in the Occupied Six that the Republic's industrial development strategies are something to envy and align with. We have ourselves heard from data centre developers in the North, for example, both in public and in private, that the Northern industry has been severely limited by its comparatively restrictive trade policies and tax incentives – a problem that would be better remedied by harmonising rather than trying to compete with the Republic. Since Brexit, this argument has only grown, with small- and medium-sized enterprises (SMEs) and multinationals alike facing punishing limitations on free trade that, in the neoliberal mindset, prevents economic development that would see 'prosperity' rise in the North, which still makes up one of the most economically and infrastructurally deprived regions of the UK and Ireland.

Data centre developers, including the founder of the Atlantic Hub, a proposed cross-border data centre campus between a proposed 'freeport' in Derry (North) and an industrial park in Letterkenny (South), argue that building such infrastructural bridges between the North and South will circumvent the challenges of Brexit and build key cross-border industries – a precondition for re-unification. Projects to fully connect the Northern and Southern electricity grids through the planned North–South 400 kV Interconnector, while a public project, is also about ensuring a greater degree of shared electricity as corporate energy demand continues to grow and wind development stalls in the South. The more effective flow of electricity from North, where capacity outstrips demand, to South, where demand risks overwhelming capacity due to 'large energy users' such as data centres, also creates more cooperation towards a decarbonised all-island economy less dependent on, for example, imported electricity from either Scotland or France (through the planned 320 kV Celtic Interconnector). Ireland also becomes once again a strategic bridge – this time not only between the US and EU, but between the EU and the UK.[5] And finally, as our comrades in Save Our Sperrins relayed to us, the mining industry already sees no border on the island. When attending a mining conference in Canada, the Northern and Southern state authorities had a booth together, selling Ireland's resources to mining companies (Cirefice quoted in in Butterly 2022). Their map was of a non-partitioned land, abundant with meticulously surveyed mineral deposits for the taking.

We would also be remiss to not deal with the fascist currents of the national question, and especially with regards to environmental issues, which have been emerging over the past few years. As mentioned in the vignette in the final chapter, fascists recruit from places of real, observable grievance with the state – a state that they also view as too 'liberal', with its 'open' borders and free trade. After all, global figures of the far right were once among the most strident critics of 'big tech', seeing the industry as a bastion of out-of-touch elites with high-minded ideals that poison the minds of the youth (or something). In the US and other parts of Europe, anti-renewable sentiment has frequently been either astro-turfed or captured by fossil fuel interests on the far right – who argue that, for example, renewable energy is a scam and the 'just transition' a phony promise for those in coal country. The arguments are actually not that far off from what we see arising as a liberal response to mineral security: bring mining (back) to the metropole. But then who does that victimise, and who does it promise to develop *for*?

Promises of development, made and broken, are extremely powerful sites of political contestation, and we can see right-wing sentiments arising within ostensibly 'liberal' movements for development, such as the mid-2010s campaigns to bring data centres to rural Ireland, where some advocates for multinational development also espoused paranoid beliefs about the role of the state, environmental objectors, and outsiders in suppressing their interests (Brodie 2020b). Anti-democratic principles promoted by those interested in 'liberal' development – in the form of suppressing dissent and 'streamlining' development to avoid delays – are within a spectrum of authoritarianism not too distant from the far-right visions of a territorial body with inside and outside groups to its expressed interests. In these ideas, the 'national resources' gained from multinational investment are great, if only their benefits are redirected back to local communities – supporting the postcolonial ecological regime and its facilitation of empire, if only that empire fulfils its promises of improvement.

In whatever picture, regression in rural environmental campaigns tends to hinge on questions of development. It becomes fertile territory for conspiracy theories and scapegoats, whether out-of-touch liberal elites, migrants, already marginalised communities, or the left – especially as rural communities frequently feel 'gaslit' for raising the issue of Irish development policy, perceived as proponents of an irrational anti-modernity. Left campaigns have tended to avoid the kinds of recruitment drives that the far right excels at around these issues, and that is a strategic imbalance that we need to take very seriously.

Our humble contribution to this contested landscape of unfolding eco-modernity – the monopoly tech-dependent vision of digitalisation and decarbonisation – is that the issue of the 'national' and the promise of development need to be re-situated towards present programmes of *anti-imperialist* environmental struggle, rather than something to be addressed at some point in the future. There are no shortages of ideas and proposals for how land, resources, technology, and labour can be deployed *differently* than the rapidly unfolding version of capitalist eco-modernity. But the only way to liberate these factors from narrowly prescribed, exploitative, and environmentally degrading modes of production is to break with dependent economic development. This is not a 'return' to autarkic self-sufficiency, but rather the socialising of ecological goods through democratic control and (re-)distribution. This then is also fundamentally a struggle for and through the state – whether its decline and re-establishment, or its radical transformation (Heron and Dean 2020). To do anything less is to cede fertile territory to the straw-grasping of official environmentalists, the smug stasis of the compradors, or, worse, to the growing force of the far right in Ireland and across the world. What the left's promise can be, against these forces of eco-modern acceleration and anti-modern regression, is an anti-imperialist politics that mobilises against the forces of monopoly capitalism for an alternative model of eco-socialist development. This will require making and strengthening links with liberation movements internationally, and recognising the antagonism of the Irish state, its compradorised organs, and the multinational corporations that have forged foundations in Ireland and in doing so have foreclosed existing horizons for meaningful environmental justice here (and abroad). These forces have historically aligned to prevent the awakening of an anti-capitalist, anti-colonial, and anti-imperialist politics on the island, politics that necessarily require an internationalist framework. Only with such a framework can we shift the thinking in this place, and a compromised transition from the bog to the cloud can cede to the creation of a just, joyous republic, from the plough to the stars.

Notes

Introduction

1. One of the key issues with these statistics is reporting – there is no centralised reporting mechanism or methodology for determining data centre resource usage, and most numbers rely on industry self-reporting. Ireland's Central Statistics Office (CSO) numbers are thought to be fairly accurate. However, Eirgrid has disputed the IEA's 'alarmist' estimate, saying that Ireland won't reach 30 per cent data centre electricity usage until nearly 2030 (O'Doherty 2024). Whatever the case, the acknowledgement is that one third of Ireland's electricity is planned to go to data centres by the end of the decade. For comparison, in most countries, this number is not higher than 1–3 per cent. In comparatively constrained countries such as the Netherlands and Singapore, moratoria were established based on percentages rising above that low bar (Brodie 2024).
2. We also identified this in one of the first things we ever wrote about this phenomenon (Bresnihan and Brodie 2019).
3. A terminological note: Ireland is one place, but partitioned into two nation-states, under two different supranational delegations. The current Republic (or South of) Ireland is an ostensibly 'independent' nation-state constituting 26 counties across all four historical Irish provinces, with membership in the European Union (EU). 'Northern Ireland' (NI) is a devolved statelet constituting the Occupied Six Counties under the United Kingdom, and is no longer a member of the EU. We refer to these six counties as the 'North of Ireland', and NI when referring specifically to the operations and institutions of the devolved government. When we say the 'Irish state', we are referring to the governing institutions of the former Free State and current Republic of Ireland. There are cooperative organisations and infrastructures across the border that have been put in place since the 1998 Good Friday Agreement. These have not re-established historical unity of Ireland still ruptured by the border, and in large part have minimal jurisdictional sway.
4. While we expand the frame to development politics more broadly, we are contributing to what has been referred to by some as 'critical data centre studies' – the analysis of the infrastructural politics of cloud computing from environmental and other perspectives (see Hogan 2018; Vonderau 2019; Burrell 2020; Brodie 2020a; Childs 2022; Gonzalez-Montserrate 2022; Johnson 2023; Velkova and Plantin 2023; Edwards et al 2024). In particular, we want to intervene in a growing area of study surrounding the politics of data centre contestation – captured in the Contested Data Territories initiative out of Oxford, which gathered academics and activists to speak about data centre contestation from Ireland, the Netherlands, and Chile, but also seeing robust expression in other transnational solidarity and action networks that have been emerging since (see Lehuedé 2022; Brodie 2023; Pasek 2023; Jansen and Cath 2024; Rone 2024).
5. Another terminological note: The 'post-' in postcolonial as we refer to it is an imperfect moniker for a particular 'state' on this colonially partitioned island, and a partial description

of a periodisation and state of affairs on the island as a whole. In addition, we return to ideas and debates surrounding the formation of a 'postcolonial' world system wherein the false commitments to 'self-determination' by Western powers instantiated a new regime of dependency, whereby colonised and so-called 'postcolonial' territories alike were subjected to the punishing discipline of an imperial world system still organised for and by the 'metropole'. The importance of recognising this common condition of 'postcoloniality' becomes evident when North and South are effectively treated as one entity from the perspective of transnational capital keen to do away with barriers to trade and investment, particularly in the context of energy and digital infrastructures and services (Chapter 6).

6   We are inspired by many who have theorised the monopoly tendencies and concentration dynamics of big tech companies and, specifically, their infrastructures. However, we do not claim that these theories are undifferentiated – for example, those discussing 'intellectual monopoly capitalism' are more interested in the market control of information than what they may see as the more external/infrastructural dynamics of energy and ecology. We hope to extend these theories more strongly into these areas, connecting the specifically infrastructural and ecological with the global economic – like any good political ecologists (see Sandvig 2015; Plantin et al 2018; Durand and Milberg 2019; Sadowski 2019; Doctorow 2021; Rikap 2021; Steinberg et al 2022; Van der Vlist et al 2024).

7   For a critique of such cyber-libertarian ideology, see Golumbia (2024).

8   We also were inspired by a conference where we presented early versions of these book chapters, 'Rethinking the Inevitability of AI', which articulated similar premises. See Hicks and Linstrum (nd).

9   See also Van der Vlist et al (2024).

10 These policies have been proliferating from the EU, to international development agencies such as the World Economic Forum, to specific countries such as Ireland – and they are being institutionalised and adopted. For example, the Irish Government Statement on the Role of Data Centres in Ireland's Enterprise Strategy states that the growth of digital infrastructure and the decarbonisation of the energy system 'can – and must be – complementary': 'These are the "twin transitions" of pervasive digitalisation and the decarbonising of our economy. While these mega-trends are truly global, they have significant implications for Ireland's economy, industrial strategy, competitiveness and prosperity. Data centre operations are at the epicentre of these transformational changes. As such, they merit and require specific policy focus, to ensure that our digital and low carbon opportunities are coherent and aligned. Both are critical to Ireland's economic future, and the success of our businesses' (Government of Ireland 2022a, 2–5; see also European Commission 2022; Fouquet and Hippe 2022; Rebellius 2023). Some books and longer studies have begun to emerge surrounding the intersections of 'green' energy politics, infrastructural development, and digitalisation (see Libertson et al 2021; Velkova 2021; Ortar et al 2022; Sareen and Muller 2023).

11 For crucial work in critical media studies on the geopolitical economies and infrastructural dimensions of big tech expansion, see Srnicek (2016); Plantin et al (2018); Couldry and Mejias (2019); Doctorow (2021). For the work in political and world ecology surrounding the energy transition, resource geographies, and contestations around 'eco-modernism', see Ajl (2021b); Heron and Heffron (2022); Hickel (2023); Tilly et al (2023); Barca (2024); Chaudhary (2024); Heron (2024). Jenny Goldstein and Eric Nost's volume *The Nature of Data* (2022) and wider project towards the 'political ecology of data' (Nost and Goldstein 2022) have come closest in bringing together these areas of research. However, our approach, rather than focus on the planetary dimensions of these industries and the regimes of datafication they represent, we are interested in how they have taken shape in a capitalist world system designed in the historical image of imperialism. This, of course,

has environmental 'impacts' and implications for regimes of knowledge and the problem of 'information' represented (and purportedly solved) by environmental data – but what about 'development' and the organising of ecologies for accumulation by tech companies? (See Lally et al 2022; Lehuedé 2024; Valdivia 2024.)

[12] For influential versions of this story, see Mosco (2014); Hu (2015).

[13] This is a strongly articulated sub-field of media studies, focussed on the technical materialities of media infrastructural expansion and, most inspiringly for us, the situation of these materialities in concrete geographical environments (see Larkin 2008; Hu 2015; Parks 2015; Parks and Starosielski 2015; Starosielski 2015; Mattern 2017; Brodie and Barney forthcoming).

[14] The US Telecommunications Act of 1996 is a key point in this narrative, in the sense that it opened the door once again to consolidated ownership of telecoms infrastructure on the back of the dotcom 'boom'. The rearticulation of monopolist telecommunications from the 1990s has been widely cited as a result of digital innovation 'demanding' monopoly – free competition, let alone state provision, could never keep up. Now, we see this concentration extending even deeper into energy infrastructure – Lenin's worst nightmare. As Paul Starr narrates: 'Out of the chaos of the telecom industry will come consolidation. Exactly how far and how fast it will go in each sector is unclear ... The big question is whether consolidation will come with or without regulation in the public interest' (2002).

[15] For a collected overview of different dimensions of Amazon's meteoric rise as an e-commerce and cloud giant, see Smith et al (2022).

[16] A clear analogue is the oil industry, which developed the corporate model of vertical integration in the US at the end of the 19th century (Hanieh 2024). Standard Oil operated not via direct ownership of crude oil supplies but through ownership and control of the infrastructures, processing facilities and markets required for transporting, refining, and developing oil-based products (for example, petrochemicals). This model of monopoly control remained the (contested) foundation of the oil industry as it internationalised throughout the 20th century.

[17] See *Merchants of Doubt* (Conway and Oreskes 2010). Monopoly tech is not far behind: the big tech lobby is now widely reported as one of the largest in the world – according to a Public Citizen report in 2021, far eclipsing big oil spending in the US (Chung 2021). This lobby has become extraordinarily powerful in shaping Irish state policy, and comes alongside a revolving door between the tech industry and the state (see Khanal et al 2024; O'Hare 2024; The Irish Times 2024; also Chapter 4).

[18] See Pedrigal and Lukić for clear overview: 'The domination of some parties by others implies, of course, an integral hierarchization of the flow of value between countries that do not retain the value they produce and others that capture and appropriate that value due to unequal exchange. The former group constitutes what is known as the periphery of the system while the latter forms the imperial core' (2024, 4).

[19] This language has become widespread in economic policy as well as industrial literature and research. Take, for example, a report on industry 4.0 and 'sustainable innovation' produced by the European Business and Innovation Centre Network in 2022, which heralds an oncoming 'fifth industrial revolution' specifically surrounding sustainability and the ability of AI to support 'environmental' action (2022).

[20] See Maxwell and Miller (2012); Gabrys (2014); Starosielski and Walker (2016).

[21] Fernando van der Vlist, Anne Helmond, and Fabian Ferrari's indispensable 2024 article 'Big AI: Cloud infrastructure dependence and the industrialisation of artificial intelligence' articulates these stakes with exceptional clarity – although without a robust analysis of world systemic dynamics.

22. Before the term became synonymous with poverty and 'underdevelopment', the 'Third World' described an anti-imperialist political project driven by the wave of national liberation movements that spread across South America, Africa and Asia in the 1950s and 1960s (Bresnihan and Millner 2023; Prashad 2007) – we use the term at precise points throughout the book to recall this vital political history.

23. The unfolding landscape of extractive enterprise geared towards 'green' policies, targets, and promises has been termed 'green extractivism', as we discuss in Chapter 6. (For further work on green extractivism and its relations to digitalisation and 'smart' economies, see Arboleda 2020; Calvão and Archer 2021; Jerez et al 2021; Chagnon et al 2022; Voskoboynik and Andreucci 2022; Bruna 2023; Hamouchene and Sandwell 2023; Jung 2023; Brodie 2024; Dunlap et al 2024; among others cited throughout this book, especially in Chapter 6).

24. One of the most important books in this recent vein has been Robbie McVeigh and Bill Rolston's *Ireland, Colonialism, and the Unfinished Revolution*, which provides rigorous contestation to the counter-revolutionary force of revisionism in promoting a conservative (or even 'liberal') agenda to position Ireland as an imperial lapdog, whether for the US or Britain (2021). McVeigh and Rolston's book has contributed to a renewed anti-imperialist intellectual left in Ireland, recovering these historical currents as vital to dismantling Ireland's subordinately supportive role in facilitating empire (see Mercier 2024).

25. As Shakir Mustafa summarises the impulses of historical revisionism, while anti-colonial nationalism has long been the ground of 'popular' resistance movements in Ireland across its history (like other colonies/postcolonies), revisionism's 'critique of nationalist politics is informed by the impulse to reconsider Irish history in the light of new research and insights on the one hand, and on the other, the pressures of continuous conflict in the North. In Ireland, certain revisionist historians and cultural critics … think that this conflict gives legitimacy to their assault on nationalism, while others tend to dismiss nationalism as a relic of a past not too helpful for Ireland's competition in a global economy' (1998, 38). Positing the rationality of 'value-free' history against the irrational mythology and zealotry of Irish republicanism, which has been the most influential left ideology on the island of Ireland for the last 150 years (Mac Bhloscaidh 2020), revisionists participate in the historical elision and forgetting of Ireland's ongoing colonial histories and postcolonial categorisation. This has origins in the early Free State Government's adoption of rhetoric against the 'irrational' and anti-progressive forces of the 'irregulars' in the anti-Treaty IRA, which during and after the Civil War marginalised republicanism (and other associated 'radical' ideologies such as socialism) in the national character. Later, during the conflict in NI (1969–98), this terminological battleground became about postcolonialism as a frame – orientated around the underlying acknowledgement that if the South was 'postcolonial', then the increasingly unpopular struggle among republicans in the North was similarly being waged on 'anti-colonial' terms. But while historical revisionism was and remains a hotly contested battleground of history and Irish studies, Irish literary and cultural studies have remained staunch reserves of colonial and postcolonial theory. Mustafa along with other contemporaries in the early 1990s such as Luke Gibbons, Declan Kiberd, David Lloyd, and the Field Day Theatre Company, agitated variously against hegemonic 'top-down elite histories' of revisionist historiography. These anti-revisionists were oftentimes sometimes aligned with the republican struggle, and always maintained the importance of anti-colonial and anti-imperialist analysis to understand unfolding contradictions of Irish modernity. (For contemporaneous and retrospective analyses, see Eagleton et al 1990; Lloyd 1993; Gibbons 1996; Kiberd 1997; Mustafa 1998; Carroll and King 2003; Mac Bhloscaidh 2020; Cleary 2022.)

26. Here, we are explicitly bringing dependency theory into conversation with more contemporary versions of world systems and world ecology thinking. Dependency theory

stems from earlier Marxist analysis of monopoly capital and imperialism, such as in the work of Lenin and Rosa Luxemburg. In the context of post-WWII Third World decolonisation, thinkers such as Wallerstein, Arghiri Emmanuel, Samir Amin, and Theotônio dos Santos theorised how relations of dependency between core and periphery were maintained even after formal independence. Through unequal trade relations and economic means, backed by threat or assertion of political force, former European colonial powers and the ascendant US subordinated formerly colonised countries to their own developmental ends. This framework of analysis, which places particular emphasis on sovereign development and national liberation in the Global South, continues in the work of Prabhat and Utsa Patnaik, Sam Moyo and Paris Yeeros, among many others. Semi-periphery within world-systems analysis, to which we and others classify Ireland, refers to those countries capable of capturing the value of other countries (in the periphery), but which are unable to retain all their value production, which, in turn, is captured by the countries at the core of the system (Pedrigal and Lukić 2024). While Ireland is a wealthy country in Western Europe, this wealth is largely generated through its semi-peripheral positioning within the world system; for example, via price transfers and corporation tax.

27 The significance of Petty's 'experimental statecraft' in Ireland goes far beyond the island of Ireland and the period of the late 17th century. Ireland served as a laboratory for British colonialism through the 19th and 20th centuries: the art of governing territory and people through technologies such as the census and the survey, institutions such as the first national police force, and later in the North through counter-insurgency, were all exported to other British colonies (see McGovern 2019; Ohlmeyer 2023).

28 It is not accidental that the development of the settler city of Derry saw the native Irish excluded to the 'Bogside', while the Protestant settlers resided within the city walls. The division in land quality between that of the Protestant planters (and the infrastructure developed there) and the native Irish is still visible across Ireland's landscape of under-development, North and South, today.

29 In this, Petty's political arithmetic is an early expression of the modern art of governmentality and biopower (Lemke 2019). In his major work, *Political Arithmetick* (published posthumously in 1690 but written some 15 years earlier), Petty sought to establish a method for the promotion of general, and at the same time individualised, welfare. As Ted McCormick shows in detail, Petty was distinct from many of his contemporaries in transposing the aims of statecraft (in a time of colonial expansion) onto the terrain of a supposedly scientific, quantitative basis (2009).

30 This petitioning resulted in key governmental innovations such as the Ordnance Surveys and the creation of the national census, which in 1851 was one of the most comprehensive national surveys undertaken anywhere in the world (Carroll 2006).

31 Mark Quigley argues that, in observing the wages of state bureaucratic and infrastructural modernisation in the Blasket Islands through what he argues is a modernist literature of the writer Tomás Ó Criomhthain, we can see how the process of nation-building was about an unequal exchange between the state and its frequently rural subjects (2003). In doing so, from a cultural perspective, Quigley helps demonstrate how multiple 'modernities' exist and have existed in Ireland, from the Blaskets to the Pale, providing nuance to perspectives surrounding mastery and enrolment in state narratives and their relations to modes of production and land use.

32 This work has been collected through Slater's website for his wider project of analysing and documenting Marx and Engels' writings on Ireland. See Slater (nd).

33 As Engels observed in 1870, 'Today England needs grain quickly and dependably – Ireland is just perfect for wheat-growing. Tomorrow England needs meat – Ireland is only fit for cattle pastures' (np).

34 The term comprador translates as 'buyer' in Portuguese and was first used to describe native house servants in China who went to market to sell their European employers' goods. The native comprador was essential for mediating and advancing European commercial interests in the colonies. In the 20th century, Marxist, anti-colonial theorists used the term to describe the class of domestic petit-bourgeois, or native elites, who work with (neo)colonial powers to advance their economic interests. For dependency theorists such as Samir Amin (1976, 1990) and Theotonio dos Santos (1970), the comprador class was essential to maintaining uneven accumulation within the world system.

35 It has elsewhere been called a time of 'conservative decolonisation', whereby certain aspects of the project of disentangling the state from Britain were achieved through Catholic theocratic state-building (Woods 2020). Most theories falsely equate these tendencies with the dominant conservative force of 'nationalism'; however, the most coherent movements towards sovereign development were led by former republicans and informed by anti-colonial politics of self-determination – as we'll discuss through the book. In interesting ways, even the project of building an FDI-led development model originated in some (misappropriated) idea of self-determination, aligning with the US to build up national industrial infrastructure.

36 See also Boyd and Allen (2021).

37 We shy away from nature/society binaries in this book in general, but it is worth noting how these distinctions grow more openly politicised across this era. The 'environment' becomes even more of a set of relations to be managed, technically and economically, in regimes of stewardship and ecological transition (see Walker and Cooper 2011; Bresnihan 2020; Nelson and Bigger 2022).

38 Besides Crotty, the tradition of dependency theory in Ireland is small, but not non-existent, and we have drawn extensively on these works throughout this book (see Regan and Walsh 1976; O'Hearn 1989; Jacobsen 1994; Yearley 1995; Boylan and McDonough 1998).

39 For examples of and those influenced by these currents, see Baker (1987); Tovey (1993); Taylor (1998); Leonard (2007, 2008); Barry and Doran (2016); Slevin (2016); Mercier et al (2022); Allen (2004); Fearon (2024).

40 In fact, Ireland's adoption of an alternative mode of 'true' national economic measurement – Modified Gross National Income (GNI), the only country in the world to do so due to the distortions wrought by its FDI dependence – speaks to the ongoing importance of dependency theory.

41 In his forensic 2021 analysis of Amin's thought, focussed on its agro-ecological dimensions, Ajl summarises Amin's theory of dependency through export-led industrialisation measures occurring across ostensibly decolonising states in the 1950s–1960s: 'thin-hulled developmental vessels built to serve the interests of local elites. Others, even the best of them, only partially democratised production without democratising the management of society' (2021a).

42 John Kurt Jacobsen (1994) emphasises the limited manoeuvrability of the Irish elite in facilitating a system of 'complex dependency', while also eliding somewhat the (post) colonial question in favour of such perceived complexity. While 'industrialisation by invitation' was certainly the result of domestic political choices by this comprador class, even orthodox dependency theory acknowledges the conditions of duress under which such decisions are taken and enter into the mainstream.

43 See Ajl 2021a; Hickel et al 2022; Arboleda 2023; Villegas Plá 2023; Franco et al 2024; Heron 2024; Molinero and Pedregal 2024.

44 For an exception, see Franco et al 2024. Sebastián Lehuedé also explores these dynamics in relation to a critique of 'extractivism' and its material and epistemic relationalities of data, albeit from a 'decolonial' perspective, drawing from theorists such as Walter Mignolo

and Aníbal Quijano (2021). While an important critique, these theories frequently tip the balance between the material and the epistemic factors in 'coloniality' – there is certainly a distinctly 'Western' treatment of territories for extraction that is distinct, but that relation also permeates through the economic and developmental motives of the capitalist world system in ways that are not resolvable through focus on discrete sites of extractivism (for example). We argue that understanding these uneven dynamics requires closer analysis of industrialisation and modernisation as *imperatives* rather than enforced paradigms – and that imperialism may be a more apt continuity. Lehuedé and collaborator Ana Valdivia appear to also come to these conclusions in more recent analysis (see Lehuedé and Valdivia 2024).

45 Hickel articulates this dynamic in a concise social media post from January 2025, in relation to the tanking of generative AI stocks with the emergence of China's cheaper and more efficient DeepSeek model, which fundamentally contradicted arguments about the scaling of AI. These arguments, it became clear, only supported the monopolisation of the infrastructure by big tech, especially in the form of cloud computing – and China's ability to provide cheaper tools for sovereign technological development challenged the core action of imperialist dependency. See also Hao (2025).

46 In spite of being at the vanguard of data centre development, Ireland is considered a laggard in the AI sphere by industrial analysts (Burns 2024) – which, whatever the ideological baggage, is significant in demonstrating the infrastructural and ecological function of dependent economies.

47 But as political economists of technology Sebastián Fernández Franco, Juan M. Graña, and Cecilia Rikap diagnose the situation, the idea of 'catching up' technologically still rests upon domestic capacities to scale up production and compete with imperialist interests on a global scale (2024).

48 This idea of Ireland as a laboratory for British colonial governance has surfaced strongly in recent scholarship between Ireland and Palestine. Bhandar, for example, argues that the logic and practice of 'improving' the boggy wastelands was tested through surveying and land transformation in Ireland, becoming formative to the colonial ideology of Zionism's imperative to 'make the desert bloom' in Palestine (2018); in 2022, Trinity College Dublin welcomed Rashid Khalidi to begin a project based on the systematic historiography of Ireland's role as a laboratory for governing Palestine (King 2022).

49 Especially, we should be clear about this in terms of the dynamics and hierarchies of colonial racialisation that differed across plantation economies in Ireland versus North America (Ohlemeyer 2022). In addition, there are other arguments citing colonial 'laboratories' that well predate the Ulster Plantation, as Tao Leigh Goffe argues in the case of the Caribbean and specifically in regards to the origins of climate crisis in colonialism (2025).

50 For an overview, see Ohlemeyer (2022), 141–69.

51 Many truisms of Irish 'modernity' – popular conceptions that modern industrial capitalism wasn't achieved in Ireland, that Ireland never had a developed 'resource base', that national infrastructure is underdeveloped, that Ireland went straight from a 'backwards' agrarian economy to one of post-industrial services – fail to adequately account for the role that Ireland played in the imperial modernity of its colonial administrator, especially through the lens of technoscience (for an exception, see Carroll 2006). For example, revisionist research often foregrounds the roles of individuals from elite backgrounds in the British Empire – flattening the location of 'Irishness' across differentiated and unevenly colonised backgrounds. The presence of relatively well-off Irish officials in positions of power within British overseas colonial holdings, for example, due to their acknowledgement in the existing historical record, is focussed on in historiographies such as Barry Crosbie's analysis of the connections between colonial Ireland and India in the 1800s (2009). The primarily

Anglo-Irish officials in the history Crosbie traces, and their 'Irish' (and comparatively liberal) stance on colonial strategy, complicates nationalist narratives of Ireland acting as a template for colonial activity abroad – the 'laboratory', in Crosbie's analysis, is one that was actually shaped by indigenously Irish expertise drawn from geographical sciences at Trinity College Dublin. However, as even other revisionist accounts such as Nicholas Whyte's *Science, Colonialism, and Ireland* (1999) unpack, such institutions only contestedly included 'Irish' students and researchers, and, at best, were the space of wealthy Anglo-Irish elite even at times of nationalist sentiment in these communities. In these examples, we see the flattening of revisionist historiography – the structures of dependency, coercion, and internal hierarchies that shaped Irish migratory histories and presence in empire are whitewashed in favour of a surface-level, 'value-free' point about what 'Irishness' within the empire looked like. To these historians, this was comparatively wealthy individuals acting as independent agents within empire. They would do well to brush up on their Aimé Césaire and Frantz Fanon to understand the epistemological and identitarian stakes of colonialism – as well as basic tenets of avoiding cherry-picked historiography.

52 Enterprise Ireland's 'Ireland's edge' campaign in the 2010s, for example, specifically mobilised the idea of 'innovation at the edge', recalling a neoliberal 'wild west' whereby state institutions and local workforces provide a robust resource base for any multinational looking to avail of such an open and deregulated environment (Brodie forthcoming).

53 With rich anthropological insight, Alix Johnson's 2023 book *Where Cloud Is Ground: Placing Data and Making Place in Iceland* makes a similar argument surrounding the role of national industry boosters and specifically postcolonial hangovers in the structure of attracting investment into data centres in Iceland. The experimental ethos seen in Ireland has strong resonance with the industrial and energy projects around these facilities in Iceland.

54 It also has an interesting relationship to 'foreign' investment and expertise – German company Siemens-Schuckert was the primary designer of the project, although it was built by an Irish workforce and planned by the state.

55 This recalls Mimi Sheller's work about aluminium and its role as a kind of packaged electricity for jurisdictions seeking to utilise 'abundant' electrical power in its refinement and manufacturing (2014). In this imaginary, Ireland cannot actually utilise its energy resources without something to export – data-driven services. Rather than what Sheller calls the 'light modernity' of aluminium, this is the eco-modernity of monopoly tech captured in and through the harnessing of electricity.

56 At points in this text, we use the term 'indigenous' in relation to, for example, indigenous industrialisation discourses, due to the fact that this is a terminology used by corporate and developmental figures in common lexicon across history. This is not to elide the importance of global Indigeneity as a political and social experience under duress by ongoing settler and internal colonialism. To differentiate, we capitalise Indigeneity and leave the industrial or developmental relationship in lower case, where necessary.

57 We don't have time to go into these debates here, but see Heron (2024) and Hickel (2023).

58 Holly Jean Buck's work has been essential in unpacking the ways that 'eco-modernisation' is enacted through emerging forms of ecological valuation such as 'geo-engineering' and the concretisation of the abstract calculabilities of 'net zero' (2019, 2021). These are battlegrounds of the climate-focussed left that need more explicit orientations attached to them – and one that we hope to provide some ideas for in this book, if not fighting in the trenches.

59 Samir Amin writes: 'A one-sided observation on the "positive" character of the development of the forces of production without a concern for the class character of this development – (in conventional terms "Development for whom?"), either generally (since

it concerns capitalism) or concretely, that is to say in a given phase of capitalist expansion – is to make an ideological, non-scientific, choice of accepting capitalism as the long term means (for centuries, millenium?) of "solving the problems of humankind"' (1990, 3).

60 Seán Fearon highlights the challenge of this in Ireland amid the unpopularity of mainstream 'climate action', especially by those recruited by the Irish far right: 'An uncompromising politics of meeting the basic needs for all, by unapologetic means of redistribution and intervention, is the only antidote to this far right poison. Perhaps we can all take hope from the French left in this regard. … The degrowth challenge is a structural one, requiring transformational change of the post-colonial model of Irish capitalism, and a radical politics inside and outside of elected institutions to advocate for this transformation' (2024).

61 We appreciate Jonathan Crary's (2024) unflinching critique of digital capitalism and the hollow-sounding calls to 'regulate' or 'reform' digital technologies: '[T]he current clamour over "surveillance capitalism" needs to be made transparent: its target is not capitalism, but the supposed excesses and violations that have been imposed on a fundamentally reformable but indispensable system. It is a deflection of critique that affirms the permanence and necessity of the existing underlying arrangements' (108). We can make a similar point about the clamour over the 'environmental excesses' of cloud computing and machine learning.

62 Fredric Jameson critiques what he might describe as the 'anti-modern' left as it emerged among the death throes of traditional Western modernism in the late 20th century. This was a moment when the modern project of the 'West' was conceptually superseded by the much-heralded postmodern condition of global and deterritorialised financial and technological paradigms (2002). The emergence of 'modernisation' as an imperative applied across First, Second, and Third Worlds post-WWII was, in Jameson's paradigm, a belated and always-incomplete project of social and technological transformation in the image of bourgeois notions of progress, as well as the connected ideology of 'catching up' to the West's socio-economic might and the play of particular kinds of cultural hegemony. To Jameson, within a 'modern' global scene, being anti-modern has historically been baptised as being anti-progress, a label with some truth wherein the belief in radical rupture is replaced by multiple and overlapping political and cultural forms united by a critique of discrete but intersecting power structures such as patriarchal society and environmental harm. However, the idea of anti-modern fragmentation among postmodernist theory was pre-emptive – and dependency theory offers a geographical corrective to this more cultural analytical tradition, as an alternative to the paradigm of phasal shifts and, most importantly, by bringing the persistence of territory back into the frame. Within any project of alternative modernity, there are elements that are worth salvaging as potential rehearsals for a different way of thinking about development – or, in the tradition of Irish environmental sociology, 'two versions of development and modernity', one elite and one popular (Tovey 1993; also Chakrabarty 2000).

63 It is worth acknowledging an unexplored relationship here between the idea of 'decoupling' in so-called green growth (as part of hegemonic eco-modernity) and 'delinking' – if decoupling is promoted as a core facet of eco-modernism, then delinking might offer a different vision of how the global economy can be re-organised *away* from unequal (ecological) exchange and over-consumption in the Global North. These are of course both imperfect, but worthwhile propositions to consider critically.

64 Ajl argues, in particular, that these were experimented with to some discrete success in Egypt and Tunisia in the 1970s and 1980s (2021a).

65 Our thinking here has been inspired by anti-colonial feminist work, especially friendship and collaboration with V'cenza Cirefice and others in the 'anti-extractivist' orbit in Ireland, who we engage with throughout this book (see Povinelli 2016; Gómez-Barris

2017; Spice 2018; Yusoff 2018; Cirefice and Sullivan 2019; LaDuke and Cowen 2020; Mercier et al 2022).

66 With this in mind, the clued-in reader will notice that most of this book is focussed on the 'Republic' or the 'South' of Ireland. That is not by design, but a result of our analytical standpoint, and the centralisation and concentration of power on the island of Ireland. Even if analysing US imperialism, power circulates through Dublin – with some rippling outwards, which includes sites in the North. Whether a wind farm in Antrim contracted to AWS or a peatslide that crosses from Donegal into Tyrone, these are still situations that tell us about how environmental power and infrastructure is distributed across Ireland. Cross-border business transactions tend to flow from South to North, as do environmental damages. Stormont, ineffective and flawed as it is in devolution, is also toothless even when `sitting, depending upon and subject to decisions made in Westminster. The North is at the same time a vacuum as well as an extreme coalescing of overlapping governance. This is why mining, fracking, illegal dumping, and intensive agriculture tend to be concentrated in the North. Our story is about tech and large-scale energy infrastructure. It is impossible to understand Ireland without this as a basis, and we hope this continues the debate about the formation of a true republic on this island.

Chapter 1

1 Charles Trevelyan, one of the key administrators involved in the British response to the Famine, described it as 'an effective mechanism for reducing surplus population' (quoted in McVeigh and Rolston 2021, 118), or what Gerry Kearns argues was a case of colonial 'mass starvation for social engineering' (2013, 23).

2 Editions of *The Marconigraph* remain accessible, and provide fascinating insight into the colonial geographies of technology: see https://www.worldradiohistory.com/Wireless_World_Magazine.htm.

3 'The more capitalism is developed', Lenin writes, 'the more strongly the shortage of raw materials is felt, the more intense the competition and the hunt for sources of raw materials throughout the whole world the more desperate the struggle for the acquisition of colonies' (1963 [1917], 728).

4 For this metaphor of the 'science fiction landscape', we credit our friend Treasa de Loughry's interview with the Irish author Mike McCormack, who proclaims to depict the west of Ireland as a 'science fiction landscape', these contrasts and contradictions a 'tiny part of that greater circum-terrestrial grid' (De Loughry and McCormack 2019).

5 Peter Anker comprehensively defines Britain's organisation of ecological science across its empire from 1895 to 1945 (2001) – and just as importantly, Frank Herbert's *Dune* (1965) features the character Liet-Kynes as the 'imperial ecologist' with the dream to 'improve' Arrakis via terraformation.

6 This is of course in addition to the thinkers sketched in the Introduction who have contributed to the most recent 'material turn' in media studies, focussing on its formative energetics and resource politics (see Maxwell and Miller 2012; Parks and Starosielski 2015; Starosielski and Walker 2016; Hogan 2018; among others too numerous to count).

7 Similar to some other adjacent disciplinary and theoretical arrangements throughout this book, we do not propose to solve ongoing debates about 'new materialism' and the importance of historical materialism – although we do perhaps more clearly align with the political project of the latter (see Lohmann and Hildyard 2014; Bellamy and Diamanti 2018; Bresnihan 2021; Jue and Ruiz 2021).

8 Historian Michael Sexton outlines the politics of Marconi's arrival (and departure) in Ireland, from Connemara to his other holdings, in his relatively rosy 2005 history *Marconi: The Irish Connection*, which we draw from in this section.

9. Elizabeth Povinelli also relates the smoggy politics of early extractive modernity across the colonies to the ephemerality of the 'cloud' (2016).
10. Taken from a newspaper archive of a reprint – see Marconi Signal Station (1907).
11. It is worth noting that Marconi had close ties with Mussolini and the Fascist regime in Italy, including actively preventing Jews from entering the Academy of Italy. On that basis, Cardiff Council in Wales removed any reference to Marconi on an installation commemorating the country's first radio broadcast (BBC 2022).
12. The rich strand of thinking around Irish modernism and the contradictions of Ireland's cultural 'modernity' exists in large part within literary studies (see, for example, Kiberd 1997; McCarthy 2000; Lloyd 2003, 2011; Quigley 2003; Cleary 2006; Rubenstein 2010). 'Modernisation theory' was popular within a particular strand of revisionist history, which equated the 'modern' in Ireland with the economic activities of Britain and, relatedly, the 'civilising' influences of the world market (see Boyce and O'Day 1996; Lee 2008). Contesting this have been environmental sociologists such as Tovey (1993) and Leonard (2007, 2013).
13. Michael Rubenstein's *Public Works: Infrastructure, Irish Modernism and the Postcolonial* (2010) takes the subject of utilities and resources in Irish modernist literature as a way of understanding cultural attitudes towards 'modern' provision in the early 20th century. One of his key insights is that Joyce's *Ulysses* models a kind of distrust of 'utility' as a colonial apparatus – delivered with compromise, and differentially across city and countryside.
14. This didn't stop Joyce from referencing the station in *Finnegans Wake* over 25 years later: 'as softly as the loftly marconimasts from Clifden sough open tireless secrets (mauveport! mauveport!) to Nova Scotia's listing sisterwands. Tubetube!' (1966, 406).
15. This was also where Alcock and Brown had crash-landed on the first transatlantic airplane flight, also from Newfoundland, in 1919 – an overlapping story of imperial technological logistics, connecting two colonies, today both commemorated by the Irish state as unique modern achievements that happened upon ready and willing Irish shores.
16. The celebration of turf-cutting and biodiversity demonstrate what are usually presented as competing ecological imperatives: small-scale, subsistence energy culture (and its association with 'traditional' livelihoods and cultural forms), versus environmental conservation and the regulatory imperatives of carbon savings.
17. This claim may be disputable, but it's also a key moment for Marshall McLuhan, who makes this claim to support his theses surrounding the socially transformative nature of technology (see McLuhan 1994).
18. Such critiques would mirror the eventual demonisation of industrial sabotage by the IRA in the North of Ireland as well, part of a legacy of intertwined media and governmental narratives surrounding irrationally violent republicans as 'anti-progressive' actors against economic and political stability (see McGovern 2010; Ó Beacháin 2014).
19. For an analysis of these emerging politics and the appeal of a kind of 'neo-Luddism' in the face of AI, see Merchant (2023), McQuillan (2022), and Mueller (2021).

Chapter 2

1. Fianna Fáil, an ostensibly anti-Treaty party founded by Eamon de Valera, took over from the pro-Treaty Cumann na nGaedheal (later Fine Gael) in 1932. The protectionist economic policies of de Valera would characterise the Free State through the 1930s–1950s.
2. For explanations of these cultural politics, see, for example, Gladwin (2016); Hitchcock (2019).
3. In the North, where infrastructural connections to the South had begun to wither away under the tourniquet of partition, the extractive economy remained centred on agriculture

as well as the industrial activities in the port cities of Belfast and Derry. As we are focussing primarily on the bogs as sites of electrical politics in this chapter, we will not necessarily discuss the North as a central factor, although much of the infrastructural development in the South during this period was part of a process of delinking from the North due to partition. The grid can thus be perceived as a site to see the durability of partition, in this period as well as in later developments in the FDI-led economy in the South, as later chapters describe in more detail.

4 These documentaries appear in the ESB archives alongside titles such as *Death of the Banshee* and *More Power to the Farmer*, both about rural electrification, the latter of which directly associates it with the land reforms of the 1880s.

5 For a famous example, see Lee (2008).

6 At the time of independence, 97 per cent of Irish exports went to the British mainland (McCabe 2011). The Cumman na Gael Minister for Agriculture, Patrick Hogan, infamously argued that 'national development in Ireland for our generation at least, is practically synonymous with agricultural development' (quoted in Kirby 2010, 16). By this he meant continued support for large, grazier farmers and the comprador middlemen who benefited from agricultural exports.

7 Throughout the 1930s, the Land Commission's work was underpinned by the creation (and expansion) of the 'small, family farm' – a unit of land, labour, and production that was envisaged as the ideological and economic backbone of De Valera's Ireland. This tallied with the stakes of the economic war with Britain in so far as such a trade war weakened the position of the grazier farmer, supporting a policy of greater agricultural subsistence. But, in the absence of capital investments, research and development, and support of alternative markets and associated industries, the 'small, family farm' was a naive, conservative relic at best, a populist rhetorical gesture to appeal to the majority rural population.

8 The link between state-building and energy is best illustrated by the creation of Ireland's Electricity Supply Board (ESB) in 1927. This was the first national, public energy utility anywhere in the world and was tasked with the construction of the Ardnacrusha dam (the largest hydroelectric dam in the world at the time) and rolling out national electricity supply (Mercier 2021). Before the ESB, limited state governance capacities ensured that local authorities, private companies, and self-organised rural communities created geographically discrete and frequently privileged modes of access and connectivity.

9 In an industrial revisionist illustration, these are still advertised and held on the BnM history website: https://www.bordnamonalivinghistory.ie/maps/. They have since been fascinatingly remediated through the EPA and DAFM-funded RePeat project at Trinity College Dublin, which uses these historical maps against recent satellite imaging to effectively identify action sites for rewetting and other 'green' uses: https://sites.google.com/view/project-repeat/home.

10 Lily Toomey's PhD dissertation deftly unpacks the labour process of turf-cutting as it was integrated into BnM institutional policies over the mid-20th century – between machine-cut and hand-won processes, these dictated the terms of the social metabolism between the worker and the soil in Ireland's energy development, especially in terms of increasing mechanisation (Toomey 2025). With peat, this is always an unavoidably transformative socio-ecological process, as peat beds are formed over thousands of years of (anaerobic) plant decomposition. In the process of draining and cutting, in whatever process, the land (and its carbon content) is degraded significantly – which is compounded when burnt, as peat burns hotter and dirtier than coal. In spite of this, it remains a go-to household fuel in many segments of the country due to cheapness and availability for many who retain

turbary (commons-based access and cutting) rights. The small-scale political economy of turf-cutting and selling remains central to rural areas, especially the midlands and west. As described in Chapter 1, driving around turbary in the summer provides insight into the liveliness of this 'small e' energy culture (Lohmann 2016), central to the national imaginary.

11 In 1935, the Coal-Cattle Pact was signed between Ireland and Britain, reducing the high tariffs placed on Irish cattle destined for Britain and British coal in Ireland.

12 Todd Andrews (2001) referred to the ESB as being full of 'free staters', a reference to the Cumann na Gael Party (later to become Fine Gael) that governed Ireland in the 1920s and was strongly associated with the interests of large grazier farmers, and was resistant to state intervention, supporting continued economic dependency on Britain.

13 This is the expression used by a former worker employed on the project, quoted in Loftus and Laffey (2015).

14 During the 2023–24 genocide in Gaza, the Israeli plan to expel Palestinians to the Sinai has been clearly connected to the famous Cromwellian line 'to Hell or to Connacht'.

15 This is a term shared with Katja Bruisch in her 2014 book on agricultural experts and economists in late imperial and early Soviet Russia (see Bruisch 2014).

16 Later experiments in planned towns were not necessarily about public provision, but rather market-based assurance of housing for workers – for example, in Shannon. This point takes on special meaning during the contemporary housing crisis across the country, where companies such as Microsoft and Ryanair provide or are planning to buy up designated housing for their workers due to housing shortages.

17 Once again, this suggests the pertinence of the idea of a 'conservative decolonisation' – however, this is ultimately inseparable from a designated national development project (see Woods 2020).

18 The original National Land League was founded in 1879 in Castlebar, County Mayo, with the slogan: 'The Land of Ireland for the people of Ireland.' Tenant organising against extractive rents, precarious leases, and evictions was a major plank not only of agrarian politics but national, anti-colonial politics in the late 19th century. In an effort to quell the land-based grievances that were fuelling the radical nationalist movement, the British Government introduced Land Acts and a Land Commission to facilitate the purchase of land by tenant farmers. While instigating the establishment of a new class of peasant-proprietors in rural Ireland, these interventions did not settle the land question – failing to address the continued dependence of Ireland's agrarian economy on British markets, the congestion in western regions, and the inter-linked questions of land redistribution and the 'men of no property' who made up the majority of the rural population.

19 Brian O'Boyle and Kieran Allen write: 'De Valera and Lemass were serious about ending the horrors of colonialism, but they never managed to wrest full control of the economy away from their own domestic bankers' (2021, 38). Conor McCabe (2011) writes that the 'value of the Irish pound was set at such a disproportionately high rate that it became a significant hurdle in the development of indigenous Irish industry'.

20 Similarly, Max Ajl summarises Samir Amin's theory of dependency as it applies to ostensibly decolonising states in the 1950s–1960s as 'thin-hulled developmental vessels built to serve the interests of local elites. Others, even the best of them, only partially democratised production without democratising the management of society. As a result, they constantly leaked value into the world capitalist system' (2021a, 82–3).

21 The results for Irish-owned industry were disastrous. Between 1973 and 1986, 85–90 per cent of the jobs in pre-1955 clothing and textiles firms were lost (O'Hearn 1990).

22 For an effective overview of the establishment and early operations of the IDA, see Barry and Ó Fathartaigh (2015).

23 After 1965, at least 70–80 per cent of all new manufacturing jobs were in 'TNCs' (O'Hearn 1987).
24 In Keller Easterling's theorisation of 'extrastatecraft' and the centrality of zones of exceptional economic policy (2014; also Ong 2006), the Shannon Free Zone is central to this story of global infrastructure and its governance. This is powerful in demonstrating Ireland's anachronistic role in modelling postcolonial economic development – more than two decades before the East Asian Tiger economies and, more importantly, China would begin experimenting with special economic zones (SEZs), this small town in Shannon formed the template of Ireland's distinct version of extreme economic liberalism that would advance over the latter half of the 20th century (Brodie forthcoming). In this way, while often purposed by revisionist histories as an example of enterprising, innovative entrepreneurialism to deliver FDI nationalism, it also offers an example of alternative alignments – the site has acted as a kind of pilgrimage for economic statesmen from China, owing a certain amount of inspiration to the zone for their own state-led development policies (Kennard and Provost 2016).
25 Another example of the new generation of Irish compradors actively working to open Ireland up to global capital from the 1960s, O'Regan would become chairman of Bord Fáilte Éireann, a semi-state tourism company. He held the position for 16 years (see O'Connell and O'Carroll 2018).

Chapter 3

1 El Putnam's multimedia work *Rituals for Circuits* (2023) visualises this landscape, especially as it is currently taking shape as a potential digital hub intended to emerge from the industrial ruin.
2 This was a preoccupation of many of the same postcolonial and anti-revisionist theorists referenced in Chapter 1, who attempted to navigate an emerging 'postmodern' Ireland within what was an observably postcolonial cultural landscape.
3 Ó Riain elsewhere refers to the post-1980s Irish state as more closely a 'flexible developmental state', investing in particular forms of production towards these ambitions (2000).
4 According to Crotty, 'Ireland's metropolitan dependence, with respect to agricultural prices, jobs, and credit is now far more complete than that of any other former capitalist colony. This extreme dependence arises from, and is the corollary of, Ireland's uniqueness among former capitalist colonies in being located in Europe' (Crotty 1977, 101).
5 This phrase is shared with Brodie's *Wild Tides: Media Infrastructure and Financial Crisis in Ireland* (forthcoming), which traces a parallel story of the specificities of Irish neoliberal development in and through the financialisation of media and culture.
6 The Telesis Report was an influential critical review of FDI strategy commissioned by the National Economic and Social Council in 1982, an 'independent' advisory of the Taoiseach that would become prominent in the social partnership paradigm later in the 1980s. As the story goes, the IDA won out, in part due to the risky pay-off of the Intel investment in 1989 (see Telesis 1983; Keenan 1999).
7 While frequently coming under fire in places such as the UK from right-wing groups fighting government 'over-spend' and pushing for lower taxes, these bodies in Ireland – we focus here on semi-states specifically – are key to managing the unique features of Irish capitalism through the mediation of multinational capital, making them due for more focussed left-wing critique.
8 Two significant new semi-states created in the 1980s were Telecom Eireann (1984), responsible for telecommunications services, and Coillte (1988), responsible for Ireland's forestry sector and land amounting to 7 per cent of the Republic's total territory.

NOTES

9. One of the striking things looking back at this period is that there was little attempt to water down what was in effect a fundamental shift from socially productive, public goods to market-focussed commodities. As the RTE news segment on the launch of Coillte in 1988 puts it: 'No longer under the straitjacket of the civil service, forestry is now entering the commercial world of the '80s' (RTÉ 1988b).
10. Tony Ryan, for example, became a manager with the state-owned airline company, Aer Lingus. In 1975, with a London-based financial services company, Ryan set up Guinness Peat Aviation (GPA), an aircraft leasing company that went on to become the largest aviation leasing company in the world. After GPA was taken over by General Electric in the early 1990s, Ryan, equipped with experience and networks, would go on to set up the new commercial airline, Ryanair. Another well-known figure was Tony O'Reilly. He became General Manager of An Bord Bainne, the state dairy company, in 1962. Having earned a PhD in agricultural marketing from the University of Bradford, O'Reilly inserted the Irish dairy industry into new international markets through the Kerrygold brand. The success of this strategy, and his networks in the US, led him to becoming the CEO of Heinz, a major multinational food processing company, in the 1970s. Ireland was not just a (neo)colonial laboratory, it was a training ground for a new entrepreneurial capitalist class in the era of neoliberal restructuring.
11. The primary historical sources in this section are the archive of *Scéal na Móna*, a monthly publication published by BnM for workers that ran from the 1970s to the early 2000s, and a series of ten oral history interviews conducted with former BnM workers.
12. O'Connor was popular with BnM workers because he not only kept the industry going, but also gave them the opportunity to make more money if they worked harder. As well as introducing bonuses for productivity, he remunerated workers for technological innovations. It is easy to dismiss these 'neoliberal' workplace practices but they grafted onto a pre-existing culture that existed in the form of sports competitions and beauty pageants developed by BnM from the 1940s.
13. Móna Engineering was set up at this time to utilise the skilled labour and factory workshops that BnM had at its disposal but were no longer required for peat production. In the mid-1990s, Móna had nearly 50 engineering projects, including manufacturing a unique waste disposal system for major drug manufacturers, including Pfizer, SmithKline Beecham, Sandos, FMC and Neway, ADM, and NEC. Known as the BnM 'commandos', Móna Engineering was pivoting to provide services to the new wave of FDI that was coming just as the peat industry went into steep decline (Scéal na Mona, 1997).
14. Commenting that BnM previously 'gave away ideas and advice for free', O'Connor expressed relief that the company had 'now developed a clear and professional approach to consultancy services, with all information, advice, and assistance provided by IPB Global at a price' (Scéal na Móna 1994).
15. Barry and O'Mahoney refer to this process that had already occurred across the workings of the state towards FDI in the 1950s as 'regime change' (2017), which O'Hearn similarly supports in his article on this earlier era (1989). Barry and Ó Fathartaigh (nd) contend that this was explicitly a result of the IDA, similarly arguing that 'a revolution in the attitudes of ministers and mandarins would be required before the IDA's role would be clearly defined. Trade liberalisation would ultimately ensue'. These 'passive revolutions', as Gramsci referred to the organised maintenance of ruling-class interests through the state, are successive across Irish history – including during the formation of the Southern state, as Beatty explains (2016).
16. The Edenderry power plant, which opened in Offaly in 2000, was Ireland's first 'independent' power station, built and owned by the Finnish Fortune Group before being sold to the energy multinational E.ON in 2003.

17. The strains of this would begin to be felt through the infrastructural landscape from the late 1980s. For example, an ESB strike in 1988 prominently affected FDI industrial production – an interesting point of reference for the power of infrastructural labour to halt the profit flows of FDI (see RTÉ 1988a).
18. See, for example, Regan and Walsh (1976); Crotty (1977); Orridge (1983); Baker (1987); O'Hearn (1989, 1990); Tovey (1993); Jacobsen (1994); Ó Grada (1997); Taylor (1998); Allen (2004).
19. Tovey cites one particular commentator who associated Ireland's cultural backwardness on environmental issues with Irish nationalism – the assumption being that Ireland closed itself off from the progressive influence of modern ideas between independence and 1970.
20. From the 1970s, major environmental organisations identified the biggest threat to Ireland's environment as rural residents, primarily farmers. This ignored that the modernisation of agriculture was highly uneven and that the intensification of dairy in particular was brought about by EEC agricultural policy and the shift of state policy towards processing and expanding export markets (for baby formula, for example).
21. The concept of postcolonial ecological regime borrows from Sharae Deckard's path-breaking work on Ireland's 'neoliberal ecological regime' (2016).
22. The shift in agricultural policy from the 1970s parallels the shift towards FDI-led industrialisation in so far as rural development, support for smaller farmers, and production of food for the Irish population shifted towards earning foreign currency via exports. Once again, it was semi-states such as An Bord Bainne that actively brought about this transition from developmental to post-developmental dependency (Crotty 1977).
23. One of the key issues in Irish economic indicators is the non-correspondence between GDP and GNP – or, in general, between GDP and social progress. O'Hearn wrote in 2001: 'In 1980, southern Irish GDP and GNP were practically equal. In 1990, GDP was eleven per cent higher than GNP. By the turn of the century, GDP exceeded GNP by about twenty per cent. In simple language, GDP overstates by a fifth how much of the material wealth created by the economic activities of the Irish people is available for their own use within Ireland' (2001b). Today, while Ireland is second in the world in GDP per capita, GDP is 50 per cent higher than GNP. This is so extreme as to throw off international indicators, deeming Ireland's GDP measures 'leprechaun economics', and leading the Irish Central Statistics Office (CSO) to generate a new measure called 'modified GNI', making it the only country in the world to officially measure its economy in this way.
24. There is a rich seam of Irish geographical literature associated with this line of thinking, which Brodie (forthcoming) examines and supplements in detail elsewhere.
25. See also Brodie (2021).
26. The Asahi plant produced synthetic fibres from highly toxic chemicals, including acrylonitrile (also known as vinyl cyanide) and methyl acrylate. In the event of a serious accident, contact with these chemicals would be fatal. Despite these risks, tanks of these chemicals were transported daily from Dublin Port to Ballina by rail. Over two decades, there were several accidents along the railway line that resulted in the evacuation of nearby residents (RTÉ 1985).
27. Host in Ireland, a data centre industry lobby group has proclaimed that Ireland has gone from 'potatoes to chips' in its export evolution since the 1970s. This is not just in terms of physical production and infrastructural transformation, but, in the tech industry narrative, the cultivation of skills and expertise through land-based productive relations that are themselves exportable prospects – similar to O'Connor's desire to export peat expertise, albeit premised on a very different productive/resource basis (Connolly 2022).

28 'If a single event can point to the birth of the Celtic Tiger, it was the Irish state's success in attracting Intel to the country in 1990, at a historically high cost to the Irish state' (O'Hearn 2003, 38).

29 This was such an exemplary case of Ireland's FDI strategies that it was chosen for a school lesson for this helpful guide: https://bantrygeography.wordpress.com/wp-content/uploads/2012/04/intel.pdf.

30 A similar but somewhat different logic comes about with telecoms and media privatisation – this is an asset that must be cashed in on during times of declining revenues, debt, and changing infrastructure/industry. Privatisation offers not only less exposure to public spending but also a shift of necessary expertise and management to private sector 'innovation' via R&D.

31 The report cited here suggests that the sustainable solution was not to build new or proprietary infrastructure to achieve stable energy needs, but rather to reduce energy consumption. This recommendation seemed to get lost in the discourses between 2003 and the mid-2010s, when the same questions arise for data centres.

32 Further, this energy use is subsidised by the state in times of crisis – for example, in 2024, when the IDA handed out massive subsidies to Intel and other multinationals in the face of energy price hikes (Whyte 2024).

33 For an interesting and multi-layered analysis of this project and its implications, featuring a voice from the data centre industry supporting it for Ireland's competitiveness, see Collins (2025).

34 Anyone familiar with Irish society in the early 2020s will be struck by this time capsule – has anything really changed, except for the roads in the FDI-intensive areas getting more connected?

35 Apple is not a story we tell here, but its location in the Holyhill Industrial Estate in Cork since 1980 – where it still locates a reasonably sized manufacturing and services facility – has been a site of controversy surrounding its use as a tax dodge for Apple globally (see McCabe 2022). Additionally, in the 2010s, the Irish state planned to allow the company to build an €850 million data centre facility on a Coillte woodland in Athenry, County Galway, that could have used 5–8 per cent of the country's electricity, daily, had it gone ahead. While the state supported the project, as did many in the region, objectors delayed the project until Apple withdrew, much to the chagrin of the government, who had organised a diplomatic mission to California to ask the company to carry the project forward (see Brodie 2020b).

36 While opposition to specific chemical facilities always carried a place-based, local force, it also developed connections with other campaigns. Baker (1987) shows that 18 different groups were involved in the Raybestos campaign – including residents associations, the Irish Anti-Nuclear Movement, and more politically radical groups such as Revolutionary Struggle. As in other parts of the world, fears of chemical pollution were linked with fears around radioactive pollution and nuclear energy. State plans to build a nuclear reactor in Carnsore Point in County Wexford were resisted in the late 1970s, with two major concerts happening in 1978 and 1979. At the same time, another campaign arose in response to the Anglo-Australian company Rio Tinto trying to mine for uranium in County Donegal. These groups helped foster an 'anti-toxic industry movement' across Ireland – and here, the connections between extractive industries such as mining, risks associated with pollution, and state regulation become apparent.

37 Concerns haven't gone away, however, nor have campaigns organised to challenge formal expertise and state and corporate assurances of risk management and control. The Aughinish refinery in Askeaton, County Limerick, for example, Europe's largest bauxite refinery, has been subject to repeated complaints and concerns from local residents about

human and animal illnesses. Despite the 350-acre site of red, hazardous waste (visible from satellite images), the EPA has granted permission for the refinery to expand its production (and toxic waste) with no clear social or environmental transition programme in place.

[38] One local farmer near the Intel site in Leixlip, for example, named Thomas Reid, has been objecting to attempted compulsory purchases of his land and pollution to local water supply by the company for over a decade. With Intel supported by successive governments, licensed by IDA attempts to requisition Reid's land, and favoured by An Bord Pleanála (ABP), Reid's uphill battle against the company (and the planning process itself) has been the subject of a documentary film and an array of news reports. Corruption in ABP has even been admonished by judges ruling in favour of Intel, with the planning body accepting unverified scientific evidence from the company. See Clifford (2022); also *The Lonely Battle of Thomas Reid* (dir. Feargal Ward 2017).

[39] It's been widely acknowledged that one of the growing ecological factors in monopoly tech's expansion is fresh water usage in times and places of drought (Dryer 2023; Lehuedé 2024) – particularly in chip manufacturing (Lev-Ram 2024).

[40] Ireland ranks 51st in the world, behind only two other EU nations (Malta and Poland, as well as of course Norway) (SWFI nd). This is a direct result of Ireland's facilitation of multinational tax evasion. Recent empirical analysis (Parnreiter et al 2024) shows the extent to which global profit repatriation functions as a mechanism of uneven development. In terms of net export of profits, Ireland ranks second (after the Russian Federation) in the world, accounting for 7.7 per cent of total exported profits. Ireland's specific role in draining surplus value from the Global South to core countries in the Global North is through its complex tax regime – skimming a significant wage in the process.

[41] As Crotty summarises: 'The ultimate consequence of the Whitaker-Gerladine policy of reintegrating Ireland's former capitalist colonial economy with the economies of the metropolitan capitalist countries has been to intensify Irish economic dependence' (Crotty 1977, 100).

Chapter 4

[1] Captured by Twitter user Mark Rooney: https://x.com/rooneymobile/status/1327581502763380736.

[2] We are here intervening in a lively discourse in political ecology, geography, and critical agrarian studies surrounding 'green extractivism', which is one geographical instantiation of green capitalism across expanding resource frontiers. In particular, as we argue in Chapter 6, there has been minimal connection between how monopoly tech and multinational renewable energy have been coalescing and intersecting (see Arboleda 2020; Calvão and Archer 2021; Jeres, Garcés, and Torres 2021; Voskoboynik and Andreucci 2021; Bruna 2023; Dunlap and Riquito 2023; Hamouchene and Sandwell 2023; Brodie 2024; Dunlap et al 2024).

[3] As the most recent Irish Government Statement on the Role of Data Centres in Ireland's Enterprise Strategy states: 'These transitions can – and must be – complementary. For this to happen, digital and climate change policies need to move in tandem and this Statement sets out how this will be achieved in respect of data centres', which the statement goes on to assure 'are core digital infrastructure and play an indispensable role in our economy and society' (Government of Ireland 2022a, 2).

[4] Many have commented on how the climate and atmosphere become territories of valorisation in green capitalism, especially as their transformation via capital becomes more entrenched and irreversible. To name a few analysts of these atmospheric politics: Cooper (2010); Howe and Boyer (2016); McCormack (2018); Furuhata (2022); Grossman (2023).

NOTES

5   For example, the Galway Wind Park operation on Moycullen Bog saw environmental opposition and planning problems since 2012, due to An Bord Pleanála's initial refusal of the project on environmental grounds and ongoing local opposition because of effects on inland fisheries and protected bog habitats.
6   Speaking to carbon offsets, Bumpus and Liverman refer to 'accumulation by decarbonisation' (2008).
7   In a public interview he gave in 1994, Eddie O'Connor stated that BnM's traditional activity as a fuel peat business was finished and there was a need to develop new initiatives, including in the 'growth area' of environmental sustainability. Asked about losing the political identity of the company if there were job losses and closures to briquette factories, he replied: 'I'm only concerned with commercial identity' (Sceal na Mona 1994, 6).
8   O'Connor was forced to step down from his position as chair of the company in 2021 after publicly stating that the energy transition in Africa was being held back by a lack of education in 'tribal societies'.
9   This clip unpacks so much about the branding of Ireland and its FDI model through continued industrialisation (Wind Energy 2016).
10 This has been both promoted and critiqued extensively in the press (see Dunphy 2022; Eirgrid 2023; O'Donoghue 2024).
11 Take, for example, another key semi-state in this story: Coillte. Holding 7 per cent of Ireland's land, the organisation in 2025 quietly, without public announcement, shut down its non-profit woodland credit scheme and handed the reins over to a start-up called Nature Trust. A news article perfectly sums up the double-speak: 'Nature Trust sells "woodland credits" to companies in return for investing in planting, but Coillte said: "This is not a carbon offsetting programme." ... However, Bank of Ireland which developed the Nature Trust woodland credit scheme describes it as being used in a "carbon offsetting social enterprise"' (O'Doherty 2025). See also Chapter 5.
12 This was evidenced in the 2024 planning Bill that has legislated for exponentially expanded gas use (see Mercier 2024b). This is on top of data centre companies applying for connection to the gas grid to make their own on-site energy generation facilities (Swinhoe 2023) – or even just using diesel generators (O'Carroll 2024).
13 These have been proposed for some time – ideas surrounding BnM Energy Parks first surfaced in 2021, building on existing plans for developing energy and industrial infrastructure in the midlands for a 'just transition'. Other post-industrial spaces, however, proposed similar measures – for example, the Killala plan discussed in Chapter 3 also plans for pairing of multinational data and energy.
14 It's worth noting that Foley's previous role was managing director of Land Solutions in Coillte, the semi-state responsible for forestry. This involved development of privately owned wind energy and telecoms infrastructure on Coillte-owned land. Prior to his involvement with Ireland's semi-states, he held a number of senior executive roles with multinationals in speciality chemicals and electronics.
15 Lantry has written similar opinion pieces, or been featured in similar pieces, multiple times since 2023. We identify him as a key player in the data centre industry lobby, but also as a kind of eco-modern comprador – as a former Eirgrid man himself.
16 Similarly, Alix Johnson (2023) discusses this landscape as one of knowledge exchange and consolidation of industrial narratives – both within the context of Iceland's industrial culture, and its geographical position globally.
17 As Ireland has become a destination for cloud storage providers, so too has it developed commercial expertise and networks within the sector, with deepening relationships to the state and transnational networks of industry. Reflecting Ireland's status as a laboratory for capitalist technology, the national industry has moved from simply hosting big tech

in Ireland to being a vector for it around the world (see Brodie 2021, 2024). For expert breakdown of the idea of the tech 'ecosystem', see Pringle (2021).

18 For this turn of phrase, we also have Lantry to thank, if the press releases are to be believed (see Leonard 2024).

19 This is of course amplifying during 'hype' around AI (Chen 2024).

20 This is exemplified by AWS' involvement in the Tallaght District Heating Scheme (TDHS). While these systems have been promoted for years, the TDHS is the only one that has been developed. This is not just about the expansion of monopoly tech into energy services, or even the 'greenwashing' of data centres. It is more fundamentally about a situation in which new energy infrastructure in Ireland is only being developed in tandem with or supported by tech investment.

21 'Eaton has launched an energy service that enables data centers to contribute to renewable energy and earn from their technology investments. Eaton's EnergyAware UPS is the data center industry's first solution to enable organisations to earn from the UPS investment. It puts data centers in control of their energy, letting them offer capacity back to the grid, and to say when and at what price' (Eaton nd). In the same video, there is an image of a data centre, surrounded by trees, wind turbines, and a hydroelectric dam, with money pouring into it from the sky. 'A data center could expect typical returns of up to 50.000 € per MW of power allocated to grid support per year.'

22 For a critical analysis of these dynamics in the context of Ireland's carbon budgets, see Daly (2024).

23 This effort to secure energy as cheaply as possible is opening up new markets for tech companies as energy providers (as alluded to above). In Ireland, this is taking the form of 'capacity payments' by Eirgrid to data storage/energy service providers paid for through household bills. In other words, rather than being a cost, control of energy infrastructure in Ireland opens up new, highly profitable revenue streams for these companies (Reynolds 2025).

24 As we detail in the Introduction, the best historical materialist work on the colonial political ecologies of Ireland comes from Eamonn Slater, Terrence McDonough, and Eoin Flaherty – Slater's 'Irish Metabolic Rifts' website remains an indispensable repository of his and his colleagues' theorisation of Marx and Engels' exchanges on the metabolic rifting of Ireland's soil ecologies and its widespread socio-ecological effects (see Slater nd).

25 As research by the Irish River Project has shown, current wind farms are overwhelmingly clustered around peatlands.

26 In Ireland, these contestations have typically taken the shape of anti-wind (turbine) or anti-pylon protests. More widely, there has been significant work on the political ecologies and geographies of energy transitions, development, and mounting inequalities, which have attempted to understand these politics from a critical perspective. For intros to two exemplary special issues on the subject, see Bridge et al (2018); Knuth et al (2022). For how this connects to the digital, there has been a smaller but growing number of studies (see Abram et al 2022; Sovacool et al 2022; Sareen and Müller 2023).

27 This includes an influential report on utilising data centres' infrastructural capacities towards decarbonisation (see Bloomberg NEF 2021).

28 This is quoted in a later planning statement for the Cloghercor wind farm – we were unable to track down a citable version of the 2022 Donegal County Development Plan.

29 We'd like to acknowledge here the help and influence from Julia Velkova, and her ongoing work looking into the politics of large-scale, extractive wind energy development to supply data centres in the north of Sweden. Her comments and support have been immensely helpful in this regard.

30 This is how we refer to this dynamic in our first article on the subject, arguments which this chapter reproduces and expands (see Bresnihan and Brodie 2021). In addition, we

have minimal space to get into it in this short chapter, but the use of smart meters and the proprietary software used to privately administer energy austerity are part of this (see Sadowski and Levenda 2020).

31 As Denis O'Hearn argues, Ireland's position as a semi-periphery within the world economy must also account for spatial variations within the country: 'not only are agrarian regions of the island of Ireland distinct from urban and more industrialized regions but each region has its own specificities. It may seem obvious to say it, but Kerry is not Donegal, nor is Cork Dublin' (Beatty et al 2016, 203).

32 AWS, for example, was quick to distance itself from the Meenbog peatslide when only months earlier it had been quick to claim the Donegal wind farm as its first renewable energy investment in Ireland (O'Brien 2019). When we wrote a short article for an online media outlet a year later, connecting AWS with the peatslide, the editor of the journal was reluctant to connect AWS directly due to fear of litigation.

33 The centrality of venture capital in both the data centre and energy sector in the development stage is something that we won't have time to comment on at length – but deserves a footnote, at least. This is largely about real estate, and developing an asset/project that will be more effectively used by a larger, industrial multinational.

34 For a recent analysis of the 'extractive mediation' of oceanic environments, see Han (2024).

35 Take, for example, Echelon's multiple energy projects and their different territorial dimensions, especially after years of delays (see Alley 2020; Swinhoe 2024a).

36 Doubtful, but ironic, if James Connolly is among them.

37 They tell a similar story about Ireland as a whole – the country was a wasteland where the choice was to either go to the US or England before the US multinationals came and rescued the economy.

38 Google was blocked from extending its Grange Castle data centre complex in August 2024. The decision by South Dublin County Council ruled that there was 'insufficient capacity in the electricity network (grid) and lack of significant on-site renewable energy to power the data centre' (Deegan 2024).

Chapter 5

1 See iCRAG (2023a).
2 At the time of writing, SFI was in the process of being absorbed (alongside the Irish Research Council, a more social science/humanities focussed funder) into Research Ireland under the Research and Innovation Act 2024. Without the ability to go into the new organisation in detail, in short, it appears to have intensified SFI's instrumental, economically orientated research focus.
3 These are the two most directly illustrative of many such projects that we will reference throughout this chapter (see AI2Peat 2024; Terrain AI 2024).
4 For excellent research surrounding the 'sustainability industry' and the misguided (but often well-meaning) landscape of climate solutionism (see Goldstein 2018; Buller 2022; Archer 2024).
5 We are of course not the first to notice the structures of dependency in Irish HEIs (Yearley 1995), and how that has shaped and deepened the 'neoliberalisation' of the university (Mercille and Murphy 2017). In addition, the commercial orientation of university research – beholden to private interests and industrial partnerships for funding and shareholder value – is a global phenomenon, related to the much-maligned 'neoliberalisation' of the university in the West and its alignment with the 'accumulation of capital' (Giroux 2014; Rikap and Harari-Kermadec 2020). The UK and the US have been the primary examples of these dynamics in the Anglo-sphere which we see playing out in Ireland

– whether the prevalence of corporate culture and knowledge exchange across global universities, which Nick Dyer-Witheford argues makes universities 'firmly entrained to market-driven economic growth – in particular, to the development of high-technology industries. Universities are now frankly conceived and funded by policy elites as research facilities and training grounds for the creation of the new intellectual properties and technocultural subjectivities necessary to a post-Fordist accumulation regime' (2005, 71). However, as we outline below, the degrees to which this has occurred in Ireland are distinct and worth drawing out in the context of contemporary eco-modernisation.

6   There has been a significant body of literature on the problematics of 'net zero' for climate politics, especially as its core value is the pricing and measurement of continued emissions in sectors seeking to exonerate themselves of climate villainy (see Buck 2021; Buller 2022).

7   While writing, SFI has become Research Ireland – which effectively continues SFI's remit, while absorbing the Irish Research Council (IRC), typically more social science, arts, and humanities focussed. At the time of writing in autumn 2024, it's yet to be seen what effect these changes will have, but our guess is further entrenchment of these existing schemes, based on familiar tokenistic language surrounding the role of these non-scientific disciplines in supporting or supplementing scientific and 'impact'-orientated ends (see Government of Ireland 2024c).

8   There are interesting connections to be made between the Dutch 'discovery' of Ireland's bogs, and the 'edenic narratives' of European scientists' 'discovery' of the Amazon discussed by Slater (1996).

9   Given Ireland's different development history, the country became something of a beacon for Irish and European environmentalists in the 1980s, who presented it as relatively untouched and pristine compared with the industrialised UK and continent. The representation of Ireland as the 'emerald isle' within Irish tourism campaigns and IDA advertising also takes off around this time.

10   In 1993, Agarwal and Narain famously called this approach 'environmental colonialism' (2019).

11   In Ireland, by the beginning of the 18th century most bogs belonged in law to individual landowners, with many of the large bogs incorporated within great estates. But long-standing customary rights were able to survive, in part because these rights of turbary can be invoked by anybody coming within the custom of the locality, even if they have no other land rights (Feehan et al 2008). This is what makes the governance of such rights, particularly via the state, so contested. Turbary rights grant individual rights of access to households living near or adjacent to specific bogs, but the 'winning' of turf via hand or machine, the drying of turf, and its final transfer to houses often involves collective labour and shared resources.

12   The Forum was convened to hear the views of turf-cutting communities who were set to have their rights to cut turf taken away by the state in the interests of peatland conservation. Captured in the Quirke Report in 2012, the testimonies from the Forum reveal a thick set of social relations, economic dependencies, and cultural attachments to the bogs – relations difficult to contain within contemporary narratives of conservation or efficiency (NPWS 2012). Similar to the previous chapter, where Donal's intimate knowledge of the plants on the bog, and its ties to history and memory, was central to his objections to large wind turbines being built there.

13   For example: carbon dynamics affected by 'previous and current land use, the residual depth of the peat, nutrient status and vegetation composition' (Wilson et al 2022). Conversely, bog rewetting can also lead to a short-term increase in methane emissions. In the long term, rewetting brings back vegetation, which in turn absorbs atmospheric carbon and

stores it in peat soils. But the timelines for such rehabilitation are highly uncertain, with one recent study suggesting that under one scenario, the rewetting of a drained raised bog site would continue to have a warming effect on the climate until 2085 but will then have a strong cooling impact (Wilson et al 2022).

14 Jennifer Goldstein (2022) distinguishes between scientific uncertainty and financial uncertainty: for private sector investors or donors, minimising financial risk, rather than determining the amount of carbon sequestered, is the measure by which a climate mitigation project succeeds or fails.

15 We can already see how these political economic shifts manifested in the orientation of engineering expertise and innovation within BnM in the 1990s – Móna Engineering was set up to utilise the skilled labour and factory workshops that BnM had at its disposal but no longer required for peat production. See Chapter 3.

16 This strategy was not without contention and difficulties at the early stages. As Jacobsen notes, the 'peripheral postindustrial' project of the IDA's courting of tech multinationals was 'eroding as a result of systematic technology gaps – systematic in terms both of internal socio-economic organization and of international exchange relations' (1994, 110). Jacobsen argues that this is related to foreign control of technology transfer, global segmentation of production and labour processes, and the obsolescence of new technologies, which, when combined, leads to an impoverished national R&D ecosystem due to the dependence upon flighty multinationals, who go where the cheap labour is rather than durably investing in a 'local' or 'national' research ecosystem (1994, 110–11).

17 Yearley narrates the history of the NBST in the early 1970s, responding to the failure of FDI to support a national R&D culture – foreshadowing the Telesis Report commissioned by the NSC in 1982. The NBST, however, was mired by controversy and overspending, especially in the crisis-ridden 1980s, and was absorbed into EOLAS as part of new Fianna Fáil austerity programmes in 1987. The organisation had effectively failed to justify direct public spending on R&D in economic or cultural terms – even though it was an early adopter of economic arguments for public science – leaving science and industry to flourish in partnership through closer association with more powerful development agencies such as the IDA (Yearley 1995).

18 In 2022, 'Science Foundation Ireland (SFI) leveraged €267m in external funding over and above a base investment of €213m'. Presumably, this means that direct public investment was €213 million, but the main strategy is to leverage external funding. Ireland ranks sixth in the world in university–industry partnerships, and the focus has also audibly shifted to 'sustainability', in both IDA and SFI copy: '"In 2022, SFI launched new programmes to facilitate our becoming a green, sustainable, deep-tech innovation leader and furthered its economic impact with €61m secured from private enterprise in 2022 and over 1,500 regional industry engagements," he added.' Half of these 'industry engagements' were from multinationals, primarily concentrated in the eastern and southern regions (see SFI 2022; Gain 2023).

19 We should be clear here that the centrality of R&D (now 'R&I' (research and innovation)) within export-led industrial development strategies in the late 20th century is by no means unique to Ireland. However, in Ireland, this mobilisation of universities as tools for industrial development – and specifically operating within a landscape of FDI-led development – has produced circumstances whereby universities and funding bodies effectively become organs of state development agencies motivated by the needs of these industries and companies. Some have tied this to austerity specifically (Mercille and Murphy 2017), while others have recently shown the deepening of this in the form of direct industry funding and its impacts on research agendas, specifically around 'sustainability' (Maonaigh et al 2025). This FDI-led logic of knowledge production has been deeply integrated into the

research culture of HEIs and associated research institutions across Ireland. Let us take one example from one of our home institutions, University College Dublin – again, by no means unique, but instructive as to the wider dynamic. Under the UCD umbrella, there exist dual bodies called NOVA and NEXUS UCD, which deal with innovation activities and support entrepreneurs and research/industry partnerships. These organisations boast support for 'knowledge transfer' and 'commercialisation', whereby the university helps researchers to 'spin-off' publicly funded research into commercial applications (frequently through existing industry partnerships, with companies such as IBM) or enables companies to 'benefit from UCD research expertise'. The website promotes four reasons to partner with UCD: 'international reputation'; 'support offered'; 'funding opportunities' through Enterprise Ireland innovation partnerships and SFI Research Centres; and 'tax incentives for R&D in Ireland', advertised as R&D tax credits of 25 per cent, EU grants, IDA RD&I grants of up to 50 per cent project costs, and an exceptionally low tax rate: 'KDB 6.25% corporation tax rate on profits arising from R&D projects relating to certain patents and copyrighted software carried out by an Irish company' (NovaUCD nd). In this model, UCD not only behaves like, but also advertises itself as a de facto organ of Ireland's developmental model.

[20] This has been absorbed into Research Ireland: a primary focus is retaining R&I competitiveness for attracting multinationals to Ireland.

[21] Along with other, somewhat more problematic applications – for example, facial recognition via AI to recognise 'diversity' in partnership with RTÉ, or simply acting as a testing centre for AI technologies prior to roll-out (through what it refers to as its 'Test Before Invest' service.

[22] Ireland's 'research centres' model has been especially proficient in producing research and partnerships across institutions and the private sector, as researchers are encouraged to seek out industrial applications – ADAPT, Insight, MAREI, Nexsys, and so on.

[23] The development of an Irish 'Peatland Code' modelled after the UK version would be intended to standardise the measurement, valuation, and application of industrial credits. https://www.iucn-uk-peatlandprogramme.org/peatland-code-0.

[24] For exceptions, see Buck's and Pasek's work cited throughout this chapter; also Wiessner (2024).

[25] There are, of course, exceptions – in particular, looking at the management of 'smart forests' and regimes of techno-ecological governance. See Jennifer Gabrys' work on 'smart forests' (2020); and Jędrzej Niklas' Data Forests project (forthcoming).

[26] 'While the project is capturing data from land types in Ireland, the intention is to design a cloud platform that can use the insights from the Irish findings and be shared with other countries to help them explore land usage and carbon reduction in their own jurisdictions' (Hallahan 2020).

[27] These ambitions speak directly to the shifting epistemologies from the 'global', central to the conception of climate change as a problem that needed both a whole-world systemic approach at the same time as the entrenchment of neoliberal capitalism (Edwards 2010), to the 'planetary', speaking to the idea that the planet can and should be engineered towards sustaining human (capitalist) life (Arboleda 2020) (see Microsoft nd).

[28] Among those already cited, many have engaged with the ways that 'accumulation by decarbonisation' is enabled via mechanisms of carbon pricing, crediting, and offsetting, all of which require the capturing, valuation, and trading of carbon via advanced technoscientific means, and introduces problematic relations for environmental governance and climate justice (see Bumpus and Liverman 2008; Lovell and Liverman 2010; Lippert 2016; Watt 2021; Dalsgaard 2022).

[29] PFI found that 90 per cent of total carbon tax payments in Ireland are paid by 10 per cent of taxpayers, mainly large energy importers (but also large energy users, such as data centre operators). They have proposed that some of this tax could be offset by investments in peatland restoration projects, thereby incentivising large carbon polluters to directly engage in these projects. This is an extension of Ireland's FDI-friendly tax regime in an era of eco-modernisation.

[30] See note 23.

[31] There was a similar response to the government announcement that they would be rewetting 80,000 hectares, resulting in 100 million tonnes of carbon being stored in perpetuity. Despite the positive news story, the announcement was met with some ambivalence by those who have worked for years, even decades, to understand the carbon cycles of peat soils and those who have worked to protect intact bogs from further drainage and extraction.

[32] Feehan is the lead author on the seminal *The Bogs of Ireland* cited throughout this chapter (Feehan et al 2008).

[33] The above is all captured in the report from the event, published as Lough Boora Parklands (1998).

[34] See, for example, Tsing (2015).

Chapter 6

[1] For specifics on extractive forestry in Leitrim, see Fitzgerald (2023).

[2] For a detailed and generous accounts and reflections of these events, see Cirefice and Mincks (2026); Fitzgerald and Murphy (2023); Making Relatives Collective (nd).

[3] We reference some of these discourses and policies in the Introduction, but key in the policy sphere are Department of the Environment, Climate and Communications (2024); Government of Ireland (2022c); in the critical research sphere, see Bruna (2023); Dunlap et al (2024).

[4] At least, not when it suits them – see Chapter 4, and the case of AWS maintaining arm's length from the Meenbog peatslide.

[5] In particular, shout-out to V'cenza Cirefice, Sian Cowman, Lynda Sullivan, and all communities taking strong and principled stances against the global injustices of extractivism.

[6] For example, across the EU, where green extractive frontiers are unfolding in peripheralised countries such as Serbia and Portugal, as well as across the Global South.

[7] In 1968, Silvermines opened in County Tipperary, and in 1965 Tynagh mines opened in East Galway. When the two mines closed, both in 1982, all that was left were hundreds of unemployed former workers and environmental damage to land that can not now be recuperated for farming or other productive use (Barry and Doran 2016). In 1983 it emerged that 2,000 acres of land were contaminated in East Galway, with lead, arsenic, and zinc, while toxic dust from tailings piles blew around the countryside (Leonard 2007).

[8] Regan and Walsh's 1976 article on dependency and under-development in the Irish mineral sector remains one of the few contemporaneous academic analyses of the Irish economy through this lens.

[9] The company appears largely focussed on its licences in Austria for the moment (see Sadden 2024).

[10] This latter company is particularly hilarious: an Australian-based 'mining incubator' that exploits deposits in Greenland.

[11] For example, as recently as 2009, an influential collection entitled *A Living Countryside? The Politics of Sustainable Development in Rural Ireland* (McDonagh et al 2016) has zero

chapters devoted to, or even significantly mentioning, mining. Between mining and chemicals manufacturing, these environmental 'villains' were far from the minds of those considering early strategies of sustainability in and through the countryside – whereas today, most mainstream climate policy discussion cedes ground to the necessity of green mining, similar to the need for data centres.

[12] See Gago and Mezzadra (2017); Gómez-Barris (2017); Cirefice and Sullivan (2019); Arboleda (2020); Jerez et al (2021); Szeman and Wenzel (2021); Chagnon et al (2022); Voskoboynik and Andreucci (2022); Bruna (2023); Hamouchene and Sandwell (2023); Jung (2023); Brodie (2024); Dunlap et al (2024).

[13] As Natacha Bruna defines it, extractivism arises in the 1950s as an extension of colonial dynamics within the resource requirements of the capitalist world system (2023).

[14] For different influential variants of these themes around climate action, colonialism, and imperialism, see Kothari (1981); Fairhead et al (2012); Agarwal and Narain (2019); Sultana (2022); Hamouchene and Sandwell (2023); Pedregal and Lukić (2024).

[15] See Arboleda (2020). Lisa Han's recent book touches on this, considering resource-making via digital tech employed on the seafloor (2024). We talk a bit about this legibility around wind and resources more broadly throughout the book (see Chapters 4 and 5), but cloud technologies are enabling the deepening of extractive relationships into these 'resource frontiers' across the board, whether wind, carbon finance, or minerals. And this is about an expansion of monopoly tech business models, not just about 'efficiency' and 'green' strategies/decision making.

[16] In particular Ajl (2023) but see also his more thorough critique of the varieties of Global North-centred Green New Deals (2021b). Common to the critique of both mainstream currents of anti-extractivism that bypass (or simply condemn) the state, and national-focussed projects of eco-modernisation, is the absence of an understanding of capitalism as a *world-system*. What matters in this analysis is not simply internal 'national production', or 'inter-state' competition, but a dialectical understanding of how imperial capital operates across and through territories supported (and resisted) by nation-states.

[17] As Álvaro García Linera argued in the context of Latin America, 'to break that colonial subordination it is not sufficient to sound off with insults against that extractivism, to stop producing and drive the people into greater misery, so later the Right returns and without modifying extractivism satisfies partially the basic needs of the population' (2013).

[18] See also Pedrigal and Lukić (2024).

[19] 'Extractivism does not seriously approach the relative rural–urban balances needed for a popular anticolonial and anti-imperialist development path nor have an answer for what is to be done for Third World poor whose basic well being is directly tied to export commodities' (Ajl 2023).

[20] Although Ireland is not known for fossil fuels (besides peat), there were similar policies of selling off a natural gas deposit to Ohio-incorporated Marathon Oil in the 1970s off the south coast, although this gas was primarily destined for domestic consumption in power plants. Whatever the case, the model of 'farming out' resource extraction (and wealth accumulation) to multinationals is the key model (see Regan and Walsh 1976).

[21] This area of West Mayo has a long association with Republicanism – dating back to the Civil War at least (Garavan 2007). The intensity of the community-based campaign against Shell and the Irish state at the turn of the 21st century cannot be fully understood without an appreciation of this Republican political culture, especially alongside the well-documented demonisation of the movement in national media as irrational and violent. We find similar links between resource politics and Republicanism in the Resource Protection Campaign also discussed in this chapter.

22 This maps in interesting ways onto disputes surrounding climate reductionism versus more comprehensive environmental justice campaigning in contemporary environmental movements.
23 At the same time, the IRA was always conscious of the infrastructural qualities of imperial control – take, for example, the sabotage of the Marconi station(s), planned or foiled attempts to destroy English electricity infrastructure, or attacks on NI grid infrastructure (see Craig 2010).
24 It is important to consider this within the global context. As Moyo and Yeros (2007) write: 'With the crisis of the 1970s and the defeat of the anti-imperialist struggle worldwide, the two historic questions [national and agrarian] were demobilised and sent into neoliberal "hibernation"' (172).
25 For example, in 1989 plans to mine for gold on Croagh Patrick, a sacred pilgrimage site, were successfully stopped due to the campaigning work of the Mayo Environmental Group made up of local community residents and farmers, who mobilised against not only the destruction of the mountain, but also primarily the toxic cyanide pollution that would be used to extract the gold. Solidarity was formed with conservationists such as David Bellamy, who travelled to the mountain in 1989 to support the anti-mining campaign. In this and other cases, the objections are clear, and ecological care is rightfully foregrounded.

Conclusion

1 This is true as of the time of writing. In 2024, Ireland was Israel's second-largest trading partner in terms of goods, primarily due to transfer pricing arrangements in multinational microchips manufacturing across the two territories.
2 In private communications, we have been told that one of the more prominent Irish ENGOs believed the messaging was 'too complex' for ordinary people.
3 Chaudhary's *The Exhausted of the Earth* (2024) was inspirational for us in writing up this book, especially in terms of the intensive dynamics of extraction and exploitation that continue to characterise the unfolding planetary imperialism that Ireland is facilitating.
4 See Srnicek (2016); Couldry and Mejias (2019); Ricaurte (2019); Siapera (2022).
5 Take, for example, a partnership between the UK and the South of Ireland in March 2025 – which would see greater cooperation on building, and securing, offshore wind developments and their connections to territorial grids (see O'Carroll 2025).

References

Abbeyleix Bog Project (nd) https://www.abbeyleixbog.ie/
Abram, S., Waltorp, K., Ortar, N., and Pink, S. (eds) (2022) *Energy Futures: Anthropocene Challenges, Emerging Technologies and Everyday Life*, De Gruyter.
Afloat (2021) 'Works on rivers impacted by Donegal/Tyrone bogslide may take "years" to complete', *Afloat*, 22 May.
Agarwal, A. and Narain, S. (2019) 'Global warming in an unequal world: a case of environmental colonialism', in N.K. Dubash (ed.) *India in a Warming World*, Oxford University Press, pp 81–91.
Agrarian South (2012) 'The agrarian question: past, present and future', *Agrarian South: Journal of Political Economy*, 1(1): 1–10.
AI2Peat (2024) 'Accelerating peatland restoration', *AI2Peat*, https://ai2peat.ie/
Ajl, M. (2021a) 'The hidden legacy of Samir Amin: delinking's ecological foundation', *Review of African Political Economy*, 48(167): 82–101.
Ajl, M. (2021b) *A People's Green New Deal*, Pluto Press.
Ajl, M. (2023) 'Theories of political ecology: monopoly capital against people and the planet', *Agrarian South: Journal of Political Economy*, 12(1): 12–50.
Ali, C. (2021) *Farm Fresh Broadband: The Politics of Rural Connectivity*, MIT Press.
Allen, L. (2024) 'State's ban on new data centres is putting 2030 climate target at risk, Engineers Ireland warn', *Business Post*, 11 January.
Allen, R. (2004) *No Global: The People of Ireland vs. the Multinationals*, Pluto Press.
Alley, A. (2020) 'Echelon DC to fund electricity substation for giant offshore Irish wind farm', *Data Centre Dynamics*, 18 November.
Amazon Team (2024) 'Amazon supports new Peatland Standard to accelerate restoration and boost Ireland's climate resilience', *Amazon News*, 5 November.
Amin, S. (1976) *Unequal Development: An Essay on the Social Formations of Peripheral Capitalism*, Harvester Press.
Amin, S. (1990) *Delinking: Towards a Polycentric World*, Zed Books.

REFERENCES

Andrews, C.S. (1952) 'Some precursors of Bord na Móna', *Journal of the Statistical and Social Inquiry Society of Ireland*, 19: 132.

Andrews, C.S. (2001) *Man of No Property*, Lilliput Press.

Anker, P. (2001) *Imperial Ecology: Environmental Order in the British Empire, 1895–1945*, Harvard University Press.

Arboleda, M. (2020) *Planetary Mine: Territories of Extraction under Late Capitalism*, Verso.

Arboleda, M. (2023) 'Development as national liberation: The experience of the Popular Unity government in Chile', *Radical Philosophy*, 215: 23–38.

Archer, M. (2024) *Unsustainable: Measurement, Reporting, and the Limits of Corporate Sustainability*, NYU Press.

Baker, S. (1987) 'Dependent industrialization and political protest: Raybestos Manhattan in Ireland', *Government and Opposition*, 22(3): 352–8.

Barca, S. (2024) *Workers of the Earth. Labour, Ecology and Reproduction in the Age of Climate Change*, Pluto Press.

Barnard, T.C. (1979) 'Sir William Petty, his Irish estates and Irish population', *Irish Economic and Social History*, 6(1): 64–9.

Barry, F. and Ó Fathartaigh, M. (2015) 'The Industrial Development Authority, 1949–58: establishment, evolution and expansion of influence', *Irish Historical Studies*, 39(155): 460–78.

Barry, F. and Ó Fathartaigh, M. (nd) 'An Irish industrial revolution: the creation of the Industrial Development Authority (IDA), 1949–59', *History Ireland*, https://historyireland.com/an-irish-industrial-revolution-the-creation-of-the-industrial-development-authority-ida-1949-59/

Barry, F. and O'Mahony, C. (2017) 'Regime change in 1950s Ireland: the new export-oriented foreign investment strategy', *Irish Economic and Social History*, 44(1): 46–65.

Barry, J. and Doran, P. (2016) 'Environmental movements in Ireland: north and south', in J. McDonagh, T. Varley, and S. Shortall (eds) *A Living Countryside?: The Politics of Sustainable Development in Rural Ireland*, Taylor and Francis, pp 321–40.

BBC (2022) 'Cardiff Bay: radio sculpture with Marconi links approved' *BBC*, 6 September.

Beatty, A. (2016) 'An Irish revolution without a revolution', *Journal of World-Systems Research*, 22(1): 54–76.

Beatty A., Deckard S., Coakley M., et al (2016) 'Ireland in the world-system: an interview with Denis O'Hearn', *Journal of World-Systems Research*, 22(1): 202–13.

Bellamy, B.R. and Diamanti, J. (2018) 'Materialism and the critique of energy', in B.R. Bellamy and J. Diamanti (eds) *Materialism and the Critique of Energy*, MCM' Publishing.

Bhandar, B. (2018) *Colonial Lives of Property: Law, Land, and Racial Regimes of Ownership*, Duke University Press.

Bloomberg NEF (2021) 'Data centers and decarbonization: unlocking flexibility in Europe's data centers', 14 October.

Bord na Móna (nd) 'Bord na Móna announces Amazon Web Services as first business to join Eco Energy Park in a strategic collaboration that will see significant investment in the Midlands', https://www.bordnamona.ie/bord-na-mona-announces-amazon-web-services-as-first-business-to-join-eco-energy-park/

Botwright, K. and Dabré, G. (2024) 'Critical minerals are in demand. How do we make sure this trend drives development?', *World Economic Forum*, 10 September.

Boyce, D.G. and O'Day, A. (eds) (1996) *The Making of Modern Irish History: Revisionism and the Revisionist Controversy*, Routledge.

Boylan, T.A. and McDonough, T. (1998) 'Dependency and modernization: perspectives from the Irish nineteenth century', in T.P. Foley and S. Ryder (eds) *Ideology and Ireland in the Nineteenth Century*, Four Courts Press, pp 113–29.

Boyle, B. and Allen, K. (2021) *Tax Haven Ireland*, Pluto Press.

Brahic, C. (2007) 'Peatland destruction is releasing vast amounts of CO_2', *New Scientist*, 11 December.

Breen, M. and Dorgan, J. (2013) 'The death of Irish trade protectionism: a political economy analysis', *Irish Studies in International Affairs*, 24: 275–89.

Bresnihan, P. (2020) 'Beyond the limits to growth: neoliberal natures and the green economy', in J.C. Keller, K. Legun, M. Carolan, and M.M. Bell (eds) *The Cambridge Handbook of Environmental Sociology* (Vol 1), Cambridge University Press, pp 124–42.

Bresnihan, P. (2021) 'Tilting at windmills', in D. Papadopoulos, M.P. de La Bellacasa, and N. Myers (eds) *Reactivating Elements: Chemistry, Ecology, Practice*, Duke University Press, pp 151–76.

Bresnihan, P. and Brodie, P. (2019) 'High-energy data centres not quite as clean and green as they seem', *The Irish Times*, 11 September.

Bresnihan, P. and Brodie, P. (2021) 'New extractive frontiers in Ireland and the moebius strip of wind/data', *Environment and Planning E: Nature and Space*, 4(4): 1645–64.

Bresnihan, P. and Milner, N. (2023) *All We Want Is the Earth: Land, Labour, and Movements beyond Environmentalism*, Bristol University Press.

Bresnihan, P., Hesse, A., and White, J.M. (2021) 'Learning from group water schemes: community infrastructures for sustainable development', EPA Research, Report No. 364.

Bridge, G. (2001) 'Resource triumphalism: postindustrial narratives of primary commodity production', *Environment and Planning A: Economy and Space*, 33(12): 2149–73.

Bridge, G. (2011) 'Resource geographies 1: making carbon economies, old and new', *Progress in Human Geography*, 35(6): 820–34.

Bridge, G, Özkaynak, B, and Turhan, E. (2018) 'Energy infrastructure and the fate of the nation: introduction to special issue', *Energy Research & Social Science*, 41(July): 1–11.

British Pathé (1950) 'Minister opens Portarlington Power Station', https://www.youtube.com/watch?v=FLT1-FPOhqM

Brodie, P. (2020a) 'Climate extraction and supply chains of data', *Media, Culture and Society*, 42(7–8): 1095–1114.

Brodie, P. (2020b) '"Stuck in mud in the fields of Athenry": Apple, territory, and popular politics', *Culture Machine*, 19.

Brodie, P. (2021) 'Hosting cultures: placing the global data centre "industry"', *Canadian Journal of Communication*, 48(2): 151–76.

Brodie, P. (2023) 'Data infrastructure studies on an unequal planet', *Big Data & Society*, 10(1).

Brodie, P. (2024) 'Smarter, greener extractivism: digital infrastructures and the harnessing of new resources', *Information, Communication and Society*.

Brodie, P. (forthcoming) *Wild Tides: Media Infrastructure and Financial Crisis in Ireland*, Duke University Press.

Brodie, P. and Barney, D. (eds) (forthcoming) *Media Rurality*, Duke University Press.

Bruisch, K. (2014) *Als das Dorf noch Zukunft war: Agrarismus und Expertise zwischen Zarenreich und Sowjetunion*, Böhlau.

Bruna, N. (2023) *The Rise of Green Extractivism: Extractivism, Rural Livelihoods and Accumulation in a Climate-Smart World*, Routledge.

Buck, H.J. (2019) *After Geoengineering: Climate Tragedy, Repair, and Restoration*, Verso.

Buck, H.J. (2021) *Ending Fossil Fuels: Why Net Zero Is Not Enough*, Verso.

Buck, H.J. (2022) 'Decarbonization as a service', *Logic(s)*, 16, 27 March.

Buller, A. (2022) *The Value of a Whale: On the Illusions of Green Capitalism*, Manchester University Press.

Bumpus, A.G. and Liverman, D.M. (2008) 'Accumulation by decarbonization and the governance of carbon offsets', *Economic Geography*, 84(2): 127–55.

Burns, J. (2024) 'Irish companies "falling behind" on AI', *Irish Independent*, 9 December.

Burrell, J. (2020) 'On half-built assemblages: waiting for a data center in Prineville, Oregon', *Engaging Science, Technology, and Society*, 6.

Butterly, L. (2022) '"There are no borders in nature": climate change resistance on the island of Ireland', *The Detail*, 14 April.

Callanan, B. (2000) *Ireland's Shannon Story: Leaders, Visions, and Networks: A Case Study of Local and Regional Development*, Irish Academic Press.

Calvão, F. and Archer, M. (2021) 'Digital extraction: blockchain traceability in mineral supply chains' *Political Geography*, 87: 102381.

Carroll, C. and King, P. (eds) (2003) *Ireland and Postcolonial Theory*, Notre Dame Press.

Carroll, P. (2006) *Science, Culture, and Modern State Formation*, University of California Press.

Carruth, A. (2014) 'The digital cloud and the micropolitics of energy', *Public Culture*, 26(2): 339–64.

Carse, A. (2012) 'Nature as infrastructure: making and managing the Panama Canal watershed', *Social Studies of Science*, 42(4): 539–63.

CeADAR (nd) 'About us', *CeADAR: Ireland's Centre for Applied AI*, https://community.ceadar.ie/

Chagnon, C.W., Durante, F., Gills, B.K., Hagolani-Albov, S.E., Hokkanen, S., Kangasluoma, et al (2022) 'From extractivism to global extractivism: the evolution of an organizing concept', *Journal of Peasant Studies*, 49(4): 760–92.

Chakrabarty, D. (2000) *Provincializing Europe*, Princeton University Press.

Chaudhary, A.S. (2024) *The Exhausted of the Earth: Politics in a Burning World*, Repeater.

Chen, Y. (2024) 'Data centre boom reveals AI hype's physical limits', *Reuters*, 4 July.

Childs, Q. (2022) '"This has nothing to do with clouds": a decolonial approach to data centers in the node pole', *Commonplace*, https://doi.org/10.21428/6ffd8432.59c985d5

Chung, J. (2021) 'Big tech, big cash: Washington's new power players', *Public Citizen*.

Cirefice, V. (2021) 'Women keeping Ireland's gold in the ground', *Ecologist*, 20 July.

Cirefice, V. and Mincks, E. (2026) 'Water protectors, flowing spirals, making relatives despite extractivism in Northwest Ireland', in Janzwood, A. and Fairbank, C. (eds) *The End of Extraction as We Know It: Learning from Extractive Resistance for Sustainable Futures*, Athabasca University Press.

Cirefice, V. and Sullivan, L. (2019) 'Women on the frontlines of resistance to extractivism', *Policy and Practice: A Development Education Review*, 29: 78–99.

Clarke, D. (2010) *Brown Gold: A History of Bord na Móna and the Peat Industry in Ireland*, Gill and Macmillan.

Cleary J. (2006) 'Introduction: Ireland and modernity', in J. Cleary and C. Connolly (eds) *The Cambridge Companion to Modern Irish Culture*, Cambridge University Press, pp 1–22.

Cleary, J. (2007) *Outrageous Fortune: Capital and Culture in Modern Ireland*, Field Day Publications.

Cleary, J. (2022) 'Irish postcolonial studies 1980–2021', *Radical History Review*, 143: 15–31.

Clifford, M. (2022) 'Farmer wants Intel planning permission revisited after Paul Hyde allegations', *The Irish Examiner*, 11 June.

Collins, J. (2025) 'The fight for Ireland's water', *DW*, 31 January, https://www.dw.com/en/irelands-water-dilemma-protecting-the-river-shannon-or-powering-the-future/audio-71458851

Collins, L. (2024) 'Airtricity founder and trailblazer Eddie O'Connor "made us all believe"', *Irish Independent*, 13 January.

Collins, P. and Pontikakis, D. (2006) 'Innovation systems in the European periphery: the policy approaches of Ireland and Greece', *Science and Public Policy*, 33(10): 757–69.

Connelly, T. (2024) 'Government may provide support to Intel for new Irish plant – McGrath', *RTÉ News*, 14 May.

Connolly, G. (2022) 'From potatoes to chips: Ireland's export evolution', *Data Centre Frontier*, 28 October.

Connolly, J. (1898) 'The Irish land question', *Workers Republic*, 24 September.

Connolly, J. (1910) *Labour in Irish History*, Marxists Internet Archive, https://www.marxists.org/archive/connolly/1910/lih/index.htm

Conway, E.M. and Oreskes, N. (2010) *Merchants of Doubt*, Bloomsbury.

Cook, M. (2024) Subjects of tradition: cultural construction and Irish comprador capitalism, *Irish Studies Review*, 32(1): 64–92.

Cooper, M. (2008) 'They turfed Eddie out of Bord na Móna — take a look at him now', *The Examiner*, 11 January.

Cooper, M. (2010) 'Turbulent worlds', *Theory, Culture & Society*, 27(2–3): 167–90.

Corr, S. (2020) 'Amazon staying tight lipped on landslide at wind farm construction site', *Belfast Live*, 28 November.

Costanza, R., d'Arge, R. de Groot, R., et al (1997) 'The value of the world's ecosystem services and natural capital', *Nature* 387: 253–60.

Costello, R. (2024) 'The rise of corporate power purchase agreements (CPPAs)', *PWC*, 8 May.

Couldry, N. and Mejias, U.A. (2019) 'Data colonialism: rethinking big data's relation to the contemporary subject', *Television & New Media*, 20(4): 336–49.

Cowen, D. (2019) 'Following the infrastructures of empire: notes on cities, settler colonialism, and method', *Urban Geography*, 41(4): 469–86.

Craig, T. (2010) 'Sabotage! The origins, development and impact of the IRA's infrastructural bombing campaigns 1939–1997', *Intelligence and National Security*, 25(3): 309–26.

Crary, J. (2022) *Scorched Earth: Beyond the Digital Age to a Post-Capitalist World*, Verso Books.

Crosbie, B. (2009) 'Ireland, colonial science, and the geographical construction of British Rule in India, c. 1820–1870', *The Historical Journal*, 52(4): 963–87.

Crotty, R. (1977) 'Britain's Irish periphery', *The IDS Bulletin*, 9(2): 29–34.

Crotty, R. (1986) *Ireland in Crisis: A Study in Capitalist Colonial Undevelopment*, Brandon Book Publishers.

CRU (2021) 'CRU proposed direction to the system operators related to data centre grid connection', *Commission for the Regulation of Utilities*, 8 June.

CSO (2019) 'Regional SDGs Ireland 2017', *Central Statistics Office*.
CSO (2022) 'Internet coverage and usage in Ireland 2022', *Central Statistics Office*, 21 December.
CSO (2024) 'Data centres metered electricity consumption 2023', *Central Statistics Office*, 23 July.
Curley, A. (2021) 'Infrastructures as colonial beachheads: the Central Arizona Project and the taking of Navajo resources', *Environment and Planning D: Society and Space*, 39(3): 387–404.
Daggett, C.N. (2019) *The Birth of Energy: Fossil Fuels, Thermodynamics, and the Politics of Work*, Duke University Press.
Dáil Éireann (1936) Committee on Finance. Turf (Use and Development) Bill, 1935—Second Stage. Tuesday 28 April 1936 (Vol. 61, No. 12).
Dáil Éireann (1952) Committee on Finance. Turf Development Bill, 1953—Money Resolution. Tuesday 16 June 1953 (Vol. 139, No. 9).
Dáil Éireann (1957) Disapproval of Government's Foreign Policy—Motion. Thursday 28 November 1957 (Vol. 164, No. 8).
Dalsgaard, S. (2022) 'Tales of carbon offsets: between experiments and indulgences?', *Journal of Cultural Economy*, 15(1): 52–66.
Daly, H. (2024) 'Data centres in the context of Ireland's carbon budgets', *EPMG*, December.
Day One Team (2019) 'Amazon announces new renewable energy project in Ireland to support AWS global infrastructure', *Amazon News*.
De Loughry, T. and McCormack, M. (2019) '"… a tiny part of that greater circum-terrestrial grid": a conversation with Mike McCormack', *Irish University Review*, 49(1): 105–16.
Deckard, S. (2016) 'World-ecology and Ireland: the neoliberal ecological regime', *Journal of World-Systems Research*, 22(1): 145–76.
Deegan, G. (2024) 'Google data centre in Dublin blocked over electricity supply concerns', *Irish Independent*, 27 August.
Dempsey, J. and Robertson, M.M. (2012) 'Ecosystem services: tensions, impurities, and points of engagement within neoliberalism', *Progress in Human Geography*, 36(6): 758–79.
Department of the Environment, Climate and Communications (2024) 'Press release: Critical Raw Materials Act comes into force', *Gov.ie*, 23 May.
Department of Housing, Local Government and Heritage (2023) 'Countries convene in Dublin for ground-breaking European peatlands Initiative', *Gov.ie*, 8 May.
Devine, F., O'Neill, M., and Booth, C. (2024) 'DECC publishes guiding principles for the development of a "Private Wires" policy', *William Fry*, 16 July.
The Ditch Editors (2024) 'US ambassador warned of "consequences" for enacting Occupied Territories Bill – 90 minutes later Micheál Martin said it would be reviewed rather than passed', *The Ditch*, 5 November.

Doctorow, C. (2021) *How to Destroy Surveillance Capitalism*, Medium Editions.

Donnelly, C. (2024) 'Dublin confirmed as world's third-largest hyperscale datacentre hub', *Computer Weekly*, 15 August.

Donnelly, M. (2024) 'Raised bogs can store 13 times the carbon of Amazon rainforest', *Irish Independent*, 24 June.

Dooley, T. (2004) *The Land for the People: The Land Question in Independent Ireland*, UCD Press.

Dos Santos, T. (1970) 'The structure of dependence', *The American Economic Review*, 60(2): 231–36.

Dryer, T. (2023) 'No AI for the Colorado River', *Water Justice and Technology Studio*, 5 March, https://waterjustice-tech.org/no-ai-colorado-river/

Duarte, M.E. (2017) *Network Sovereignty: Building the Internet across Indian Country*, University of Washington Press.

Duffy, C. (2022a) 'Anger at the low fine for the "catastrophic ecological disaster" at Meenbog', *Ireland Live*, 27 July.

Duffy, C. (2022b) 'Development plan decision "a slap in the face for local democracy", says councillor', *Donegal Live*.

Duffy, P. (2011) 'Wiring the countryside: rural electrification in Ireland', in S.D. Brunn (ed.) *Engineering Earth*, 1885–1899, Springer.

Dunlap, A. and Riquito, M. (2023) 'Social warfare for lithium extraction? Open-pit lithium mining, counterinsurgency tactics and enforcing green extractivism in northern Portugal', *Energy Research & Social Science*, 95.

Dunlap, A., Verweijen, J., and Tornel, C. (2024) 'The political ecologies of "green" extractivism(s): an introduction', *Journal of Political Ecology*, 31(1): 436–63.

Dunphy, L. (2022) 'Ireland has to move quickly if we are to become the Saudi Arabia of wind energy', *Irish Examiner*, 3 September.

Durand, C. and Milberg, W. (2019) 'Intellectual monopoly in global value chains', *Review of International Political Economy*, 27(2): 404–29.

Dyer-Witheford, N. (2005) 'Cognitive capitalism and the contested campus', *European Journal of Arts Education*, 2: 71–93.

Eagleton, T., Jameson, F., and Said, E. (1990) *Nationalism, Colonialism, and Literature*, University of Minnesota Press.

Easterling, K. (2014) *Extrastatecraft: The Power of Infrastructure Space*, Princeton University Press.

Eaton (nd) Eaton EnergyAware UPS, *Eaton*, https://www.eaton.com/gb/en-gb/products/backup-power-ups-surge-it-power-distribution/backup-power-ups/backup-power-solutions/eaton-energyaware.html

Edwards, D., Cooper, Z.G.T., and Hogan, M. (2024) 'The making of critical data center studies', *Convergence*, 31(2).

Edwards, P.N. (2010) *A Vast Machine: Computer Models, Climate Data, and the Politics of Global Warming*, MIT Press.

Eirgrid (2023) 'Celtic Interconnector project aims to make Ireland the "Saudi Arabia of Europe for offshore wind"', *Breakingnews.ie*, 27 January.

Els, F. (2024) 'Mining vs AI – it's not even close', *Mining.com*, 28 October, https://www.mining.com/mining-vs-ai-its-not-even-close/

Engels, F. (1856) 'Engels to Marx in London', *History Is a Weapon*.

Engels, F. (1971 [1870]) History of Ireland, https://www.marxists.org/archive/marx/works/1870/history-ireland/ch01.htm

ESRI (nd) 'Strategic alliances', *ESRI*, https://www.esri.com/en-us/about/partners/our-partners/strategic-alliances

European Business and Innovation Centre Network (2022) *Industry 4.0: The Digital Wave of Sustainable Innovation*, SmartEEs.

Explore Intel (nd) 'Ireland campus', https://www.exploreintel.com/ireland

Fadul, L.G. (2023) '"What we see in Gaza is the rehearsal of the future": Colombian President at UN climate summit', *AA*, 2 December.

Fairhead, J., Leach, M., and Scoones, I. (2012) 'Green grabbing: a new appropriation of nature?', *Journal of Peasant Studies*, 39(2): 237–61.

Fearon, S. (2024) 'Decolonisation, dependency and disengagement—the challenge of Ireland's degrowth transition', *CUSP: Centre for the Understanding of Sustainable Prosperity*, 24 July.

Feehan, J., O'Donovan, G., Renou-Wilson, F., and Wilson, D. (2008) *The Bogs of Ireland: An Introduction to the Natural, Cultural and Industrial Heritage of Irish Peatlands*, University College Dublin.

Ferraro, P.J. and Kiss, A. (2002) 'Ecology. Direct payments to conserve biodiversity', *Science*, 298(5599): 1718–19.

Fingleton White (2003) 'Intel Ireland sustainable energy report', Fingleton White & Co., 5 June.

Finn, D. (2019) *One Man's Terrorist: A Political History of the IRA*, Verso.

Fitzgerald, L. (2023) 'What's the impact of large-scale forestry on Irish communities?', *RTÉ Brainstorm*, 1 February.

Fitzgerald, L. and Murphy, J. (2023) 'Making relatives: Earth protectors in Leitrim building international solidarity', *The Irish Examiner*, 7 June.

Foster, J.B. (2000) *Marx's Ecology: Materialism and Nature*, Monthly Review Press.

Foster, J.B. and Holleman, H. (2014) 'The theory of unequal ecological exchange: a Marx–Odum dialectic', *Journal of Peasant Studies*, 41(2): 199–233.

Fouquet, R. and Hippe, R. (2022) 'Twin transitions of decarbonisation and digitalisation: a historical perspective on energy and information in European economies', *Energy Research & Social Science*, 91: 102736.

Foxe, K. (2024) 'EirGrid's warning over possible "mass exodus" of data centres from Ireland', *The Story.ie*, 13 August.

Franco, S.F., Graña, J.M., and Rikap, C. (2024) 'Dependency in the digital age? The experience of Mercado Libre in Latin America', *Development and Change*, 55: 429–64.

Freeman, T.W. (1943) 'The congested districts of western Ireland', *Geographical Review*, 33(1): 1–14.

Furuhata, Y. (2022) *Climatic Media: Transpacific Experiments in Atmospheric Control*, Duke University Press.

Gabrys, J. (2009) 'Sink: the dirt of systems', *Environment and Planning D: Society and Space*, 27: 666–81.

Gabrys, J. (2014) 'Powering the digital: from energy ecologies to electronic environmentalism', in R. Maxwell, J. Raundalen, and N.L. Vestberg (eds) *Media and the Ecological Crisis*, Routledge, pp 3–18.

Gabrys, J. (2016) *Program Earth: Environmental Sensing Technology and the Making of a Computational Planet*, University of Minnesota Press.

Gabrys, J. (2020) 'Smart forests and data practices: from the internet of trees to planetary governance', *Big Data & Society*, 7(1): 1–10.

Gago, V. and Mezzadra, S. (2017) 'A critique of the extractive operations of capital: toward an expanded concept of extractivism', *Rethinking Marxism*, 29(4): 574–91.

Gain, V. (2023) 'SFI reports an increase in Irish research funding in 2022', *IDA Ireland*, 18 September.

Gaonkar, D. (1999) 'On alternative modernities', *Public Culture*, 11(1): 1–18.

Garavan, M. (ed.) (2007) *Our Story: The Rossport 5*, Small World Media.

Garland, P. (2023) 'The ionosphere – undermining Britain's imperial power: wireless and its impact on geopolitics and naval operations (1919–1927)', *International Journal of Maritime History*, 35(1): 71–97.

Gibbons, L. (1996) *Transformations in Irish culture*, Notre Dame Press.

Gifford, L. (2020) '"You can't value what you can't measure": a critical look at forest carbon accounting', *Climatic Change*, 161: 291–306.

Giroux, H. (2014) *Neoliberalism's War on Higher Education*, Haymarket Books.

Gladwin, D. (2016) *Contentious Terrains: Boglands, Ireland, Postcolonial Gothic*, Cork University Press.

Global Peatlands Initiative (2019) https://globalpeatlands.org/

Goffe, T.L. (2025) *Dark Laboratory: On Columbus, the Caribbean, and the Origins of the Climate Crisis*, Random House.

Goldstein, J.E. (2018) *Planetary Improvement: Cleantech Entrepreneurship and the Contradictions of Green Capitalism*, MIT Press.

Goldstein, J.E. (2022) 'More data, more problems? Incompatible uncertainty in Indonesia's climate change mitigation projects', *Geoforum*, 132: 195–204.

Goldstein, J.E. and Nost, E. (eds) (2022) *The Nature of Data: Infrastructures, Environments, Politics*, University of Nebraska Press.

Golumbia, D. (2024) *Cyberlibertarianism: The Right-Wing Politics of Digital Technology*, University of Minnesota Press.

Gómez-Barris, M. (2017) *The Extractive Zone: Social Ecologies and Decolonial Perspectives*, Duke University Press.

Gonzalez-Monserrate, S. (2022) 'The cloud is material: on the environmental impacts of computation and data storage', *MIT Case Studies in Social and Ethical Responsibilities of Computing*, January.

Goodbody, W. (2024) 'EU critical materials rules could lead to new Irish mines', *RTÉ*, 23 May.

Gorey, C. (2020) 'SSE Renewables and Echelon Data Centres to build €50m Arklow substation', *Silicon Republic*, 17 November.

Government of Ireland (2003) Industrial Development (Science Foundation Ireland) Act 2003, *Irish Statute Book*.

Government of Ireland (2022a) *Government Statement on the Role of Data Centres in Ireland's Enterprise Strategy*.

Government of Ireland (2022b) Territorial Just Transition Plan: EU Just Transition Fund.

Government of Ireland (2022c) Policy Statement on Mineral Exploration and Mining: Critical Raw Materials for the Circular Economy Transition.

Government of Ireland (2023) 'Private Wires consultation', *Gov.ie*, 18 August.

Government of Ireland (2024a) *Climate Action Plan: 2024*.

Government of Ireland (2024b) *Powering Prosperity: Ireland's Offshore Wind Industrial Strategy*, Department of Enterprise, Trade and Employment.

Government of Ireland (2024c) Research and Innovation Act 2024, *Irish Statute Book*.

Grappiolo, C., Gurusiddappa, V., Regan, S., Boydell, O., and Holohan, E. (2024) 'A satellite-derived peatland ecotype classification method using artificial neural network hierarchical ensembles', *AI2Peat*, https://ai2peat.ie/wp-content/uploads/2024/07/Grappiolo_et_al_Satellite-derived-Peatland-Ecotype-Classification-Method-Using-Artificial-Neural-Network-Hierarchical-Ensembles.pdf

Greenpeace International (2017) 'Clicking clean', *Greenpeace*, 10 January.

Grossman, S.J. (2023) *Immeasurable Weather: Meteorological Data and Settler Colonialism from 1820 to Hurricane Sandy*, Duke University Press.

GSI (2022) 'Eoin McGrath talks lithium exploration on The Hard Shoulder', *Geological Survey Ireland*, 18 January, https://www.gsi.ie/en-ie/events-and-news/news/Pages/Eoin-McGrath-Talk-Lithium-Exploration-on-The-Hard-Shoulder.aspx

Günel, G. (2019) *Spaceship in the Desert: Energy, Climate Change, and Urban Design in Abu Dhabi*, Duke University Press.

Habib, W. and Connolly, J. (2023) 'A national-scale assessment of land use change in peatlands between 1989 and 2020 using Landsat data and Google Earth Engine – a case study of Ireland', *Regional Environmental Change*, 23(4): 124.

Hallahan, C. (2020) 'Terrain AI, accelerating our understanding of carbon reduction', *Microsoft Pulse*, https://pulse.microsoft.com/en-ie/sustainable-futures-en-ie/na/fa3-terrain-ai-accelerating-our-understanding-of-carbon-reduction/

Halpern, O. and Mitchell, R. (2022) *The Smartness Mandate*, MIT Press.

Hamouchene, H. and Sandwell, K. (2023) *Dismantling Green Colonialism: Energy and Climate Justice in the Arab Region*, Pluto Press.

Han, L.Y. (2024) *Deepwater Alchemy: Extractive Mediation and the Taming of the Seafloor*, University of Minnesota Press.

Hanieh, A. (2024) *Crude Capitalism: Oil, Corporate Power, and the Making of the World Market*, Verso Books.

The Hard Shoulder (2022) 18 January.

Healy, J. (1988) *No One Shouted Stop!*, Octavo.

Healy, J. (2018) 'Asahi and the Mayo venture', *Mayo News*, 18 April.

Herbert, F. (1965) *Dune*, Chilton.

Heron, K. (2024) 'Forget eco-modernism', *Verso Blog*, 2 April.

Heron, K. and Dean, J. (2020) 'Revolution or ruin, *e-flux Journal*.

Heron, K. and Heffron, A. (2022) 'Towards the abolition of the hinterlands', *Architectural Design*, 92(1): 120–7.

Hickel, J. (2021) 'The anti-colonial politics of degrowth', *Political Geography*, 88: 102404.

Hickel, J. (2023) 'On technology and degrowth', *Monthly Review*, 1 July.

Hickel, J., Dorninger, C., Wieland, H., and Suwandi, I. (2022) 'Imperialist appropriation in the world economy: drain from the Global South through unequal exchange, 1990–2015', *Global Environmental Change*, 73:102467.

Hicks, M. and Linstrum, E. (nd) 'Rethinking the inevitability of AI: historicizing climate impact and discussing best practices for energy and water consumption', *University of Virginia Environmental Institute*, https://environment.virginia.edu/ai-and-society

Hitchcock, M. (2019) '"Earth pantry, bone vault": a critical analysis of the peat bog as an archaeological archive', *Journal of Wetland Archaeology*, 19(1–2): 21–31.

Hogan, M. (2018) 'Big data ecologies', *Ephemera: Theory and Politics in Organization*, 18(3): 631–57.

Horgan, J. (2001) *Irish Media: A Critical History since 1922*, Routledge.

Horner, A. (2005) 'Napoleon's Irish legacy: the bogs commissioners, 1809–14', *History Ireland*, 24–8, https://historyireland.com/napoleons-irish-legacy-the-bogs-commissioners-1809-14/

Horner, A. (ed.) (2019) *Documents Relating to the Bogs Commissioners, 1809–1813*, Irish Manuscripts Commission.

Horrigan, M. (2021) 'Stigma damages', https://michelehorrigan.com/project/stigma-damages/

Host in Ireland (2021) 'Event replay: empowering change: the challenges and opportunities for Ireland's decarbonised grid', *Host in Ireland*, 1 December.

Howe, C. (2011) 'Logics of the wind: development desires over Oaxaca', *Anthropology News*, 52: 8.

Howe, C. (2014) 'Anthropocenic ecoauthority: the winds of Oaxaca', *Anthropological Quarterly*, 87(2): 381–404.

Howe, C. and Boyer, D. (2016) 'Aeolian extractivism and community wind in Southern Mexico', *Public Culture*, 28(279): 215–35.

Hu, T.H. (2015) *A Prehistory of the Cloud*, MIT Press.

Hughes, D.M. (2021) *Who Owns the Wind?: Climate Crisis and the Hope of Renewable Energy*, Verso.

ICOS (nd) https://www.icos-cp.eu/

iCRAG (2023a) 'iCRAG hosts Future of Ireland's Peatlands: Science, Engineering & a Just Transition workshop', *iCRAG: SFI Research Centre in Applied Geosciences*, https://www.icrag-centre.org

iCRAG (2023b) 'iCRAG launches Writing the Earth', *iCRAG: SFI Research Centre in Applied Geosciences*, 7 February, https://www.icrag-centre.org/news-and-media/icraglauncheswritingtheearth.html

IEA (2017) *Energy Technology Perspectives 2017: Catalysing Energy Technology Transformations*, International Energy Agency.

IEA (2022) 'The role of critical minerals in clean energy transitions: executive summary', *International Energy Agency*, https://www.iea.org/reports/the-role-of-critical-minerals-in-clean-energy-transitions/executive-summary

IEA (2024) *Electricity 2024: Analysis and Forecast to 2026*, International Energy Agency.

IGI (nd) 'A more diverse, sustainable supply of critical raw materials in Europe', *Institute of Geologists of Ireland*, https://igi.ie/assets/uploads/2024/05/IGI-CRM-FINAL-01.05.24.pdf

Intel (nd) 'Water restoration in Ireland', *Intel*, https://www.intel.ie/content/www/ie/en/company-overview/ireland-water-restoration.html

Irish Independent (1925) 'The fruits of folly. Clifden Marconi Station abandoned', 17 July.

Irish Independent (2000) 'Microsoft chief warns on shortage of IT personnel', *Irish Independent*, 7 April.

Irish Independent (2007) 'Going, going, gone', 15 October.

Irish Tech News (2023) 'Artificial intelligence solutions to protect Ireland's peatlands are being explored', 18 April. https://irishtechnews.ie/artificial-intelligence-protect-irelands-peatland/

The Irish Times (2001) 'Keeping the Republic sweet for IT investors Intel's John McGowan tells Jamie Smyth that escalating labour costs and infrastructure problems are eroding our attractiveness', 8 June: 59.

The Irish Times (2022) 'Microsoft plans private power plant on €900m data centre site in response to energy concerns', *The Irish Times*, 4 December.

The Irish Times (2023) 'Drawing from the river: how a multinational relies on nature's resources for its technology. Multinational Intel takes in about 660 million litres of water a month – the equivalent of 264 Olympic-sized swimming pools – from the river for its chipmaking facility', *The Irish Times*, 1 November.

The Irish Times (2024) 'The Irish Times view on business lobbying on data centres: a tone of entitlement', *The Irish Times*, 17 June.

Irwin-Hunt, A. (2020) 'fDi diaries: "attracting foreign direct investment is a contact sport"', *FDI Intelligence*, 9 September.

ISIF (nd) 'Irish Minerals Fund', *National Treasury Management Agency*, https://isif.ie/portfolio/irish-minerals-fund

Jacobsen, J.K. (1994) *Chasing Progress in the Irish Republic: Ideology, Democracy and Dependent Development*, Cambridge University Press.

Jameson, F. (2002) *A Singular Modernity*, Verso.

Jansen, F. and Cath, C. (2024) *Down with Data Centres: Developing Critical Policy*, Critical Infrastructure Lab.

Jerez, B., Garcés, I., and Torres, R. (2021) 'Lithium extractivism and water injustices in the Salar de Atacama, Chile: the colonial shadow of green electromobility', *Political Geography*, 87: 102382.

Johnson, A. (2023) *Where Cloud Is Ground: Placing Data and Making Place in Iceland*, University of California Press.

Joyce, J. (1966) *Finnegan's Wake*, The Viking Press.

Jue, M. and Ruiz, R. (eds) (2021) *Saturation: An Elemental Politics*, Duke University Press.

Jung, M. (2023) 'Digital capitalism is a mine not a cloud', *Transnational Institute*, 10 February.

Kadri, A. (2023) *The Accumulation of Waste: A Political Economy of Systemic Destruction*, Brill.

Kama, K. (2020) 'Resource-making controversies: knowledge, anticipatory politics and economization of unconventional fossil fuels', *Progress in Human Geography*, 44(2): 333–56.

Kamiya, G. and Bertoldi, P. (2024) 'Energy consumption in data centres and broadband communication networks in the EU', *European Commission*.

Kearney, R. (1996) *Postnationalist Ireland: Politics, Culture, Philosophy*, Routledge.

Kearns, G. (2013) 'Historical geographies of Ireland: colonial contexts and postcolonial legacies', *Historical Geography*, 41: 22–34.

Kearns, K.C. (1976) 'Ireland's mining boom: development and impact', *The American Journal of Economics and Sociology*, 35(3): 251–70.

Keenan, B. (1999) 'The genesis of Telesis now an almost forgotten memory', *Irish Independent*, 23 June.

Kelly, A. (2019) 'Apple and Google named in US lawsuit over Congolese child cobalt mining deaths', *The Guardian*, 16 December.

Kennard, M. and Provost, C. (2016) 'Story of cities #25: Shannon – a tiny Irish town inspires China's economic boom', *The Guardian*, 19 April.

Khanal, S., Zhang, H., and Taeihagh, A. (2024) 'Why and how is the power of Big Tech increasing in the policy process? The case of generative AI', *Policy and Society*.

Kiberd, D. (1997) *Inventing Ireland: The Literature of the Modern Nation*, Harvard University Press.

Kiernan, A. (2019) 'Donegal group "baffled" by Amazon deal to wind farm awaiting planning permission', *Wind Watch*, 11 April.

King, A. (2022) 'Ireland "a laboratory" for colonialism in Palestine', *Trinity Long Room Hub Arts & Humanities Research Institute*, 21 March.

Kirby, P. (2009) 'The competition state – lessons from Ireland', *Limerick Papers in Politics and Public Administration*, 1: 1–24.

Kirby, P. (2010) *Celtic Tiger in Collapse: Explaining the Weaknesses of the Irish Model*, Palgrave Macmillan.

Knuth, S., Behrsin, I., Levenda, A., McCarthy, J. (2022) 'New political ecologies of renewable energy', *Environment and Planning E: Nature and Space*, 5(3): 997–1013.

Kothari, R. (1981) 'On eco-imperialism', *Alternatives*, 7(3): 385–94.

LaDuke, W. and Cowen, D. (2020) 'Beyond Wiindigo infrastructure', *South Atlantic Quarterly*, 119(2): 243–68.

Lally, N., Kay, K., and Thatcher, J. (2022) 'Computational parasites and hydropower: a political ecology of Bitcoin mining on the Columbia River', *Environment and Planning E: Nature and Space*, 5(1): 18–38.

Landscape Finance Lab (nd) https://landscapefinancelab.org/

Lantry, P. (2023) 'Data centre moratorium could strangle digital growth and impact carbon targets', *The Irish Times*, 27 November.

Larkin, B. (2008) *Signal and Noise: Media, Infrastructure, and Urban Culture in Nigeria*, Duke University Press.

Lee, J. (2008) *The Modernisation of Irish Society 1848–1918*, Gill and Macmillan.

Lehuedé, S. (2021) *Governing Data in Modernity/Coloniality: Astronomy Data in the Atacama Desert and the Struggle for Collective Autonomy*, London School of Economics, PhD thesis, July.

Lehuedé, S. (2022) 'Big tech's new headache: data centre activism flourishes across the world', *London School of Economics*, 2 November.

Lehuedé, S. (2024) 'An elemental ethics for artificial intelligence: water as resistance within AI's value chain', *AI and Society*.

Lehuedé, S. and Valdivia, A. (2024) 'Peripheries on the rise: eco-imperialism in the race for technology resourcing', pre-print, https://ssrn.com/abstract=5085112

Leifeld, J. and Menichetti, L. (2018) 'The underappreciated potential of peatlands in global climate change mitigation strategies', *Nature Communications*, 9(1): 1–7.

Lemke, T. (2019) *Foucault's Analysis of Modern Governmentality: A Critique of Political Reason*, Verso.

Lenin, V. (1963 [1917]) *Imperialism, the Highest Stage of Capitalism*, in Lenin's Selected Works (Vol 1), Progress Publishers, pp 667–766.

Lenin, V. (2024) *Imperialism and the National Question*, Verso.

Leonard, L. (2007) 'Environmentalism in Ireland: ecological modernisation versus populist rural sentiment', *Environmental Values*, 16(4): 463–83.

Leonard, L. (2008) 'Rapid development & community mobilisation in the Republic of Ireland', *Community Development*, 39(3): 59–74.

Leonard, L. (2013) 'Ecomodern discourse and localised narratives: waste policy, community mobilisation and governmentality in Ireland', in M.J. Zapata and M. Hall (eds) *Organising Waste in the City: International Perspectives on Narratives and Practices*, Policy Press.

Leonard, R. (2024) 'Techxit: Equinix's Peter Lantry warns of fallout from data centre moratorium', *Irish Tech News*, 29 February.

Leonardi, E. (2017) 'For a critique of neoliberal green economy: a Foucauldian perspective on ecological crisis and biomimicry', *Soft Power*, 4(1): 168–85.

Lev-Ram, M. (2024) 'The chip industry's dirty little secret: it's very dirty', *Fortune*, 29 January.

Libertson, F., Velkova, J., and Palm, J. (2021) 'Data-center infrastructure and energy gentrification: perspectives from Sweden', *Sustainability: Science, Practice and Policy*, 17(1): 152–61.

Liboiron, M. (2021) *Pollution Is Colonialism*, Duke University Press.

Lillington, K. (2013) 'Intel turned Leixlip into Ireland's Silicon Valley', *The Irish Times*, 12 November.

Linera, A.G. (2013) 'Once again on so-called "extractivism"', *Monthly Review*, 29 April.

Lionhead Resources (nd) 'We are investors in the minerals critical to a prosperous, clean energy future', https://lionheadresources.com/

Lippert, I. (2016) 'Failing the market, failing deliberative democracy: how scaling up corporate carbon reporting proliferates information asymmetries', *Big Data & Society*, 3(2).

Lloyd, D. (1993) *Anomalous States: Irish Writing and the Post-Colonial Moment*, Duke University Press.

Lloyd, D. (2003) 'Ireland's modernities: introduction', *Interventions*, 5(3): 317–21.

Lloyd, D. (2011) *Irish Culture and Colonial Modernity 1800–2000: The Transformation of Oral Space*, Cambridge University Press.

Loftus, C. and Laffey, J. (2015) *Powering the West – a History of Bord na Móna and ESB in North Mayo*, Crossmolina-Bord na Móna/ESB Commemoration Committee.

Lohmann, L. (2016) 'What is the "green" in "green growth"', in G. Dale, M.V. Mathai, and J.A.P. de Oliveira (eds) *Green Growth: Ideology, Political Economy and the Alternatives*, Zed Books, pp 42–71.

Lohmann, L. and Hildyard, N. (2014) *Energy, Work and Finance*, The Corner House.

Lough Boora Parklands (1998) *The Future Use of Cutaway Bogs*, Bord na Mona, https://collinsandgoto.com/wp-content/uploads/2020/07/The-future-use-of-Cutaway-Bog-Lough-Boora-Parklands-Conference.pdf

Lovell, H. and Liverman, D. (2010) 'Understanding carbon offset technologies', *New Political Economy*, 15(2): 255–73.

Lyne, L. (2025) 'Half of Dublin's electricity supply being eaten up by data centres', *Dublin Live*, 19 February.

Mac Bhloscaidh, F. (2020) 'Objective historians, irrational Fenians and the bewildered herd: revisionist myth and the Irish revolution', *Irish Studies Review*, 28(2): 204–34.

MacNamee, D. (2024) 'Shannon water pipeline delays a "threat" to foreign investment', *Business Post*, 10 March.

Madden, J. (2012) *Fr. John Fahy: Radical Republican and Agrarian Activist (1893–1969)*, Columba Press.

Making Relatives Collective (nd) 'Looking back, looking forward', *Making Relatives Collective*, https://makingrelativesireland.wordpress.com

Marconi Signal Station (1907) *Wagga Wagga Advertiser*, p 6, https://trove.nla.gov.au/newspaper/article/145073841

Mattern, S. (2017) *Code and Clay, Data and Dirt: Five Thousand Years of Urban Media*, University of Minnesota Press.

Maxwell, R. and Miller, T. (2012) *Greening the Media*, Oxford University Press.

Mbaria, G. (2023) 'Anatomy of a multi-million dollar colonial carbon project in Kenya', *Survival International*, 15 March.

McAfee, K. (1999) 'Selling nature to save it? Biodiversity and green developmentalism', *Environment and Planning D: Society and Space*, 17(2): 133–54.

McCabe, C. (2011) *Sins of the Father: Tracing the Decisions that Shaped the Irish Economy*, The History Press.

McCabe, C. (2015) 'False economy: the financialisation of Ireland and the roots of austerity', in C. Coulter and A. Nagle (eds) *Ireland under Austerity: Neoliberal Crisis, Neoliberal Solutions*, Manchester University Press.

McCabe, C. (2022) 'Apple and Ireland, 1980–2020: a case study of the Irish comprador capitalist system', *Radical History Review*, 143: 141–8.

McCabe, C. (2024) *The Lost and Early Writings of James Connolly, 1889–1898*, Iskra Books.

McCabe, F. (2018) *Ambition and Achievement – The Civic Visions of Frank Gibney*, Castles in the Air Publications.

McCarthy, C. (2000) *Modernisation: Crisis and Culture in Ireland 1969–1992*, Four Courts Press.

McCormack, D.P. (2018) *Atmospheric Things: On the Allure of Atmospheric Envelopment*, Duke University Press.

McCormick, T. (2009) *William Petty and the Ambitions of Political Arithmetic*, Oxford University Press.

McDonagh, J., Varley, T., and Shortall, S. (eds) (2016) *A Living Countryside?: The Politics of Sustainable Development in Rural Ireland*, Taylor and Francis.

McGovern, M. (2010) 'The IRA are not Al Qaeda: new terrorism discourse and Irish republicanism', in K. Hayward and C. O'Donnell (eds) *Political Discourse and Conflict Resolution: Debating Peace in Northern Ireland*, Routledge, pp 192–208.

McGovern, M. (2019) *Counterinsurgency and Collusion in Northern Ireland*, Pluto Press.

McGowran, L. (2022) 'Digital platform helps Bord na Móna restore Ireland's peatlands', *Silicon Republic*, 10 November.

McGrath, E., O'Donnell, E., and Torremans, K. (2023) 'Digging our way to a Just Transition', *Geological Society, London, Special Publications*, 526: 175–82.

McGrath, P. (2020) 'Cabinet approves €108m for midlands peatland restoration', *RTÉ*, 24 November.

McGuinness, K. (2023) 'A supercharged tech research ecosystem will help meet the challenge of achieving net zero', *Irish Tech News*, 3 April.

McLaughlin, J. (2015) 'Data: clouds and precipitation', in G.A. Boyd and J. McLaughlin, *Infra-Eireann: Infrastructure and the Architectures of Modernity in Ireland 1916–2016*, Actar.

McLuhan, M. (1994) *Understanding Media: Extensions of Man*, MIT Press.

McQuillan, D. (2022) *Resisting AI: An Anti-fascist Approach to Artificial Intelligence*, Bristol University Press.

McVeigh, R. and Rolston, B. (2021) *Ireland, Colonialism, and the Unfinished Revolution*, Beyond the Pale.

McWilliams, D. (2024) 'Ireland should not be blocking data centres, we need more of them', *The Irish Times*, 31 August.

Meleisea, E. (2022) 'The Abbeyleix Bog Project: a model for community-based peatlands restoration and management', *Global Peatlands Initiative*, 24 October.

Melia, P. (2019) 'Intel will use four times as much power as Galway city in Leixlip', *Irish Independent*, 12 January.

Merchant, B. (2023) *Blood in the Machine: The Origins of the Rebellion Against Big Tech*, Little, Brown.

Mercier, S. (2021) 'Ireland's energy system: the historical case for hope in climate action', *New Labor Forum*, 30(2): 21–30.

Mercier, S. (2023) 'What would private electricity wires mean for Ireland's energy system?', *RTÉ*, 21 September.

Mercier, S. (2024a) 'Analysis – state failures: siding with north against south, with colonisers against the colonised', *The Ditch*, 24 January.

Mercier, S. (2024b) 'Comment: the planning bill – here comes the most fossil fuel infrastructure in the history of the state', *The Ditch*, 8 October.

Mercier, S., O'Dochartaigh, A., and Cirefice, V. (2022) 'Resistance to mining and pathways to a sustainable rural environment: rewriting the maps', in A. Attorp, S. Heron, and R. McAreavey (eds) *Rural Governance in the UK: Towards a Sustainable and Equitable Society*, Routledge, pp 99–119.

Mercille, J. and Murphy, E. (2017) 'The neoliberalization of Irish higher education under austerity', *Critical Sociology*, 43(3): 371–87.
Mezzadra, S. and Neilson, B. (2019) *The Politics of Operations: Excavating Contemporary Capitalism*, Duke University Press.
Microsoft (nd) 'A planetary computer for a sustainable future', https://planetarycomputer.microsoft.com/
Microsoft News Centre (2017) 'Microsoft, GE sign agreement on new wind project in Ireland', *Microsoft Source*, 9 October.
Molinero, A.G. and Pedregal, A. (2024) 'The early socio-ecological dimensions of tricontinental (1967–1971): a sovereign social metabolism for the Third World', *Agrarian South: Journal of Political Economy*, 13(3): 368–400.
Moore, J. (2015) *Capitalism in the Web of Life: Ecology and the Accumulation of Capital*, Verso.
Mosco, V. (2014) *To the Cloud: Big Data in a Turbulent World*, Routledge.
Moyo, S. and Yeros, P. (2007) 'The radicalised state: Zimbabwe's interrupted revolution', *Review of African Political Economy*, 34(111): 103–21.
Mueller, G. (2021) *Breaking Things at Work: The Luddites Are Right about Why You Hate Your Job*, Verso.
Murray, D. (2024) 'Ireland can be a "key player" in Europe's push for new mines to supply critical and rare minerals', *Business Post*, 23 May.
Murray, D. (2025) 'Ireland part of New Fortress Energy's plans to develop data centres on "more than 1,000 acres of land"', *Business Post*, 20 March.
Mustafa, S. (1998) 'Revisionism and revival: a postcolonial approach to Irish cultural nationalism', *New Hibernia Review*, 2(3): 36–53.
Nally, D. (2008) '"That coming storm": the Irish Poor Law, colonial biopolitics, and the Great Famine', *Annals of the Association of American Geographers*, 98(3): 714–41.
Nelson, S.H. and Bigger, P. (2022) 'Infrastructural nature', *Progress in Human Geography*, 46(1): 86–107.
Niklas, J. (forthcoming) 'Data ecopolitics: negotiating citizenship and expertise in environmental governance', *Science, Technology, & Human Values*.
Nkrumah, K. (1966) *Neo-colonialism: The Last Stage of Imperialism*, International Publishers.
Nost, E. (2024) 'Governing AI, governing climate change?', *Geo: Geography and Environment*, 11: e00138.
Nost, E. and Goldstein, J.E. (2022) 'A political ecology of data', *Environment and Planning E: Nature and Space*, 5(1): 3–17.
Nova UCD (nd) 'Collaborate and access research expertise', *Nova UCD*, https://www.ucd.ie/innovation/industry-and-business/collaborate-and-access-research-expertise/
NPWS (2012) 'The Quirke Report', *National Parks and Wildlife Service*, https://www.npws.ie/sites/default/files/publications/pdf/QUIRKE%20REPORT.pdf

Ó Beacháin, D. (2014) 'Book review: from guns to government – the IRA in context [review of the book *The IRA: The Irish Republican Army*, by J. Dingley]', *Studies of Transition States and Societies*, 6(1): 68–74.

O'Brien, Ciara. (2019) 'Amazon to invest in Donegal wind farm as it eyes renewable energy goal', *The Irish Times*, 8 April.

O'Callaghan, C., Kelly, S., Boyle, M., and Kitchin, R. (2015) 'Topologies and topographies of Ireland's neoliberal crisis', *Space and Polity*, 19(1): 31–46.

O'Carroll, C. (2024) 'Ireland's data centres turning to fossil fuels after maxing out country's electricity grid', *The Journal*, 28 November.

O'Carroll, L. (2025) 'UK and Ireland announce deal connecting offshore windfarms to energy networks', *The Guardian*, 6 March.

O'Connell, B. and O'Carroll, C. (2018) *Brendan O'Regan: Irish Visionary, Innovator, Peacemaker*, Irish Academic Press.

O'Connor, F. (2024) 'Energy supply can't keep up with demand of big employers – and it could cost thousands of new jobs, warn Kildare businesses', *Irish Independent*, 18 May.

O'Doherty, C. (2024) 'Eirgrid disputes "alarmist" prediction that power demand by Irish data centres is set to double within two years', *Irish Independent*, 30 January.

O'Doherty, C. (2025) 'Questions raised as Coillte quietly shuts down its non-profit Nature branch', *Irish Independent*, 22 March.

O'Donnell, P. (1933) 'And now—what? On with the good work!', *An Phoblacht*, 18 February.

O'Donnell, P. (1965) *The Role of Industrial Workers in the Problems of the West*, Docas Co-operative Society.

O'Donnell, P. (2017) *There Will Be Another Day: The Inside Story of the Land Struggle in 1920s Ireland*, Red Sky Books.

O'Donoghue, P. (2024) 'Why Ireland's vision of being the "Saudi Arabia of offshore wind" is in trouble', *The Journal*, 10 August.

O'Dwyer, R. (nd) *Whitespaces: A Political Economy of Radio Spectrum*, unpublished manuscript.

Ó Grada, C. (1997) *A Rocky Road: The Irish Economy Since the 1920s*, Manchester University Press.

O'Halloran, B. (2019) 'Eirgrid plans €30m investment to boost Intel's power supply', *The Irish Times*, 15 January.

O'Halloran, B. (2024) 'Data centres not to blame for squeeze on electricity supply, expert claims: planner says industry has become a "whipping boy" for state's shortcomings', *The Irish Times*, 20 August.

O'Hare, E. (2024) 'Big tech companies lobby government almost thirty times in three years', *Business Post*, 19 August.

O'Hearn, D. (1987) 'Estimates of new foreign manufacturing employment in Ireland (1956–1972)', *Economic and Social Review*, 18(3): 173–88.

O'Hearn, D. (1989) 'The Irish case of dependency: an exception to the exceptions?', *American Sociological Review*, 54(4): 578–96.

O'Hearn, D. (1990) 'The road from import-substituting to export-led industrialization in Ireland: who mixed the asphalt, who drove the machinery, and who kept making them change directions?', *Politics & Society*, 18(1): 1–38.

O'Hearn, D. (2000) 'Globalization, "New Tigers," and the end of the developmental state? The case of the Celtic Tiger', *Politics and Society*, 28(1): 67–92.

O'Hearn, D. (2001a) *The Atlantic Economy: Britain, the US, and Ireland*, Manchester University Press.

O'Hearn, D. (2001b) 'Economic growth and social cohesion in Ireland', https://library.fes.de/fulltext/id/01135c01.htm

O'Hearn D. (2003) 'Macroeconomic policy in the Celtic Tiger: a critical reassessment', in C. Coulter and S. Coleman (eds) *The End of Irish History? Critical Reflections on the Celtic Tiger*, Manchester University Press, pp 34–55.

Ó Maonaigh, C., Reilly, L., and Stephens, J.C. (2025) 'Industry funding of Irish universities', *Public Policy.ie*, 25 February.

Ó Riain, S. (2000) 'The flexible developmental state: globalization, information technology, and the "Celtic Tiger"', *Politics and Society*, 28(2): 157–93.

Ó Riain, S. (2004) *The Politics of High-Tech Growth: Developmental Network States in the Global Economy*, Cambridge University Press.

O'Sullivan, K. (2018) *Ireland, Africa and the End of Empire: Small State Identity in the Cold War 1955–75*, Manchester University Press.

O'Toole, F. (2021) *We Don't Know Ourselves: A Personal History of Ireland Since 1958*, Liveright.

Offaly Independent (1922) 'Clifden Marconi Station destroyed by Irregulars', Irish Newspaper Archives, 5 August.

Ohlmeyer, J. (2023) *Making Empire: Ireland, Imperialism, and the Early Modern World*, Oxford University Press.

Ong, A. (2006) *Neoliberalism as Exception: Transformations in Citizenship and Sovereignty*, Duke University Press.

Orridge, A.W. (1983) 'The blueshirts and the "economic war": a study of Ireland in the context of dependency theory', *Political Studies*, 31(3): 351–69.

Ortar, N. Taylor, A.R.E., Velkova, J. Brodie, P. Johnson, A., Marquet, C., et al (2022) 'Powering "smart" futures: data centres and the energy politics of digitalisation', in S. Abram, K. Waltorp, N. Ortar, and S. Pink (eds) *Energy Futures: Anthropocene Challenges, Emerging Technologies and Everyday Life*, De Gruyter, pp 125–67.

Parks, L. (2015) '"Stuff you can kick": toward a theory of media infrastructures', in P. Svensson and D.T. Goldberg (eds) *Between Humanities and the Digital*, MIT Press.

Parks, L. and Starosielski, N. (eds) (2015) *Signal Traffic: Critical Studies of Media Infrastructures*, University of Illinois Press.

Parnreiter, C., Steinwärder, L. and Kolhoff, K. (2024) 'Uneven development through profit repatriation: how capitalism's class and geographical antagonisms intertwine', *Antipode*, 56: 2343–67.

Pasek, A. (2019) 'Managing carbon and data flows: fungible forms of mediation in the cloud', *Culture Machine*, 18.

Pasek, A. (2023) *Getting into Fights with Data Centers: Or, a Modest Proposal for Reframing the Climate Politics of ICT*, White Paper, Experimental Methods and Media Lab, Trent University, July, https://emmlab.info/Resources_page/Data%20Center%20Fights-_digital.pdf

Pasek, A., Lin, C., Cooper, Z.G.T., and Kinder, J. (2023) *Digital Energetics*, University of Minnesota Press.

Patnaik, U. and Patnaik, P. (2021) *Capital and Imperialism: Theory, History, and the Present*, Monthly Review Press.

Peatland Finance Ireland (2021) 'Baseline Report. Deliverable 2 of TA Assignment No. AA-010612-001 for the EIB Natural Capital Finance Facility', https://drive.google.com/file/d/1E_D94Bmng9yD-YxObf0Y3hojx-qMV5pR/view.

Pedregal, A. and Lukić, N. (2024) 'Imperialism, ecological imperialism, and green imperialism: an overview', *Journal of Labor and Society*, 27(1): 105–38.

Pillaia, A., Reañosa, M.T., and Curtis, J. (2022) 'Fuel poverty in Ireland: an analysis of trends and profiles', *ESRI: Economic and Social Research Institute*, June.

Plantin, J.-C., Lagoze, C., Edwards, P.N., and Sandvig, C. (2018) 'Infrastructure studies meet platform studies in the age of Google and Facebook', *New Media & Society*, 20(1): 293–310.

Pollock, S. (2024) 'The utility regulator is now deciding on Ireland's economic future – but it's not their job to do that', *Irish Independent*, 31 August.

Port of Ventspils (2005) 'The Ventspils High Technology Park (VHTP)', *Port of Ventspils*, https://www.portofventspils.lv/en/invest-in-ventspils/industrial-clients/ventspils-high-technology-park-vhtp/

Povinelli, E. (2016) *Geontologies: A Requiem to Late Liberalism*, Duke University Press.

Prashad, V. (2007) *The Darker Nations: A People's History of the Third World*, The New Press.

Pratt, M.L. (1992) *Imperial Eyes: Travel Writing and Transculturation*, Routledge.

Preston, P., Kerr, A., and Cawley, A. (2009) 'Innovation and knowledge in the digital media sector: an information economy approach', *Information, Communication & Society*, 12(7): 994–1014.

Pringle, D. (2001) 'Ireland catches its breath – tech slowdown may give overstretched country a chance to regroup – now it has time to address strains on labor market, infrastructure', *Wall Street Journal*, 30 May.

Pringle, T.P. (2021) 'The tech ecosystem and the colony', *Heliotrope*, 12 May.

Putnam, E. (2023) *Rituals for Circuits*, YouTube, 8 October, https://www.youtube.com/watch?v=WH4QwlLxuhs

Quigley, M. (2003) 'Modernity's edge: speaking silence on the Blasket Islands', *Interventions*, 5(3): 382–406.

Radiokerrynews (2021) 'Claims proposed North Kerry data centre campus will devour energy from LNG terminal', *Radio Kerry*, 24 June.

Radovanovic, A. (2020) 'Our data centers now work harder when the sun shines and wind blows', *The Keyword*, 22 April.

Ramsar Convention (nd) https://www.ramsar.org/

Rasmussen, M.B. and Lund, C. (2018) 'Reconfiguring frontier spaces: the territorialization of resource control', *World Development*, 101: 388–99.

Rebellius, M. (2023) 'How digital technologies will help the EU meet its energy efficiency targets', *World Economic Forum*, 22 November.

Regan, C. and Walsh, F. (1976) 'Dependence and underdevelopment: the case of mineral resources in the Irish Republic', *Antipode*, 8: 46–59.

Renou-Wilson, F., Bolger, T., Bullock, C., Convery, F., Curry, J., Ward, S., et al (2011) 'Bogland: sustainable management of peatlands in Ireland', *STRIVE report series*, 181.

Renou-Wilson, F., Moser, G., Fallon, D., Farrell, C.A., Müller, C., and Wilson, D. (2019) 'Rewetting degraded peatlands for climate and biodiversity benefits: results from two raised bogs', *Ecological Engineering*, 127: 547–60.

Renou-Wilson, F., Byrne, K.A., Flynn, R., Premrov, A., Riondato, E., Saunders, M., et al (2022) 'Peatland properties influencing greenhouse gas emissions and removal', *EPA Research*, January.

Resource Protection Campaign (1975) 'Ireland's resources: the case for state control. RPC publication', https://www.leftarchive.ie/document/7105/

Resources Study Group (1970) 'The need for Irish mining. A case study of exploitation', https://www.leftarchive.ie/document/1191/

Resources Study Group (1972) 'Navan and Irish mining documentation of an £850,000,000 robbery', https://www.leftarchive.ie/document/2478/

Reynolds, J. (2025) 'Consumers' energy bills set to rise further as more data centres will add to costs', *Irish Independent*, 16 March.

Ricaurte, P. (2019) 'Data epistemologies, the coloniality of power, and resistance', *Television & New Media*, 20(4): 350–65.

Richter, F. (2024) 'Amazon maintains cloud lead as Microsoft edges closer', *Statista*, 1 November.

Rikap, C. (2021) *Capitalism, Power and Innovation: Intellectual Monopoly Capitalism Uncovered*, Routledge.

Rikap, C. and Harari-Kermadec, H. (2020) 'The direct subordination of universities to the accumulation of capital', *Capital & Class*, 44(3): 371–400.

Riofrancos, T. (2020) *Resource Radicals: From Petro-Nationalism to Post-Extractivism in Ecuador*, Duke University Press.

Riofrancos, T. (2023) 'The security–sustainability nexus: lithium onshoring in the Global North', *Global Environmental Politics*, 23(1): 20–41.

Roach, J. (2022) 'Microsoft datacenter batteries to support growth of renewables on the power grid', *Microsoft Source*, 7 July.

Robertson, M. (2006) 'The nature that capital can see: science, state and market in the commodification of ecosystem services', *Environment and Planning D: Society and Space*, 24(3): 367–87.

Robertson, M. (2012) 'Measurement and alienation: making a world of ecosystem services', *Transactions of the Institute of British Geographers*, 37(3): 386–401.

Robinson, T. (2012) *Connemara after the Famine: Journal of a Survey of the Martin Estate by Thomas Colville Scott, 1853*, Lilliput Press.

Rodney, W. (2022) *Decolonial Marxism: Essays from the Pan-African Revolution*, Verso.

Rone, J. (2024) 'The shape of the cloud: contesting date centre construction in North Holland', *New Media & Society*, 26(10): 5999–6018.

RTÉ (1978) 'Peaceful protest turns violent', *RTÉ Archives*, 15 May.

RTÉ (1983) 'Social conscience of the Land League', *RTÉ Archives*, 10 March.

RTÉ (1985) 'Chemical Tanker Leak', *RTÉ Archives*, 28 May.

RTÉ (1987) 'Campaign to save Irish bogs goes Dutch', *RTÉ Archives*, 5 October.

RTÉ (1988a) 'ESB strikes impacts', *RTÉ Archives*, 4 May.

RTÉ (1988b) 'Launch of Coillte', *RTÉ Archives*, 21 December.

RTÉ (1989) 'O'Malley on Intel jobs', *RTÉ Archives*, 2 October.

RTÉ (1990) 'Electronics jobs for Dublin', *RTÉ Archives*, 17 September.

RTÉ (nd) 'Mother operated on successfully today', *RTÉ*, https://1916.rte.ie/relevant-places/they-were-told-they-would-have-to-advance-at-all-costs/

RTÉ News (2024) 'Echelon secures grid connection for Co Wicklow data centre', *RTÉ News*, 6 September.

Rubenstein, M. (2010) *Public Works: Infrastructure, Irish Modernism, and the Postcolonial*, Notre Dame Press.

Ruuskanen, E. (2018) 'Encroaching Irish bogland frontiers: science, policy and aspirations from the 1770s to the 1840s', in J. Agar and J. Ward (eds) *Histories of Technology, the Environment and Modern Britain*, University College London Press.

Sachs, W. (ed.) (1997) *The Development Dictionary: A Guide to Knowledge as Power*, Orient Blackswan.

Sadden, E. (2024) 'UK's Technology Minerals to sell Irish lithium exploration licenses', *S&P Global: Commodity Insights*, 22 April.

Sadowski, J. (2019) 'When data is capital: datafication, accumulation, and extraction', *Big Data & Society*, 6(1).

Sadowski, J. and Levenda, A.M. (2020) 'The anti-politics of smart energy regimes', *Political Geography*, 81: 102202.

Sandvig, C. (2015) 'The internet as the anti-television: distribution infrastructure as culture and power', in L. Parks and N. Starosielski (eds) *Signal Traffic: Critical Studies of Media Infrastructures*, University of Illinois Press.

Sareen, S. and Muller, K. (eds) (2023) *Digitisation and Low-Carbon Energy Transition*s, Palgrave Macmillan.

Scanlon, C. (2021) 'Revealed – river damaged by landslide is one of most polluted in Ireland', *Donegal Daily*, 14 July.

Scéal na Móna (1994) National Library of Ireland.

Scéal na Móna (1995) National Library of Ireland.

Scéal na Móna (1997) National Library of Ireland.

Schwab, K. (2016) *The Fourth Industrial Revolution*, Penguin.

Sexton, M. (2005) *Marconi: The Irish Connection*, Four Courts Press.

SFI (2017) 'Technology Foresight Ireland Report', *Science Foundation Ireland*.

SFI (2022) 'Annual Report and Accounts', *Science Foundation Ireland*, https://www.sfi.ie/Annual-Report-2022/SFI_AnnualReport_2022_Website.pdf

Sheller, M. (2014) *Aluminum Dreams: The Making of Light Modernity*, MIT Press.

Shiel, P. (2003) *The Quiet Revolution: The Electrification of Rural Ireland, 1946–1976*, O'Brien Press.

Siapera, E. (2022) 'AI content moderation, racism and (de)coloniality', *International Journal of Bullying Prevention* 4: 55–65.

Siemens (2023) 'Offaly in the Irish Midlands ready to rival Europe's key cities as green data centre hub', *Siemens*, 20 June.

Slater, C. (1996) 'Amazonia as Edenic narrative', in W. Cronon (ed.) *Uncommon Ground: Rethinking the Human Place in Nature*, Norton, pp 114–31.

Slater, E. (nd) 'Irish metabolic rifts – Marx and Engels on Ireland', *Irish Metabolic Rifts*, https://www.irishmetabolicrifts.com/

Slater, E. and Flaherty, E. (2023) 'Marx on the reciprocal interconnections between the soil and the human body: Ireland and its colonialised metabolic rifts', *Antipode*, 55: 620–42.

Slevin, A. (2016) *Gas, Oil and the Irish State: Understanding the Dynamics and Conflicts of Hydrocarbon Management*, Manchester University Press.

Slevin, A. (2019) 'Assessing the Corrib gas controversy: Beyond "David and Goliath" analyses of a resource conflict', *The Extractive Industries and Society*, 6(2): 519–30.

Smith, P., Monea, A., and Santiago, M. (eds) (2022) *Amazon: At the Intersection of Culture and Capital*, Rowman and Littlefield.

Sovacool, B.K., Chukwuka, G.M., and Upham, P. (2022) 'Making the internet globally sustainable: technical and policy options for improved energy management, governance and community acceptance of Nordic datacenters', *Renewable and Sustainable Energy Reviews*, 154: 111793.

Spice, A. (2018) 'Fighting invasive infrastructures: indigenous relations against pipelines', *Environment and Society*, 9: 40–56.

Srnicek, N. (2016) *Platform Capitalism*, Polity Press.

Starosielski, N. (2015) *The Undersea Network*, Duke University Press.

Starosielski, N. and Walker, J. (eds) (2016) *Sustainable Media: Critical Approaches to Media and Environment*, Routledge.

Starr, P. (2002) 'The great telecom implosion', *The American Prospect*, 8 September, https://www.princeton.edu/~starr/articles/articles02/Starr-TelecomImplosion-9-02.htm

Stefanović, S. (2024) 'Holistic security for environmental defenders?', *Green Web Foundation*, 5 February.

Steinberg, M., Mukherjee, R., and Punathembakar, A. (2022) 'Media power in digital Asia: super apps and megacorps', *Media, Culture & Society*, 44(8): 1405–19.

Sullivan, L. (2021) 'Our existence is our resistance: mining and resistance on the island of Ireland', *Yes to Life No to Mining*, https://yestolifenotomining.org/wp-content/uploads/2021/09/Comp-IoI-1.pdf

Sultana, F. (2022) 'The unbearable heaviness of climate coloniality', *Political Geography*, 99: 102638.

Svampa, M. (2019) *Neo-extractivism in Latin America: Socio-environmental Conflicts, the Territorial Turn, and New Political Narratives*, Cambridge University Press.

SWFI (nd) 'Top 100 largest sovereign wealth fund rankings by total assets', https://www.swfinstitute.org/fund-rankings/sovereign-wealth-fund

Swinhoe, D. (2023) '11 data centers in Dublin set to rely on Ireland's gas network for power', *Data Centre Dynamics*, 24 April.

Swinhoe, D. (2024a) 'Echelon "frustrated" with EirGrid negotiation over planned Arklow campus', *Data Centre Dynamics*, 8 January.

Swinhoe, D. (2024b) 'Investment firm Starwood launches data center-focused unit', *Data Centre Dynamics*, 23 January.

Swinhoe, D. (2024c) 'Starwood acquires $850 million stake in Echelon Data Centers', *Data Centre Dynamics*, 15 February.

Szeman, I. and Boyer, D. (2017) 'Introduction', in I. Szeman and D. Boyer, *Energy Humanities: An Anthology*, Johns Hopkins University Press.

Szeman, I. and Wenzel, J. (2021) 'What do we talk about when we talk about extractivism?', *Textual Practice*, 35(3): 505–23.

Taylor, G. (1998) 'Conserving the Emerald Tiger: the politics of environmental regulation in Ireland', *Environmental Politics*, 7(4): 53–74.

Telesis (1983) 'A review of industrial policy', National Economic and Social Council.

Terrain AI (2024) 'Terrain-AI: uncovering new insights to support effective climate change decision-making', *Terrain AI*, https://terrainai.com/

Threshold (nd) 'Energy poverty', *Threshold: Preventing Homelessness*, https://threshold.ie/advocacy-campaign/energypoverty/

Tipton, G. (2010) 'Culture in the cutaway', *The Irish Times*, 3 April.

Tobin Consulting Engineers (2023) *Cloghercor Wind Farm Planning Statement*, March.

Toomey, L. (2025) *'A National Resource of Primary Importance': Transforming Ireland's Peatlands in the Twentieth Century*, unpublished PhD thesis, Trinity College Dublin.

Tovey, H. (1993) 'Environmentalism in Ireland: two versions of development and modernity', *International Sociology*, 8(4): 413–30.

Tsing, A. (2015) *The Mushroom at the End of the World: On the Possibility of Life in Capitalist Ruins*, Princeton University Press.

Tuam Herald (1922) 'The Marconi Station at Clifden', Irish Newspaper Archives, 23 September.

Turf Development Bill Deb, Second Stage (Resumed) (1997) Wednesday 3 December 1997 (Vol. 484, No. 1).

UK Parliament (nd) Irish Congested Districts Board, Volume 105: debated on Friday 14 March 1902.

Valdivia, A. (2024) 'The supply chain capitalism of AI: a call to (re)think algorithmic harms and resistance through environmental lens', *Information, Communication & Society*: 1–17.

van der Vlist, F., Helmond, A., and Ferrari, F. (2024) 'Big AI: cloud infrastructure dependence and the industrialisation of artificial intelligence', *Big Data & Society*, 11(1).

van Egeraat, C. and Jacobson, D. (2004) 'The rise and demise of the Irish and Scottish computer hardware industry', *European Planning Studies*, 12(6): 809–34.

Velkova, J. (2021) 'Thermopolitics of data: cloud infrastructures and energy futures', *Cultural Studies*, 35(4–5): 663–83.

Velkova, J. and Plantin, J.-C. (2023) 'Data centers and the infrastructural temporalities of digital media: an introduction', *New Media & Society*, 25(2): 273–86.

Villegas Plá, B. (2023) 'Dependency theory meets feminist economics: a research agenda', *Third World Quarterly*, 45(8): 1325–42.

Vonderau, A. (2019) 'Scaling the cloud: making state and infrastructure in Sweden', *Ethnos*, 84(4): 698–718.

Voskoboynik, D.M. and Andreucci, D. (2021) 'Greening extractivism: environmental discourses and resource governance in the "Lithium Triangle"', *Environment and Planning E: Nature and Space*, 5(2): 787–809.

Walker, J. and Cooper, M. (2011) 'Genealogies of resilience: from systems ecology to the political economy of crisis adaptation', *Security Dialogue*, 42(2): 143–60.

Walsh, J. (2018) *Higher Education in Ireland, 1922–2016: Politics, Policy and Power – A History of Higher Education in the Irish State*, Palgrave Macmillan.

Watt, R. (2021) 'The fantasy of carbon offsetting', *Environmental Politics*, 30(7): 1069–88.

Wenzel, J. (2019) *The Disposition of Nature: Environmental Crisis and World Literature*, Fordham University Press.

Weston, K. (2012) 'Political ecologies of the precarious', *Anthropological Quarterly*, 85(2): 429–55.

Whyte, B.J. (2024) 'IDA gives Intel €30m to offset energy price spike', *The Irish Times*, 3 May.

Whyte, N. (1999) *Science, Colonialism, and Ireland*, Cork University Press.

Wiessner, M. (2024) 'The ecologistics of carbon tracking: environmental accounting software and industrial media practices', *Journal of Environmental Media*.

Wilkins, N.P. (2016) *Alexander Nimmo, Master Engineer, 1783–1832: Public Works and Civil Surveys*, Irish Academic Press.

Williams, E. (2022 [1944]) *Capitalism and Slavery*, Penguin Classics.

Wilson, D., Mackin, F., Tuovinen, J.-P., Moser, G., Farrell, C., and Renou-Wilson, F. (2022) 'Carbon and climate implications of rewetting a raised bog in Ireland', *Global Change Biology*, 28: 6349–65.

Wind Energy (2016) 'Wind energy – the power to power ourselves', *YouTube*, https://www.youtube.com/watch?v=eqKZkcxeKR8

Woodcock, N. (2024) 'Prioritising AI over climate change would be catastrophic', *Tech Informed*, 28 October.

Woods, M. (2020) 'A conservative decoloniality?: On the limitations of Irish decolonization', *Contending Modernities*, 15 December.

Yearley, S. (1995) 'From one dependency to another: the political economy of science policy in the Irish Republic in the second half of the twentieth century', *Science, Technology, & Human Values*, 20(2): 171–96.

Yusoff, K. (2018) *A Billion Black Anthropocenes or None*, University of Minnesota Press.

Index

References to figures appear in *italic*.

A

Abbeyleix 141–2, 161–3
Act for the Employment of the Poor in certain Districts of Ireland 40
Aer Lingus 57–8
Africa 177
Agrarian South 118
agriculture, 13, 15, 64, 74, 85; *see also* land
AI (artificial intelligence) 1, 8, 20, 150, 154
Aiken, Frank 80
Airtricity 94, 120
Ajl, Max 27, 96, 182, 185
Alibaba 5
Allen, Robert 107
Alphabet 5
Amazon 5, 6–7, 26
Amazon Web Services (AWS) *see* AWS
Amin, Samir 19, 27, 183
An Gorta Mór 41
Andrews, Todd 58, 62–4, 67–71, 73, 92–3, 95, 124
Anglo-Irish Treaty 51–2
'anti-toxic' campaigns 107
anti-Treaty forces 52–3
Apple 5, 192
Arab states 91
Arboleda, Martin 181–2
Ardnacrusha hydroelectric dam 23, 57, 64, 83
Arklow 136
Arrighi, Giovanni 9
artificial intelligence (AI) *see* AI
Asahi chemical plant 87, *87*, 100, 134
atmospheric exploitation 118
Avaio Capital 134
AWS (Amazon Web Services) 128–30
  catastrophic peat slide at Meenbog 3, 114, 129–32; *see also* Meenbog
    quickly dissociates itself from disaster 130
  cloud and 6
  first infrastructure region outside US 98
  hyperscale data centres 2
    in Dublin 4
  nature of data centres 8
  privileged access 128
  transformative role of 117

B

BBC 54
Béaslaí. Piaras 52
Bellacorick 67–8, 74, 86, 120, 184
Bellamy, Brent Ryan 45
Berridge, Richard 41
Bezos, Jeff 3
Bhandar, Brenna 13
'big tech' 5–7
Black Lives Matter (BLM) 11, 203
Bog Commission 14, 40, 63, 64
bogs 3–4, 145–50; *see also* Derrigimlagh bog; peat; turf-cutting
  Abbeyleix 161–2
  attitudes to 64
  become synonymous with the backward 13
  carbon sinks, as 143, 148
  colonial administrators' views of 59
  'Future Use of the Cutaway Bogs' (John Feehan and Bernard Kaye) 162
  largest programme of 'rehabilitation' 143
  Lough Boora 162
  monopoly tech and 160
  most prominent extractive landscape 59
  national grid construction lays groundwork for future green development 60
  reclamation proposals 13, 14
  re-wetted bogs 33, 148–9
  sphagnum moss 114
  storage uses 146, 148
  surface area of as percentage of whole 143
  surveys of 13
  west coast bogs and Irish self-determination 68
Wicklow 109

INDEX

Boland's Mill 136–7
Bord Failte 50
Bord na Móna (BnM) 91–5; *see also* Turf Development Board
  cast as a villain 17
  compradors and 112
  cutting edge technology (Experimental Station) 66–7
  Derrinlough briquette factory 138
  described 3
  Eco-Energy Park 134–6
  housebuilding activities, unique nature of 70, *70*
  institutional transformation (Third Development Programme) 91
  international expansion 93
  remit in west 59
  sabotage of 83
  'Some Precursors of …' (Todd Andrews) 62
briquette factories 138, *139*
Britain 11
  currency parity 77
  exports 11, 16, 63, 73–4
  facing new competition after breaking with 60
  French attempt to liberate Ireland from 87
  Ireland as colonial laboratory 21
  Irish modernisation projects and 59
  preventing Ireland becoming self-sufficient 76–7
  science dominated by 151
  South continues dependence on Britain 11–12
  telegraph station (Valentia, County Kerry) 51
British Pathé 66
broadcasting 54
Buck, Holly Jean 149
Bytedance 5

C

Cabral, Amilcar 27, 183
capitalism
  accumulation strategies 43
  as an ecology 9
  communism undermined by 26
  eco-modernity and 20
  fourth industrial revolution and 181
  imperial powers and environmentalism 8, 9
  Ireland re-inserts into 10, 16, 80–1, 203
  Irish capitalism, nature of 3
  produces rather than affects ecologies 131
  railways reveal true character of 44
  world capitalism and Irish environmentalism 17, 118
  see also colonialism; imperialism
carbon *see* decarbonisation
carbon, global accounting 129, 144, 150

carbon, present and future 149
carbon emissions 53, 143, 148–9, 157
carbon from drained bogs 143
carbon mitigation 160
Carlow Land War 75, 190
cattle 11, 16, 101
CeADAR 154
Celtic Otherworld 146
Celtic Tiger 11, 16, 24, 90, 94–5, 109
censorship 54
Chaudhary, Ajay Singh 26
Childers, Erskine 74
China 5, 10, 80
Civil War 52
Clan na Gael 51
clearances 41, 44
Cleary, Joe 82
Clifden (Connemara) 36–7, 48
Climate Action Plan 2003 143, 175
climate mitigation 143–4, 148–50, 155, 160
cloud, the
  AWS investing in 7
  big tech and 6
  Donegal wind farm disaster 3
  growing centrality of 122
  nature of 1
  operationalised as global carbon accounting ledger 144
coal 65, 76, 92
colonial capitalism 17; *see also* capitalism; colonialism; imperialism
colonialism
  anti-colonial land based history of 1
  capital dominates 46
  continuing currents in Ireland 11–12
  dependency and 4
  Enlightenment thermodynamics 45
  from Marconi to modern digitalisation, an example 39
  histories of 39
  late burst (late 19th, early 20th centuries) 43
  neo-colonialism 79–80
  postcolonial Ireland 3, 19, 97
  remoteness, concept of 44
  unfinished project of decolonialisation 2
  see also capitalism; imperialism
Commission for the Regulation of Utilities (CRU) 2, 108, 123, 134
communism 26
communities 4, 18, 33, 73–5, 100, 107, 128–9, 142, 160–71, 205
comprador classes 110–12
  and the postcolonial formation of Irish capitalism 96
  BnM and 112
  bourgeoisie accept 19
  comprador capitalism 23
  export of cattle by 16

FDI-led development and 25, 96–7, 108, 110
Fianna Fáil and 77
function of in Ireland 108
inherited privilege 76
mobile and influential 20
nature of 65
new generation of 92
Congested Districts Board (CDB) 42
Connemara
  agrarian economy, history and significance 42
  demographics 42
  journey through 36
  Marconi's broadcast 8, 39
    entanglement with local ecology 31
    partial nature of Marconi's industrial 'success' in 48
  sale of 41
Connolly, Garry 22, 24, 28, 124
content and carrier consolidation 6
Control of Manufacturers Act (1932) 63
convergence (of economies) 18
Cork Harbour 107
corporate power purchase agreements (CPPAs) 114, 123–4, 126–7, 131–2, 138
Corrib gas field 85, 184–5
Cosgrave, W.T. 65
Coveney, Simon 125
Cowen, Deborah 39
Crotty, Raymond 17–18, 90, 110, 136

D

Daggett, Cara New 45
Dalradian 170, 194
data centres 1–4, 123–5
  AWS's dominance 7
  enormous electricity needs of 23, 29, 123
  Google 137–8
  Irish locations and type 2
  history of 89–90
  need to provide their own onsite energy 123
  post-colonial Ireland and 97
  questioning the necessity of 27
  sustainability and 23, 118
Data Centres Ireland 22, 24, 125
datafication 156
De Valera, Éamon 82
decarbonisation
  and digitalisation 6, 20–1, 24, 29, 90, 107, 112, 118, 121; *see also* carbon, increasingly institutionalised 154
  data centres allegedly vital to 124
  digital cloud providers and 25
  imperative of 8
  meeting targets (according to a Taoiseach) 136

Deckard, Sharae 9, 16, 17, 19
decolonisation, compromise and contradiction 60; *see also* colonisation
demonstrations 197–9
Department of Scientific and Industrial Research 62
dependency 17–21
  agricultural exports to Britain 63
  deepening structures of 118
  Ireland a classic case of 90
  minimal intellectual tradition 96
  state development models and monopoly tech 194–5
  theorists of 203
Derrigimlagh 36–9
  Bog 37, *38*, 44–5, *47*
  enhanced visitor experience 50–1
  briquette factory 138, *139*
development 10–11, 33–4
  developmental to post-developmental 89
  state strategies 109–10
Devoy, John 51
Diamanti, Jeff 45
digital capitalism 7, 10, 29, 53–4; *see also* capitalism
Digital Energetics (Anne Pasek et al) 8
digital media 4, 180
'digital rights' 5
digitalisation 6
  and decarbonisation 6, 20–1, 24, 29, 90, 107, 112, 118, 121
  increasingly institutionalised 154
  fourth industrial revolution 117
  infrastructures for 88, 105
  platforms 6
  reactions to
    confused critiques levelled at anti-colonialists 53
  unprecedented times 29
Do Sheep Dream of Electric Ruins? (Matt Parker) 37
Doctorow, Cory 5
'Donal' 116–17
Donegal 3, *115*, *128*
  County Development Plan 130
Dos Santos, Theotônio 18
dotcom boom and crash 104, 105
Down Survey 13; *see also* land: surveys
Dublin 2, 4, 136–7
  Dublin Docklands Development Authority (DDDA) 137

E

East Asia 18
Easter Rising 51, 137
Echelon Data Centres 135
Eco-Energy Parks 3
  BnM 132–4, 138

INDEX

eco-modernity 10, 12, 20, 21–8
  inheritance of colonial-extractive logic 176–7
  what it looks like in Ireland 138–9
Economic Development (T.K. Whitaker) 76
eco-socialism 6, 10, 26, 30
  blind spot of 27
education 73, 93, 97, 102, 127, 144–5, 151, 153
EEC (European Economic Community) 75, 83, 101; *see also* EU
Eirgrid 2, 22, 23, 122–4
electricity
  data centres: proportion of amount consumed 2
  digital infrastructure and 23–4
  Marconi signal and 49
  mining and 177
  Moyle Interconnector 123
  national grid 59
  Power for Progress 61
  rural 75
  turf powered 64
Electricity Supply Board (ESB) 3, 57, 59, 61, 83
emigration 18, 73–4, 76, 90
energy
  electronic media's need for 180
  for transmission of information 8
  Ireland's dependence on Britain 14, 123
  materialism of 45
  mining and 177
  offshore and renewable 135
  problems caused and solutions sought 23
Engels, Friedrich 15, 59
Enlightenment thermodynamics 45
Ennis 134, 192
Enterprise Ireland 23
Environmental Protection Agency (EPA) 108
Environmental sociology 18
environmentalism, types of 14–15, 96–8, 107–9, 185–93
  data-tech-as-solution 156
  green colonial discourses 147
  planning departments and 108–9
  rendered as services 136
  world capitalism and 17
Equinix 22
EU 138, 162, 202; *see also* EEC
Europe 61, 98, 99
Eurozone 12
exports 73–8
extraction/extractivism 180–5; *see also* mining
  Ajl on 182
  appropriation of land for 15
  carbon fuel 47
  colonial capitalism and 42
  dominant motive, the 122
  fourth industrial revolution and 7
  from periphery to core 19, 22, 27–8
  green extractivism 178, 181
  important concept for international left 181
  of peat 3, 17, 31
  political economy of Ireland 59
  'socially necessary extraction' 176
  struggles against 33
  wind 131

F

Facebook 5
Fahy, Father 73
Famine 41, 44, 68
Fanon, Frantz 27
farmers, small 73–4, 75; *see also* land
Fianna Fáil 62–5, 76–7, 82, 110
Finance Services Centre (IFSC) 16
Finland 92
Finn Valley Wind Action Group (FVWAG) 128–9
Flaherty, Eoin 15
Foley, Mark 22, 124
foreign direct investment (FDI) 95–6
  a 'contact sport' 22
  crux of Irish development 25, 32
  development strategies 110
  environmental contradictions 19
  as an ecological project 106
  facilitation 4
  Ireland navigates its place in 88
  manipulation of environmental factors 95–6
  1990s 16
  popular discontent with 108
  QUANGOs and 90–1
  Sean Lamass and 60
  state mobilised 11
  Telesis Report 100
  towards a green digital transition 21
  university research and 154
'fourth industrial revolution' 7, 117, 150, 181
fracking 168
France 40, 87
Free State Army 52, 53
Fukuyama, Francis 18

G

Gaonkar, Dilip 28
Garden Cities 71, 81
General Post Office (GPO) 51
Geological Survey of Ireland 14
Germany 61
Gibney, Frank 70–3, 72, 75, 81
Glencolumbkille 74
global communication 46

Global North and South 6, 101, 118, 158, 182–3, 186
Google
  Boland's Mill 136–7
    microcosm of postcolonial ecological regime 137
  cloud and 6, 117
  data centres 2
  Google Maps 37
  Grange Castle Business Park South 137–8
  grid-responsive computing 126
  market power 5
Goulding, Cathal 189
Grange Castle Business Park South 137
'green' politics
  digital transition 6
  nature of `38
  imperialism 6
  industrial parks 135
  policies and imperial power through monopoly-finance capitalism 118
  political economy 19
  transition, aligned with post-colonial ecology, multinationals and neoliberalism 136
Greenpeace International 1
Griffith Purser, John 61–2, 63
growth without development 136
Guinea-Bissau 10
Günel, Gökçe 164

H

Halligan, Brendan 92
hemp 40
Heron, Kai 26, 27
historical materialism 45
historical revisionism 61, 76, 83
Host in Ireland 22, 124, 125
How to Destroy Surveillance Capitalism (Cory Doctorow) 5
Huawei 5
hyperscale data centres 2; *see also* data centres

I

ICT Ireland 103
ideology of improvement *see below* improvement, ideology of
Illawi, Ibrahim 27
imperialism
  capitalism, environmentalism and 8, 9
  energy at heart of 45–6
  'free markets' 46
  histories of 39
  location, choice and considerations 46
  see also capitalism; colonialism
Imperialism, the Highest Stage of Capitalism (Vladimir Lenin) 43–4
'improvement', ideology of 12–15
  extraction at heart of 42
  from Marconi to the digital age 39–40
  improvement projects, colonial and national-sovereign 61
  processes involved 43
Industrial Development Authority (IDA) 98–101, *99*, 103
  experimental governance 23
  Grange Castle Business Park South 137–8
  nature and perspective of 22
  producing graduate engineers 151–2
industrialisation, from state-driven to FDI led 60
  Fianna Fáil's legacy 110
  import-substituting 63
  multinational capital and 195
information flows 6, 8
infrastructures
  centrality of the digital 23
  Irish Times on 103
  meeting the need of multinationals 88, 118
  nature of in Ireland 2–3
  peat-driven national grid 59
  provision to multinationals without investment from them, consequences of 119
  rural communities 73, 74
  state faces challenges 104–6
integration, lack of 19
Intel 101–5, 109, 155–6
International Convention on Wetlands 146
International Energy Agency (IEA) 2
International Financial Services Centre (IFSC) 101
iPhone 181
IRA 31, 51–2, 189
Ireland
  AI, use of 20
  as laboratory for 'innovative' technology 5, 119
    and for new forms of expropriation 19–20
  Britain's colonial laboratory 21
  Britain and, a compare and contrast situation 92–3; *see also* Britain
  Celtic Tiger *see* Celtic Tiger
  conservative elements within 77
  contradictions of imperial ecology played out in 171
  dependency on monopoly tech 9; *see also* monopoly tech
  extraction *see* extraction
  financial crash 98
  Free State 51, 59
  free trade speedily adopted 78–9
    world's first free trade zone 81
  GDP 98
  Gibney's vision 71

INDEX

innovation 9, 59
land-based *see* land; rural areas
mapping of 14
marketing aestheticized 'development' 136
metabolic rift, the 15
midlands 4, 134
modernity, its nature in 49–50
narratives of its history 24
national projects 60
neoliberalism of 14, 17
1980s debt 91–2
offshore marine sector 135
partition 11, 204
   sustained relationship with Britain 11–12
pasture-based agriculture 15
private enterprise 79
re-inserts itself into capitalist world system 10; *see also* capitalism
reliance on multinationals 25
resources 59
revisionist histories of benefit to 49
self-determination through turf 68; *see also* bogs; peat; turf-cutting
semi-periphery, the 15
six counties 51
soil exhaustion 26
sovereign wealth fund 111
state positioning 25
tax haven, as 97
US aid post-World War II 77–8
western Ireland 74
Ireland's Resources: The Case for State Control (RPC) 189
Irish Independent 52
Irish Nationalist Party 42
Irish Peat Board Global Consultancy Service 93
Irish Times 103
Israel 197–9, 203

J

Japan 87
Joyce, James 31, 50
'just transitions' 4, 31, 127, 132, 136–8, 141–2, 165

K

Keating, Seán 5, 60
   mural 57, *58*, 82
Kennedy, John F. 79, 121
Kildare 66
Killala 87, 100, 134
Kirkintilloch 65
knowledge 23, 144, 164

L

Labour in Irish History (Garry Connolly) 28
Lakota Nation 168–9, *169*

land 15–17
   agitation 16, 73
   annuities 63
   Carlow Land War 75
   continuity of land management 19
   distribution to small farmers 63
   enclosing 59
   exploitation of Ireland 15
   export of cattle 16
   foreign ownership 74–5
   landlords 41
   National Land League 75
   surveys 12–13, 14
      Down Survey 13
   transitioning towards technology 24
   value/waste and civilised/savage 13, 14
Land Acts
   1881 42
   1933 63
Land Commission 42, 63, 73, 75
Land League 41, 42, 190
Lantry, Peter 22, 23, 124–5
Latin America 180, 182
Leitrim 168–9
Leixlip 102, 109
Lemass Seán, 60, 64, 68, 81–2
Lenin, Vladimir 7, 43–4, 111
Lia Fáil 73
Lough Boora 162
Lowry, Barry 22
Lundon, William 42

M

Mainstream Renewable Power 120
Making Relatives 168, 170
Marconi, Guglielmo 36–8, 42–53; *see also* Derrigimlagh; radio; wireless telegraphy
   experimental technology of 8
   Wireless Telegraph Company
   BnM projects compared to 68–9
   choice of location 30–1
   description of working Station 47–8
      materials required for 48
      security for 50
   essential aims of, and today's comparisons 43
Marconi Station 47–8, *47*, 50
   destruction of, and reaction to 52–3
   final transmission from 53
Marconigraph 43
Marshall Plan 66, 70, 77
Marx, Karl 15, 26, 59
Marxism 6, 95, 96, 127
materialism 45
McCabe, Conor 16, 96, 108
McCarron, Sister Majella 169–70, *191*
McDonough, Terrence 15
McDyer, Father 74

McVeigh, Robbie 2
media technologies, energy driven nature of 45
Meenbog wind farm 3–4, 114–16, *115*, 128–32
Meta 2, 5
Microsoft
  cloud and social media 2, 6, 117, 150
  first CPPA 131
  grid flexibility experiments 126
  market power 5
  opens up in Ireland 105
  proposals for power plant outside Dublin 134
  Terrain-AI 157
mining 171–80; *see also* extraction
  dubious practices 179
  first case linking monopoly tech to 172–3
  history of 174
  lithium 176
  other vital extractable metals 177–8
  researchers' in danger of becoming industry's mouthpieces 179
  state company 186
modernisation
  development and 10–11
  neoliberalism and 96
  problems and contradictions 28
  theory of in Ireland 18, 61, 176
modernism, literary 50
modernity 50, 82–3
Molinero, Alberto García 10
monopolies 44
monopoly tech 4, 7, 25, 106, 122
  campaigning against 173
  central role in peatlands and climate mitigation 143
  climate mitigation and 149–50
Moore, Jason 9, 16
Mourne Beg River 116
multinational companies
  critique of 188
  'data centre land' and 32
  encouragement to remain in Ireland 104
  Irish capitalism, from land to 16–17
  Robert Allen's book on 107
  use of land and technology by 88–9
  varying types of location within Ireland need mediation 132, 137–8
Musk, Elon 5

N

Nally, David 41
Napoleonic Wars 40
National Agricultural Soil Carbon Observatory (NASCO) 149
national grid
  building the infrastructure 59

  connecting to 75
  multinationals efforts on 126
  overwhelmed by data centres 123
  see also electricity; infrastructure
National Land League 75
National Parks and Wildlife Service (NPWS) 109, 155
Neo-colonialism, the Last Stage of Imperialism (Kwame Nkrumah) 79;
  see also colonialism
neoliberalism
  Celtic Tiger and 90
  comprador class produced from 20
  fixations and suitability 14
  modernisation and 96
  privatisation by 111
  ways of looking at things 92
Netherlands 146–7
New Fortress Energy 134
Niger Delta 85
'Night Candles are Burnt Out' (Seán Keating) 57
Nimmo, Alexander 40
Nkrumah, Kwame 79
No Global: The People of Ireland v the Multinationals (Robert Allen) 107

O

O'Brien, Conor Cruise 51
O'Connor, Eddie 67, 92–4, 112, 120
O'Donnell, Peadar 63, 73–4
Offaly 134, 138
offshore renewable energy 135;
  see also energy
O'Hearn, Denis 18, 60, 76
Ongar 53
O'Regan, Brendan 81
O'Toole, Fintan 76
Oweninny bog complex 67, 87, 120, 184–5

P

Palestine 11, 80, 170, 171, 197–200, 203
paramilitary republicanism 30
Parker, Matt 37, *37*
Parnell, Charles Stewart 42
partition 11, 204
Pasek, Anne 8, 45, 150, 156
Pearse, Padraig 51
peat
  AI2Peat project 157
  Bord na Móna 17
  catastrophic slide 3, 129; *see also* Meenbog
  committee to examine uses of 62
  conference attended 141–2
  Dutch Government initiative 146
  failures to prevent imports of British coal 76
  International Peat Symposium 67

last briquette factory 138, *139*
library of international research on 67
national grid construction 59–60
national politics of reserves 31
reclamation proposals 13
restoration 166
rewetting 33, 148–9
sustainability the word 155
tensions between conservation and usage of 147–8
Territorial Just Development Plan 138
Third Development Programme 91
transported to US 93
see also bogs; turf-cutting
Peatland Finance Ireland (PFI) 159–61, 163
Pedregal, Alejandro 10
Petro, Gustavo 200
Petty, William 12–13, 150
planning system 108–9
pollution 108
Portarlington, County Laois 66, 67
Pratt, Mary Louise 64
privatisation 25, 32, 60, 104, 111, 144, 157, 176, 203
production 27, 63
Protestant Ascendancy 13
protests 197–9
public debt 90
Puerto Rico 78

R

radio
  construction and destruction 39
  first transmission 49, 51
  Marconi's control through patents 43
  wireless or carbon fuel extraction 46–7
railways 44
raw materials 44, 165, 172, 174–80
Raybestos Manhattan 107, 193
resource nationalism 22, 32, 60, 71, 79, 111–12, 119, 190, 192
Resource Protection Campaign (RPC) 186–90
Ring, Eugene 51
Ring, Tim 51
Rio Earth Summit (1992) 97
Role of Industrial Workers in the Problems of the West (Peadar O'Donnell) 73
Rolston, Bill 2
Rosslare Europort 135
Roundstone, South Connemara 40–1
Royal Canal 62
Royal Dutch Shell 169, 184
rural areas
  'boosterism' 135
  Gibney's vision 71
  growth without development 136

infrastructure issues 73, 74
lack of development 75–6
rural sociology 96
see also bogs; land
Rural Electrification Scheme 61
rural resistance 14
Ruuskanen, Esa 13

S

sails, material for 40
Sandvig, Christian 6
Saro-Wiwa, Ken 85
Schmidt, Eric 1
Schouten, Matthijs 146
Schwab, Klaus 7
science 150–5
  centrality of economic development in policy 152
  National Board for Science and Technology (NBST) 152
  National Science Council (NSC) 152
  Science Foundation Ireland (SFI) 124, 141, 144–5, 157, 163
  importance of 153–4
Scott, Michael 58–9
semi-periphery 17–21
  core and 18
  core imports to 19, 176
  extraction from 27
semi-states 91–2, 122
SFI *see* Science Foundation Ireland
Shannon Free Zone 81
Shannon Hydroelectric Scheme 23, 57
Shannon/Kerry LNG project 134
Shell 169, 184
Siemens 134
Silicon Docks 137
Sinn Féin 186, 203
Slater, Eamonn 15
software 103, 105–6, 149, 156–7
soil exhaustion 26
sovereign social metabolism 10
Soviet Union 60
sports metaphors 22
Starwood Capital 136
Statcraft 130
state developmental dynamics 6
stress diagrams 72
supply chains
  Amazon and others 26–7
  preference for managing inhouse 132
  geographies of 4
  global nature of 16
  green digital transition and 179
  Marconi's aid to 43, 49
  national grid 59
surveys (of land) 12–13
  Geological Survey of Ireland 14

sustainability
  data centres and 23, 118
  monopoly tech and 144, 157
  peatlands now governed by considerations of 155
  publicly funded science working towards 144

T

T50 fibre-optic cable 105
technology
  rejected politicisation of 53
  what is the point of? 55
Telesis Report 90, 100, 153
Tencent 5
Terrain-AI 157
Territorial Just Transition Plan 138
Thatcher, Margaret 93
Third Development Programme 91
Tír na nÓg 146
Tovey, Hilary 14–15, 96–7, 103, 107, 109, 164, 186
toxicity (chemical and pharmaceuticals) 18
Trump, Donald 5
turf-cutting 44–5; *see also* bogs; peat
  electric power from regarded as ambitious 64
  process industrialised 59
  rights to 114
  traditional practice of 64–5
Turf Development Acts
  1946 66
  1950 70
  1998 94–5
Turf Development Board 14, 58, 62, 64–6; *see also* Bord na Móna
Turf Use and Development Bill 64, 65
Turraun bog 62, 64

U

Ukraine war 121
United States
  dangers of antagonising 33–4
  dominates world capitalist system 16
  enormous pressure from 10
  first radio broadcast in Europe sent to from General Post Office (1916) 51
  hegemony of 12
  imperialist monopoly capitalism 22
  Irish dependency 20
  Marshall Plan 66, 70, 77
  post-World War II involvement in Europe 77–8
  transporting peat to 93
  violence of hegemony 19
university sector 144–5
  dubious partners involved 178
  University College Dublin 154, 202

V

Valentia, County Kerry 51
value extraction 27–8, 42–4
Vapo 92
Varadkar, Leo 3
Ventspils Industrial Park (Latvia) 135

W

Wallerstein, Immanuel 9
War of Independence 51
water 100, 104, 109, 168–71
We Don't Know Ourselves (Fintan O'Toole) 76
Weismoor 69
Whitaker, T.K. 76
Wicklow 109, 155
Wiessner, Megan 144–5
wind 32
wind farms 3, 119, 127
  first wind farm in Ireland 120
wireless telegraphy 43, 46; *see also* Marconi, Guglielmo
Wireless Telegraphy Bill 54
Worker Solidarity Movement 86
World Fair (New York 1939) 57–8
Wynter, Sylvia 27

Y

Young, Arthur 13, 161

Z

Zuckerberg, Mark 5

www.ingramcontent.com/pod-product-compliance
Lightning Source LLC
Chambersburg PA
CBHW051531020426
42333CB00016B/1877